Language in Society 39
Principles of Linguistic Change, Volume 3

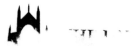

Language in Society

GENERAL EDITOR

Peter Trudgill, Chair of English
Linguistics, University of Fribourg

ADVISORY EDITORS

J. K. Chambers, Professor of
Linguistics, University of Toronto

Ralph Fasold, Professor of Linguistics,
Georgetown University

William Labov, Professor of Linguistics,
University of Pennsylvania

Lesley Milroy, Professor of Linguistics,
University of Michigan, Ann Arbor

Principles of Linguistic Change

VOLUME 3: COGNITIVE AND CULTURAL FACTORS

William Labov

A John Wiley & Sons, Ltd., Publication

This edition first published 2010
© 2010 William Labov
Figure 15.9 © 1949, reprinted by permission of the University of Michigan Press.
Kurath, Hans. 1949. *A Word Geography of the Eastern United States.*
Ann Arbor: University of Michigan Press

Blackwell Publishing was acquired by John Wiley & Sons in February 2007.
Blackwell's publishing program has been merged with Wiley's global Scientific,
Technical, and Medical business to form Wiley-Blackwell.

Registered Office
John Wiley & Sons Ltd, The Atrium, Southern Gate, Chichester, West Sussex,
PO19 8SQ, United Kingdom

Editorial Offices
350 Main Street, Malden, MA 02148-5020, USA
9600 Garsington Road, Oxford, OX4 2DQ, UK
The Atrium, Southern Gate, Chichester, West Sussex, PO19 8SQ, UK

For details of our global editorial offices, for customer services, and for information
about how to apply for permission to reuse the copyright material in this book please
see our website at www.wiley.com/wiley-blackwell.

The right of William Labov to be identified as the author of this work has been asserted
in accordance with the UK Copyright, Designs and Patents Act 1988.

Library of Congress Cataloging-in-Publication Data is available for this book.

ISBN 978-1-4051-1215-4 (hardback); ISBN 978-1-4051-1214-7 (paperback)

British Library Cataloging-in-Publication Data
A CIP catalog record for this book is available from the British Library.

Set in 10/12pt Erhardt by Graphicraft Limited, Hong Kong
Printed and bound in Malaysia by Vivar Printing Sdn Bhd

1   2010

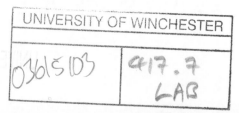

For Uriel Weinreich

Contents

List of Figures

List of Tables

Foreword

This third volume of *Principles of Linguistic Change*, dealing with *Cognitive and Cultural Factors*, appears a decade after the second, and some accounting for the delay might be in order. The first volume, on *Internal Factors*, in 1994 was followed by the second one, on *Social Factors*, in 2001. The next five years were largely occupied with the publication of the *Atlas of North American English* (ANAE). The *Atlas* radically transformed our view of linguistic change in progress in North America, and much of the present volume is devoted to understanding the impact of its findings. ANAE built upon the solid and reliable work of Kurath and McDavid in the Eastern United States, and many chapters of this volume will show how strongly their fundamental insights are confirmed. But that traditional base was not embedded in a systematic analysis of linguistic structure. It did not employ the approach to structural change generated by Martinet, Weinreich and Moulton, nor the principles of accountability used in the study of change and variation. Prior to the Telsur study that is the basis of ANAE, those tools had been applied in the study of a relatively small number of speech communities: Martha's Vineyard, New York City, Detroit, Panama City, Norwich, Montreal, Philadelphia, and in exploratory studies of a few dozen cities in England and America as reported in Labov, Yaeger and Steiner in 1972. The selection of those cities was the result of a series of historical accidents stemming from the personal history of the researchers. The larger linguistic landscape of North America, outside of the Eastern United States, was left in darkness until ANAE appeared.

Three major findings were surprising both to linguists and to the general public. (1) It was found that dialect diversity is not diminishing: the larger regional dialects, each defined by active changes in progress, are becoming increasingly more different from each other. (2) Several of these regions, especially the Inland North, display an extraordinary homogeneity across great distances and across large populations. (3) The boundaries separating many of these communities are sharply defined by the coincidence of many phonological and lexical isoglosses. In the four years since the publication of the *Atlas*, I have pursued many paths towards the explanation of these phenomena. Various chapters of this volume are engaged with the effort to account for them by settlement histories, cultural patterns and general principles of linguistic change. I am more than ever indebted to my co-authors of the ANAE, Sherry Ash and Charles Boberg, for their help in constructing the solid foundation on which the current volume is built.

The second to fourth chapters set the stage for the investigation by demonstrating that the cognitive consequences of linguistic change are a serious reduction in intelligibility within and across dialects. Here too I am indebted to Sherry Ash, my partner in the experimental studies of cross-dialectal comprehension, which date from the 1980s.

The seventeen chapters of this volume were given the most intensive scrutiny by two reviewers. I have spent the last five months in radical revisions in response to their comments, corrections and suggestions. Gregory Guy and Ronald Kim have allowed me to name them and to acknowledge my deep indebtedness to them for this effort. I have footnoted only a few of their contributions, which are found literally on every page.

In this volume I have built upon the recent research of Maciej Baranowski, Jeffrey Conn, Aaron Dinkin, Keelan Evanini, Joseph Fruehwald, Matt Gordon, Kirk Hazen, Daniel Johnson, Jamila Jones, Paul Kerswill, Dennis Preston, Gillian Sankoff, and Tonya Wolford. The work of Peter Trudgill on language change and diffusion is a point of reference throughout the volume. The insights of Penelope Eckert on the social meaning of variation are fundamental to this volume. Much of my effort is devoted to the challenge of applying her findings in the Detroit area to a wider context, and each exchange with her has led to an advance in my own thinking.

For all these contributions, many thanks. I hope I have made good use of them.

Every effort has been made to trace copyright holders and to obtain their permission for the use of copyright material. The publisher apologizes for any errors or omissions in the above lists and in the text, and would be grateful if notified of any corrections that should be incorporated in future reprints or editions of this book.

Preface

Those of us associated with Blackwell's Language in Society series over the thirty years of its existence have been delighted that we were able to publish so many titles which have been, and remain, highly significant and extremely influential in the development of linguistics. Many of them indeed have become classics in the field. But I am sure that few of the authors who have so far contributed to this series – and up till now we have published nearly forty different titles – would object to my saying that Labov's now completed work is very likely to prove to be the most important of all. When the first volume of his trilogy was published in 1994, I wrote that without William Labov there would have been no Language in Society series. And most of the scholars who have published books in this series will, I am sure, readily acknowledge their own scholarly debt to him and his work.

Now, sixteen years later, the appearance of the long-awaited final part of William Labov's massive trilogy can be seen in context for what it is: an event of immense importance for linguistics, and more especially, of course, for the study of linguistic change. We are now in a position to say that the three volumes of *The Principles of Linguistic Change* – devoted respectively to *Internal Factors*; *Social Factors*; and *Cognitive and Cultural Factors* – represent the product of an academic lifetime of outstanding accomplishment in our discipline which has few parallels: this really is a magnum opus. Labov's is a remarkable achievement; not only did he initiate a whole new field of research, he has also subsequently remained at the very forefront of innovative research in the field, over a period spanning five decades. In particular, his empirical linguistic research into language as it is really used by real speakers in real situations has produced exciting insights into the intricate mechanisms that lie behind language change. Bill has truly succeeded, to use his own phrase, in employing the present to explain the past. Linguistic change has always been one of the most intriguing and little understood features of human language. After Bill Labov's three-volume masterpiece, it still remains intriguing; but thanks to him it is now significantly better understood.

Peter Trudgill

Abbreviations

AAVE	African–American Vernacular English
ACS	animal communication systems
ANAE	*Atlas of North American English* (Labov, Ash and Boberg 2006a)
CDC	Cross-Dialectal Comprehension
DARE	*Dictionary of American Regional English*
IPA	International Phonetic Alphabet
JASA	*Journal of the Acoustical Society of America*
LANE	*Linguistic Atlas of New England* (Kurath et al. 1931)
LCV	Project on Linguistic Change and Variation in Philadelphia, 1972–9
LSA	Linguistic Society of America
LVC	Study of Linguistic Variation and Change in Philadelphia
LYS	Labov, Yaeger and Steiner 1972
MSA	Metropolitan Statistical Area
NBC	National Broadcasting Company
NCS	Northern Cities Shift
OH68	Telephone survey of low back merger in 1968
ONZE	Project on Origins of New Zealand English
PEAS	Pronunciation of English in the Atlantic States (Kurath and McDavid 1961)
RP	Received Pronunciation
RWT	Ringe, Warnow and Taylor 2002
TS	Telsur number for ANAE subjects
UMRP	Urban Minorities Reading Project

Criteria for the Northern Cities Shift and the North/Midland Boundary

O2	Short *o* fronted: F2(o) > 1450 Hz
AE1	Short *a* raised: F1(æ) < 700 Hz
EQ	Short *a* higher and fronter than short *e*: F1(æ) < F1(e) and F2(æ) > F2(e)
ED	Short *e* backed and short *o* fronted: F2(e) − F2(o) < 375 Hz

UD   Short *u* backed and short *o* fronted:
          $F2(\Lambda) < F2(o)$
ON   The word *on* is in the short *o* class in the North.

Vowel subsystems
V   short vowels
Vh   long and ingliding vowels
Vhr   long and ingliding vowels before /r/
VN   vowels before nasal consonants
Vw   back upgliding diphthongs
Vy   front upgliding diphthongs

1

Introduction to Cognitive and Cultural Factors in Linguistic Change

This third volume of *Principles of Linguistic Change* (henceforth PLC) has a broader scope and a broader database than the first two. Volume 1 investigated the internal factors that control change, beginning with a review of completed changes in the historical record and continuing with studies of change in progress. It examined the regularity of sound change and reviewed the evidence for functional explanations of linguistic change. Volume 2 looked at the social factors governing linguistic change and searched for the social location of the leaders of change, largely through a detailed study of ten Philadelphia neighborhoods. That volume also proposed models for the transmission and incrementation of change.

In the interim, there has appeared the *Atlas of North American English* (Labov, Ash and Boberg 2006: henceforth ANAE). The Atlas provided the first national (and continental) view of the phonology of English as spoken in North America, on the basis of a study of 332 North American cities. It expanded the previous views of change in progress to a panorama of changes in vowel systems on a vast scale – changes that drive neighboring regions in opposing directions.

The *Atlas* finding of steadily increasing regional divergence in North American English sets the problem for Volume 3: What are the consequences of this increasing divergence? What are its origins? And what are the forces which continue to drive divergence over time? To answer these questions, the present volume will explore more deeply the internal factors considered in Volume 1, focusing on the cognitive factors that determine the capacity of the linguistic system to transmit information. It will also expand the social factors considered in Volume 2, moving from the study of face-to-face interaction in local neighborhoods to the development of large-scale cultural patterns across vast regions and over a time span of several centuries.

1.1 Cognitive Factors

In its most general sense, *cognition* denotes any form of *knowing*. The most relevant *OED* definition of cognition is "the action or faculty of knowing taken in its widest sense, including sensation, perception, conception, etc., as distinguished from feeling and volition." *Cognitive factors* will here be used in a more limited sense: as factors that influence the acquisition of the linguistic system that conveys information on states of affairs – on *what* is being said rather than on the manner or style of expression. The study of the cognitive effects of sound change calls for a measure of listeners' abilities to identify the phonemes in the stream of speech and so to retrieve the words intended by the speaker. Chapters 2 to 4 of this volume will draw upon a series of observations and experiments that preceded and indeed motivated the *Atlas*. These chapters will examine the cognitive consequences of the sound changes that differentiate the dialects of the major cities of Philadelphia, Chicago and Birmingham.

Cognitive factors will be further explored in Chapter 6, which reviews the general principles governing chain shifts and mergers, along with the underlying mechanism of probability matching. The cognitive basis of phonemic categories will be the focus of Chapters 13 and 14. Chapter 13 uses the massive database of ANAE to address the question of the regularity of sound change and to determine whether the fundamental unit of sound change is the phoneme or the word. Chapter 14 examines the *binding force* that unites the allophones of a given phoneme and operates so as to counter the disruptive effects of coarticulation. Age differences in cognitive processing will be central to Chapters 15 and 16. These chapters distinguish the *transmission* of linguistic forms by children from the *diffusion* of forms by adults, and so distinguish the family-tree model from the wave model of change.

1.2   Cultural Factors in Linguistic Change

Cognition is of course not limited to the content of what is being said, but is sensitive to systematic variation in the way in which the message is delivered, yielding information on the speakers' social characteristics and relations to the addressee or audience. Volume 2 was concerned with such social factors in the study of linguistic change in ten Philadelphia neighborhoods from 1972 to 1979. The interviews, the narratives and the long-term ethnographic observations were focused on the effects of face-to-face interaction, as they are reflected in the studies of neighborhood effects in Chapter 7 and of social networks in Chapter 10. Cognitive aspects of that social variation were reported in Chapter 6 of Volume 2: they were the results of matched-guise experiments on the social values attributed to various stages of linguistic changes in progress. Philadelphians rarely referred to these vowel shifts when they talked about the city dialect, but showed greater sensitivity than expected to their social status in the matched-guise responses. Thus there was evidence of *social cognition* of linguistic change in Philadelphia – evidence which was parallel to the findings of field experiments in New York City (Labov 1966) – and this cognitive effect was partly responsible for the systematic differentiation of change

Table 1.1 Tensing and laxing of short *a* before /d/ in the spontaneous speech of 112 adults in the Philadelphia Neighborhood Study

	Tense	Lax
bad	143	0
mad	73	0
glad	18	1
sad	0	14
dad	0	10

by social class and gender. Section 10.4 of Volume 2 argued that the diffusion of linguistic change throughout the city followed the two-step model of influence of Katz and Lazarsfeld (1955), and the leaders of linguistic change located in Chapter 12 were comparable to the opinion leaders defined in that model.

Volume 2 did not, however, resolve the problem of accounting for the uniform direction of sound change throughout the Philadelphia speech community, or for the uniformity of its structural base (Labov 1989b). Thus the raising of (æh) showed sharp stratification by social class, but no social differentiation at all as to which vowels were raised, as shown in the near-total agreement of Table 1.1.

The problem is to deduce what form of communication is responsible for the uniformity of this pattern. Our oldest upper-class speaker has the same short-*a* system as our oldest lower working-class speaker, and the chain of events that links them would be difficult to trace. At the time that Volume 2 was completed, enough evidence had emerged from ANAE to show that the problem was broader than Philadelphia, extending to the "extraordinary uniformity of the Northern Cities Shift throughout the Inland North, and the regional shifts of the South and Canada." At the end of section 16.4 of Volume 2, the question was posed:

> If the incrementation of these changes is driven by socially motivated projections, how can we explain the fact that they affect so many millions of people in widely separated cities who have no connection with each other? (p. 511)

Chapter 16 of Volume 2 developed the concept of "abstract polarities which may take the same form in many widely separated communities" (p. 514). The "abstract polarities" will here be termed *cultural factors*. In the terminology adopted here, cultural factors will be distinguished from other social factors in their generality and remoteness from simple acts of face-to-face communication. Thus neighborhood, ethnicity, social network and communities of practice can be considered social factors in linguistic change in the light of the transparency of the social processes responsible for the diffusion of change. At the same time, they are not as strongly correlated with change as the larger categories of gender and social class.

Throughout this volume, the term *cognitive factors* will be used to designate the processes of cognition in the limited sense defined in the preceding section: the ability to decode what is being said through the accurate identification of linguistic categories. The relationship between these factors and linguistic change will bear in both directions: the effect of linguistic change on cognitive factors, as in Chapters 2–4; and the effect of cognitive factors on linguistic change, as in Chapter 6. *Social factors* will designate the effects of linguistic interaction among members of specific social groups, including the recognition of these effects by members and nonmembers. *Cultural factors* will designate the association of linguistic change with broader social patterns that are partly, if not entirely, independent of face-to-face interaction. These must involve the cognitive processes that recognize such cultural patterns, though this volume has less to say about them.

In this terminology, are *gender* and *social class* to be categorized as social or as cultural factors? It depends on what we consider to be the main route in the diffusion of these traits. While children certainly learn gender roles from their parents, they also acquire a broader cultural construct of how men and women differ in their speech. Social class differences in language behavior are also more general and wide-ranging than any particular mechanism generated by face-to-face contact.[1]

This volume will continue the line of thought developed in the final chapter of Volume 2, searching for the larger cultural factors responsible for the uniformity and continuity of linguistic change. Chapter 5 will examine the historical matrix in which current North American English sound changes originated, searching for their "triggering events." Chapter 9 will review the various proposals for the social factors that motivate linguistic change, and conclude that the extent and uniformity of these changes must be accounted for by a cultural history that is at least in part independent of face-to-face interaction.

This uniformity represents only half of the deeper problem of explanation that emerges from the ANAE data. The other half concerns the divergence of neighboring regions which have been and remain in close contact. The sections to follow will outline the relevance of cognitive and cultural factors to our understanding of this most problematic aspect of linguistic change.

1.3   Convergence and Divergence

Efforts to understand human language over the past two centuries may be sharply divided into two distinct undertakings. Both spring from an acknowledgment that language, like the species that uses it, had a single origin. Given this perspective, one task is to discover those constant properties of language that reflect the innate biological endowment of the human species – the language faculty. The other, equally challenging, task is to discover the causes of the present diversity among the languages of the world. As part of a general redirection towards a historical perspective on the understanding of language, this volume will focus on the problem of *divergence*: how linguistic systems that were once the same have come to be different.

The mere fact of diversity is usually not a challenge to our understanding of the mechanisms of linguistic change, even when we cannot trace the exact historical paths leading to such divergence. When two groups of speakers become separated over time through migration to distant parts, and communication between them is drastically reduced, we expect their linguistic systems to diverge. The many sources of variation in vocabulary, grammar and phonology will inevitably lead them to drift apart. We are not surprised that the phonology of English, transplanted from continental Europe in the fifth century AD, is now much different from that of the West Germanic languages Frisian or Low German. One would not expect, for instance, that the same lexical replacements that operate at the rate of 15 percent per millennium, as predicted by glottochronology, would occur on both sides of the North Sea. The normal work of historical linguistics is then devoted to describing the divergence that follows from reduced contact and to extracting the general principles that determine what form and direction this divergence will take. When such distant relatives converge on parallel paths, we are surprised and puzzled. Trudgill's studies of the convergence of postcolonial English dialects in the Southern Hemisphere (2004) are a case in point.

On the other hand, we are not surprised when neighboring dialects converge. The diffusion of linguistic features across dialects has been studied in considerable detail by Trudgill (1986) and more recently reviewed by Auer and Hinskens (1996). They show how the effects of dialect contact lead to the reduction of dialect diversity in the form of "dialect leveling" or, in more extreme cases, koineization: the formation of new patterns of an "historically mixed but synchronically stable" dialect (Trudgill 1986: 107). Bloomfield's principle of accommodation leads us to expect such dialect leveling:

[1]   Every speaker is constantly adapting his speech-habits to those of his inter-
      locutors. (Bloomfield 1933: 476)

However, when two groups of speakers living side by side, in daily communication, begin to speak differently from one another, we encounter a type of divergence that calls for an explanation. To sum up,

[2a] When two speech communities are separated so that communication between
      them is reduced, then divergence is expected, and any degree of convergence
      requires an explanation.

[2b] When two speech communities are in continuous communication, linguistic
      convergence is expected, and any degree of divergence requires an explanation.

This volume will confront the problem of explanation for a number of changes of the type [2b], as they are described in ANAE.

1.4   The Darwinian Paradox Revisited

An inquiry into the causes of divergence returns us to the issue raised in Chapter 1 of the second volume of this series, the "Darwinian Paradox" – an issue repeated here as [3]:

[3]   The evolution of species and the evolution of language are identical in form, although the fundamental mechanism of the former is absent in the latter.

The fundamental mechanism referred to here is natural selection. Darwin cited Max Müller's argument that words become better (more fit) as they become shorter; but the vast majority of linguists have been skeptical of such claims. The position of Hermann Paul on the functionality of sound change is prototypical of that of the the many scholars cited in Chapter 1 of Volume 2:

[4]   [T]he symmetry of any system of forms meets in sound change an incessant and aggressive foe. It is hard to realize how disconnected, confused, and unintelligible language would gradually become if it had patiently to endure all the devastations of sound change. (Paul 1970: 202)

Paul's evaluation of sound change is based on its relation to the fundamental cognitive function of language: to convey information about states of affairs across temporal and spatial dimensions. One can indeed find many analogies between social variation and communicative acts among nonhuman species in the signaling of territoriality, of local and personal identity, and of accommodation in terms of domination and submission (Cheney and Seyfarth 1990, 2007). However, an understanding of human language demands an accounting of how linguistic change and diversity relate to the unique capacity of human language to convey truth-conditional information and thereby adapt successfully to real-world conditions. Chapters 2, 3 and 4 will report observations and experiments that evaluate the effect of the sound changes discussed in Volumes 1 and 2 on the capacity to transmit information across and within the community. The results confirm the prediction of serious interference with that capacity. To the extent that we find that language change interferes with communication, we will have to agree with Paul in rejecting Müller's naïve optimism on the operation of natural selection in language change.

One way of salvaging the functionality of change is to argue that change optimizes ease of communication, responding to the principle of least effort:

[5]   It is safe to say that we speak as rapidly and with as little effort as possible, approaching always the limit where our interlocutors ask us to repeat our utterance, and that a great deal of sound change is in some way connected with this factor. (Bloomfield 1933: 386)

Most of the changes referred to by Bloomfield are cases of lenition that reduce phonetic information; mergers that simplify the phonemic inventory; or interlocking allophonic changes that disrupt the transparency of phonemic relations (see also Jespersen 1946, Saussure 1949). All such changes lead to a loss of contrast, which seems normal and predictable, as in the case of vowel reduction. The unstressed vowels of English, as in most other languages, occupy a smaller area of phonological space than the stressed vowels, have smaller margins of security available, and maintain fewer contrastive categories.

The chain shifts studied in Volume 1 and the changes in the Philadelphia vowel system that are the main focus of Volume 2 do not as a whole involve lenition, but rather exhibit fortition – an increase in effort. The general raising of /æ/ in the Inland North that initiated the Northern Cities Shift involves lengthening, fronting and raising, and breaking into two morae of equal length (ANAE, Ch. 13). Southern breaking of the same vowel involves the creation of a triphthong that moves from a low front steady state to a high front glide and back to a low central target. The London and New York development of /ay/ involves a steady state of 60 msec in low back position, a shift to a point of inflection in low central position, and a final glide with a high front target. Once the nature of these shifts and their vigorous development in real and apparent time are clearly defined, the principle of least effort recedes into the background, and the impact on comprehension returns to the foreground.

1.5 Divergence and the Central Dogma

The central dogma of sociolinguistics is that the community is prior to the individual. This means that, in linguistic analysis, the behavior of an individual can be understood only through the study of the social groups of which he or she is a member. Following the approach outlined in Weinreich et al. (1968), language is seen as an abstract pattern located in the speech community and exterior to the individual. The human language faculty, an evolutionary development rooted in human physiology, is then viewed as the capacity to perceive, reproduce and employ this pattern.

It follows that the individual is not a unit of linguistic analysis. Though the recordings and judgments on which the present work is based are gathered from individual speakers, the focus is not on their idiosyncratic behavior, but rather on the extent to which they conform to widespread community patterns.

Divergence, a central theme of this volume, is also a phenomenon of communities, not of individuals. Individuals do diverge from the pattern of their main speech communities as a function of their personal histories, but their idiosyncrasies are not instruments of linguistic communication. The divergence problem arises when different patterns of communication are generalized across individuals in neighboring communities. That problem concerns the effect on the main cognitive function of language, as defined above in section 1.1. For that function to be preserved in the face of linguistic divergence, speakers must develop a pandialectal grammar (Bailey 1972), which enables them to decode and comprehend the speech of neighboring communities. Chapters 2–4 will report the results of experiments which reveal that this ability is in fact quite limited.

1.6   The Community Orientation of Language Learning

The communal perspective applies equally to language learning. All of the factors referred to here concern the ability of the language learner to detect and grasp community patterns in the social environment and to modify linguistic behavior so as to fit that pattern. Granted that the language learning ability is constrained biologically in each individual (Hauser et al. 2002), linguistic change is change in the pattern of the speech community, not of the individual.

The ability to grasp social patterns is not constant across the life span. When children learn their first language from their caretakers, their cognitive abilities (in the sense defined in section 1.1) are at a maximum. These abilities decline rapidly in late adolescence (Sankoff 2002, 2004). Since children's view of the social differences in linguistic patterns does not expand until they move beyond the influence of their immediate family, the window of opportunity for acquiring social and cultural patterns is limited. There is ample evidence that a native-like command of a linguistic pattern different from that first learned is possible only for children who move into the new community before the age of nine or ten.

In the study of the New York City dialect, children who spent the first half of their formative years (ages 4 to 13) in the city displayed the characteristic NYC phonological system; but not those who arrived after 9 years of age (Labov 1966). Oyama (1973) also found that children of Italian background who arrived in New York City before the age of 9 showed the basic NYC pattern. Similarly, Payne found that children who had come to Philadelphia before the age of 9 acquired the characteristic Philadelphia sound changes; but not those who moved there at a later age (Payne 1976, 1980). In England, 4-year-old children in the new town of Milton Keynes showed the typical pattern of their parents, but 8-year olds acquired the new community pattern (Kerswill 1996, Williams and Kerswill 1999).

Though 9–10 appears to be a critical age for entering a new community, this does not imply that the language learning mechanism declines abruptly at that age. It seems rather that it is the proportion of the formative years exposed to the new system that counts. Thus children who moved into Philadelphia at the age of 8 did not acquire Philadelphia phonology in the single year that remained before age 9. Their behavior when interviewed at ages 13 to 17 registered the effects of 5–9 years of exposure to the new system.

The central fact of language learning is that children are not programmed to learn the language of their parents, or the language of any other individuals. Children accept the linguistic forms of their parents only when they are convinced that their parents are representative of the broader speech community. This is most obviously demonstrated when parents are not native speakers of the language that children are acquiring. The children's language learning faculty drives them towards the speech pattern they perceive as the most valid instrument of communicative exchange.

Given this tendency to adopt stable community patterns, the mechanism of transmission becomes even more problematic. When change is occurring rapidly, local children are in the same situation as newly arrived immigrants. Having learned their parents' system, they must adjust to the new community system between the ages of 5 and 17. The most precise evidence on early language learning of a changing pattern comes from the real-time studies of the shift from apical to uvular /R/ in Montreal French (Sankoff et al. 2001, Sankoff and Blondeau 2007). Of 11 speakers between age 15 and age 20 in 1971, 6 had replaced the 100% apical /r/ of their parents with 90–100% uvular /R/. Four of the others had acquired a variable use of more than 20% /R/ in 1971, but went on to a categorical use of /R/ by the time they were restudied in 1984. For variables such as these, it is clear that the formative period can extend to early adulthood.

The largest body of evidence on the acquisition of community patterns comes from ANAE. The vowel systems of North American English were studied by a sample of 762 subjects in 323 communities, representing all cities with a population of over 50,000 in 1990. It was not possible to confine the study to speakers whose parents were local to the area, since in many regions of the South and West these form a very small percentage of the population. The first two speakers who answered their telephone and answered "Yes" to the question "Did you grow up in (the city being studied)?" were accepted as representative of that city. Given the mobility of the North American population, it was inevitable that a large proportion of these subjects grew up in households where a dialect was spoken which was quite different from that of the surrounding community. If we add to this the influence of non-local friends and neighbors, one might expect the end result to be maps of a pepper-and-salt pattern in which the local dialect was obscured by individual variation. Instead, the *Atlas* shows remarkably uniform displays. Measures of homogeneity (percent within the isogloss that are X) and consistency (percent of all Xs within the isogloss) are almost all above .8 (ANAE, Ch. 11; see Figures 5.19, 8.3, 10.3 in this volume).

Within the speech community, change in progress is reflected by the steady advance of younger speakers over older speakers within each social group. This incrementation within social classes can be seen in Figures 9.5, 9.6, and 9.10, which trace the acquisition of the newer patterns by youth as they increase the levels of sound change that they acquired in first-language learning.

The recurrence of common patterns in ANAE makes even more problematic its central findings: increasing diversity of regional dialects in North American English and divergence among speakers who are in continuous contact. The task of the present volume is to explain these findings within a broader framework of cognitive and cultural factors in linguistic change.

1.7   The Argument of this Volume

Part A (Chapters 2–4) looks directly at the cognitive consequences of sound change in studies of cross-dialectal comprehension. The observations and experiments reported all lead to the conclusion that the consequences of sound change interfere severely with the primary function of the linguistic system: the transmission of information. It then becomes even more urgent to search for the origins, causes and driving forces behind linguistic change.

Part B examines the life history of linguistic change, beginning with the triggering events in Chapter 5. Chapter 6 reviews and revises the governing principles of change that were first launched in Volume 1. Chapter 7 deals with forks in the road, locating those choice points where change can go in either one direction or another. Chapter 8 then deals with conditions for divergence – the conditions under which two neighboring dialects in full communication become more different from each other over time.

Chapter 9 searches for the driving forces behind change, considering the many social and cultural factors that have been associated with particular changes: local identity, gender asymmetry, reference groups, communities of practice. Again, it is the great extent and uniformity of the Northern Cities Shift [NCS] that offers the most severe challenge to local explanations. Chapter 10 searches for larger-scale ideological correlates of the NCS in Yankee cultural imperialism, confronting the striking coincidence between the NCS and the Blue States in the presidential elections of 2000 and 2004. Chapter 11 provides some experimental evidence to support the existence of such ideological correlates. Chapter 12 observes that almost all features of currently spoken languages are the *endpoints* of completed changes, and aims at an account of how such endpoints are achieved.

Part C returns to a consideration of the units of linguistic change, pursuing further the questions raised in Volume 1. Chapter 13, "Words Floating on the Surface of Sound Change," re-engages the regularity issue, taking advantage of the massive ANAE database to search for lexical effects in sound change. The results support the neogrammarian view of change as affecting all words in which a phoneme appears; yet there remain slight fluctuations from word to word that remain to be accounted for. Chapter 14 raises the question as to whether the allophone is a more fundamental unit of change than the phoneme, and looks for evidence of allophonic chain shifting. The negative results of this inquiry leads us to estimate the strength of the binding forces which hold allophones together in the course of change.

Part D distinguishes between the transmission and the diffusion of linguistic change. *Transmission* is seen as the product of children's cognitive capacities as language learners: it is the basic process responsible both for stability and for the regularity of change within the speech community. *Diffusion* across speech communities, on the other hand, is seen as the product of the more limited learning capacity of adults. Because adults acquire language in a less regular and faithful manner than children do, the results of such language contact are found to be less regular and less consistent than transmission within the community. Chapter 15 deals with diffusion across geographically separate communities, and Chapter 16, with diffusion across segregated communal groups within the community.

1.8   The English Vowel System and the Major Chain Shifts of North American English

THE SUBSYSTEMS OF INITIAL POSITION   Most chapters in this volume will make reference to one or more of the major chain shifts that are responsible for the increasing divergence of North American English dialect regions. The mechanism and motivation of these chain shifts are best approached through the concept of *subsystem*, the domain of the general principles of chain shifting (Vol. 1, Chs 5–6). Figure 1.1a

		LONG						
	SHORT	Upgliding				Ingliding		
		Front upgliding		Back upgliding				
	V	Vy		Vw		Vh		
nucleus	front	back	front	back	front	back	front	back
high	i	u	iy		iw	uw		
mid	e	ʌ	ey	oy		ow		oh
low	æ	o		ay		aw	oh	ah
high	*bit*	*put*	*beat*		*suit*	*boot*		
mid	*bet*	*but*	*bait*	*boy*		*boat*		*bought*
low	*bat*	*pot*		*bite*		*bout*	*halve*	*father*

Figure 1.1a   Organization of North American English vowels in initial position

shows the feature-governed organization of English vowels in their initial position, from which current sound changes depart.[2] Vowels are divided into two major categories: long and short. This distribution depends upon a vocabulary distribution that is invariant across dialects and independent of phonetic realization: long vowels appear in free (word-final) or checked (word-nonfinal) position, while short vowels appear only in checked position. This is the binary notation common to most phonological treatments of English: long vowels are analyzed as bimoraic, with the second mora as a [−consonantal, −vocalic] glide. This permits the major generalization: no words end with a [+vocalic, −consonantal] segment. The three vowel subsystems are divided into two upgliding sets, distinguished by the direction of their glides, and one ingliding set.[3] In addition, they are organized by a trinary dimension of height[4] and a binary dimension of fronting. In various dialects, the inventory of these subsystems is altered through shortening, lengthening, diphthongization, monophthongization, and merger across subsystems. Change in the inventory within a subsystem initiates chain shifting in the direction of maximum dispersion.

The /h/ notation for the long and ingliding vowels identifies a subset that plays an important role in the dynamics of English sound change. The /h/ glide is realized phonetically as length for low vowels and as the inglide [ə] for mid and high vowels.[5]

The ANAE notation is useful for all English dialects that underwent diphthongization of the Middle English high and mid long vowels /iː, eː, uː, oː/. The chief consequence of this diphthongization is that they become integrated into subsets with the "true diphthongs" /ay, oy, aw/, and so participate in chain shifts with them. This is most evident in the "Southern Shift" (to be described below), which is common to the southern US, the South of England, Australia, New Zealand and South Africa.

Figure 1.1a is not a useful notation for those dialects which did not develop such diphthongization, as for example Scots, Caribbean English, traditional upper-class Charleston English, or forms of American English with a German or Scandinavian substrate (such as those spoken in Eastern Pennsylvania, Wisconsin, Minnesota). Dialects with monophthongal long vowels have a different phonological hierarchy and do not participate in the various shifts to be described here, but move in other directions.[6] The binary notation does not therefore provide an initial position for all English dialects and does not predict the directions of change in those which do not have glides /y/ and /w/ in hiatus (V to V transitions).

Many of the oppositions shown in Figure 1.1a will play a major role in the discussions of sound change in the chapters to follow. A few comments on the features of North American English that motivate this framework may be helpful here. In the short vowel subset, the low back phoneme is shown as /o/, even though it is pronounced as an unrounded [ɑ] in most North American dialects. However, the original back rounded [ɒ] is retained in Eastern New England, Canada and Western Pennsylvania (after the merger with /oh/), and we have no reason to think that the unrounding process ever took place in those dialects, as it did in Western New England. Unrounding of /o/ plays a major role in the reconstruction of the history of the Northern Cities Shift in Part B.

The opposition of /iw/ and /uw/ was for some time a stable consequence of the loss of the /y/ glide after coronals in *dew*, *tune*, *tutor*, *suit* and so on (Kenyon and Knott 1953), which opposed *dew* [dɪu] to *do* [duu]. ANAE shows that this opposition remains strong in only a few areas; but the merger is a major component of the history of the continent-wide fronting of /uw/ (as presented in Chapter 5 on triggering events).

In *r*-pronouncing dialects, the Vh subset consists of two large classes with limited distribution, /ah/ and /oh/. The /ah/ class is centered on a small lexical set (*father*, *ma*, *pa*, *bra*, *spa*), but has expanded greatly with the accretion of large numbers of loanwords containing "foreign *a*" (*taco*, *pajama*, *Rajah*, *Fujiyama*; see Boberg 1997). It also includes *palm*, *calm*, *balm* and the like when the /l/ in these words is not pronounced. In Eastern New England, /ah/ includes a subset of the "broad *a*" class of southern British English (*half*, *aunt*, *past*).

For much of North America, where /o/ does not merge with /oh/ it merges with /ah/.[7] It will be argued that both the merger of /o/ and /ah/ and the merger of /o/ and /oh/ represent the migration of /o/ to the subset of long and ingliding vowels, with the consequent acquisition of phonological length (Labov and Baranowski 2006). The third member of the Vh subset, /æh/, is indicated in only a few words, which (for some dialects) participate in the opposition of short /æ/ (as in *have*, *Sam*) to long and ingliding /æh/ (as in *halve*, *salve*, *Salmon*).[8] This opposition is amplified in the short-*a* split in New York City and the Mid-Atlantic states, discussed in detail in Chapter 16 and elsewhere. In *r*-less dialects, the long and ingliding subset is of course greatly expanded to include /ih, eh, uh/ (as in *here*, *there*, *moor* etc.).

Figure 1.1b inserts into the framework of Figure 1.1a the word class labels of J. C. Wells (1982), which are familiar to many readers in the British tradition. A more detailed definition and history of the word classes of Figure 1.1a is given in Chapter 2 of ANAE.

	SHORT		LONG					
			Upgliding				Ingliding	
			Front upgliding		Back upgliding			
	V		Vy		Vw		Vh	
nucleus	front	back	front	back	front	back	front	back
high	KIT	FOOT	FLEECE			GOOSE		
mid	DRESS	STRUT	FACE	CHOICE		GOAT		THOUGHT
low	TRAP	LOT		PRICE		MOUTH		FATHER

Figure 1.1b ANAE vowel categories identified with the word classes of Wells (1982)

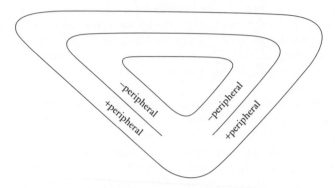

Figure 1.2   Structure of West Germanic phonological space

PHONOLOGICAL SPACE   The connection between the abstract categories of Figure 1.1a and our descriptions of current sound changes is through their realization in a phonological space that is here portrayed by the first two formant values of the resonant portion of the sound wave. The outer limits of this space are defined by the outer limits of formant values, and the internal organization, by distance from that periphery. The [±peripheral] dimension was first introduced in Labov, Yaeger and Steiner (1972: henceforth LYS), where it was found that the vowel systems and sound changes of West Germanic languages showed peripheral and non-peripheral tracks in both front and back regions. In chain shifts, vowels were found to rise along the peripheral track and fall along the nonperipheral track. Chapter 6 reviews the evidence for this analysis and tests it through the superposition of the mean values of all vowels for twenty-one North American English dialects, on the basis of the 130,000 measurements of ANAE vowels (Figure 6.18). The conclusion is that peripherality is defined in terms of formant values for high and mid vowels, but not for low vowels, where duration may be the major factor. The end result is the view of phonological space in Figure 1.2.

INSERTION OF NORTH AMERICAN ENGLISH SUBSYSTEMS INTO PHONOLOGICAL SPACE   The general principles of chain shifting (PLC, Vol. 1, Chs 5–6) and the large-scale acoustic investigation in Chapter 6 show that, in initial position, the long subsystems are located on the peripheral track and the short subsystem on the nonperipheral track. Thus Figure 1.3 inserts the abstract schemata of Figure 1.1 into the phonological space of Figure 1.2.

THE MAJOR NORTH AMERICAN ENGLISH CHAIN SHIFTS   The Northern Cities Shift [NCS] involves the rotation of six vowels, as shown in Figure 1.4. The NCS involves the general tensing, raising and fronting of /æ/, the fronting of /o/, the lowering and fronting of /oh/, the falling and backing of /e/, and the backing of /ʌ/.[9] The most advanced versions show the reversal of the relative positions of /e/ and /æ/,

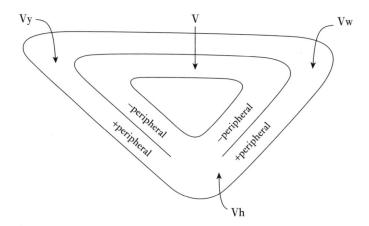

Figure 1.3 Insertion of North American English vowel subsystems into West Germanic phonological space

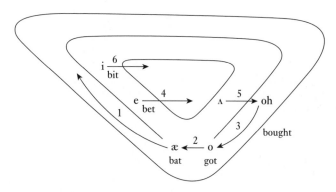

Figure 1.4 The Northern Cities Shift

the front–back alignment of /e/ and /o/ and the reversal of the relative positions of /o/ and /ʌ/.

The ordering of events in the NCS is a matter of ongoing investigation. Chapter 5 will show that the general raising of /æ/ in Western New York State was a triggering event for the shift. Yet the unrounding of /o/ in New York State may be considered a precondition for this general raising of /æ/. Boberg (2001) points out that several preconditions for the NCS are found in Southwestern New England (see also ANAE, section 14.2 and Map 14.9).

The Southern Shift, shown in Figure 1.5, is initiated by the monophthongization of /ay/, followed by the lowering and backing of the nucleus of /ey/ along with the tensing, raising and fronting of /e/ This is followed by the lowering and backing of the nucleus of /iy/ and the tensing, raising and fronting of /i/.[10]

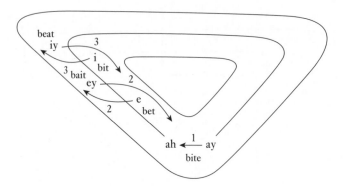

Figure 1.5   The Southern Shift

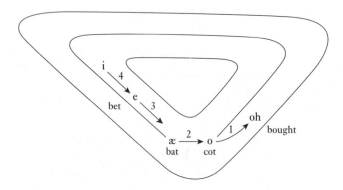

Figure 1.6   The Canadian Shift

The Canadian Shift is displayed in Figure 1.6. It is initiated by the low back merger of (o) and (oh) in lower mid back position, close to cardinal [ɔ]. This was followed by the backing of /æ/ to low central position [a] and by the backing and lowering of /e/. In some systems the movement of /e/ is only to the back, thus appearing as a parallel backing rather than as a chain shift.[11] More recent studies have confirmed the initial finding that lowering (and/or backing) of /i/ is involved as well.

The Pittsburgh Shift, first reported in ANAE, represents a different response to the low back merger, as shown in Figure 1.7. In Pittsburgh, as in Canada, the low back merger takes place in lower mid back position; but, instead of a shift of /æ/ into the space vacated, we observe a downward movement of /ʌ/.

The Back Shift Before /r/, shown in Figure 1.8, is found widely in the Midland and South, which together make up the the Southeastern superregion (ANAE, Chs 17–19). It appears to be initiated by the backing and raising of /ahr/ to lower mid

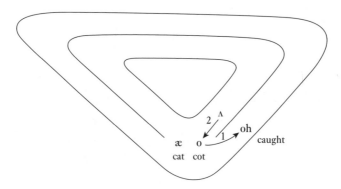

Figure 1.7 The Pittsburgh Shift

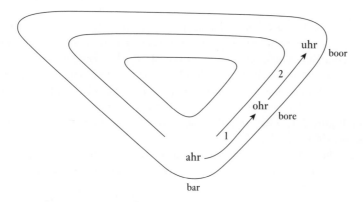

Figure 1.8 The Back Shift Before /r/

back position [ɔːr], which is completed in Philadelphia for all ages and social groups; this movement is followed by the upward shift of /ohr/ (which is long since merged with /ɔhr/). This shift resembles the most common pattern of vowel shifting in Western Europe, discussed in Haudricourt and Juilland (1949) and Martinet (1955). In Western Europe it is frequently accompanied by the fronting of /o/ and /u/. Since no North American dialect shows fronting of back vowels before /r/, /ohr/ fully or partially merges with /uhr/.[12] A row of communities along the Eastern Seaboard show a parallel raising of /oh/ to upper mid position, but no coupling with a movement of /ah/ has been demonstrated.

The Back Upglide Shift of Figure 1.9 is a phenomenon peculiar to the South: a phonological reinterpretation of the fronting of /aw/, general across the South-eastern superregion. It represents the logic initiated by the southern development of long open *o* to a back upgliding form [ɔo] instead of an ingliding form [ɔə], as in other areas. The shift to [ɔɑ] must have followed the lengthening of short *o*

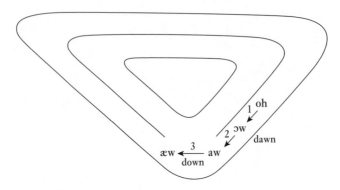

Figure 1.9   The Back Upglide Shift

before voiceless fricatives and velar nasals (as in *lost*, *song*, etc.). Among younger speakers, the rounded nucleus tends to give way to an unrounded one as a form of nucleus–glide differentiation. The result is [ɑɔ], which would be identical with the phonetic reflex of /aw/ in the North. However, the diphthong /aw/ is realized with a fronted nucleus in the South, [æo, ɛo, eo] – a development which justifies the phonemic categorization of the /aw/ of initial position as /æw/ in the framework of Figure 1.1. The same development of /aw/ in the Midland does not support rewriting /aw/ as /æw/.

These schematic views of the major chain shifts taking place in present-day North American English will be a point of reference for all the chapters to follow.

Part A
Cross-Dialectal Comprehension

2

Natural Misunderstandings

The study of language in everyday life cannot proceed very far without encountering many inefficiencies, miscommunications and misunderstandings, which lead us to the general conviction that language does not work as well as we would like it to. This chapter pursues the question as to whether linguistic changes in progress are major contributors to misunderstanding. Each of the speech communities studied in the 1960s and 1970s – New York, Philadelphia, Norwich, Panama City, Detroit, Chicago – showed vigorous sound changes in apparent time, as documented in LYS and in Volumes 1 and 2 of this work. But it does not follow automatically that generational change in the community, reflected in a gradient series of values in apparent time, will confuse members of that community. Such change might be considered equivalent to adding one more dimension – age – to the major variables of the speech community: social class, gender and contextual style. Speakers are normally not confused by this variation. If they know a value on one dimension of the matrix – say, style – they should be able to identify the probable social class of the speaker by the values of the variants. If change is in progress, they may be able to adjust their judgments by taking the speaker's age into consideration. The same logic might apply to the identification of the phonemic category of a sound change in progress.

Recent research indicates that members of the speech community store remembered tokens with associated information on the age, gender, social class and personal identity of the speakers who uttered them. Thus Hay, Warren and Drager (2006) showed that listeners were influenced by such information in responding categorically to the ongoing merger of *fear* /ihr/ vs *fair* /ehr/ in New Zealand English. Judgments of whether a token with a mid front ingliding vowel was a member of the /ihr/ or /ehr/ category were influenced by the age and social class of the person who was supposed to have uttered it. These findings were interpreted as support for an exemplar theory: that episodic memories are preserved as the basis of speech perception and production (Pierrehumbert 2002). Indeed, exemplar theory might explain why "inefficiencies in communication" had not been observed as a result of changes in progress (Weinreich et al. 1968).

A very extensive range of linguistic events that might produce misunderstanding has been found in recent sociolinguistic studies. We often find radical shifts in the phonetic realization of a given phoneme, in which the newer forms overlap the positions of one, two or even three neighboring phonemes of the same speakers' phonological systems. Thus for younger New York City speakers /æh/ in *bad* overlaps the distribution of /eh/ in *bared* and of /ih/ in *beard* (Labov 1966). The chain shifts displayed in section 1.5 exhibit many such radical shifts. In Chicago and other cities of the Inland North, the fronting of /o/ has reached a position close to that of low front /æ/ among the oldest speakers, and is almost identical to the normal pronunciation of /æ/ in the neighboring Midland areas. In Birmingham and other cities of the Inland South, advanced values of /ey/ have descended to a position equivalent to that of diphthongal /ay/, as the latter is pronounced within and outside of the area. Even more pressing challenges to the efficiency of communication appear in the rapid expansion of mergers across the North American continent: the low back merger of /o/ and /oh/; the collapse of /w/ and /wh/; and the growing tendency to merge vowels before /l/.

Two questions arise in regard to these developments:

1   Do conservative and advanced speakers understand each other's productions within the community?
2   Do members of other speech communities understand these local forms when they come into contact with them?

2.1   The Collection of Natural Misunderstandings

One common response to these questions is to assert that context will resolve any ambiguity produced by such overlapping distributions (Eliasson 1997). Another is to measure the functional load of an opposition and the consequences of its loss by a count of minimal pairs (Martinet 1955) – a procedure which King (1969) finds, in a first approximation, to be inadequate. Rather than argue from the effect of completed changes, it may be more fruitful to examine how people deal with changes in progress – which is the main strategy of these volumes. As a first step to an empirical assessment of the cognitive consequences of sound change in progress, the Project on Cross Dialectal Comprehension[1] (henceforth CDC) undertook the collection of misunderstandings that take place in everyday life. Linguists and linguistic students were asked to note down any observation of misunderstandings on a pad of printed forms, as in Figure 2.1.

The analysis of these data are far from systematic, but certain generalizations will emerge from this sizeable data base and they will give us some insight into everyday behavior, which will be examined more systematically in the controlled experiments to follow in Chapters 3 and 4.

```
┌─────────────────────────────────────────────────────────────────┐
│ MISUNDERSTANDINGS              Date _____              │
│ Speaker _____           Hearer _____             │
│ Dialect area _____              _____            │
│ Speaker said [continue on back for full setting]:                │
│                                                                   │
│ Hearer heard:                                                     │
│                                                                   │
│ Hearer corrected mishearing after ____sec ____min                │
│ ____ before utterance was over                                   │
│ ____ by speaker's response to look or query                      │
│ ____ by inference from further utterances                        │
│ ____ by accidental events that followed                          │
└─────────────────────────────────────────────────────────────────┘
```

Figure 2.1   Standard form used by the CDC for recording natural misunderstandings

The following examples will illustrate the various modes of correction, using conventions that will hold throughout this chapter. A colon introduces a spoken utterance and the double arrow ⇒ introduces an interpretation in the mind of the observer (or, if the listener is not the observer, the listener's later account of what they were thinking). Unless otherwise noted, the observer is the second speaker. What follows after a colon is spoken. The geographic background of each participant is given, whether or not it is relevant to the misunderstanding. The initials WL refer to the author.

2.2   Modes of Correction

A   *Before the utterance was over*   Observers and listeners often report themselves as correcting their first misunderstanding before the sentence is finished, in less than a second.

(1)   Dana M. [NYC]: [...] in the Sunday Inquirer.
Ruth H. [CT] ⇒ and this Sunday in choir [She was wondering what choir Dana belongs to.]

(2)   John S. [Southern IL]: [...] accountable to the data [...]
Debbie S. [Philadelphia] ⇒ [...] a cannibal to the data [...]

(3)   WL [Northern NJ]: You oughta see Frank's crow when you rub his head.
Gillian S. [Montreal] ⇒ [problem of anaphora: whose head gets rubbed, Frank's or the crow's.]

(4)   Claudia M. [OR]: Is Dwight Bolinger a Canadian?
Ruth H. [CT] ⇒ Is Dwight Bolinger a comedian?

B *By speaker's response to look or query* The most common situation is that the utterance is perceived as pragmatically odd or incomprehensible, and some form of query leads to a correction within seconds.

(5) Pat D.: I hated dissecting (frogs and worms) in science so the second time my class dissected I dissected an apple instead, and the time after that I dissected a carrot.
Lois K. ⇒ I dissected a parrot: You dissected a what?

(6) Black guy: I feel like ten nails.
White guy: You feel like tin nails.
Black guy: [slowly] No, ten nails.
[observed by Robin S. in Georgia]

(7) Susan M. [CA]: Can I pour us both juice?
Ruth H. [CT]: What's a spoke juice?

(8) Alice G. [Philadelphia] [to WL]: That's a great shirt!
Gillian S. [Montreal]: What do you mean, "grapefruit"?

C *By inference from further utterances* Almost as common is the situation where no pragmatic anomaly is sensed at first, but the error is uncovered in the course of the ensuing conversation. This may take from ten seconds to several minutes.

(9) Dana M. [NYC]: What are you giving up for Lent?
Caroline H. [UK] ⇒ What are you giving out for Lent?
Caroline [annoyed]: Pancakes.
Dana: You're giving up PANCAKES?

(10) Charlotte M. [VA]: Every time Robin takes a picture of me she gets a "telephone pole" in the picture.
Maureen S. [PI] ⇒ telephone call
Charlotte: Yes, she gets a telephone pole in the pictures, even in the living room.
Maureen: Well, maybe she has call forwarding, you know.
Charlotte: Call forwarding?
Maureen: Yes, you know that service.
Charlotte: No, no, telephone pole.
Maureen: Pole? What pole?

D *By accidental events that followed* The data base shows a smaller number of items where the misunderstanding was not uncovered during the conversation at all, but only by accident, in an event that occurred some time later, sometimes after many days.

(11)   Otto S.A. [NM]: Hit carriage return.
       Elise M. [Western MA] ⇒ caricature: Otto hit the key that I call "ENTER"
       or just "RETURN," and I thought, "How odd, he calls it caricature."
       A couple of hours later, he said it again and I understood it.

(12)   Dr B. [East Coast]: What are all complexities in life due to? Sets.
       Amy K. [Madison, WI] ⇒ sex [This made no sense, so I asked a person
       nearby.]

(13)   Loudspeaker at O'Hare airport: Milwaukee passenger report to the Eastern
       Airlines counter.
       Franz S. [Chicago] ⇒ lucky [He wonders what was lucky about this
       passenger. Some time later, the announcement was repeated, and he
       understood it.]

(14)   The following incident is reconstructed from an article in the *Philadelphia
       Inquirer* on January 18, 1989:
       Gas station manager: It looks like a bomb on my bathroom floor.
       Robin Corder, dispatcher: I'm going to get somebody [that somebody included
       the fire department]
       Manager: The fire department?
       RC: Well yes, that's standard procedure on a bomb call.
       Manager: Oh no, ma'am, I wouldn't be anywhere near a bomb. I said I have
       a bum on the bathroom floor.
       [8 firefighters, 3 sheriff's deputies and the York Co. emergency preparedness
       director showed up at the gas station to escort the homeless transient out.]

E   *Not at all*   In a much smaller number of cases the misunderstanding was not
detected by the participants, but observed by a third person, who did not communicate it to them.

(15)   John Baugh reported to Louise Feagin that a non-Texan told a Texan the
       name of her son was "Ian." The Texan couldn't understand why anybody
       would name a child something so strange as the preposition IN.

The following incident was observed by WL at the house of the D. family in South
Philadelphia.

(16)   Rosemarie D.: All right, come to dinner! [carrying out the food on a tray]
       WL: You run a tight ship.
       Tom D. [Rosemarie's husband]: She makes us slave.
       Rosemarie: Why would I want you to leave?
       Tom D.: One day, we'll explain it all to Rosemarie.

The misunderstanding displayed in (16) is the result of an ongoing change in progress in Philadelphia: the raising of checked /ey/ to high position, overlapping with /iy/ (Vol. 2, Chs 4, 5). The vowel of *slave* approximates the vowel of *leave*, and the initial /s/ that differentiates the two words is neutralized by the phonetic context.

Tom: [ʃimeˈɪksəsleˈɪvz]
Rosemarie ⇒ [ʃimeˈɪksəsliˌɪv]

A humorous remark was interpreted as a bad-tempered insult. The irritation produced by this misunderstanding simmered below the surface for some time. Neither party realized that there had been a misunderstanding.

2.3   How Common Are Misunderstandings?

Since one of the main goals of this study is to determine how much misunderstanding is actually caused by change in progress, the distribution of these five types is relevant to our undertaking (Table 2.1).

It seems clear that the least serious disruptions to communication and understanding are the first two types, and with increasing delay the consequences become more serious. A moment's reflection shows how difficult it is to estimate the extent of miscommunication in everyday life, since the more evidence there is, the more likely is it that it will be observed and corrected. How can we estimate the frequencies of types C, D and E? The situation is most severe with type E. There is no way to calculate how often two people miscommunicate and go their ways with different views of what was intended, said and understood. Tom did not realize that Rosemarie had misunderstood him, and wearily decided not to explain his joke, which was hardly worth his trouble.

These 872 observations were collected over fourteen years, which is a little more than one a week. This does not seem to reflect a very high rate of

Table 2.1   How misunderstandings were detected

During the utterance	108
By an immediate query	374
By inference after	204
From observation of later events	74
Never	17
Not reported	95
Total	872

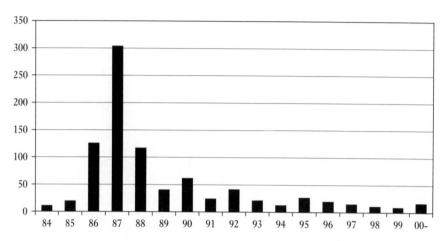

Figure 2.2 Numbers of observations of natural misunderstandings over time

misunderstanding, but it turns out that a considerable degree of concentration is required to record the mishearings of everyday life. If we ask someone to recall whether they had had such an experience in the past week, the answer is normally no. The main effort to concentrate these observations was exerted in 1986–8, as shown in Figure 2.2. Armed with a pad of forms for recording errors and with constant reminders, an observer returned regularly each week with two, three or four cases. One of our regular observers, Ruth Herold, recorded sixty misunderstandings in this period. The collection continued over time, at a lower rate. There is of course a danger that these later observations will concentrate on dialect-motivated misunderstandings, so that the rate during the main period of collection, 1986–8, is the best indicator: 27 percent of the 544 observations recorded then were dialect-motivated, and this projects an overall proportion of 235 out of 869. These figures, then, seem to give a reasonable estimate of the frequency of misunderstandings that are the result of linguistic change.

2.4 What Is the Role of Sound Change in Misunderstanding?

Our records regularly show that a little more than one quarter of the natural misunderstandings can be attributed to dialect differences. This proportion did not vary over the years in which the observations were made. Some of these dialect differences are due to stable variables, like the presence of flapping in American dialects versus its absence in British English; but the great majority are due to

Table 2.2　Major contributors to the collection of natural misunderstandings

	Home dialect	Total observations	Dialect-motivated	% Dialect-motivated
Robin Sabino	Long Island City	137	43	31
Gillian Sankoff	Montreal	137	26	19
William Labov	Northern NJ	123	27	22
Ruth Herold	Connecticut	88	30	34
Mark Karan	Northern NJ	67	14	21
Sherry Ash	Chicago	63	22	35
Tom Veatch	California	31	2	6
Charles Boberg	Edmonton	12	10	83
Corey Miller	NYC	6	3	50
Other		205	59	28
Total		869	236	

sound changes in progress. The proportion of dialect misunderstandings may certainly have been influenced by the observers' interest in sound change, though every effort was made to avoid this bias. The main observers were linguists with good phonetic training, as shown in Table 2.2.

Most of the observers came close to the general mean of 27 percent dialect-motivated errors, with the exception of Boberg and Miller, whose contributions are the smallest in number.[2] The area in which observations were made is of course relevant. The good majority occurred in Philadelphia, but observers also traveled widely outside of that area. A strategic contributor was Robin Sabino, who moved to the Auburn University in Alabama shortly after the project began, and the database benefits from many of her observations of cross-dialectal contact with speakers of the Southern Shift. Another major source of cross-dialectal contact was the encounter between the Canadian dialect of Sankoff and the Northern New Jersey dialect of Labov, with considerable geographic movement to the Montreal area. The least well represented among the major sound changes in North America is the Northern Cities Shift; but, as we will see, there is still considerable evidence of misunderstanding from that source.

We can conclude that the proportion of misunderstandings due to dialect differences is in the area of 25 percent.

2.5　The Linguistic Focus of the Misunderstandings

Each of the misunderstandings was classified according to the relative effects of lexicon, phonology, syntax and pragmatics, as well as by dialect differences (that

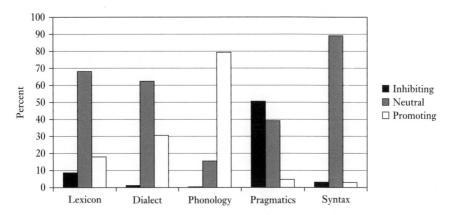

Figure 2.3 Effect of linguistic factors on misunderstanding: Percent inhibiting, neutral to or promoting misunderstanding for five factors

is, whether this aspect of the utterance contributed to the misunderstanding, inhibited it, or was neutral in this respect). Figure 2.3 shows the distribution of these factors. As noted above, about 25–30 percent of the cases were promoted by dialect differences. But overall phonology was overwhelmingly the major contributor to misunderstanding, and mismatch with the pragmatic situation was the most common factor that brought it to the listener's attention and led to its being recorded.

A   *Variation in the syntactic analysis of homonymous sequences*   See (3) and (16) above, as well as the following examples:

(17)   Philadelphia newscaster: leaving a third passenger too dazed to escape.
       Ruth H. [CT]: [. . .] leaving a third passenger two days to escape.

(18)   Tom V. [CAL]: [writing down items to buy] Two "c"s in broccoli?
       Ruth H. [CT]: What's two-season broccoli?

(19)   Judy S. [Philadelphia]: We'll go down to Knights St.
       Mark K. [Northern NJ] ⇒ We'll go down tonight's street.

Some near-homonymous cases involve the failure of small prosodic differences to take effect:

(20)   Robin S. [Long Island City]: They have toucans there.
       Lisa B [Long Island City] ⇒ They have two cans there.

B   *Loss or insertion of a segment*

(21)   Charlotte T. [VA]: I was at Brooks & Company
       Robin S. [Long Island City]: ⇒ at Books & Co. [She knows Charlotte sells
       books.]

(22)   WL [Northern NJ]: especially if you travel in twos.
       Katie S. [WI] ⇒ especially if you travel in tubes.

C   *Wrong identification of a single segment*   See items (5), (6), (12), (14) above.

D   *Wrong identification of two segments in a word*   See (10) above and the following
example:

(23)   Bambi S. [NYC]: What tapes are in the car?
       WL [Northern NJ] ⇒ What keeps her in the car?

E   *Error at the word level*   See (4), (9), (13) above.

F   *Re-analysis of word sequences with phonological adjustments*   See (1), (2), (7), (8),
(11), (15) above.

In writing, these misunderstandings produce the most comic effects. But close
examination of the phonetics involved shows that they often are produced by minimal phonetic mismatches. Thus we have:

(1′)	inquirer	[ɪŋkwaɪrɚ]
	in choir	[ɪŋkwaɪr]
(2′)	accountable	[əkaonəbl]
	a cannibal	[əkanəbl]
(7′)	us both juice	[əsboθdʒɪus]
	a spoke juice	[əsbokdʒɪus]
(11′)	carriage return	[kærɪdʒritɝrn]
	caricature	[kærɪkətʃɚ]

The misunderstanding in (1) involved a simple loss of a /shwa/; in (2), the loss of
the glide on /aw/ – a frequent occurrence in polysyllables; in (7), the mishearing
of interdental [θ] as velar [k]; and in (11), a mishearing of a palatal affricate as a
velar stop, with loss of the final nasal.

   Some of these mechanisms involve the processes of morphophonemic condensa-
tion in rapid speech, which are common across the major dialects studied here.
Others involve syntactic re-analysis, which is generally not subject to dialectal
variation. We can therefore expect major differences in the distribution of these

Table 2.3 Percent distribution of focus of misunderstanding for dialect-motivated errors and others

	Homonyms	Segment lost	One segment	Two segments	Whole word	Re-analysis	Total
Dialect-motivated	2.1	2.1	62.3	15.9	13.4	4.2	100
Other	11.3	3.4	31.6	15.9	14.4	22.6	100

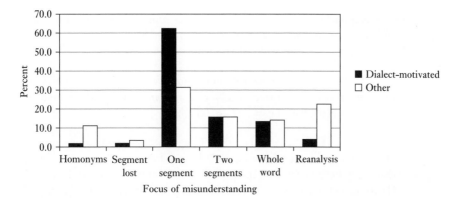

Figure 2.4 Percent distribution of focus of misunderstanding for dialect-motivated errors and others

mechanisms of misunderstanding when we tabulate the dialect-motivated cases against others, as in Table 2.3 and Figure 2.4.

There appear to be polar differences in the mechanisms involved in dialect-motivated versus other misunderstandings. The dialect-motivated examples are heavily concentrated in the single-segment category, while the cases involving re-analysis and restructuring across word boundaries are almost free of dialect influence.

It follows that most dialect-motivated misunderstandings will be influenced by phonological features, and that the smaller number of cases that are syntactically motivated will be concentrated among those with no specific dialectal origin (24 out of the 26 cases, chi square 6.00, p = .01). There is no significant difference in the lexical sources of misunderstanding between dialect motivation and motivation of other kinds. Pragmatic factors are the major route to the discovery of misunderstanding, for dialect-motivated cases and others, and it is rare to find pragmatic factors favoring misunderstanding. Here is one dramatic case, which involved a displacement of a final /d/. The pragmatics of the medical examination favored *tender* in place of the actual utterance, *tenure*.

(24)   Resident, examining Gillian: Are you tenured?
        Gillian S. [Montreal] ⇒ tender: Yes.
        Resident: For how long?
        Gillian: What?
        Resident: How long have you had it?
        Gillian: What do you mean?
        Resident: How long have you had tenure?
        Gillian [She laughs, and nurse too, who understood "tender"]

Another rare pragmatic motivation appears in (25):

(25)   Answering machine: You've reached Sam and Ann's. Please leave a message
        after the tone and we'll call you back.
        Atissa Banuazizi ⇒ Ann will call you back.

Only 9 out of the 42 cases of pragmatic motivation were also dialect-motivated.
Here is one remarkable case reported by a New Yorker in Chicago, which involves
the Northern Cities Shift backing of /e/ to /ʌ/:

(26)   Corey Miller [NYC]: Perceived on the Chicago commuter train this morning:
        "I've got a mutual fund coming in." This didn't sound so strange, given
        that many of the people on the train are financial folks. I heard the person
        clarify to her associate, who also misperceived the utterance, "a mutual
        FRIEND."

If these analyses of the pragmatic situation are correct, this means that most reports
of dialect-motivated misunderstandings are heard as contrary to the probable inferences that are made from the social and linguistic context. This of course is how
most are detected and reported, as is shown in Table 2.2. The great majority were
so out of key with the immediate situation that the listener responded with a query,
as in (5)–(8) and (27).

(27)   Mark Karan [Northern NJ]: Have a good day at school.
        Jeremie [Northern NJ] ⇒ Have a good day, scum.
        What did you call me?

When the misunderstanding persists, the pursuit of understanding may lead to
considerable social friction. This is evident in (28) and (29):

(28)   Alice Goffman, 7 years old [Philadelphia]: I want to talk to you about the kitty.
        Gillian Sankoff [Montreal] ⇒ about the cake: You want a piece of it?
        Alice: Are you out of your mind?
        Gillian: Don't say that to your mother.
        Alice: Why would you want to cut the kitty?

(29)   Leighton W., boss: I'm going home for about an hour kitty-cats.
       Shelah, employee ⇒ take a nap [When someone called for LW, she told him
          he had gone to take a nap. LW's wife called afterwards and wanted to
          know, angrily, where her husband was going to take a nap.]

We have already seen that any estimate of the frequency of misunderstandings is
lower then the actual figure, since our observations are bound to be skewed towards
the most detectable events. It can also be said that deferred or undetected misunderstandings, now matter how infrequent, are those that put the greatest strain on
the fabric of sociability.

   We can now turn to the specific mergers, chain shifts and other sound changes
that have been the major focus of our studies of linguistic changes in progress, and
see how and to what extent they are sources of misunderstanding.

2.6   The Effect of Mergers

2.6.1   *The low back merger*

The largest single group of dialect-motivated misunderstandings has to do with
the one major unconditioned merger in North American English: the low back
merger of /o/ and /oh/ in *cot* and *caught*, *Don* and *dawn*. ANAE shows this merger
as dominant in Eastern New England, Canada, Western Pennsylvania and the
West, with transitional status in the Midland and sporadic merger in the South
(Maps 9.1–4). The low back merger accounted for 32 out of 235 cases, or 14 percent.
Ten of them involved the same pair of words: *coffee* and *copy*.[3]

(30)   Carl R. [Boston]: How did the coffee machine work out?
       Sherry A. [Chicago] [She began a story about her copy machine.]

(31)   Gillian S. [Montreal]: We won't save any time to come here for a copy
          shop.
       WL [Northern NJ]: Coffee shop?

(32)   Gillian S. [Montreal]: Oh! Copy shop! Here it is!
       WL [Northern NJ] [He looks around for a coffee shop.]

(33)   Gillian S. [Montreal]: I wonder if there's a copy place near the airport?
       WL [Northern NJ] [Why would she need coffee?]

(34)   David S. [Montreal]: It's time to make the copies.
       WL [Northern NJ]: But I've already had my coffee.

(35) David S. [Montreal]: I'll get your copy right away.
WL [Northern NJ] [Why is he getting us coffee?]

(36) Ann T. [Vancouver]: Do you have the copy key?
Don R. [KY]: Is there a key to the coffee?

(37) David B. [OK]: There is a nice coffee stain on this one.
Mark K. [Northern NJ] ⇒ There is a nice copy stain on this one.

(38) Ruth H. [CT]: These are copied from Maurice Sendak.
Woman [?]: I thought you said you were getting coffee for Maurice Sendak.

(39) Edward L. [?]: Do you know any place where I can get some coffee?
Robin S. [NYC] ⇒ [. . .] get some copies

This series has several points of interest for our current inquiry. *Copy* and *coffee* would not appear in any list of minimal pairs for /o/ and /oh/. However, the /p/~/f/ contrast is not salient in intervocalic position. When the merged vowel is produced by a speaker from Canada or New England, as in (30)–(36), it is in back rounded position, with heightened allophonic rounding from the following labial: this leads to the automatic identification with /oh/ by speakers of the unmerged dialect. When the merged vowel is produced by a Western speaker, usually in an unrounded position, it is interpreted as unrounded /o/ by an unmerged speaker, as in (37). Mark K. afterwards noted the [ɑ] quality of the misunderstood *coffee*.[4]

The comical nature of this series, which creates prolonged laughter in oral presentations, is an important part of the story.[5] The characters involved are linguists, who know more than anyone else about the low back merger. Yet they have not learned from repeated experience and continue mechanically to misunderstand, time after time. In many cases the pragmatics of the situation strongly supported the correct interpretation, yet did not affect the outcome. In (31), (32) and (33), I knew very well that they were searching for a copy shop and I had already had coffee, yet heard the merged production of *copy* [kɔpi] as *coffee*.

Another series of repeated misunderstandings involved the minimal pair *Don* and *Dawn*. At the time of our collection of samples, the Penn Department of Linguistics included a graduate student Dawn Suvino and the faculty member Don Ringe.

(40) Gillian S. [Montreal]: It would be even better if Don could take her to the airport.
WL [Northern NJ] ⇒ Dawn [wondered for some time about how Dawn, who is blind, could take her.]

Table 2.4 Distribution of /o/ ~ /oh/ errors by speaker and hearer

Speaker	Hearer	Cases
Merged	Unmerged	20
Unmerged	Merged	5
Merged	Merged	0
Unmerged	Unmerged	0

(41) Mary A. [RI]: I started sneezing in Greek meter and after a while I figured Dawn's dog must've been in there.
Ann T. [CA]: Don doesn't have a dog.
Mary: No, DAWN!

(42) Ann T. [CA]: [at the meeting of new students] Elise spent quite a long time talking to Dawn.
Ruth H. [CT]: What do you mean? [since Don is not a new student]

(43) Sherry A. [Chicago]: I've been talking to Dawn here [...]
Carl R. [Boston] ⇒ Don Hindle: [...] Hindle?

(44) Peter P. [GA]: I'm working for Dawn.
Carol C. [Philadelphia]: Don Ringe?

Here we have a small community, all fully aware of the presence of the two individuals and of the homonymy of their names, whose members repeatedly confuse them even when the pragmatics of the situation point to the correct identification. Again, the majority are trained phoneticians, yet they do not use their knowledge of the linguistic situation to avoid misunderstanding.

We can now apply these data to the general question of the mechanism of the low back merger. In Herold's well-known proposal (1990), the expansion of the merger in a contact situation is the result of repeated misunderstandings of productions of one-phoneme speakers by two-phoneme speakers who try to map the former's allophonic differences into separate phonemic categories. On the other hand, one-phoneme speakers do not make such mistakes, as they do not rely upon phonetic differences to distinguish the /o/ and /oh/ classes. The data from natural misunderstandings gives reasonable support to Herold's position. Out of 35 cases, we can be certain of the status of the merger of both speaker and hearer in 25.[6] Table 2.4 shows the distribution of errors by speaker and hearer.

A full 80 percent of the misunderstandings recorded conform to Herold's model. This support is encouraging. However, the result does suggest that adults learn from their mistakes and abandon their reliance on the /o/ ~ /oh/ distinction in interpreting the productions of others. There still remains the question of how such a shift in speech perception may lead to a collapse of the distinction between /o/ and /oh/ in their children's speech production.[7]

Even more striking in Table 2.4 is the fact that there are no clear cases of misunderstanding between merged speakers or between unmerged speakers. This situation leads us to believe that mergers – even the unconditioned merger of word classes like /o/ and /oh/ – are not a major source of misunderstanding within the community. The misunderstandings produced by the low back merger are a contact phenomenon, not the result of a loss of contrast within the dialect of the speech community.

2.6.2   The pin/pen merger

Among the conditioned mergers of North American English, one of the most vigorously expanding is the loss of the distinction between /i/ and /e/ before nasals – usually in favor of /i/, but sometimes with /e/. It is characteristic of the South generally and of the South Midland, as well as of African–American speakers everywhere, and it occurs sporadically in the West (ANAE, Map 9.5). There are 11 cases in the data set; some involve the classic *pin/pen* confusion, others are in less expected positions.

(45)   Bank teller [African–American]: You have your Penn ID?
         Sherry A. [Chicago]: PIN ID?
         Teller: Your Penn ID?
         Sherry: PIN ID?

(46)   Melissa H. [TN]: Every time I say "INsurance" [. . .]
         Ruth H. [CT] ⇒ Every time I say "entrance"

Here the distributions of speakers and hearers resembled that found for the low back merger. Out of the 11 cases, 8 involved merged speakers and unmerged hearers, and only 1 the reverse. But 2 such confusions occurred between speakers of the unmerged dialect.

2.6.3   Mergers before /l/

ANAE shows a variety of mergers taking place before /l/ (pp. 69 ff.). A good 10 percent of the 762 speakers show a complete merger, both of /il ~ iyl/ and of /ul/ ~ /uwl/, but in very different geographic regions. Misunderstandings between *feelings* and *fillings*, or *pull* and *pool*, occur in the data set of natural misunderstandings, reflecting ongoing mergers; but the most common cases involve misplacement of the mid low back and mid back vowels, which occurs as a result of different phonetic realizations across dialects: Canadian *bowl* heard as *ball* by Mid-Atlantic hearers, Mid-Atlantic *called* heard as *cold* by Canadian hearers.

2.7 Chain Shifts

The major sources of divergence in North American English are the chain shifts, which rotate vowel systems in opposing directions: the Northern Cities Shift, the Southern Shift, the Canadian Shift, the Pittsburgh Shift, the Southern Back Upglide Shift, and the Back Chain Shift before /r/ – as described in LYS, in PLC, Vol. 1 and in ANAE, and as displayed in the current view of phonological space at the end of Chapter 1 of this volume. Chain shifts are well represented among the dialect-motivated misunderstandings.

2.7.1 The Northern Cities Shift

Since none of our major observers was located in Northern Cities Shift (NCS) territory, we did not expect to observe as many misunderstandings motivated by this chain shift as by the low back merger. However, almost as many appeared: 22, representing all five stages of the NCS (Figure 1.4). The first stage, the general raising of /æ/, is most likely to be misunderstood when it occurs before voiceless stops. In this position it can be misheard by speakers of other dialects as prenasal, since for them that is the predominant raising environment. Thus when Patty Plum from Syracuse introduced herself, Robin Sabino understood her first name to be "Candy." When I asked Linda Novak of Rochester where her father worked, she answered [kodiək], which I understood as "Coding" until on repetition it appeared to be the more expected "Kodak."

The second stage, the fronting of /o/, is represented in a number of remarkable misunderstandings: Beatrice Santorini heard a news announcer saying, "The Eden Expressway is jammed salad." It was a good ten seconds into the broadcast before she realized what had actually been said. She also heard a hotel functionary say, "In the morning, we serve complimentary coffee and tea next to the padded plant." Another linguist, raised in Cincinnati, was listening to a radio broadcast from Oshkosh, and heard a factory worker say, "The plant doesn't get enough orders to maintain aberrations." It was not until some time later in the broadcast that she stopped wondering why the plant would want to maintain aberrations, and understood that he had said *operations*. A Canadian phonetician heard a student from St Louis say, "I did the casting for a play," but only after he asked her how she got that job did he come to understand that she had done the *costumes* for that play.

A woman from Kansas recorded a misunderstanding between her Kansas-raised sister and a Michigan-raised cousin, in a discussion of what kinds of things can go into a dishwasher. She could not understand why the Michigander was ready to put *chapsticks* into the machine, until she finally realized that it was *chopsticks* that he had in mind. This confusion of short *o* with short *a* can become encapsulated in print. A Michigan newspaper reported a local politician as saying he was sure whose "axe would be gored." Others may come to think that *axe* is found in this fixed expression, but somewhere along the line there has been at least one misunderstanding of *ox* as *axe*.

These misunderstandings involve the mishearing of the rotated vowels by speakers of other dialects. We also get the reverse, where people from the Inland North wrongly categorize the speech of others. Suzanne Wagner (UK speaker) asked an employee of the Target store in East Lansing, Michigan: "Where can I find baby sleep sacks?" and then he quickly pointed to a display of baby socks. The same misunderstanding recurred two days later at the J. C. Penny department store. Jane Goodheart reports:

(47)   "Neither my boyfriend Dave nor I are natives to Michigan, and we are not NCS speakers. Dave had the following misunderstanding happen three times in the Lansing area, at two different grocery stores, with two different workers: he asked for 'catfish' and the man behind the counter gave him cod, thinking he said 'codfish.'"

The shifts of NCS /e/ provide two different sources for misunderstanding. The early lowering of /e/ towards low front position created considerable overlap with the /o/ tokens, which are fronting to the same position (Labov and Baranowski 2006). This leads to the confusion of /e/ and /o/ reflected in (48):

(48)   Telephone surveyor [Chicago]: Do you have any pets in the house?
       Brian T. [Eastern US] ⇒ pots [He thought that "pot" was not likely, since everyone has pots and pot = marijuana was too personal; he asked for repetition several times, until understood.]

Five other misunderstandings of Inland North /e/ reflect backing to overlap with the /ʌ/ of older speakers and other dialects: *Betty* ⇒ *Buddy*, *best* ⇒ *bus*, *Tech Net* ⇒ *Tech Nut*, and the example of (49). Here one can see how the phonetic facts lead to a misinterpretation, though all elements of the context support an /e/ reading:

(49)   Laura W. [Madison]: They make Treks in Wisconsin [while pushing bike along and talking about where she got it]
       Charles B. [Edmonton] ⇒ trucks

The lowering of /oh/ can lead to confusion with the /o/ of other dialects, but more likely with /ʌ/. The lowering and backing of /i/, the least prominent of the NCS stages, appears in the misunderstanding of *Hicks* as *Hex*.

Of the twenty-two cases of misunderstanding due to the NCS, nineteen were from outsiders' perception of NCS productions; one was the reverse case of (46); and one happened within the NCS community (13). It appears that the origin and location of our observers is responsible for the absence of misunderstandings within the NCS; the experiments to be reported in the next chapter testify to their prevalence.

2.7.2 The Southern Shift

The other major rotation of North American vowels is the Southern Shift, as displayed in Figure 1.5. The first stage is the monophthongization of /ay/, which is accompanied by a slight fronting movement. A number of misunderstandings are involved this process: *right* ⇒ *rot*, *right* ⇒ *rat*, *nice* ⇒ *nots*, *diet* ⇒ *dat*, and *alibis* ⇒ *alabaster*. It is notable that the most common pattern is misunderstanding of monophthongization before voiceless consonants, which (except in the Inland South) is a socially marked and stigmatized feature. Thus the most common expression, "Well right now . . . ," spoken by a Missourian, was briefly misunderstood by Robin S. as "rot now." One case of an inverse error was observed: "blond joke" was heard as "blind joke," both being equally likely.

The second stage of the Southern Shift, the lowering of /ey/ along the non-peripheral track, is represented by the mishearing of *space suit* as *spice suit*, a less likely combination. In the El Paso airport, Joanna Labov heard it announced that "the plane was going to be light" (instead of "late").

The raising of the short front vowels to peripheral position, stages 3 and 5 of the Southern Shift, appear in the mishearing of *Glenn* as *grand*, *sped up* as *spit up*, *Ding* as *Dean*, *wings* as *weenies*. Listening to Michael Montgomery discuss Varbrul, Robin Sabino heard "when you make a sale file," but quickly corrected this to "cell file."

Most of these mishearings of the Southern Shift were made by the New York observer Robin Sabino in Alabama. However, she did report a misunderstanding within a Southeast Alabama family. Nancy H. was describing a new comb to her daughter Jane, and asked "Do you want to see it?." Jane answered that she did not want to sit. This reflects the development of the inglide with peripheral /i/, which is characteristic of the Southern Shift and will play a major role in the next chapter. Sabino also observed the following case (50):

(50) Kevin H. [Crossville, AL]: We have no right [. . .]
        Christina J. [Atlanta] ⇒ We have no rat [. . .]

Chapter 3 will present more systematic evidence on how well Southerners understand the output of the Southern Shift. Sledd (1955) argued that the fronting that accompanies the monophthongization of /ay/ establishes a distinct phoneme for Southerners which allows them to distinguish /æh/ in *baa'd* from the vowel of *lied* and *ah'd* (as in "The woman ah'd and oh'd"). This would force the notation /lahd/ in *lied* vs /ɑhd/ in *ah'd*. Thus, within the community, *blind* would not be confused with *bland*, or *blond* or *right* with *rat* or *rot*. However, (50) suggests that the distinction between *rat*, *right* and *rot* may not always be maintained in the South.

It may be useful to examine the whole set of mishearings involving the word *right*. In addition to the misunderstandings of Southern *right* as *rot* and *rat*, a Missourian misunderstood a New Yorker's *all right job* as *wrote job*. Examples (51) and (52) show errors outside of the South that have nothing to do with monophthongization of the vowel. They both depart from the homonymy of *write* and *right*, which is the product of the much earlier and now universal merger of /wr/ and /r/.

(51) Alice G [Philadelphia]: I have to do that writing sample.
      Gillian S. [Montreal] ⇒ I have to do that right example: ?
      Alice G.: I have to do like a big-ass writing sample.

(52) Gillian S. [Montreal]: Would you help me right the table again? [referring
           to an outside table that had been tilted over to drain the water off]
      WL [Northern NJ] ⇒ Would you help me write my paper again? [Puzzled,
           he looks for repetition.]
      Gillian S. [Montreal] [repeats.]
      WL [First misunderstands, and finally gets it.]

2.7.3   The Canadian Shift

The downward and backward shift of /e/ and /æ/ is triggered in Canada by the merger of /o/ and /oh/ in lower mid back position (Figure 1.6). It is represented in the data on misunderstanding by the mishearing of *black* as *block* and by the example of (53), which shows how the phonetics of Canadian /æ/ can force a wrong interpretation against all contextual likelihood.

(53) Ruth H. [CT]: [looking at a bed frame] What supports the mattress?
      Saleswoman [Canada]: There's a rack underneath.
      Ruth: A rock?
      Saleswoman: No, a rack.

2.8   Philadelphia Sound Changes

Chapters 4 and 5 of Volume 2 presented a detailed view of three new and vigorous sound changes in the city of Philadelphia. Since many of our observations were made in that city, one would expect a good representation of naturally occurring misunderstandings motivated by these changes in progress.

2.8.1   The Back Vowel Shift before /r/

In Philadelphia as in many parts of the US, the low central vowel before /ahr/ shifts to mid back position, with an accompanying shift of /ohr/ to high back position usually merging with /uhr/ (Figure 1.7). This shift is complete in Philadelphia, with no significant variation by social class, gender or age (PLC, Vol. 2: 134). Accordingly, we have outsiders hearing Philadelphia *farms* as *forms*, *far* as *four*, and *card* as *court*.

(54)   Steve N. [Philadelphia]: We better get hold of him soon, because his [dɛ:ns kɔrd] is going to be filled up.
Gillian S. [Montreal] ⇒ dance court [She couldn't figure out what he meant; but after she hung up, realized that he had meant *dance card.*]

2.8.2   The fronting and raising of /aw/

In the 1970s, conservative older speakers in Philadelphia realized /aw/ with a low front nucleus [æʊ]. Younger speakers have shifted to [ɛo], and in more advanced forms to [eɔ] with a low back glide target. Conn's re-study of Philadelphia (2005) shows that this process of fronting and raising reached a maximum among those born in the 1950s and is receding steadily among younger speakers. Wagner (2008) confirms this recession of (aw).

Our data set shows six misunderstandings of Philadelphian /aw/ that reflect the upper mid position of the nucleus. Typically, the upper mid front nucleus is identified with a vowel in that area, and the back rounded glide is lost. Thus /aw/ is misheard as the vowel of /æh/, which is usually higher and fronter but has an inglide that descends only to [ə]. Thus *frown* is heard as *fan*, *ground* as *grand*. When *sound* is heard as *sales*, we note a confusion of the rounded [ɔ] glide with back unrounded [ɤ] (see below on the vocalization of /l/). When *mouse* is heard as *mess*, the glide is not observed at all. A fully articulated glide can lead to a re-analysis – a misunderstanding that takes some further events to reverse.

(55)   Mother of toddler [Philadelphia]: Get up [off the floor] and sit down!
Charles Boberg [Edmonton] ⇒ sit day-old [as in day-old bread]

One result of the /aw/ shift is the homonymy of *crown* and *crayon*, which is pervasive throughout the city even among conservative speakers, being facilitated by the use of /oh/ in the second syllable. The reverse misunderstanding, displayed in (56), suggests that Philadelphian /aw/ may be re-analyzed as /eyoh/:

(56)   Brian K. [Phila suburbs]: You know what else is there [in Easton, PA]?
       The Crayola Crayon factory.
       Sherry Ash [Chicago] ⇒ The Crayola crown factory.

In (57) we see a Philadelphian repeating *crown* in such a way that a non-Philadelphian
interprets it as *crayon.*

(57)   Laurel M. [Philadelphia] [having looked up the name *Stephen*]: Oh, it's from
          the Greek for *crown.*
       Jean F. [Philadelphia]: Right, cr[æw]n.
       Kyle G. [Cincinnati]: What? Crayon?
       Jean F.: No, cr[æw]n, like a king wears!
       Kyle G.: Ohhh, cr[aw]n!!

A similar development of /aw/ as [ɔ] in the Inland South produced the misunderstanding in (58):

(58)   Christine K. [TN]: Laurel leaves were used to make crowns.
       Robin S. [NYC] ⇒ to make crayons

2.8.3   The raising of checked /ey/

Among the new and vigorous sound changes in Philadelphia is the raising of /ey/
in checked syllables, to the point that it largely overlaps the distribution of /iy/.
Conn (2005) shows that this change has continued to progress in the twenty-first
century. This was the basis of the misunderstanding of *slaves* for *leave* in (16).
Further misunderstandings of Philadelphia (eyC) have appeared: *eight* as *eat*, *snake*
as *sneak*, *fashion mate* as *fashion me*, and *train* as *tree* "*n.*"
     A misunderstanding over many years is reported by Ron Kim. In the early 1990s,
he listened to a local rock station that frequently broadcast ads for a Philadelphia
jewelry store which he understood as "Robbins Ethan Walnut," with the slogan
"Our name is our address!" Over the years, he remembered "Ethan Walnut Street"
as a strange address. In 1998 he was walking west on Walnut Street in Philadelphia's
Old City, passed 8th Street, and saw the store with its sign reading "Robbins 8th
and Walnut."

2.8.4   The lowering of /e/

In the 1970s, the lowering of /e/ appeared as an incipient change in the vowel
system of Philadelphia, part of the general re-orientation of the front vowel system to
a Northern rather than Midland model, which was consistent with the raising of

/ey/ in checked syllables. There are many indications that this change is progress-ing in Philadelphia, and the natural misunderstanding data set confirms this.

(59)   Hairdresser [Phila]: [...] dress an' everything.
       Gillian S. [Montreal] ⇒ grass an' everything.
       Hairdresser: I was wearing a silk dress.
       Gillian S. ⇒ suck grass [...] [She quickly realizes the woman meant silk dress]

The case of (59) is paralleled by the mishearings of *req[uisition]* as *rack* and of *Jerry* – as *Jarry* in one case and as *Jared* in another.

2.8.5   The vocalization of /l/

In many areas of the US, syllable-final /l/ is undergoing vocalization. ANAE does not trace this variable, since it is not reliably recorded in telephone interviews, but does report on a number of mergers of vowels before /l/ that appear to be largely associated with vocalization. The vocalization of /l/ is one of the main contributors to misunderstanding in this data set, with 25 instances. In coda position, the unrounded glide representing /l/ is often heard as a rounded glide. Thus *hold* was heard as *who?* and *Bill* as *who's*; *rental* as *Reno*; *Strassel* as *Strasso*. Conversely, an /l/ not intended can be supplied, as in the mishearings of *go* as *goal*, *O-negative* as *all negative*, *omissions* as *all missions*, and *sulking* for *soaking*. In pre-consonantal coda position, /l/ is most often lost, as in *boats* for *bolts* and *office* for *alpha's*.

The most numerous and dramatic examples of misunderstanding appear in intervocalic position, and the 13 cases found are heavily concentrated in Philadelphia, where the vocalization of /l/ is extended to this position (Ash 1982a, b).[8] A leading and paradigmatic item is the confusion of *balance* and *bounce*. It has been observed experimentally that if customers walk into a running shoe store in Philadelphia and ask for "New Bounce" shoes, they will be shown "New Balance" shoes without further question. In the data set we observe:

(60)   Jeffrey W. [Philadelphia]: [...] to see if the payroll sheets balance
       Corey M. [NY] ⇒ to see if the payroll sheets bounce.

(61)   Larry B. [Philadelphia] [speaking to his 4-year-old son Jonathan]: [...] balance.
       Jonathan, 4: Bounce. [repeats, and begins to bounce up and down.] [observed by Ruth H.]

(62)   John M. [Philadelphia]: You meet two kinds of people in life, some can balance their checkbooks and some can't.
       Mark K. [Northern NJ] ⇒ bounce.

The phenomenon is not confined to Philadelphia:

(63)   Mary Ann [TX, travel agent]: There's a small balance due.
       Ruth H. [CT]: There's a *what* due? [adds that she had no idea what was
       intended, it sounded like "bounce" if anything.]

We have recorded a long string of misunderstandings of intervocalic /l/ spoken
by Philadelphians. A teller reading my name "William" was heard to say *WHAM.*
A man on the phone said "Tell him it's Harvey," and the listener heard *Thomas
Harvey. Volleyball courts* was heard as *Bible courts.* A Philadelphian asking for a
cooler was understood as asking for a *Coor* (one of the minority cases in which the
pragmatic situation favored the misunderstanding). *Spelling* was heard as *spine.*
   The converse error is also found with intervocalic /l/. Thus in the course of her
work Ruth Herold asked a man in Eastern Pennsylvania where his father was born.
Having heard many deletions of intervocalic /l/, she heard him say "Williamsburg,"
and only after some time did she find out that he had said "Waynesburg." Though
most of these errors arise in communication between Philadelphians and others, (64)
occurred in a conversation between two Philadelphians observed by an outsider.

(64)   Instructor [Philadelphia]: Tell me what this sentence implies to you:
       "Mr. Williams strode into the office."
       Student [Philadelphia]: It means he was real casual.
       Instructor: For *strode?* As in *stride?* Do you know what "stride" means?
       Student: I'm sorry, I thought you said "strolled." "Strode" means
       "forcefully."

2.9   r-less vs r-ful Dialects

There is some tendency towards the vocalization of /r/ codas in Philadelphia
(Myhill 1988), but the chief sources of r-lessness in our data are from British, New
York City and African–American speakers. Thus one New Yorker heard the *floor*
of another New Yorker as *flaw,* and a listener raised in upper New York State heard
another New Yorker's *yarn* as a *yawn.* The *Carl* of one African–American speaker
was heard as *call* by another African–American listener. As is well known, the
insertion of /r/ where it was not intended is also quite frequent. A New Yorker
heard a Mid-Atlantic *autistic* as *artistic,* and another New Yorker heard Midland
Aubie's as *Arbie's.* Given the general variation of /r/ with zero, even a Midland
listener may hear /r/ where it was not intended.

(65)   Jill N. [NYC]: They have a new pawn shop now.
       Naomi N. [NE] $\Rightarrow$ They have a new porn shop now.

It was a good 30 seconds before this misunderstanding was straightened out by succeeding events.

2.10   Sound Changes General to North America

To this point we have been examining the effect on comprehension of regional differences, and primarily the effect of dialect contact. Some sound changes general to all or most of North America produce misunderstandings. Short *a* is raised before nasal consonants to one extent or another in all American dialects, to mid and high ingliding position, so that *Ian* is in many areas homonymous with *Ann*. Thus a New Yorker heard a Philadelphian pronouncing *Ann Arbor* as *Ian Arbor*, and a Southerner heard a New Yorker's *Ian Hancock* as *Ann Hancock*. This high ingliding /æh/ can be truncated and is most commonly misheard as /i/:

(66)   Charlotte A. [VA]: Is Ann coming?
        Marybeth L. [Philadelphia suburbs]: Incoming? Incoming from where?

It is also not uncommon for tensed short *a* to be heard as short /e/. Thus we find *Kennedy* for *Canada*, *pens* for *pans*, *bed* for *bad* and *bread* for *grass*.

2.10.1   The fronting of back vowels

ANAE, Chapter 12 shows that /uw/ is generally fronted throughout North America, with the exception of limited areas in Eastern New England and in Wisconsin/Minnesota. This fronting frequently reaches high front nonperipheral position, with a nucleus at [ü]. When the back glide is truncated or fronted, this vowel can be misheard as /iy/. Thus Philadelphia *scooter* was heard by another Philadelphian as *skeeter*. We also note *youth* misheard as *yeast*, *shoe* as *cheese*, and *boozey* as *beesy*.

    The parallel fronting of the nucleus of /ow/ is general to the Mid-Atlantic region, the Midland and the South. The fronted nucleus is heard as an unrounded vowel. Thus a Philadelphian's *Ocean City* was misheard as *Nation's City*; a Pittsburgher's *phones* as *films*. Ruth H. observed the following struggle to understand the Philadelphia version of *boat*:

(67)   Philadelphia woman [boarding Piedmont Flight from Philadelphia to Florida]:
            I'm going down to Lauderdale and then on a boat.
        Stewardess [mimicking extreme Philadelphia pronunciation as if it were a
            place name] Abewte? where's that?
        Passenger: A boat.

Stewardess ⇒ ?
Passenger: A boat.
Stewardess [finally understands.]

2.11   An Overview of Natural Misunderstandings

The set of 869 natural misunderstandings collected yields some insight into the nature and extent of cross-dialectal comprehension, but it plainly has limitations. We have only occasional records of the phonetic form of the input, which we largely project from the dialect background of the speakers. We have no information on the absolute frequency of misunderstandings as compared to correct understanding. The data do give us an idea of the relative number of misunderstandings due to dialect motivation, though we cannot be sure of the extent to which the observers' attention was biased towards cases of this type. Most of the misunderstandings noted here crossed dialect boundaries; there are relatively few among speakers of the same dialect, but the comparison is not a controlled one.

These limitations will be corrected in Chapters 3 and 4, which report controlled experiments on cross-dialectal comprehension. Conversely, the results from natural misunderstanding will serve to correct the limitations of these controlled experiments, which evoke responses in an environment that is inevitably associated with the norms of careful, nonlocal speech patterns. The data on natural misunderstandings are free from such effects. We can of course project other methods of studying misunderstanding. One can examine errors in the transcriptions of recorded texts, or search through tape recordings of sociolinguistic interviews. From past experience, however, it seems that the first will provide too many errors, the second too few. With all its limitations, the method we used here emerges as one valid way of capturing the cognitive consequences of linguistic change.

These results run counter to the common illusion that North American English speakers have no trouble understanding other North American dialects of English. If the stored memories of our previous experience were available for search and comparison, along with our memories of who said what, as exemplar theory argues, we would not go on repeatedly confusing the Canadian allophones of *coffee* and *copy*. Instead we hear these utterances through the filter of our own categories: the allophone [ɔ] in *copy* is heard as the phoneme /oh/ in *coffee*. This result gives little support to the notion that, over the years, we construct a pandialectal phonology in the spirit of C.-J. Bailey (1972), to translate from one system into another. The study of natural misunderstandings displays a persistent, mechanical and comical incompetence on the part of the most highly trained and knowledgeable observers. Why are these errors so comical? It is because they show us to be victims of our own habitual behavior, unable to make use of the rich store of knowledge that we access through conscious reflection. We can return to the observation that a very large part of these natural misunderstandings come from linguists whose professional competence rests on their knowledge of dialect differences. I write in the third person about these mishearers, though I was myself a prominent member of the group. If anyone should be able to draw upon a pandialectal grammar, built over years of study and experience, to interpret the productions of speakers of other dialects, we should have been able to do so. But we did not.

This view of the cognitive consequences of linguistic change makes it even more urgent that we pursue the search for the driving forces responsible for these large-scale rotations, mergers and confusions. Part B of this volume will make an effort to do so. But it seems that, whatever forces are operating to produce the results displayed in this chapter, they are outside of our control. It would be comforting to think that linguistic change is the work of active agency, in which we all maximize our status through the manipulation of social variants. But these 869 observations of natural misunderstandings show considerable distance between intention and achievement in linguistic interaction. We observe no desire to be misunderstood or to misunderstand, but, to the extent that we recognize it, there is a sense of strong dismay that something has upset the linguistic applecart.

3

A Controlled Experiment on Vowel Identification

This chapter will pursue the investigation of the cognitive consequences of linguistic change that was initiated in Chapter 2. While Chapter 2 examined evidence on the effect of dialect differences in everyday life, this chapter will present the results of controlled experiments that measure with greater precision the effects of sound changes in progress on the ability to recognize the vowel phonemes of English. If nineteenth-century grammarians were right in asserting that sound change has a destructive effect upon the central functions of language (Chapter 1 of Volume 2), we should find that changes in progress interfere with the identification of words and their meanings, not only across communities but within the community as well.

The experiments reported here were carried out by the project on Cross-Dialectal Comprehension [CDC],[1] which focused on three cities in which sound changes were moving in radically different directions:

- Philadelphia, the site of the new and vigorous changes described in Chapters 4 and 5 of Volume 2;
- Chicago, the largest city undergoing the Northern Cities Shift [NCS], as defined in Volume 1; in ANAE, Chapters 11 and 14; and in Figure 1.4 of this volume;
- Birmingham, prototypical site of the Southern Shift, as defined in Volume 2; in ANAE, Chapters 11 and 18; and in Figure 1.5 of this volume.

To create the stimuli for the experiments, we located and recorded in each city speakers who could be expected to represent the leading edge of sound change in the speech community. Volume 2 found that the leaders of linguistic change are most likely to be found among upwardly mobile women from the upper working class and lower middle class. The Project on Linguistic Change and Variation [LCV] of the 1970s had identified and recorded leaders of linguistic change in Philadelphia, using open reel Nagra tape recorders and high-fidelity lavalier microphones. To obtain comparable recordings in the other two cities, we selected in Chicago and Birmingham the major local state-supported commuter colleges, with a high proportion of local residents, many of them being the first in their families to go to college. These were the University of Illinois in Chicago (UIC) and the University of Alabama in Birmingham (UAB). Sharon Ash carried out interviews with first-year women in both of these colleges in 1988.[2]

3.1   The Peterson–Barney Experiment

The title of this chapter is taken from the well-known experiment of Peterson and Barney in 1952, designed to test listeners' ability to identify the vowels of words spoken in isolation. Peterson and Barney presented ten vowels in the frame / h_d / : *heed, hid, head, had, hod, hawed, hood, who'd, hud, heard*, as pronounced by 76 different speakers, including men, women and children. Most of the speakers were said to be speakers of "general American," a category no longer recognized in American dialectology, but confusion in the *hod/hawed* area points to the fact that some speakers exhibited the low back merger.

  Peterson and Barney raised the issue of determining the reference grid by which listeners interpret the vowels they hear. One possibility is that this grid is their own vowel system and that each vowel produced by a speaker is heard as if it were produced by the listener. At the other extreme lies the hypothesis of a pandialectal grammar, comprising all of the vowel systems that the listener has heard and interpreted (Bailey 1972). Such overall constructs may be the result of interdialectal experience or of a general understanding of what changes are possible or likely to occur. To the extent that such a pandialectal competence exists, sound changes may not interfere seriously with communication across communities. Within a given speech community, we may ask whether all of its members shift their reference grids to include the most recent changes, or whether only those who are participating in the change do so.

3.2   Replicating the Peterson–Barney Experiment

Given the lack of definition of the Peterson–Barney data in regard to dialect differences, the CDC project replicated this experiment with speakers and judges from the three identified dialect areas. This was largely the work of Sharon Ash, and much of the analysis given here is drawn from Ash (1988). Instead of the ten / h_d / words of the Peterson–Barney framework, fourteen vowels were selected in the / k_d / environment:

SHORT		FRONT UPGLIDING		BACK UPGLIDING		INGLIDING	
/i/	kid	/iy/	keyed				
/e/	Ked	/ey/	cade				
/æ/	cad	/ay/	kide	/aw/	cowed		
/o/	cod	/oy/	koid	/ow/	code	/oh/	cawed
/ʌ/	cud						
/u/	could			/uw/	cooed		

Though this framework introduced three non-words (*cade, kide, koid*) and one trade name (*Ked*), it had the advantage of using the established words *cooed* and *cawed* where Peterson and Barney used *who'd* and *hawed*.

In preliminary work in Chicago and Birmingham, a number of students at the host universities were recorded reading the list of fourteen words. All tape recording was done in a quiet room, using a Nagra IV-S open reel tape recorder at 7 1/2 ips and a Sennheiser 415 directional microphone. Of those recorded in Chicago and Birmingham, the two speakers who were most advanced in the sound changes under study were selected for the test stimuli. In Philadelphia, two speakers were selected from the LCV Neighborhood Study carried out in the 1970s (Volume 2).

Figure 3.1 shows the F1 and F2 positions of the six vowels involved in the Northern Cities Shift – /i, e, æ, o, ʌ, oh/ – as pronounced by the six speakers.[3] Given the formal character of word-list pronunciation with a high degree of attention to speech, it is a matter of interest whether the extreme rotations of the NCS would be reflected in these tokens. The figure shows that this is in fact the case. The raising and fronting of Chicago /æ/ is represented by the location of *Ccad1, Ccad2*, which appear at a level with the mid and high vowels of other dialects. The fronting of Chicago /o/ is evident in the approximation of *Ccod1* with *Pcad2* and of *Ccod2* with *Pcad1*. The lowering and backing of Chicago /e/ is reflected in the positions of *Cked1* and *Cked2*. The latest stage of the NCS, the backing of /ʌ/, does not appear in the controlled utterances of Figure 3.1.

Subjects for the experiment were drawn from class groups recruited at each of the selected sites. The test words were presented in dialect sets, and the twenty-eight words in each set were presented in random order. The randomized sets of words were copied onto a Sony WM-D6C cassette tape recorder for playback on the same recorder through a Nagra DSM loudspeaker. Answer sheets were prepared with the fourteen words printed at the top. These words were first read to the subjects by Ash, with the admonition that the reading represented her own speech and might differ from the listeners' speech or from that of the speakers who were recorded on the test tape. The listeners were then asked to write, for each item, the word they believed was being pronounced, using the spellings given at the top of the answer sheet.

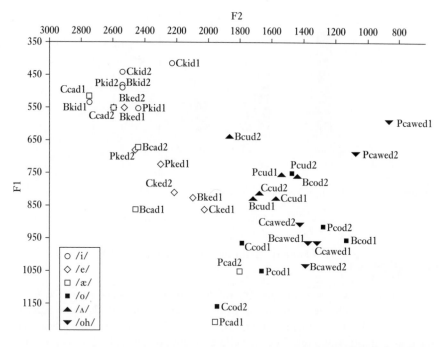

Figure 3.1 Vowel nuclei of the stimuli in the Peterson–Barney replication for *kid*, *ked*, *cad*, *cod*, *cud*, *cawed*. Initial consonant of vowel label: P = Philadelphia, C = Chicago, B = Birmingham

Table 3.1 Percent correct vowel identifications by city of speakers and listeners in the Peterson–Barney replication

| | Speakers | | | |
	Philadelphia	Chicago	Birmingham	All
Listeners	N = 27	N = 25	N = 42	N = 94
Philadelphia	**89**	77	64	77
Chicago	81	**81**	71	78
Birmingham	77	69	**77**	75
Total	82	76	71	**77**

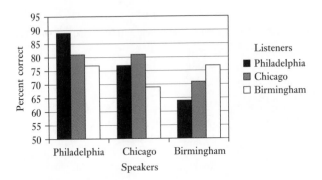

Figure 3.2   Overall correct responses to Peterson–Barney replication

3.3   Overall Success in Identification

The general success in identifying the intended phonemes is shown in Table 3.1 and Figure 3.2. The first comparison with Peterson–Barney (1952) is the percent correct overall. The high figure of 95% correct in the original experiment has been the center of attention ever since, and efforts to develop normalization systems are often judged by the translation of the Peterson–Barney data to reflect that level of success. The overall success rate in the dialect-controlled replication was much lower, only 77%. There were no significant differences in the overall performance of judges from the three cities: all three means were close to the general rate of 77% correct.

Local listeners did better than non-locals, as shown in Table 3.1 by the bold figures in the diagonal of the matrix. This effect held for each city. The local advantage is significant by t-test for all cases, except that the difference between Chicago and Birmingham listeners to the Birmingham speaker (71% to 77%) is not significant. On the whole, this local advantage is only moderate: the best re-cognition rate in the series, Philadelphians listening to Philadelphians, reaches only 89%, well below the Peterson–Barney level of 95%.

To understand why the success rate was so much lower in this replication, we need to examine the phonetic realization of the stimuli for particular phonemes.

3.4   Responses to the Chicago Speakers

The responses of subjects to the Chicago stimuli are shown in Table 3.2. The numbers in each cell show the percentage of correct identifications; the parentheses

Table 3.2   Percent correct vowel identifications of Chicago speakers in
the Peterson–Barney replication (errors > 15% in parentheses)

Vowel Phoneme	Percentage of Correct Responses by Listeners		
	Philadelphia	Chicago	Birmingham
iy	100	96	90
i	98	80 (16 u)	88
ey	72 (22 iy)	68 (18 iy)	52 (30 iy)
e	39 (15 æ, 44 ʌ)	40 (56 ʌ)	55 (36 ʌ)
æ	78	90	60 (18 e)
ay	98	92	86
aw	94	94	88
o	78	90	38 (38 æ, 13 ay)
oh	11 (11 æ, 76 o)	40 (54 o)	8 (83 o)
oy	98	94	80
ow	61 (15 oh)	82	79
u	63 (35 ʌ)	74 (24 ʌ)	71 (23 ʌ)
uw	89	92	85
ʌ	94	96	88
Mean	77	81	69

following show any tendency to misidentify a given phoneme that is greater than
15%. The pattern of errors reflects the rotation of vowels by the NCS, as displayed
in the general schema of Figure 1.4 and in the phonetic realization of the experimental stimuli in Figure 3.1.

The raising and fronting of *cad* is shown by a drop from 90% correct for Chicago
listeners to 72% in Philadelphia (split among /e/ and /i/ in responses) and to
only 60% in Birmingham (largely /e/). The inglide usually heard in fully stressed
NCS /æ/ is only partially effective in preserving the distinction between the tense
vowel (best represented as /æh/) and the lax front vowels.[4]

The fronted Chicago /o/ was recognized by a high percentage of Chicago listeners
(90%), and again by a lower percentage of Philadelphia listeners (78%). Recognition
by Birmingham listeners was even lower (38%). An equal number of Birmingham
listeners heard Chicago /o/ as /æ/, which is consistent with the equivalence
indicated in Figure 3.1.

Chicago /oh/ was generally heard as /o/, even in Chicago, where 54% of the
listeners did so. This lowered and fronted phoneme is located between the
Philadelphia and Birmingham /o/. The fact that the majority of Philadelphia and
Birmingham speakers heard it as /o/ – 76% and 83%, respectively – may be related
to the lexical preference for *cod* over *cawed*.

The most extraordinary mismatch between the vowel intended and the vowel identified occurred in the case of /e/. In Figure 3.1, Chicago *ked* is relatively back and low, but quite distinct from the group of /ʌ/ measurements. Nevertheless, the majority of Chicagoans identified this vowel with *cud*, and a sizeable percentage of other listeners did so as well. This must be related to the non-word status of the trade-name *Ked*, a limitation of the experimental design. Nevertheless, it is consistent with the evidence of Chapter 2 and with the Gating experiments (to follow in Chapter 4): the NCS produces considerable confusion of /e/ and /ʌ/.

As a whole, Table 3.2 shows that the vowel rotations of the NCS interfere with the capacity of speakers from other dialects to recognize the vowels produced by Chicagoans.

3.5 Responses to the Birmingham Speakers

Table 3.3 shows the patterns of identifications of the vowels spoken by the residents of Birmingham for judges from the three cities.

The most striking phenomenon is the set of low figures for the recognition of /e/. The great majority hear Birmingham *ked* as *kid*. A glance at Figure 3.1 shows

Table 3.3 Percent correct vowel identifications of Birmingham speakers in the Peterson–Barney replication (errors > 15% in parentheses)

Vowel Phoneme	Percent response by listeners		
	Philadelphia	Chicago	Birmingham
iy	96	94	96
i	89	82	94
ey	69	78	81
e	6 (80 i)	12 (74 i)	25 (69 i)
æ	65	70	73 (21 e)
ay	43 (20 æ, 24 o)	48 (32 o, 16 ʌ)	51 (15 æ, 14 o, 14 ʌ)
aw	70 (22 æ)	78	81
o	39 (11 ay, 33 oh)	52 (38 oh)	61 (20 oh)
oh	37 (44 aw)	48 (28 aw, 12 ow)	74 (15 aw)
oy	93	100	88
ow	74	94	98
u	76 (19 ʌ)	88	88
uw	76	86	94
ʌ	69 (28 u)	60 (36 u)	76 (23 u)
Mean	64	71	77

that this is an accurate perception of the acoustic realization of /e/ in *ked* by both speakers. The symbols *Bked1* and *Bked2* are in the center of the *kid* area and are heard as *kid* by most listeners. Nevertheless, the number of local judges who correctly identified the vowel as /e/ was twice as high as the figure for Chicago and four times as high as in Philadelphia.

The second greatest cause of confusion is in the area of the low back vowels: /o/ in *cod* and /oh/ in *cawed*. Recognition of /o/ ranged from 39% (Philadelphia) to 61% (Birmingham). This is consistent with the fact that the Southern realizations of /o/ and /oh/ are highly skewed from those in other dialects: both have the same low back rounded nucleus, but /oh/ is marked by a back upglide (Figure 1.9; ANAE, Map 18.8). A glance at Figure 3.1 shows that the Birmingham tokens are both well into the [ɔ] region (*Bcawed2* is somewhat centralized). About a third of the nonlocals identified this [ɔ] as /oh/, but a smaller number of the locals did so (20%).

As the pattern of the Southern Back Upglide Shift (Figure 1.9) would predict, the biggest single difference between Birmingham judges and others was in the recognition of the back upgliding *cawed* tokens produced by Birmingham speakers as [kɑod]. The local recognition rate was 74%, versus 48% for Chicago and only 37% for Philadelphia. Most of the Northern judges heard this back upgliding vowel as /aw/ in *cowed*, consistent with the fact that their nucleus for /aw/ is the back [ɑ], used by Birmingham speakers for the vowel of *cawed*.

The most generally recognized feature of Southern speech is the monophthongization of /ay/. Since the eighteen words were heard in blocks, the Southern identity was salient for the Southern section. There is every reason to think that the nonlocal subjects could use any knowledge they had of Southern speech to identify [ka:d] as *kide*. However, less than half did so. The fact that *kide* is not an existing English word undoubtedly played a role here, though it was clearly identified in print and in reading by the experimenter and had high recognition rates in the Chicago version of Table 3.2. In the chapter to follow, we will see that this difficulty in identifying salient features of Southern speech extends to forms extracted from the spontaneous speech of Birmingham speakers. The conclusion is that our subjects do not display the knowledge base necessary to build a pandialectal grammar for cross-dialectal comprehension.

Table 3.3 also reveals considerable difficulty in the identification of Birmingham /ʌ/. This reflects ANAE's finding that /ʌ/ is a relatively back vowel in the North and the Mid-Atlantic states, and relatively front in the Midland and the South, and that this difference is accelerating among younger speakers (ANAE, Ch. 11). There are only small differences among the three groups of judges, and the major error was to hear the intended unrounded vowel as if it were rounded: *cud* as *could*. Since the /ʌ/ ~ /u/ opposition is not salient for many speakers,[5] confusion was not unexpected. But the confusions are reversed in Chicago and Birmingham: Birmingham /ʌ/ has a notable tendency to be taken for /u/, and Chicago /u/ for /ʌ/. This remains to be explained.

3.6   Responses to the Philadelphia Speakers

Table 3.4 gives the percentages of correct responses to the Philadelphia speakers for judges in the three cities. The most striking difference between local and non-local listeners is found in reactions to /æ/ in *cad*. This may seem surprising since Philadelphia does not show tensing and raising of /æ/ (unlike New York City). However, recent studies of Philadelphia report a tendency in apparent time to backing of lax /æ/ (Conn 2005), and the two tokens of *Pcad* in Figure 3.1 are further back than the Birmingham or Chicago versions. Most importantly, the strong fronting of Chicago /o/ leads to the coincidence of Philadelphia *cad* with Chicago *cod*. Both Chicago tokens of *cod* are overlapped with Philadelphia *cad*. As a result, 32% of the Chicago listeners assigned Philadelphia *cad* to *cod*. Almost as many, 28%, heard this as a variant of *kide*. It can be noted here that one of the regular features of the Inland North (Chicago) dialect is the identification of the nuclei of /o/ and /ay/: both are equally fronted.

Birmingham listeners did not have much greater success in identifying Philadelphia /æ/: only 44% of their judgments were correct. Here the majority of the errors assigned the Philadelphia /æ/ to /ay/, understandable in the light of the fact that Birmingham monophthongal /ay/ is shifted to the front, close to Philadelphia /æ/.

Table 3.4   Percent correct vowel identifications of Philadelphia speakers in the Peterson–Barney replication (errors > 15% in parentheses)

Vowel Phoneme	Percentage of correct responses by listeners		
	Philadelphia	Chicago	Birmingham
iy	98	98	93
i	96	92	85
ey	72 (22 iy)	66 (32 iy)	60 (33 iy)
e	76	68	62 (15 ey)
æ	76 (15 o)	32 (28 ay, 32 o)	44 (32 ay)
ay	93	86	82
aw	87	80	82
o	89	88	82
oh	89	82	76
oy	93	88	80
ow	89	70 (18 uw)	68 (30 uw)
u	98	96	95
uw	94	92	81
ʌ	98	92	92
Mean	89	81	77

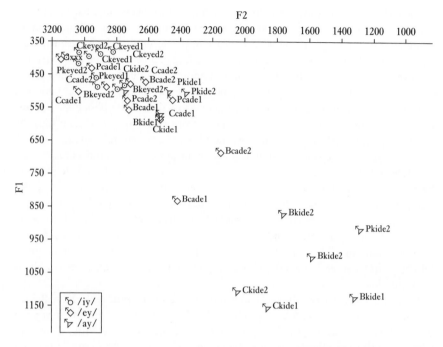

Figure 3.3   Vowel nuclei of the stimuli in the Peterson–Barney replication for front upgliding vowels in *keyed*, *cade* and *kide*. Initial consonant of vowel label: P = Philadelphia, C = Chicago, B = Birmingham

The downward shift of /e/ and /æ/ in Philadelphia also led to difficulty in the interpretation of /e/, which was only 76% correct among local listeners and somewhat less among nonlocal listeners.

One of the new and vigorous changes in Philadelphia is the raising of checked /ey/, overlapping with /iy/ (Volume 2, Chapter 4; Conn 2005). Figure 3.3 shows the F1/F2 positions of *keyed* and *cade*; one token of Philadelphia *cade* is very close to Birmingham *keyed*. As a result, a good 22% of Philadelphians heard their own *cade* as *keyed*, and a full third of the judges from Chicago and Birmingham heard the same.

3.7   Overview

It is generally recognized that the Peterson–Barney experiment would have benefited from closer control of the speakers' dialect. This experiment controls dialect variation within North American English, selecting advanced speakers of the three major regional dialects. The purpose is to further the inquiry begun in Chapter 2: what are the consequences of ongoing sound change for comprehension within the larger boundaries of the English language? In place of the naturally occurring misunderstandings of Chapter 2, we have the careful reading of a controlled list of syllables. This reduces the chance that the misunderstandings are due to unintended errors of articulation, and also eliminates the effects of varying and unusual contexts. Given the understanding that the fundamental function of the phonemic oppositions such as /æ/ ~ /o/ is to distinguish one word class from another, it must be admitted that, when this function fails, the phonemic system has failed.

In each of the three cities a significant local advantage was found. This reflects an increased likelihood of misunderstanding when residents of Philadelphia are brought into sudden contact with speakers from Chicago. These events may not bulk large against the sum total of communications in everyday life. It is often assumed that, if such cross-dialectal contacts are frequent and habitual, listeners will adjust their perceptual and interpretive systems so as to lower the rate of misunderstanding. The repeated instances of *copy* ~ *coffee* confusion in items (30)–(39) in Chapter 2 suggest that this adjustment may not happen as readily as we would like to think.

In each particular case, the local advantage was explained through the match or mismatch of the phonetic tokens produced by the six speakers, and the mismatch was in all cases explained by the opposing direction of the chain shifts, defined in Chapter 1. But the effect of sound change on comprehension appears to be even larger when we consider the error rates of the local listeners.

56% of the Chicago listeners heard Chicago /e/ as /ʌ/
54% of the Chicago listeners heard Chicago /oh/ as /o/
74% of the Birmingham listeners heard Birmingham /e/ as /i/
48% of the Birmingham listeners heard Birmingham /ay/ as /o/ or /ʌ/
40% of the Birmingham listeners heard Birmingham /oh/ as /aw/ or /ow/
22% of the Philadelphia listeners heard Philadelphia /ey/ as /iy/
15% of the Philadelphia listeners heard Philadelphia /æ/ as /o/.

These figures are lower for Philadelphia than for Birmingham and Chicago. But Philadelphians, like the others, fall short of the expected mark in interpreting the speech that they hear around them in everyday life. It is important to bear in mind that the persons who made the recordings were from the same socioeconomic and age groups as those who served as judges.[6] The results of this chapter agree with the findings of Chapter 2 on the extent of cross-dialectal miscomprehension. These results go further, showing that sound change reduces comprehension within the speech community as well as across communities.

4

The Gating Experiments

The replication of the Peterson–Barney experiment in Chapter 3 showed the extent to which changes in progress produced variation in the categorization of words pronounced under formal and controlled conditions. For some dialects of American English, it has been amply demonstrated that sound changes are modified and corrected when attention is fully focused on speech in word lists and minimal pairs. The tendency to correct vernacular speech patterns appears maximal in New York City (Labov 1966), moderate in Philadelphia (PLC, Vol. 1) and quite variable in the South (Feagin 1979). On the other hand, the comparison of word lists and spontaneous speech in ANAE interviews showed that the raising of short *a* in the Northern Cities Shift (NCS) was more advanced in word lists for seven out of the ten speakers examined, and none showed the opposite tendency (Ash 1999).[1] Whether or not we find stylistic correction, speakers will often display variation in the form of outliers in the direction of the change in progress, especially in stressed, highly emphatic articulations. It is possible that such advanced forms would have a considerable effect on cross-dialectal comprehension.

4.1   Construction of the Gating Experiments

The Project on Cross-Dialectal Comprehension [CDC] designed a series of Gating Experiments that would test the ability of listeners from Philadelphia, Chicago and Birmingham to recognize advanced forms of the Philadelphia sound changes, the Northern Cities Shift and the Southern Shift, in words taken from the most spontaneous and emphatic forms of vernacular speech. When Ash administered the Peterson–Barney replication in Chicago and Birmingham, she asked the subject groups for volunteers to be interviewed. Since it has been found that the great majority of sound changes are led by upwardly mobile young women (Labov 1990, PLC, Vol. 2; Haeri 1996), Ash selected six to seven young women from the local colleges in each city and carried out sociolinguistic interviews in which a variety of techniques serve to reduce the effects of observation (Labov

1984). The speakers that Ash interviewed were expressive, voluble and eloquent exponents of the local scene. High-quality recordings were made with the Nagra IV-S Stereo recorder and Sony lavaliere ECM-55 microphones.

From the Chicago interviews, Ash selected eighteen examples of advanced forms for each of the elements of the Northern Cities Shift.[2] In each case the target vowels were extracted as the only stressed vowel in a one or two-syllable word. A larger section was then extracted, in which the target word was heard embedded in a phrase. Finally the full sentence in which the phrase appears was extracted. The same procedure was followed for Birmingham and Philadelphia. Comprehension was tested with groups of subjects at each of the three local colleges where the original recordings had been done.

In each city, subjects first heard the series of eighteen isolated words from a given city and then were asked to write down whatever word they heard. The sounds were played from a Nagra IV-S open reel tape recorder, with a Nagra III loudspeaker, which has been found to reach all areas of a typical classroom with approximately equal clarity. Subjects were advised that some of the tokens might not sound like English words, but they should write down the sounds they heard using ordinary English spelling. Each word was played three times. After the series of words was transcribed, subjects were given a fresh page with eighteen blanks and asked to transcribe the phrases containing the same words. A third transcription page then showed the full sentences, with a blank left for the phrase. Subjects were asked to fill in the blank with their understanding of the phrase, as heard in the full sentence context.

In each city, a second series of group experiments were carried out in a local high school with the population of white, upwardly mobile students oriented to college. In Chicago, experiments were carried out in Mother Theodore Guerin High School in the suburb of River Grove. In Birmingham, Fultondale High School was selected – a public school in the town of Fultondale, just north of Birmingham.[3] In the 1990 census, Birmingham proper had a population of 264,000, with 36 percent white and 63 percent black. Fultondale had a population of 6,400, with 98 percent white and only 1.7 percent black. In Philadelphia, subjects for group experiments were recruited at Nazareth Academy, a private Catholic school in the Northeast section of Philadelphia.

4.2 Overall Responses to the Gating Experiments

Figure 4.1 and Table 4.1 show the overall pattern of responses to the speakers of the three cities by the six groups of subjects. The main effects are the same throughout: the expected upward steps of recognition with the increase of context from word to phrase to sentence. However, three unexpected aspects of these results have made these experiments the most effective and dramatic means for acquainting linguists as well as the general public with the extraordinary nature of the sound changes involved.[4]

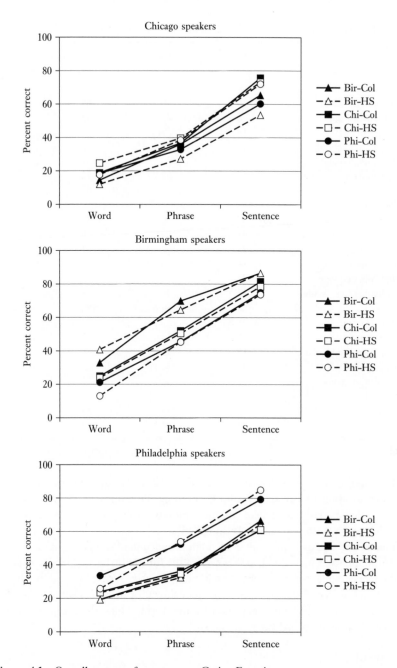

Figure 4.1 Overall pattern of responses to Gating Experiments

Table 4.1 Overall percent correct in comprehension of Gating items

	Word	Phrase	Sentence	N
Chicago speakers				
Birmingham college	15	36	66	37
Birmingham high school	13	28	54	45
Chicago college	18	37	75	94
Chicago high school	24	40	73	38
Philadelphia college	17	32	61	30
Philadelphia high school	17	38	72	43
All listeners	18	35	67	
Birmingham speakers				
Birmingham college	33	70	87	37
Birmingham high school	41	64	86	45
Chicago college	25	52	81	94
Chicago high school	24	50	78	38
Philadelphia college	21	46	75	30
Philadelphia high school	13	45	74	43
All listeners	26	54	80	
Philadelphia speakers				
Birmingham college	20	35	67	37
Birmingham high school	19	32	61	77
Chicago college	22	36	62	99
Chicago high school	22	34	61	38
Phliadelphia college	33	53	79	31
Philadelphia high school	26	54	85	39
All listeners	24	41	69	

The first of these results consists in the uniformly low rates of success in the identification of isolated words. Combining all groups of listeners, correct identification is only 18 percent for the Chicago sound changes, 24 percent for Philadelphia, and 26 percent for Birmingham.

The second unexpected result is the high proportion of errors that remain when the full sentence is played to listeners. When the full context is supplied, a majority of the listeners identify the word for what it obviously was intended to be. But in Chicago 33 percent failed to do so. The item shown below as (1) is the word *block* pronounced by a Chicago speaker in a fronted form, which the great majority of listeners hear as the word *black*.

(1)   Word: [blæ:k]
      Phrase: living on one [blæ:k]
      Sentence: senior citizens living on one [blæ:k][5]

When Philadelphia college students heard (1) in the word context, only 10 percent heard it as *block*. In the phrase context, 29 percent more sudents correctly identified it as *block*, filling in the phrase blank with "living on one block." But the full sentence context convinced only 32 percent more to change their minds. In sum, 71 percent finally realized that this speaker was saying "block" in the same way that they said "black," but 29 percent would not recognize this possibility. Table 4.1 shows that 33 percent of all the listeners failed to correct their original misunderstandings of Chicago speakers; 31 percent, of Philadelphia speakers; and 20 percent, of Birmingham speakers. This result supports the natural misunderstandings of Chapter 2, which show sequences of dialect-motivated errors that resist the interpretations provided by the full context of the speech situation.

The third remarkable aspect of these overall results is that the advantage of local listeners over outsiders is small. In each section of Figure 4.1, one can observe that the two groups of local subjects show a higher rate of correct responses than the others. The important point is that, whatever the consequences of sound change may be for cross-dialectal comprehension, they are not radically different for members of the speech community who listen to other members. While the data from natural misunderstanding in Chapter 2 were generated largely across dialect lines, the results of Chapters 3 and 4 point to a more general effect of change on comprehension within the community.

The low proportion of correct responses for isolated words may not be entirely the product of sound change, but may be in part caused by the well-known difficulty of extracting isolated sections from the stream of speech without affecting intelligibility. If the consonants preceding and following the vowel are not clearly identified, this will affect the perception of the vowel, which takes into account consonant transitions (Cooper et al. 1952). In fact, the proportion of errors due to imperfect perception of the segmental environment is small. Figure 4.2 shows the total number of responses according to the schema of (2).

(2) *Dialect motivated error*: misidentification of the vowel in the direction predicted by the sound change and by no other changes, for example *sacks* for *socks*.

    Consonant motivated error: vowel correct but consonants wrong, for example *docks* for *socks*.

    Other errors: wrong word not related to sound change, for example *besides* for *socks*.

    Blank: no response.

    Correct: *socks* for *socks*.

It is evident that the proportion of dialect errors is much greater than that of non-dialect errors: subjects are responding to these advanced forms in a way that is predicted by their phonetic character. Consonant-motivated errors, reflecting problems with the extraction of the syllable from context, are very low, for both

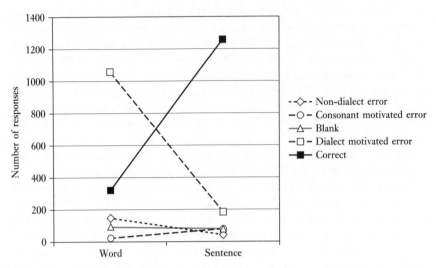

Figure 4.2   Number of response types for all Chicago listeners to Chicago speech. Speakers: word and sentence. [N = 1602]

word and sentence contexts. As the dashed black line shows, dialect-motivated errors in the word context are heavily concentrated in the segment that is affected by the change in progress. Such single-segment errors are maximal in the word context and relatively low in the sentence context.

4.3   Comprehension of the Northern Cities Shift in Chicago

In (3), the various items in the Chicago section of the Gating Experiment are grouped according to their relation to six stages of the NCS (see Figure 1.4). In this and similar displays, the item in the word context will be in caps, and the phrase context underlined.

(3)   Sound changes in the Chicago Gating items

    1   THE GENERAL RAISING AND FRONTING OF /æ/   This is most clearly exemplified by the high front position of *that* [ðiɐt], gliding to a central shwa, and less so by the upper mid position of *rafts* [reᵊfts], strongly modified by the initial /r/ and the following consonant cluster.

      •   Nobody really got <u>scared of THAT</u>.
      •   Oh we <u>went out on the RAFTS</u>, and we went out where the boats were, and they were circling around us like that.

2 THE FRONTING OF /o/ Three items focus on this variable: *block* [blæ:k] and *socks* [sæks] and *locks* [læˀks].

- Y' hadda <u>wear SOCKS</u>, no sandals.
- Old senior citizens <u>living on one BLOCK</u>.
- Oh yeah, <u>he went in the LOCKS</u>; and he got stuck in there; and they had to tow him out.

3 THE LOWERING AND FRONTING OF /oh/ See *off* [ɒf] and *talk* [tɑk].

- To <u>top it OFF</u>, her nephew came on the trip also.
- We had all these conversations and <u>TALKS</u> about it.

4 THE BACKING AND LOWERING OF /e/ Backing is shown in *steady* [stʌˤdi] and, *better* [bʌɾər]; lowering in *head* [hæd], *said* [sæd], *met* [mæt] and *red* [ræd]. The low realizations of /e/ are in the same region as /o/ in *block* and *socks*, but slightly fronter and not as long.

- And I didn't know there was such a thing as an air pocket, and we kept going up and down in the air, and uh you get to a point where <u>you're STEADY</u> for a while and there's this massive drop.
- Mostly I write, <u>I write BETTER</u> than I do anything else.
- The light is shining into his eyes, and <u>they looked RED</u>.
- I dreamed about somebody <u>that I later MET</u>, a couple of times, like in my last year of high school.
- My mother corrected me the other night and I don't know <u>what I SAID</u>.

5 THE BACKING OF /ʌ/ This is heard most clearly in *busses* [bɔsəz], which is identified by almost all listeners as "bosses."

- I can remember vaguely, when we had <u>the BUSES with the antennas</u> on top.

6 THE LOWERING AND BACKING OF /i/ This is heard in *rich* [rətʃ] and in *sick* [sæk]. There is also one token of an extremely low /i/ in *hit* [hæt].

- They were obnoxious; they didn't speak French; <u>they were all RICH</u> and scummy.
- But I never get <u>sea-SICK</u>; and I love the ocean.
- He made bathtub gin here, and they used to have a maid and a telephone, and then, they repealed prohibition <u>and then the depression HIT</u>; so it was lean times.

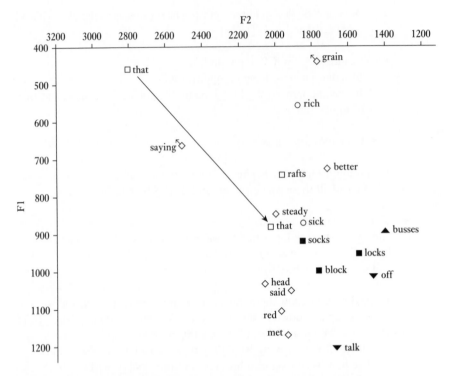

Figure 4.3   Location of vowels of Chicago Gating words in F1/F2 space

Figure 4.3 shows the location of the nuclei of the eighteen words in the CDC Chicago series In addition, Figure 4.3 shows the relatively high position of /ey/ in *saying* [se̩ɪn] and *grain* [griːn], which is characteristic of the Northern dialect.

- Well the way he died, he had a heart attack, he was <u>shoveling GRAIN</u>, down at the docks, I think.
- And you say, "I believe in baby blue eyes," and then sooner or later after <u>SAYING it so many times</u> you see two blue eyes [...] in your arms.

The oldest and most salient feature of the NCS is the general raising of short *a* in all environments, which reaches the same level as the raising before nasal consonants in many neighboring dialects. The most extreme example in the stimuli is the high ingliding vowel [ðiɐt] from an exploratory recording of 1968. The second mora is not a centering inglide, but a low front vowel of equal duration to the first.[6] It is often heard as "the act," "the fact" or "to be at," reflecting a shift of syllabicity that may be a candidate for the next stage of sound change after the first mora has reached cardinal [i].

Figure 4.4 shows a strong local advantage in the interpretation of this vowel. Both Chicago groups show a significant advantage (p < .0001) in phrase and sentence

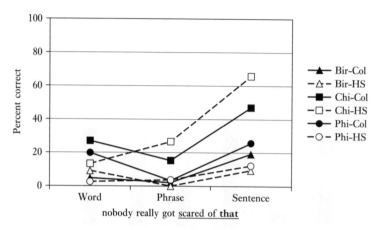

Figure 4.4 Gating responses to Chicago raised and broken /æ/ in *that*

context. Here we also note a superiority of the Chicago high school listeners over the Chicago college group, a difference that is significant at the .05 level for sentence context.

In order to understand this local advantage better, we can compare the distribution of responses in the phrase context for high school students from Philadelphia and Chicago. Figure 4.5 shows the frequency of correct responses; correct vowel but wrong consonants (*scared of dad, scared of cats*); interpretation as a succession of two phonemes /iyæ/ (*scared of the act, scared of the ice*); a high front vowel /iy/ (*scared of bees, scared of the…*); blank (no response, or ?), and other. The main differences between the two groups of listeners is in the much higher rate of correct responses in Chicago and in the large bulk of non-responses for Philadelphia. About the same percent of subjects in both cities perceived the broken vowel as two phonemes. We must assume that breaking was perceived by the Chicago listeners who gave their correct responses, but it was automatically converted to the phoneme /æ/ by those who have incorporated Northern breaking into their own systems. The high proportion of non-response from Philadelphians reflects the opposite: near-total unfamiliarity with Northern breaking before voiceless stops. There was no significant improvement for Philadelphians in sentence context: percent correct rose from 4 percent to only 12 percent.

The second stage of the NCS, the fronting of *block, socks, locks*, also displays a strong local advantage, as shown in Figure 4.6. Here the local high school students are well ahead of local college students. The difference is strongest in the word context, and diminishes as Chicagoans reach a ceiling effect. On the other hand, 29 percent of the Birmingham high school students could not accept the idea that [blæ:k] could stand for "block," and 27 percent of the Philadelphia college students could not, either.

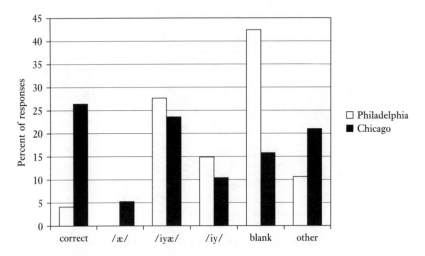

Figure 4.5 Responses to phrase context "scared of that" from high school listeners in Chicago and Philadelphia

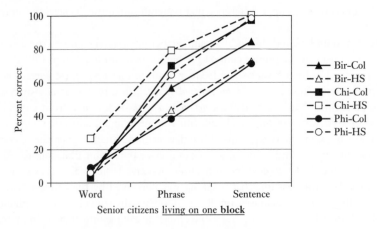

Senior citizens <u>living on one **block**</u>

Figure 4.6 Gating responses for Chicago fronted /o/ in *block*

A similar pattern appears in Figure 4.7; the fronted *socks* is interpreted as *sacks* by the overwhelming majority of listeners. A significant degree of recognition in the word context is shown by the Chicago high school students (34 percent). The pattern for *socks* is quite different from that of *block* in one respect: there is much less information provided in the phrase context, so the recognition rate is flat from word to phrase. Here again the superior ability of the Chicago high school students to recognize the characteristic forms of their own speech is quite marked. Though the college students reached 83 percent correct in the sentence context, only 11 percent recognized the isolated *socks* – less than a third of the level for high school students.

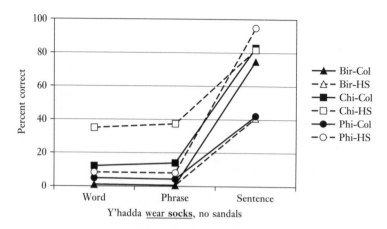

Figure 4.7 Gating responses for Chicago fronted /o/ in *socks*

Table 4.2 Regression coefficients for all responses to Chicago speakers

Factor	Coefficient	Probability
Phrase	−34.9	< .0001
Word	−52.6	< .0001
Chicago High School	8.2	.038
Unpaired	7.7	.009

Table 4.2 is a regression analysis of correct responses to the Chicago speakers. The largest factors are of course the negative effects of limited context: word and phrase as compared to the residual context, sentence. There is a small local advantage only for Chicago high school, not for Chicago college. The local advantage for Chicago shown in Table 4.2 holds for only ten of the eighteen items, and there is only a handful where it holds for both college and high school groups. High school students have an advantage over college students in the word context for eight of the eighteen items, and college students are ahead of high school students for only two items. It appears that there is no general local advantage in Chicago: sound change reduces communicative efficiency within the community as well as across communities.

4.4 Recognition of Chicago Sound Changes in the Word Context

Figure 4.8 compares success in identifying Chicago vowels in the word context across the six subject groups. In this diagram, "correct" refers to success in identifying

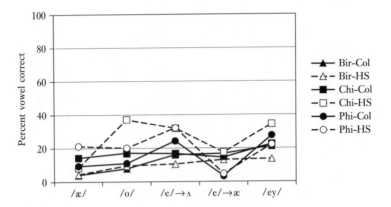

Figure 4.8 Percent responses with correct identification of the vowel in the word context by city and school. /æ/ = mean score for *rafts, that*; /o/ for *socks, block, locks*; /e/ → ʌ for *better, steady*; /e/ → æ for *met, said, red*; /ey/ for *saying, green*

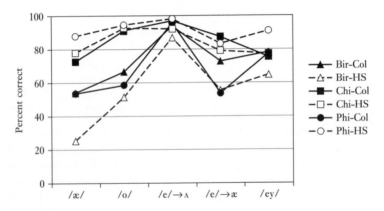

Figure 4.9 Percent responses with correct identification of the word in the sentence context by city and school. (Categories on the horizontal axis as in Figure 4.8)

the vowel, including the small number of responses in which the vowel is correct but the surrounding consonants are misidentified. The Chicago high school group is significantly superior to the college group for three of the five categories. We also observe that the Philadelphia high school group shows an advantage for three vowels. On the whole, the similarities in response are much greater than the differences. The one response which stands out from the rest comes from the 37 percent of the Chicago high school students who recognized the fronted /o/ tokens correctly: the figure is almost twice as high as for the second best group.

Figure 4.9 gives the corresponding display for the sentence context. Here the high school advantage for Chicago and Philadelphia has disappeared, and we see a strong advantage for both local groups in the first two categories. The Philadelphia high school group has the highest score in four of the five categories. On the other hand, the Birmingham high school group is at a severe disadvantage throughout.

4.5   The Effect of Lexical Equivalence

In the word context of the Gating Experiments, subjects were primarily trying to identify words, though they were told that, if they could not, they should try to indicate the sound they heard. Thus some subjects recorded "blatts" or "blatz" for *locks*; "broch" for *rich*; and one entry given for *that* was "dias." It stands to reason that, when the vowel is shifted in the direction of another phoneme, listeners would tend to hear that phoneme more often if there existed a lexical equivalent with that vowel. Thus the nine items on the left are paired with known lexical items of comparable frequency, but the nine items on the right are not.

Paired			*Unpaired*		
block	→	black	rafts	→	?
socks	→	sacks	that	→	?
locks	→	lax	seasick	→	?
better	→	butter	rich	→	?
steady	→	study	off	→	?
grain	→	green	talks	→	?
busses	→	bosses	red	→	?
met	→	mat	hit	→	?

To check the effect of such lexical equivalences, membership in the right-hand list – unpaired – was added as a factor in the regression analysis of Chicago shown in the left-hand column of Table 4.2. A significant effect emerges, with a positive coefficient of 7.7, $p < .01$, with no changes in any other figures. In other words, the absence of a lexical equivalent with the shifted vowel lowers by a good 7 percent the tendency of subjects to err in that direction of word identification. However, this leaves a large majority who continue to err in that direction, that is, who refuse to assign the shifted vowel to its intended word class even though this is the only choice that makes semantic sense. Such subjects will often hear other lexical items with different segmental environments. For example, listeners who hear the lowered and backed vowel in *rich* do not record the rare word *wretch* or *retch*, but note instead *bread*, *words* or *roads*; and, for *rafts*, the most frequent responses are *rest* and *arrest*.

4.6 Comprehension of Southern Sound Changes in Birmingham

From this point on we will consider only the word and sentence contexts. From one item to another, the increase in understanding in the phrase context will vary according to the amount of context supplied and according to the extent to which it predicts the identity of the word. For example the context _____-watchers points heavily to the word "weight," while the phrasal context "I did not _____" does not project as strongly the word "buy." Figure 4.10 supplies the acoustic measurements of the eighteen Birmingham Gating items. The various stages of the Southern Shift are represented here. Many of these vowels exhibit complex movements, and measurements at two or three points are shown as numbered series.

1 MONOPHTHONGIZATION OF /ay/ At the lower right of Figure 4.10 there appear the purely monophthongal versions of final /ay/ in *buy* and *guy*, which do not have any lexical equivalents along with an equally monophthongal token before a voiceless consonant, *nights*, which sounds to most listeners like "nice."

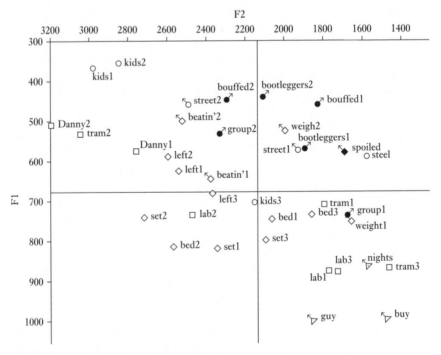

Figure 4.10 Location of vowels of Birmingham Gating words in F1/F2 space. Numbers indicate stages in the vowel trajectories

- And I <u>knew the GUY.</u>
- <u>I did not BUY</u> any kind of Hawaiian print.
- If he <u>works NIGHTS</u> at the <u>STEEL plant</u>, then he'll come in and sleep a couple of hours, then go work all day.

2 LOWERING OF THE NUCLEUS OF /ey/ This vowel falls along a nonperipheral track in the direction of /ay/. It appears in *weight1*, located well below the midline and centralized under the influence of initial /w/, then gliding to the endpoint of *weight2*. This word sounds like "white" to most listeners.

- She's on a <u>WEIGHT-watchers</u> diet now, so she eats a lot of cottage cheese.

3 THE LOWERING OF THE NUCLEUS OF /iy/ This vowel falls in the direction of /ey/, as seen in in upgliding *beatin'1,2* and *street1,2*. This realization of *beating* sounds like "baiting" to most listeners.

- No, <u>he started BEATIN' me</u> and then he said, "I let you win."
- There's <u>this one STREET</u>, called Broad Street.

Figure 4.11 shows the percent correct identification of the vowel in isolated words by the six sets of listeners for stages 1–3 of the Southern Shift, as described above. In the great majority of cases, the word is identified correctly as well; the number of cases where only the vowel is correct are minimal in this series.

Figure 4.11 displays an extraordinary advantage of the Birmingham high school subjects over all others. Though the Birmingham college students show a higher

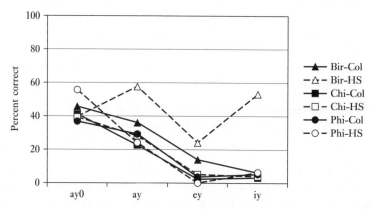

Figure 4.11 Percent correct identification of vowel in the word context of the Gating Experiment by context, city and school for the first three stages of the Southern Shift in Birmingham

correct score than others, the difference is nowhere a significant one, while /ay/, /ey/ and /iy/, the high school students differ from the rest at p < .00001 (by chi-square).

4 THE RAISING, FRONTING AND TENSING OF SHORT /i/ This appears at the upper left of Figure 4.10, with *kids1,2* ingliding to *kids3*. While Birmingham subjects uniformly hear this as "kids," Chicago listeners often hear "keys" or convert the velar onset to a labial, as "P.S."

- I was with a bunch of KIDS.

5 SOUTHERN BREAKING OF OTHER FRONT SHORT VOWELS /e/ and /æ/ undergo "Southern breaking" (ANAE, Ch. 13), where the first part of the nucleus is relatively low and lax, moving to a high tense glide and then gliding back down, to a position not far from the origin. This can be traced in Figure 4.10 in *set1,2,3, bed1,2,3, left1,2,3, lab1,2,3, tram1,2,3*. The breaking is only moderate in *left* but strong in *set*, which is commonly heard as "say it." In the polysyllable *Danny* the inglide is truncated, and the vowel is often heard as /iy/: "dainty, Zany, Danish."

- Yes, and everybody's so upSET.
- "Melanie's downstairs." No she's not, she's in the BED."
- Where the LEFT-hand keys are? Those are numbers too, and you have...
- My biology class didn't have a LAB.
- Like DANNY says some things like...
- Last time I went to Albuquerque it was in March, and there was snow, and we rode the TRAM.

6 THE GENERAL FRONTING OF /uw/ This is a continent-wide, on-going process in which the nucleus of /uw/ shifted, from high back to front of center. The South frequently shows an additional fronting of the glide to [ü] (ANAE, Ch. 12). This can be observed in Figure 4.10 in the trajectories of *group1,2, bootleggers1,2* and *bouffed1,2*. These words all glide towards high front position and are often perceived as unrounded /iy/, /ey/ or /i/.

- Every once in awhile you hear about some BOOTleggers.
- You know, their hair all BOUFFED out.
- If you want to see a diversified GROUP sit in UAB cafeteria.

A substantial local advantage appears in responses to the second and third items, as displayed in Figure 4.13. The two Birmingham groups are significantly and clearly higher than others, close to 100 percent, while the four other groups are clustered around 50 percent.

Table 4.3 gives results on two items that are quite different from the chain shifts we have been considering. The first is the merger of /i/ and /iy/ before /l/. This

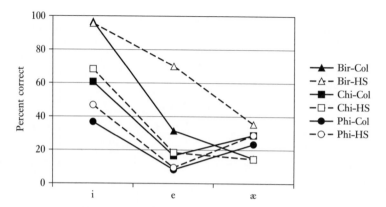

Figure 4.12 Percent correct identification in the word context of the Gating Experiment by city and school for the breaking of short front vowels in Birmingham speech

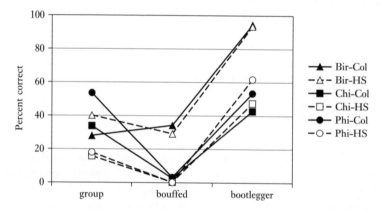

Figure 4.13 Percent correct identification in the word context of the Gating Experiment by city and school for the fronting of /uw/ in Birmingham speech

Table 4.3 Percent correct identification of Birmingham *steel* in the word context of the Gating Experiment by city and school

Birmingham Col	5
Birmingham HS	4
Chicago Col	2
Chicago HS	0
Philadelphia Col	0
Philadelphia HS	0

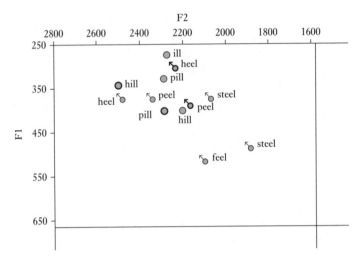

Figure 4.14   Distribution of /i/ and /iy/ tokens in the vowel system of Belle M., 67 [1995], Birmingham AL, TS 340. Highlighted tokens: minimal pairs

merger originally took place in the South in the tense position, where "fill" sounded like "feel," but the merger is now occurring in many areas in the lax position, so that *feel* sounds like *fill* to those who make the distinction, even in the South. (LYS, Di Paolo 1988, Di Paolo and Faber 1990).

• If he <u>works</u> <u>NIGHTS</u> at the STEEL plant [...]

This merger of /i/ and /iy/ before /l/ is close to being complete in Birmingham. ANAE, Map 9.7 shows that /iy/ and /i/ are "the same" in production and perception for three of the five subjects, and clearly distinct for only one. Figure 4.14 shows the distribution of /i/ and /iy/ for a 67-year-old woman from Birmingham, with tokens from both spontaneous speech and minimal pairs. The total merger is evident.

Since the merger is close to complete in Birmingham, we might expect 50 percent correct from local judges in the word context, given the fact that both *still* and *steel* are well-known words. The result is quite different: almost everyone judges the production [stɪl] to represent the word *still*, and there are no significant differences among groups. Part of the reason is frequency: *steel* is registered at only 45 in the Brown corpus, while *still* is listed at 782. In Figure 4.14, the tokens of *steel* are on the back and low end of the distribution, which would favor the interpretation of a lax vowel for listeners who expect a contrast. In any case, judgments are not significantly different from listeners from Birmingham, who have the merger, and from listeners from other cities, who do not.

The second item in Table 4.4 concerns the diphthong /oy/, which undergoes monophthongization as much as /ay/, in this case in the most favored position – before /l/.

Table 4.4 Percent correct identification of Birmingham *spoiled* in the word context of the Gating Experiment by city and school

Birmingham Col	100
Birmingham HS	100
Chicago Col	70
Chicago HS	71
Philadelphia Col	57
Philadelphia HS	55

Table 4.5 Local advantage for Birmingham sound changes in word context; ++ strong; + moderate; – none

	ay0	ay	ey	iy	i	e	æ	ruw	uw	oy
College	–	–	+	–	++	+	–	–	++	++
High school	–	+	++	++	++	+	+	–	++	++

• Everybody says that <u>only children are SPOILED</u>.

The results for this item are also strikingly different from any others, but in the opposite direction from responses to *steel* in Table 4.4. It is the only item where the local listeners show a perfect score. The nonlocal listeners are far off the mark, and high school and college groups have identical scores.

This result is what we would expect from a static situation, where members of the local community are perfectly attuned to the local dialect and outsiders are at a great disadvantage. It serves to illustrate the fact that most of our results are quite different from any such expectation.

Local advantage in the study of cross-dialectal comprehension in Birmingham is summed up in Table 4.5. The item *group* is distinguished from *bouffed* and *bootlegger* with the heading *ruw* as opposed to *uw*, since the results are so different. For college students, local advantage is quite variable; for high school students it is much more consistent. The superior performance of the high school students shows up in eight of the ten items, with no results pointing in the opposite direction.

4.7 Comprehension of Philadelphia Sound Changes

The sound changes operating in Philadelphia are not like the chain shifts of Birmingham and Chicago, which rotate vowels to a phonetic position equivalent to that of the unrotated vowels of other dialects. Instead, the characteristic Philadelphia change shifts phonetic qualities to an extreme position, quite different from the sounds that the out-of-state listener is familiar with. The vowel shifts are

described in some detail in Volume 2, Ch. 4: four of them are represented in the
CDC stimuli, along with the vocalization of intervocalic /l/.

1   CANADIAN RAISING OF /ay/   In the 1970s, the centralization of /ay/ before
voiceless consonants was a new and vigorous change in Philadelphia, one of the
two male-dominated variables. Backing and rounding of the nucleus was particularly characteristic of young working-class men. The CDC items included
a male speaker saying:

- Well <u>ridin' my BIKE</u> [bɔˤɪk] on a rainy day, and the brakes never work
  when you have hand brakes.
- They stopped at a <u>red LIGHT</u> [lʌit].
- [. . .] that go out <u>lookin' for a FIGHT</u> [fɔit].

2   RAISING AND FRONTING OF (æh)   As in most other areas, Philadelphians have
tense /æ/ before nasals in closed syllables. The extreme Philadelphian form
shows a high fronted nucleus followed by an inglide, which is often hard for
others to recognize.

- That's why <u>HALF [hi:əf] of the things</u>, I don't know, I can't understand
  how they sell them!
- In fact, that girl got beat <u>really BAD</u> [bi:əd] with a chain and they put her
  in the hospital for that.
- The hospital nowadays, they want you to have at least <u>HALF [hɛ:əf] of it
  down</u> before you go *in* the hospital.
- <u>There's a BAND</u> [be:ənd], and they have like beer, and whiskey sours.

3   RAISING AND FRONTING OF (aw)   Older Philadelphians of the 1970s realized
/aw/ as [æo]; younger Philadelphians moved the nucleus to upper mid peripheral
position, and shifted the glide target to [ɔ].

- We <u>have HOUSE [hɛ:os] parties</u> like we had a pollyanna party here.
- She used to have eh a very <u>LOUD [le:əd] voice.</u>
- Well years ago, people around here were <u>too PROUD [pre:oˤd] to get it</u>.

4   THE FRONTING OF /ow/ IN CHECKED SYLLABLES   As in the Midland and South
generally, the nucleus of /ow/ is strongly fronted in Philadelphia. It is especially
unrounded, so that, when the syllable is compressed, the vowel is often mistaken
for a front unrounded vowel.

- Like, <u>I'll tell you</u>, <u>MOST [mɪs] of them</u> talk about their families.
- Yeah <u>MOST [mɛˀst] of them</u> are steady 'cause we have all trucking com-
  panies up there.

5 THE VOCALIZATION OF /l/   As pointed out in Chapter 2, Philadelphia has an unusual extension of the vocalization of /l/, which applies freely in intervocalic position. This is a major source of miscomprehension.

- About the woman who lived in a house, <u>they were CALLIN' [kɔːɪn]</u> her the old witch.
- So she <u>took a RULER [rʊɣr]</u> and smacked my hands.
- Before I had the baby I fell <u>down the CELLAR [sɛːɝ]</u> steps, 'n' she was right there to help me.

The overall results of the Gating Experiments with Philadelphia speakers are shown in Figure 4.15 for the word context and in Figure 4.16 for the sentence context. The overall pattern seems clear. Birmingham and Chicago are not differentiated, while Philadelphia shows a strong local advantage, except for variables that are close to zero or 100 percent.

This result makes it evident that the local advantage in Philadelphia is greater than that found in Chicago and Birmingham. This was first indicated in Figure 4.1. The local advantage shown in Figures 4.4, 4.10 and 4.11 is less consistent than that displayed in Figures 4.13–4.14 and Table 4.6. This difference between the

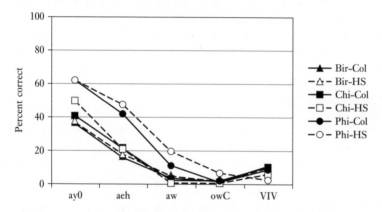

Figure 4.15   Percent correct identification of five Philadelphia sound changes in the word context by city and school

Table 4.6   Significance by chi-square of advantage of Philadelphia vs other listeners in percent correct identification of Philadelphia speakers

	ay0	aeh	aw	ow	VIV
Word	0.001	< .0001	0.0003	ns	ns
Sentence	ns	0.02	0.002	< .0001	< .0001

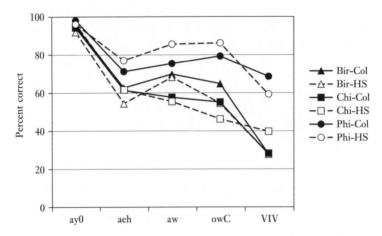

Figure 4.16   Percent correct identification of five Philadelphia sound changes in the sentence context by city and school

cities is most likely to be connected with the difference in the character of the sound changes concerned. Chicago and Birmingham are involved in chain shifts, where the younger, more advanced speakers realize a given vowel in such a way that it overlaps another vowel as spoken by the older, more conservative speakers. Thus 73 of the 89 Chicago college students heard the advanced token of *socks* as *sacks*, as compared with 28 out of the 31 Philadelphia college students; the difference is not significant. In Birmingham, 36 out of 37 college students wrote *sacks*, a result which differs from the Chicago subjects at the .05 level.

The Philadelphia sound changes are not chain shifts but radical phonetic developments of individual elements of the system, and this makes identification particularly difficult in spontaneous speech. In Figures 4.15 and 4.16, the (æh) variable shows a significant local advantage, and it may be instructive to see what the main sources of difficulty are in the outsiders' identification of these vowels. The fact that the tense vowels involved are phonemically distinct from the lax set in Philadelphia (Ferguson 1975, Labov 1989b) is not necessarily relevant, since raising and fronting of short *a* is also found in the allophonic distributions of Chicago and Birmingham. Figure 4.17 locates the nuclei of the test items *bad, band, half* in a plot of all the stressed vowels in the sentences spoken by the female Philadelphian. One can observe a tight clustering of five phonemes in the upper front peripheral area: the nuclei of /iy/ in *beat*; /ihr/ in *beer, cheer*; /eyC/ in *chain*; /aw/ in *down, thousand, sours, how, proud*; and tense /æh/ in *bad, band, baskets, half*. All of these are higher and fronter than the lax nucleus of /i/ in *this*, so that they will be heard phonetically as beginning with [i]. This tense initial is distinctly higher and fronter than the lax vowel of *this*, which is close to the unrounded nucleus of /ow/ in *go* and *most*.

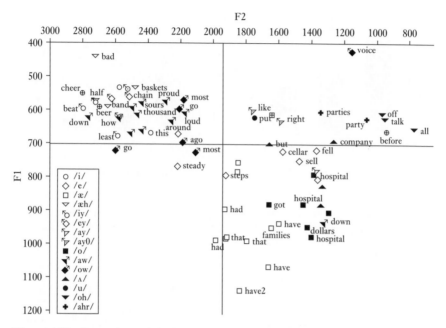

Figure 4.17 Stressed vowels in Gating Experiment sentences spoken by female Philadelphian

However, responses to the Gating item *half* do not reflect this tense initial. It is identified overwhelmingly in the word context as a lax short *i*. The word "if" is most prominent in the responses: 37 percent of the responses in Philadelphia, 52 percent in Chicago, 67 percent in Birmingham. However, there is little local advantage here. In each city only one person gave the correct response to the word "half." The lower incidence of "if" in Philadelphia reflects the fact that Philadelphians were more likely to submit a blank response than the other listeners were.

Much of the local advantage in Philadelphia stems from the Philadelphians' ability to recognize tensed short *a* in *bad* and *band*. Figure 4.18 a and b shows the percent responses for college students from the three cities. On the left hand, it is evident that Philadelphians are superior in their ability to identify this form: Philadelphia registers 94 percent correct, as against 58 percent for Chicago and 46 percent for Birmingham. The dominant tendency in Chicago and Birmingham is to report the tense, raised *band* as having a mid lax phoneme /e/, as in *bend, fend, end, pen*. It appears that tensed short *a* is heard as a lax vowel, despite the fact that the onset of the vowel is higher than the high front tense /iy/. We can attribute this to the general tendency in North American English to identify ingliding tokens with short vowels, no matter how long they become. Indeed the vowel of *band* is very long: 534 msec. But, as Figure 4.19 shows, the nucleus of *band* is a high front

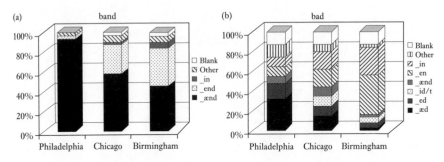

Figure 4.18a and b   Gating Experiment responses to *band* and *bad* in the word context

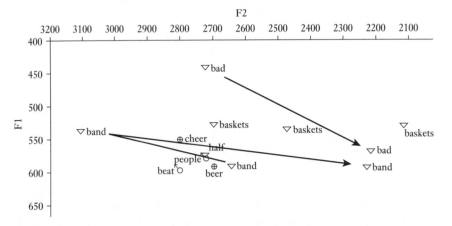

Figure 4.19   Trajectories of *bad* and *band* in the Philadelphia CDC stimuli

vowel, close to *beer*; it then moves rapidly to a central inglide. It is then uniformly interpreted as a lax vowel – phonemically mid or sometimes high, as in *thin, in, pin*.

In Figure 4.18 a and b, the pattern of responses to Philadelphian *bad* adds another feature to the picture. Philadelphians are much ahead of others in the percent of correct identifications of *bad* (and words that rhyme with *bad*). Yet the correct response represents only a minority of the total (32 percent). Almost as many listeners (26 percent) hear a word with a nasal consonant (*and, band, ben, den, din, thin...*). In the subjective reaction tests of the LCV project, tense /æh/ was the main item to receive overt comment, and it was not uncommon for Philadelphians to refer to the "harsh nasal a" in *bad* as well as in *Camden*. A tense high front nucleus is associated with the prenasal allophone more than with any other. Again, we note that this tense ingliding form is assigned only to lax nuclei, with or without a nasal consonant following.

The tendency to hear *bad* with a nasal consonant is stronger in Chicago (45 percent), even though the difference between oral and nasal allophones of /æ/ is smaller in the Northern cities than anywhere else. The tendency is overwhelming in Birmingham (71 percent). The Birmingham short-*a* system is continuous. Following nasals show the most raising and fronting, but following voiced consonants show considerable shift in this direction as well. We might well conclude that the Philadelphia tense /æh/ before oral consonants is pronounced with a significant opening of the nasal passage.

These patterns of local advantage are opposed to other Philadelphian advanced forms, which are difficult for everyone to recognize. In Figure 4.15 no group has more than 6 percent success in recognizing checked /ow/ in the word context. The unrounded and truncated nucleus of /ow/ in the two instances of *most* was recognized as /ow/ by only two Philadelphia subjects: the great majority of responses from all three cities showed a short /i/ nucleus: *miss, missed, mist*. In Figure 4.16, this opaque situation in word context is translated into a strong local advantage in the sentence context. Nevertheless, we find nine of thirty-two Philadelphia college students hearing /ow/ as /i/, in transcriptions of *I'll tell you most of them*...as "I tell you miss them," "I'll tell you listen," or "I'll tell him you missed him."

Even though this token of *most* is fully stressed, it is a function word subject to reduction, and this may account for the truncation of the glide. This does not apply to the last item in Figures 4.14–4.16, the vocalization of intervocalic /l/ in *callin'*, *ruler*, and *cellar*. No group showed more than 10 percent recognition of these words in the word context, and the non-Philadelphians did not exceed 40 percent correct in the sentence context. These results mesh with the proliferation of natural misunderstandings of *balance, cooler, spelling, Tell him, volleyball* in Chapter 2 (items (59)–(63)). Of the thirty-two Philadelphia college students, twenty heard *cellar* as "sorry" and four as "sir" in the word context. They guessed at *ruler* in a wide variety of forms: "roar, more, walk, work, wall, roll, roy, boy, rural, raw," and only one heard "ruler." In the phrase context, *took a ruler* was heard as "took a walk" by twenty out of thirty-two, and as "to the wall" by four. The isolated word *callin'* was reported most often as "coin" or "point." In the sentence context, *they were callin' her* remained opaque for 31 percent. Nine of the thirty-two subjects heard *callin'* as *corner*, in such transcriptions as "on the corner." The mishearing as *corner* is facilitated by the fact that this is a dissimilating word in Philadelphia, like *quarter*, and the first /r/ is regularly vocalized.

These results confirm earlier indications that the vocalization of intervocalic /l/ is very far below the level of social consciousness in Philadelphia, though it is firmly rooted in the phonological practice of that community.

4.8   Overview of the Gating Experiments

The results of the CDC Gating Experiments show major interference with the communicative function of language as a consequence of the Northern Cities Shift, of the Southern Shift, and of the Philadelphia sound changes. The local advantage, which appears at one point or another of these investigations, is encouraging because it confirms the initial impetus for the experiments, which focused on the ability of speakers from one city to understand the output of sound changes of another city – sound changes that were alien to them and firmly rooted in that other speech community. If the members of that second community are significantly better in their ability to recognize these advanced forms, it is because they have frequently produced them, heard them and recognized them in interaction with their peers in everyday life.

At the same time, this local advantage is limited. It is significant for less than half of the items where it could be expected to appear. This is true not only for new sound changes in progress, but for well-established regional features like the monophthongization of /ay/. In many cases, local subjects fail to recognize pronunciations like [ga:] for *guy*, which are the normal and dominant form of their own phonetic realization. If the local advantage were everywhere strong, we could then conclude that the interference of sound change with the communicative function of language was limited to cross-dialectal communication. However, the confusion introduced by sound change affects local speakers in the same way as nonlocal speakers.

One model that has been advanced for the perception of phonemic categories would predict a stronger local advantage. The exemplar model developed by Pierrehumbert (2002) argues that perceived instances of a labeled sound are stored in episodic memory with detailed phonetic and social information. Hay, Warren and Drager (2006) investigated the ability of New Zealanders to identify a word as /ihr/ or /ehr/ – given the ongoing merger of these two vowels. Their subjects' decisions were significantly influenced by the perceived age and social class of the speaker. Storage of age information from remembered tokens should allow members of the community to interpret advanced tokens of a sound change as they are normally spoken by the younger people they know. We would expect a very large advantage for these locally embedded listeners over subjects in another city who have little or no experience with their local phonology. If our subjects have stored their daily experience in a form to which they have ready access, why is the local advantage not greater?

One avenue to an understanding of this question is to consider the number of contexts in which high school students outperformed college students – in Figures 4.4, and 4.6 through to 4.10. The most striking cases are in Figures 4.6–4.7, where local college students are well behind high school students in the word context, but recover their ground once more context is supplied. It seems likely that the loss of college students' ability to recognize their own speech patterns is the result of more extensive contact with competing norms: the conservative patterns of older academic figures and the increased contact with nonlocal speakers, who are closer to the norms of broadcast standard. The experiment itself is carried out in an academic setting, where vernacular norms are disfavored. Our experimenter, Sharon Ash, delivered her instructions in all three cities in her conservative Chicago dialect, without the radical rotation of /æ, o, e, ʌ, oh/ characteristic of advanced forms. All of these factors would help to explain why local advantage is so limited.

One might also explain the high error rates of the word context as a product of the experimental methodology. We normally do not hear words in isolation, excerpted from the stream of speech. But this methodology is the appropriate way of testing the phonological efficiency of the system, in which the alternation of a single distinctive feature should be enough to trigger the interpretation of the morpheme, phrase, and sentence.[7]

Furthermore, the results of the Gating Experiments are consistent with the view of cross-dialectal comprehension derived from the study of natural misunderstandings. Dialect differences lead to confusion, and language change compounds it. Even those with the most intimate knowledge of cross-dialectal relations fail to apply that knowledge in the rapid interchanges of everyday life. The view of the speaker-listener that emerges from these studies is quite remote from that of the sensitive agent who is said to monitor, store and retrieve dialectal information from the accumulated memories of previous experience. Rather this speaker-listener comes across as a more simple-minded individual, whose reactions are dominated by the salient categories of the moment, who hears what he or she expects to hear.

Given the limitations of the machinery for processing dialect differences, we return to the ever-puzzling questions of the causes of language change.

Part B

The Life History of Linguistic Change

5

Triggering Events

The preliminary chapters of this volume have been devoted to an examination of the cognitive consequences of linguistic change. This pursuit was in part driven by the desire to resolve the Darwinian Paradox of Volume 2, repeated below:

> The evolution of species and the evolution of language are identical in form, although the fundamental mechanism of the former is absent in the latter.

That fundamental mechanism is of course natural selection. No matter what view we have of the mechanism of linguistic evolution, it is clear that human language has evolved the capacity to transfer propositional information about near and remote times and places.[1] To identify a cognate of natural selection in the sound changes now in progress, we would have to find a mechanism through which the capacity to communicate such truth-conditional information was enhanced – or at least preserved – by the innovative forms. In our studies of the cognitive consequences of linguistic change in Chapters 2–4 we might have discovered a general capacity for dealing with the effects of change, perhaps in the form of a pandialectal phonology that assigned each new variant its proper interpretation. But no such mechanism was found in the natural misunderstandings of Chapter 2 or in the CDC experiments of Chapters 3 and 4. Instead, we found people repeatedly confused by the new forms, even those that matched their own productions. These results can only reinforce the negative view of change that was dominant in the nineteenth century reviewed in Chapter 1 of Volume 2. Sound change does interfere with the primary function of language as an instrument for conveying truth-conditional information. Both our evolutionary perspective and our sociolinguistic orientation lead us to reject the earlier attribution of change to laziness, carelessness and ignorance. What, then, are the forces that initiate, shape and drive to completion the sweeping linguistic changes described in Volumes 1 and 2? The present chapter is the first in a series that attempts to answer this question.

5.1   Bends in the Chain of Causality

There is general agreement that the heart of the study of language change is the search for causes. It is what we generally mean by the explanation of change. While we would like to apply to this search the universal principles that govern grammar as a whole, it is also understood, following Meillet (1921), that no universal principles can account for the sporadic course of change, in which particular changes begin and end at a given time in history. The actuation problem demands that we search for universals in particulars.

However, the pursuit of the causes of any given change might, on further reflection, involve us in an unsatisfactory and endless recursion. It goes without saying that any given state of a language is the outcome of a previous state of that language, and so on – back in time as far as our knowledge can carry us. The title of this chapter needs, then, some justification if it refers to linguistic events. In an endless chain of causes, every state of the language is a triggering event for the one that follows. Even if there is no detectable change in a given system, the system itself has a cause: the state of equilibrium that was reached in the preceding period. And when there is change, as Martinet (1955) has argued, the evolving system reflects a series of earlier readjustments, which spiral backward in time.

I would like to defend the concept of "triggering event" by arguing that this sequence of preceding causes is not smooth and uniform. Rather, there are bends in the chain of causality at which the triggering events are located, as suggested in Figure 5.1. Around the bend there are further chains of causality, but they are often orthogonal to the question that drives the original search. A nonlinguistic example may illustrate the point. We are all interested in the prehistory that gave rise to mammalian evolution, and in this causal sequence we encounter the extinction of dinosaurs, along with plesiosaurs, mosasaurs, and a majority of all other existing families at the K-T boundary between the Cretaceous and Tertiary Periods. What caused this massive extinction? The most strongly supported theory is that of Luis and Walter Alvarez, originally proposed in the 1980s: that the K-T extinction was the result of the impact of a large meteor with the earth.

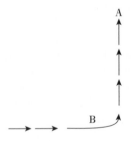

Figure 5.1   A bend in the chain of causality

While the exact killing mechanisms may or may not yet have been identified, all the data – including the rate of extinction, the nature of the recovery, and the patterns of survivorship – are concordant with the hypothesis of extinction by asteroid impact. (Fastovsky and Sheehan 2004)

The hypothesis of a meteor impact, if it continues to be supported, provides a satisfactory answer to the search for the triggering event that gave rise to mammalian predominance in the evolutionary sequence. But what, then, were the causes of this intersection of asteroid and earth? It is an important question for the future of the human race, which would be profoundly influenced by a potential major impact of this kind. Yet the pursuit of that question would not further illuminate the later history of biological evolution. The triggering event in this case is the joint result of many other historical events whose concatenation is not relevant to our original question. A triggering event of the linguistic changes we have been studying may indeed be an earlier linguistic event, one which represents a terminus a quo for the historical development as well as a terminus ad quem for the inquiry.

Chain shifts are a natural subject for the study of causal sequences and for the search for triggering events. Section 1.5 of Chapter 1 describes six such chain shifts, which involve two to six events. In each case we can posit an earliest event in the chain. Though there is always some uncertainty on this, we can ask in each case: what preceding event brought about this initial element of the chain shift?

We might think, again following Martinet, that this triggering event must be an external event impinging on the linguistic process, like the Norman Invasion or World War II – an event outside of the realm of autonomous linguistic explanation. For some shifts, this is indeed the case. But in others it will appear that there are linguistic bends in the chain of causality, and I will argue that there are triggering events of a purely linguistic character. Their explanation calls upon a different set of principles from those that operate on the changes they initiate.

First, however, it can be shown that bends in the linguistic chain are essential characteristics of chain shifts. In fact, without such shifts of direction it will be difficult to defend the very concept of a chain shift.

Consider the simplest kind of chain shift.

(1) B → A →

Here A is the *leaving* element and B is the *entering* element.[2] A causal connection might be said to exist if A moved away because B approached A, reducing the margin of security, or if A moved away, increasing the margin of security, and B consequently moved in the direction of A. However, such chain shift events are subject to an alternative interpretation. The movement of A may be generalized to B, just as a change affecting a front vowel may be generalized to the corresponding back vowel without any relevant change in margins of security. In (2) below, if A is a vowel /e/ moving in the vowel space from mid to high, and B is a low vowel

/æ/ moving from low to mid behind it, one could argue that the movements of A and B are causally related. But this can also be conceived of as a single expression, as in (3): an expression in which all front vowels undergo the loss of one degree of openness. Whatever factor C acted on /e/ to make it less open, it came to act equally on /æ/, so that the causal relationship is seen as in (4) rather than (1).

(2)   A   e → i
       B   æ → e

(3)   α open → α-1 open / _____
       [+ant]

(4)   C
          ╱ ╲
       B   A

However, option (4) is not available if A and B are different kinds of linguistic processes. Thus, in the Southern Shift (Figure 1.5), A is the monophthongization of /ay/ and B is the lowering and centralization of the nucleus of /ey/ (ANAE, Ch. 18) – as represented in (5). In A, /ay/ is a vowel from the subsystem of front upgliding vowels that moves to the system of long and ingliding vowels, while B is an adjustment entirely within the set of front upgliding vowels.

(5)   A   ay → ah
       B   ey → ay

Here we must accept a chain shift of type (1), since there is no single process that can be generalized in order to unite the behavior of A and B. The causal relationship seems clear: the removal of /ay/ from the front upgliding system has led to a re-adjustment by the well-recognized principle of maximum dispersion: the tendency of vowels to achieve equidistant positions within a subsystem (Martinet 1955,

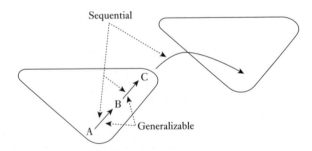

Figure 5.2   Generalizable and sequential chain shifts within and across subsystems

Liljencrants and Lindblom 1972, Disner 1978, Lindblom 1988).[3] Figure 5.2 sums up the characterization of these two situations: generalizable shifts within a subsystem, and sequential shifts across subsystems.

The type of causal explanation applied to chain shifts is not in question here. In this search for triggering events, one may take a teleological position, like that of Martinet (1955) or Jakobson (1972), and argue that speakers shift their vowels to minimize misunderstanding. Or one can attribute these linked movements to the mechanical effects of misunderstanding on the probability matching of the language learner (Volume 1, Chapter 20). Evidence for the causal link may come from temporal sequencing, geographic nesting or internal correlation (ANAE, Chs 14, 18). However, the order of events is crucial to the present discussion: whether we are dealing with a drag chain or a push chain will be a determining factor in the search for triggering events.

5.1.1 Subsystems of English vowels

Much of the logic of chain shifting involves movements out of and into subsystems. The binary notation used throughout Volumes 1 and 2 and developed in most detail in ANAE, Ch. 2 is designed to characterize these subsystems in a coherent and systematic manner. Figure 1.1 outlined the four subsystems of North American English: short vowels, front upgliding vowels, back upgliding vowels, and the smaller set of long and ingliding vowels. The notation does not describe the set of contrasts in any one dialect, but rather the initial position from which present-day dialects can be derived. In that sense, the individual units are historical word classes comparable to the lexical key words presented in Wells (1982).[4]

The principles of maximal dispersion and maintenance of margins of security, developed in Martinet (1955), operate within subsystems. Chapter 9 of Volume 1 presented data from natural misunderstandings (the same data set as in Chapter 2 of this volume), which show that confusions occur primarily within members of a subsystem, rather than across subsystems. There is for example more confusion between /i/ and /e/ than between /e/ and /ey/, and more between /ey/ and /ay/ than between /ay/ and /aw/.[5]

5.2 Causes of the Canadian Shift

The Canadian Shift, first shown in Figure 1.6, is reproduced here as Figure 5.3. It involves three events, as shown: the backing and raising of /o/, the backing of /æ/, and the lowering and backing of /e/.

This chain shift was first described by Clarke et al. in 1995, on the basis of word lists read by sixteen college students, and has since been confirmed by several

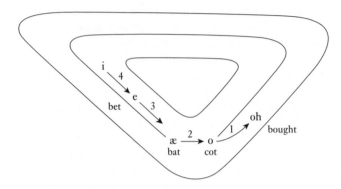

Figure 5.3   The Canadian Shift

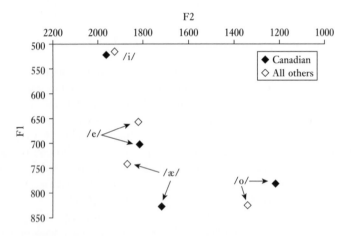

Figure 5.4   Mean values of vowels in the Canadian Shift for the Canada region [N = 25] and all other dialects combined [N = 414]

other studies of Canadian English (ANAE, Ch. 16, De Decker and Mackenzie 2000, Boberg 2005, Hollett 2006, Hagiwara 2006, and Roeder and Jarmasz 2009). It is the most consistent marker of the Canadian English dialect in ANAE, and it is the basis for the isogloss defining the Canada region of North American English (including all points in Canada outside of the Atlantic Provinces).[6] Figure 5.4 compares the Canada dialect region with the combined means for all other regions for the vowels involved in the shift. There is no significant difference for /i/ in the ANAE, though other studies find backing and/or lowering. Canadian /e/ is significantly lower than the general mean, and an even greater difference appears for /æ/. One can also observe that /o/ is well back of the general average.

It was clear from the outset that the lowering and backing of the short front vowels was a response to the low back merger of /o/ and /oh/ in *cot* and *caught* or *Don* and *dawn*, well established in Canada. To which subsystem do we assign the collapsed vowel phonologically? The decision is dictated by phonological facts. While the original short *o* was a checked vowel, which cannot occur in stressed word-final position, the merged vowel occurs in free as well as in checked position: that is, the vowel of *cot* is now an allophone of the vowel of *caw*. Though both vowels may shift position in the course of the merger,[7] it is /o/ that moves to the long and ingliding subsystem rather than /oh/ to the short subsystem. Figure 5.3 embeds the Canadian Shift in the acoustically defined phonological space characteristic of the modern West Germanic languages, with a peripheral region enclosing a nonperipheral region. By the principles of chain shifting developed in Chapters 5 and 6 of Volume 1, tense or long vowel nuclei rise along the peripheral track, and lax or short nuclei fall along the nonperipheral track. A shift from a short to a long subsystem appears as a movement towards a peripheral track, as indicated in Figure 5.3.[8] The remaining short vowels then readjust their positions along the nonperipheral track, to achieve maximal dispersion.

The temporal relations of the low back merger and of the Canadian shift are consistent with the causal assignment to the merger as prior. As noted above, the first report of the shift of /e/ and /æ/ dates from 1995. The low back merger in Canada was firmly documented well before then (Scargill and Warkentyne 1972, Gregg 1957). Chambers (1993: 11–12) cites literary sources for the merger already in the middle of the nineteenth century.

The geographic distributions of the Canadian Shift and of the low back merger are also consistent with the causal connection inferred; here we encounter the nesting relation that plays an important role in the application of dialect geography to historical sequencing. Figure 5.5 maps the distribution of ANAE subjects who satisfy the acoustic criteria for the Canadian Shift (grey symbols) and the isogloss that defines the region in which these symbols predominate. The homogeneity of this isogloss – the proportion of speakers within the area who satisfy the criteria – is .84. Twenty-one of the twenty-five Canadians within the isogloss satisfy it, producing an even more reliable definition of the Canadian dialect than Canadian Raising (ANAE, Ch. 15). However, consistency – the proportion of speakers showing the trait who fall within the isogloss – is quite low, since the same forces are operating wherever the low back merger is found. The implicational relation between the Canadian Shift and the low back merger is evident, in that only three of the sixty speakers who show the Canadian Shift have /o/ and /oh/ as distinct. The important geographic relation is that the Canadian Shift isogloss is strictly contained within the low back merger isogloss on Figure 5.5. The low back merger extends to a much wider territory, covering the West, Western Pennsylvania and Eastern New England in the US. A total of 123 speakers produced /o/ and /oh/ as the same in minimal pair tests, and only sixty showed the back shifting of /e/ and /æ/. At the same time, the Canadian Shift does appear among a minority group of speakers in other low back merger areas: twelve in the West; five in Western Pennsylvania; four in Texas, where the merger is reported to be in progress (Bailey

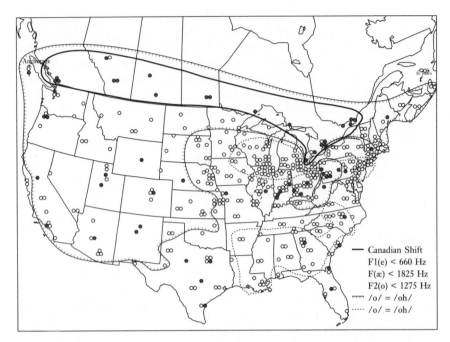

Figure 5.5   Nesting of Canadian Shift within the Low Back Merger isogloss.
Grey symbols = satisfies three conditions of the Canadian Shift

et al. 1991); and seven in the Midland, where the merger is generally in transition.[9] However, only two grey symbols appear within the dashed isoglosses: these outline the areas of greatest resistance to the merger: in the Inland North, the Mid-Atlantic states and the South. The two exceptional cases are in cities of the South with strongest Midland influence: Atlanta and Raleigh-Durham.

Both temporal evidence and spatial evidence thus indicate that the low back merger is a prior condition for the backing of /æ/ and accompanying backing and lowering of /e/.[10] In removing /o/ from the subset of short vowels, it acts as the triggering event for the Canadian Shift.

5.3   Causes of the Pittsburgh Shift

ANAE reported a chain shift in the city of Pittsburgh, first shown as Figure 1.7 and reproduced here as Figure 5.6.

The low back merger is solidly entrenched in Pittsburgh, as it is in Canada. But in Pittsburgh the phoneme /ʌ/ moves downward on the nonperipheral track from mid back-of-center position, while /æ/ remains in place in the low front area.

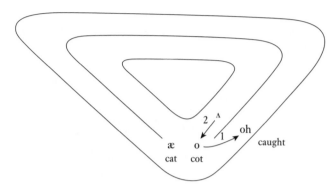

Figure 5.6   The Pittsburgh Shift

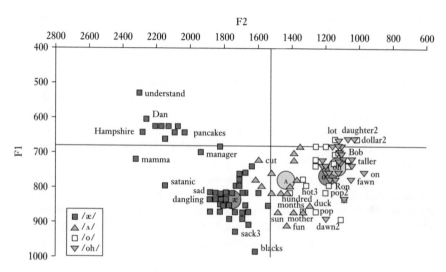

Figure 5.7   The Pittsburgh Shift in the system of Kenneth K., 35 [1996], TS 545

Figure 5.7 provides a detailed view of this downward movement in the vowel system of a 35-year-old man from Pittsburgh, interviewed in 1996. On the left, the short-*a* vowels follow the nasal system: words with nasal codas are raised to mid and upper mid position, while all others are in a tight cluster in low front position. In the back, /o/ is clearly merged with /oh/ in the same lower mid back position as in Canada. Between /æ/ and /o/~/oh/ are located the majority of the tokens of /ʌ/. Words with /ʌ/ before /n/ are particularly low (*sun, mother, fun, months*); the token of *duck* is regularly heard as *dock* by speakers of other dialects.

Figure 5.8 places this Pittsburgh development against the mean values of the low vowels for Canada and eighteen other North American dialects.[11] It can be

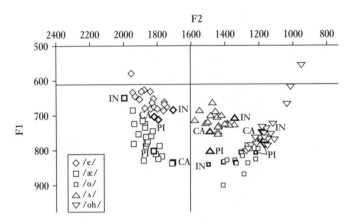

Figure 5.8   Mean positions of low vowels for twenty ANAE dialects, with Canadian Shift labeled for Canada [CA], Pittsburgh Shift labeled for Pittsburgh [PI] and Northern Cities Shift labeled for the Inland North [IN]

seen that the mean position of /æ/ in Canada is well to the back of other dialects while Pittsburgh /æ/ is in normal low front position.[12] At right, both Canada and Pittsburgh show the merger of /o/ and /oh/ in lower mid back position (the two Canada tokens practically coincide). In the center, the Pittsburgh mean for /ʌ/ is much lower than that of any other dialect, not far from the general distribution of /o/.

The low back merger is evidently the conditioning event for the Pittsburgh Shift, just as it is for the Canadian Shift. Here, however, we have the same cause with two different effects. In the search for causes of linguistic change, it seems reasonable to expect that the same cause will have similar or comparable effects. Why is it that /ʌ/ instead of /æ/ moved into the empty space created by the back shift of /o/ and merger with /oh/?

Among North American English sound changes, there are other cases of two neighboring phonemes competing to fill the empty space in the pattern.[13] One might say that these are two equal possibilities, and it is a matter of chance which one is realized. But these choices are not equally probable: there are sixty communities which show evidence of the Canadian Shift, and only one city with the Pittsburgh Shift.[14] To account for the unique Pittsburgh development, it is not unreasonable to turn to the other unique feature of the Pittsburgh dialect: the monophthongiza-tion of /aw/. The Pittsburgh long monophthong in *down, town, south, out* and *house* is located in low central position, partially overlapping with /ʌ/. There is no danger of confusion between /ʌ/ and /aw/, however, since monophthongized /aw/ has twice the length of /ʌ/, so that typically the longest /ʌ/ is shorter than the shortest /aw/ (ANAE: 273). One hypothesis is that the lowering of /ʌ/ is the result of a change in the organization of the vowel system of Pittsburgh speakers in which

/ʌ/ is re-analyzed as /a/, the short counterpart of /ah/. This would oppose the long and short pairs *down* ~ *dun, about* ~ *but, howl* ~ *hull* as /dahn/ ~ /dan/, /baht/ ~ /bat/, /hahl/ ~ /hal/. If further evidence supports such an abstract re-analysis, then both the low back merger and the monophthongization of /aw/ appear to be triggering events for the Pittsburgh Shift. Both are movements of a word class into the long and ingliding subsystem from other subsystems.

5.4 Causes of the Low Back Merger

Given our understanding of the effect of the low back merger on other linguistic events, the question that naturally arises is: what are the causes of the low back merger? Herold (1990, 1997) has provided a convincing social account of the actuation of the low back merger in Northeastern Pennsylvania, namely the influx of large numbers of immigrants from Eastern Europe into coal-mining communities. However, no linguistic mechanism for a substratum effect has yet been established, and the inquiry we are conducting here calls for a much more general solution. We must account for the linguistic antecedents of the collapse of /o/ and /oh/ in more than half of the North American continent, with its wide variety of vowel systems, and in Scotland as well. Why, then, is the distinction between /o/ and /oh/ so likely to collapse? If there is a linguistic answer to this question, then the low back merger is not the triggering event we are looking for, but only a link in the causal chain.

A first thought as to the cause of a merger is the functional load of the distinction. In the case of /o/ and /oh/, there is no problem in finding minimal pairs. We can generate sizable numbers, in the style of (6).

(6)	cot	caught	cock	caulk
	rot	wrought	tock	talk
	tot	taught	odd	awed
	sot	sought	nod	gnawed
	cotter	caught her	cod	cawed
	dotter	daughter	mod	Maud
	Don	dawn	sod	sawed
	yon	yawn	Sol	Saul
	pond	pawned	moll	maul
	fond	fawned	collar	caller
	hock	hawk	holler	hauler
	stock	stalk	odd ability	audibility

However, this proliferation of minimal pairs masks the odd skewing in the distribution of /o/ and /oh/ that can be seen in Table 5.1. Almost all of the contrasts

Table 5.1 Distribution of /o/ and /oh/ contrasts

	/o/	/oh/
APICALS		
t	cot, tot, hot, got, dot	**caught, bought, taut, fought**
d	odd, hod, god, sod	**awed, hawed, gaud, sawed**
s	toss, moss, floss, cost, loss	**sauce, exhaust, caustic**
z	(Oz, positive)	cause, clause, hawser, pause, paws
n	don, Ron, pond	**dawn, awn, yawn, lawn**
l	doll, moll, collar	**all, tall, maul, caller**
NON-APICALS		
p	hop, pop, top, sop	– – – – –
b	rob, hob	(daub, bauble)
tʃ	Scotch, botch, watch	– – – – –
j	lodge, dodge, Roger	– – – – –
g	log, hog, cog, dog	(auger, augment, augur, August)
k	stock, hock, clock	**stalk, hawk, talk**
f	(boff, toff)	*off, doff, scoff* (cough, trough)
θ	(Goth)	*cloth, moth*
ʃ	(gosh, bosh)	(wash)
ð	(bother)	– – – – –
ʒ	– – – – –	– – – – –
m	bomb, Tom, prom	– – – – –
ŋ	(pong, Kong)	*strong, song, wrong, strong*
#	– – – – –	law, saw, flaw, thaw, claw

between /o/ and /oh/ occur before a set of five apical consonants (/t/, /d/, /s/, /n/, /l/) and one non-apical (/k/), as indicated by the bold items. Occurrences of /o/ before /z/ are limited to special lexical items and words in which inter-vocalic /s/ is voiced. In the lower half of Table 5.1 there are six environments where /oh/ is not represented at all, and one – final position – where /o/ does not appear.

Three sets of /oh/ words in Table 5.1 are italicized. These are /o/ words that are tensed in American English before front voiceless fricatives and nasals – the same core phonetic conditioning that operates in the tensing of short *a* in the Mid-Atlantic region and of broad *a* in Britain (Ferguson 1975, Labov 1989b).[15] This tensing process, which typically proceeds by lexical diffusion (including words with coda /g/), produces an enormous amount of dialect differentiation, but does not substantially increase contrast between /o/ and /oh/. In sum, there is a total of six environments in which one side or the other is represented by a small number of learned, colloquial or specialized vocabulary items, so that in twelve environments contrast is marginal and minimal pairs are not to be found.[16]

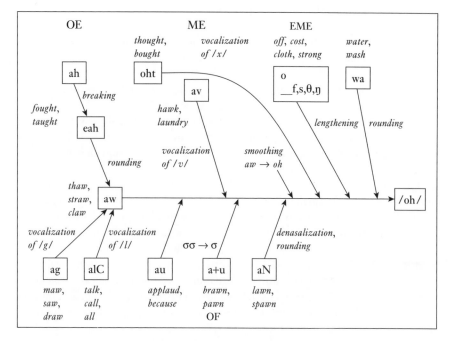

Figure 5.9 Historical development of the long open *o* word class

In order to see how this bizarre distribution came about, it will be helpful to review the historical formation of this word class, summarized schematically in Figure 5.9. Proceeding from left to right, the diagram shows:

1 an original /aw/ diphthong in Old English (*thaw, straw, claw*);

2 additions to Old English /aw/ through Early Middle English sound changes:

    a breaking and rounding of /a/ in verb preterits before complex codas beginning with /x/ (*fought, taught*);

    b vocalization and rounding of /l/ in complex codas (*talk, call, all*);

    c vocalization of coda /g/ to [ɤ] (*maw, saw, draw*);

3 additions to /aw/ in Middle English through vocalization of /v/ (*hawk, laundry*; the latter is a borrowing from Middle French, see 4 below);

4 accretion of new /aw/ forms from Middle French loan words:

    a original back upgliding diphthongs (*applaud, because*);

    b collapse of bisyllabic /a + u/ words to single syllables (*pawn, brawn*);

    c denasalization and rounding of nasal vowels (*lawn, spawn*);

5 smoothing (monophthongization) of /aw/ to /oh/:

6 lengthening of /o/ to /oh/ in Early Modern English before voiceless fricatives and velar nasals (*cloth, off, loss, lost, strong, song, wrong, long*);

7 lexically irregular rounding of /a/ after /w/ (*water, warrant, walrus*).

The /aw/ class traced here is not a reflex of Proto-Germanic /aw/, which is realized in Old English as **e:a**, in **le:af, he:ap, de:aw** (modern *leaf, heap, dew*). Because it was cobbled together by a series of conditioned sound changes, its distribution is a matter of historical accident.

The general sound change that set the stage for the low back merger was the smoothing of Middle English /aw/ to /oh/.[17] It must have anteceded the tensing of /o/ before voiceless fricatives and nasals, since these join in the further history of this category. We can argue that it must also have preceded the completion of the Great Vowel Shift in the back vowels, by which Middle English *u:* diphthongized to /aw/. The smoothing of /aw/ created the juxtaposition of /o/ and /oh/ – two lower back mid vowels differentiated only by length, which is unstable on two counts. First, it is well established that length distinctions without accompanying differences in vowel quality tend to collapse, in English and in many other languages (Chen and Wang 1975). The second reason for the instability of the contrast is the highly skewed distribution of Table 5.1. Given this situation, the merger of the opposition is a likely outcome, unless qualitative differences develop to support it. Such qualitative differentiation of /o/ and /oh/ did develop in three areas outlined by the dotted isoglosses of Figure 5.5: (1) the unrounding and fronting of /o/ in Western New England and New York State;[18] (2) the raising of /oh/ to upper mid position in East Coast dialects from Providence to Baltimore; (3) the restoration of the back upglide of /oh/ in the South.[19] Outside of these areas, the low back merger is either complete or in transition. It follows that the juxtaposition of long and short *o* created by the smoothing of /aw/ to /oh/ was the triggering event of the low back merger.

What is the relationship of the other events captured in Figure 5.9 to the low back merger? The /aw/ class originated in final position, where it could not contrast with short open /o/. The changes that followed were largely conditioned by the vocalization of /l/, /g/, /x/ and /v/ in coda position in a variety of situations. They created limited contrasts, which resisted the merger to a certain extent; one could say that it was the absence of sound changes conditioned by other consonants that favored the merger.

If the smoothing of /aw/ was the triggering event for the low back merger, and ultimately for the Canadian Shift and the Pittsburgh Shift, we must ask if it in turn had a relevant predecessor. I argued that the smoothing of /aw/ must have preceded the completion of the Great Vowel Shift, on the assumption that this shift was a drag chain. But it is also possible that a push chain was involved, and that /uː/ as a descending diphthong [ʊu] → [əu] → [au] → in *out*, *south*, *down* reduced the margin of security of /aw/ [ɑu] in a way that promoted the shift of the latter to [ɔː]. If that is the case, we would have to expand our inquiry into the triggering event of the Great Vowel Shift, a question that has been much discussed (Luick 1903, Martinet 1955, Stockwell and Minkova 1997). There is not enough evidence to pursue this connection here, except to emphasize the possibility of a chain of linguistic triggering events receding into the distant past. In any case, there is no reason to believe that any one external event intervened to produce any of these chain shifts.

5.5   The Fronting of /uw/

In the two cases just studied, the low back merger was seen to initiate subsequent changes in the vowel system, which were responses to the tendency of subsystems to maintain equidistant spacing or maximal dispersion. We will now consider a sound change that appears to be inconsistent with previous explanations based on these principles. This is the fronting of /uw/, an ongoing shift that covers 90 percent of the North American continent. The various phonetic forms involved are shown in (7).

(7)   ʊᵘ ⟶ ᵼᵘ ⟶ üᵘ ⟶ ü
                              ↘ ɪᵘ

Martinet (1955) advanced an explanation for what is now recognized as a general principle of chain shifting: back vowels move to the front.[20] He argued that the repeated fronting of /u/ and /o/ is the result of the fact that the preference for front–back symmetry in the vowel system is countered by the asymmetry of the supraglottal tract, there being less articulatory space in the back than in the front. Fronting is then the result of pressure to relieve overcrowding among the back vowels. Specifically, this happens when, through one linguistic process or another, a vowel system develops four degrees of height among the back vowels. Haudricourt and Juilland (1949) applied this logic to a wide range of sound changes in Western Europe and confirmed Martinet's prediction in every case. Labov (1991), defining three major dialects of English, argued that the third dialect, characterized by the low back merger, would be stable and would resist the fronting of /uw/ and /ow/, predominant in the South and the Midland.

Figure 5.10 shows that the completed ANAE data do not satisfy this expectation. The grey symbols identify speakers for whom /uw/ after coronal consonants, in *do*, *too*, *two*, *soon*, *noon*, etc., is front of center – that is, the mean second formant is greater than the midpoint of 1550 Hz in this normalized system. This group includes 89 percent of the population studied; there are only forty-nine of the 439 ANAE subjects for whom this is not the case. Furthermore, these forty-nine are concentrated

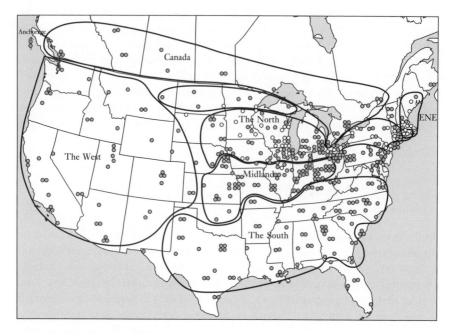

Figure 5.10   Fronting of /uw/ after coronal consonants. Grey symbols: F2 > 1550 Hz

in two narrowly circumscribed areas, New England and Minnesota–Wisconsin. In general, Eastern New England is a conservative area in regard to the fronting of both /uw/ and /ow/, and its behavior is consistent with what we would expect from the low back merger in that area. The Minnesota–Wisconsin area shows considerable variation in regard to the low back merger. But the conservative character of the vowel system, with back /uw/ and /ow/ often monophthongal, must be accounted for by a strong Scandinavian and German substratum (Allen 1973).

Once we have dispensed with these two areas, it is apparent that /uw/ is fronted in all other regions: in the Midland, the Mid-Atlantic states, the South and, most importantly, in three areas where the low back merger is complete: Canada, the West, and Western Pennsylvania. There is no reason to think that this massive, continent-wide fronting is a response to overcrowding among the back vowels.

Although the structural approach to the causes of /uw/ fronting in North American English seems to have failed in this case, we can open a structural inquiry into the causes of this phenomenon from another direction. Because /uw/ fronting is so widespread in North America, it is unlikely that we will find a triggering event in a specific population movement – like the migration of Slavic-speaking coal miners into Northeastern Pennsylvania, identified by Herold (1990). The antecedent event must be one of great generality. One clue to the problem may be found in the very large difference between the extreme fronting of /uw/ after coronal

Table 5.2   Regression coefficients for F2 of /uw/ and /ow/ for all of North American English (vowels before /l/ excluded)[21]

	/uw/ [N = 4747]		/ow/ [N = 6736]	
	Coefficient	Probability	Coefficient	Probability
Constant	1547		1386	
SOCIAL				
Age * 25 yrs	−101	< .0001	−24	< .0001
Female	42	< .0001	46	< .0002
PHONETIC				
Onset				
Coronal	**480**	< .0001	94	< .0001
Velar	181	< .0001	43	< .0001
Liquid	151	< .0001	−	n.s.
Obstruent + Liquid	164	< .0001	−	n.s.
Labial	104	< .0001	−70	< .0001
Nasal	−54	.0020		
Coda				
None	−	n.s.	31	< .0003
Coronal	70	< .0001	−	n.s.
Nasal	−193	< .0001	−101	< .0001
Fricative	−137	< .0001	−21	.0023
Stop	−89	< .0001	−39	< .0002
Voiced	40	.0095	−	n.s.
Following syllables	−	n.s.	−75	< .0001

consonants – which is the focus of Figure 5.10 – and the limited fronting of /uw/ after noncoronal consonants in *roof*, *boots*, *coop*, *food*, *move*, etc. While 390 ANAE subjects shifted /uw/ after coronal consonants front of center, only 130 did so for the noncoronal class. Table 5.2 includes the output of a regression analysis of the second formants of all 4,747 tokens of /uw/ in ANAE. Columns 2 and 3 display the very large effect of coronal onset for /uw/.

The age coefficient in the first row of Table 5.2[22] indicates vigorous change in progress for the fronting of /uw/ in apparent time. With each generation of speakers, twenty-five years younger than the last, the fronting of /uw/ as a whole advances by 101 Hz. The second row shows that, as in most sound changes in progress, women are in the lead, in this case by half a generation. Among the internal constraints, the effect of a preceding coronal stands out at 480 Hz, more than twice the effect of any other factor. This means that, for the average speaker with a mean F2 for /uw/ after coronal consonants of 1800 Hz, the value of /uw/ after noncoronals is around 1300 Hz, halfway between the values for a back and for a central vowel.

This preponderant effect of preceding coronals is a striking exception to the general rule that English vowels are influenced by the following environment more than the preceding one.[23] It is not difficult to explain the tendency for preceding coronals to promote the fronting of /uw/, which is a widespread effect. It appears strongly in Lennig's (1978) analysis of sound change in progress in Parisian French. Melchert (1983) derives Hittite second singular pronoun *zi:g* [tsi:g] from pre-Indo-European **tu:* by a conditioned sound change of fronting after apical consonants, followed by palatalization of /t/.[24] The F2 locus of apical consonants is generally close to 1800 Hz, so that a following back /uw/ requires a rapid transition of 1000 Hz from that locus to the F2 of the vowel nucleus. Articulatory ease will favor the raising of this vocalic second formant. If sound change begins to front /uw/, allophones after coronals will be in advance of others. Yet the size of this effect, 480 Hz, is more than one would expect from a phonetically motivated influence.

One way of evaluating the coronal effect on /uw/ is to compare it to the coronal effect on the fronting of the mid back vowel /ow/. This parallel process is not as widespread as the fronting of /uw/, but it is vigorously in progress throughout the Midland, the South and the Mid-Atlantic states (ANAE, Ch. 12). The right-hand side of Table 5.2 reports the age coefficients for /ow/. To ensure comparability for phonetic effects, all regions of North America are included, even though there is no active fronting for about half the population. The coefficients for /ow/ are therefore generally lower, since sound changes in progress magnify phonetic effects.

In general, the effects on /uw/ and /ow/, both external and internal, are in the same direction. The point of interest is the relation of the coefficient for preceding coronals to other effects on /ow/. While this coefficient for/uw/ is two and a half times greater than any other, the one for /ow/ is comparable to other phonetic effects and is less than the influence of following nasals. If the effect of a preceding coronal on /uw/ were the result of the same mechanism as the /ow/ effect, we would expect it to be only 20 percent greater, since the distance between second formants and the apical locus for extreme back /ow/ is only 20 percent more for /uw/ than for /ow/: 1000 Hz as opposed to 800 Hz. It follows that mechanical effects are not likely to account for the 480 Hz coronal coefficient for /uw/: this appears to be a phonological effect, not a phonetic one.

The suggestion of a phonological effect leads us to consider the relevance of the /yuw/ class of high rising diphthongs, which is historically quite distinct from the class of falling /uw/. The /yuw/ class was derived from a variety of different sources (Jespersen 1949, 3.8).

- Old English i:w, as in *Ti:wesdæg* "Tuesday"
- Old English e:ow, as in *e:ow* "you" (pl. acc./dat.)
- Middle French iu, as in *riule* "rule"
- Middle French unstressed e+u, as in *seur* "sure"
- Middle French u, as in *rude*
- Middle French ui, as in *fruit*
- Middle French iv, as in Old French *sivre* → M.E. *sewe* "sue"

In Early Modern English, these seven sources were joined by an eighth one, which was distinct in Middle English:

- OE e:a, as in *de:aw* "dew"

Although some scholars believe that this vowel was once equivalent to French front rounded [y], Jespersen argues that it has consistently been a rising diphthong [ju], noted /yuw/ in ANAE. In modern dialects, the /y/ glide is generally maintained after labials and velars, except in Norfolk and a few other sites in England (Trudgill 1974b, 1986). In North America the glide has long been variable after apicals. In many cities it became a marker of refined speech and it varied according to the preceding context: the likelihood of a /y/ glide is greatest after /t/ as in *tune*, and lowest after /l/ and /r/ as in *lewd* and *rude* (where it is also frequently deleted in British English today, including in RP).[25]

The development of the /yuw/ class is closely aligned to the problem under study. In current North American English, the historical /y/ glide has all but disappeared after coronal consonants such as in *tune, dew, suit, stupid*. In the middle of the twentieth century, Kurath and McDavid (1961) found widespread use of the glide after coronals in the South, while the characteristic Northern form was [ɪu], an unrounded front vowel moving back towards a high back target (see also Kenyon and Knott 1953, who represent this vowel generally as [iu]). This vocalic realization set up the contrast indicated in Figure 1.1 as /iw/ versus /uw/ exemplified by such minimal pairs as *dew* and *do, lute* and *loot, tutor* and *tooter*. Chapter 8 of ANAE investigated the contrast with the minimal pair *dew ~ do*, and mapped both word classes in spontaneous speech as well. Figure 5.11 shows that the distinction has almost disappeared in North America. It is mainly confined to two limited areas in the South, one in central North Carolina, the other in the smaller cities of the Gulf states. Only an occasional trace of the /y/ glide was found.

This merger of course took place only after coronals, since the contrast existed only after coronals. In other environments the distinction is not a vocalic one; that is, the difference between *beauty* /byuwtiy/ and *booty* /buwtiy/ does not depend upon vowel quality, since the front position of the vowel in the first word is the result of its proximity to /y/. The merger after coronals was accomplished by the fronting of /uw/ in those environments. It is only when the merger is complete that the binding force of the phoneme /uw/ (see Chapter 8) brings the noncoronal allophones to the front.

Figure 5.12 shows the high back vowel of a speaker of the most conservative dialect in regard to the fronting of /uw/ and /ow/: that of Providence, Rhode Island. (In this diagram and in the ones to follow, /Tuw/ indicates /uw/ after coronals and /Kuw/ indicates /uw/ after noncoronals.) Here the means for all vowels are back of center, including /iw/ in *stupid* and *Tuesday*. The vowels after noncoronals are further back, not far from the benchmark of vowels before /l/ (which are not included in the calculation of /Kuw/ means).

Figure 5.13 shows more advanced fronting in three different patterns. Typical for the North, Canada and the West is Figure 5.13a, which displays the /uw/ and

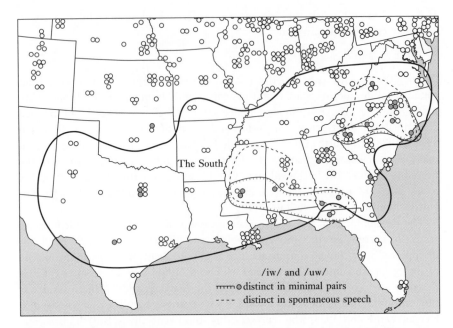

Figure 5.11 Retention of the /iw/ ~ /uw/ contrast in North American English. Grey symbols and oriented isogloss: speakers with /iw/ and /uw/ distinct in production and perception on minimal pair tests. Dashed isogloss encloses communities where acoustic measurements show a significant difference between /iw/ and /uw/ in spontaneous speech. Solid isogloss defines the South as the area where /ay/ is monophthongal before obstruents

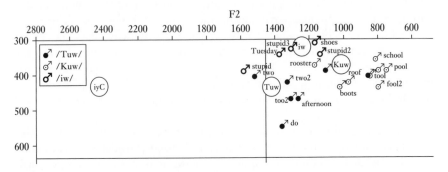

Figure 5.12 High back upgliding vowels of a conservative speaker from Providence, Rhode Island: Alex S., 42 [1996], TS 474

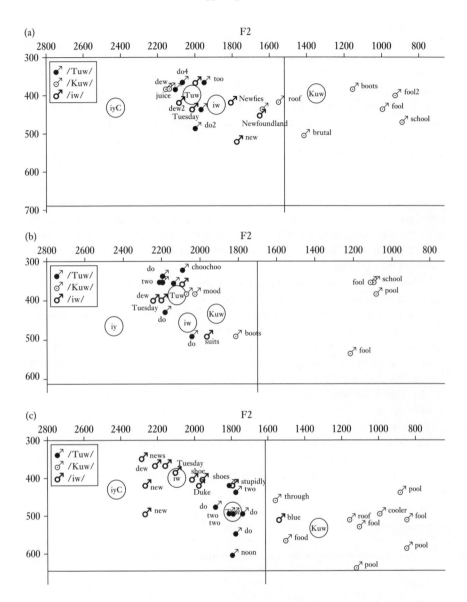

Figure 5.13 Three fronting patterns of the high back upgliding vowels: Figure 5.13a Differentiation of /uw/ after coronals (Tuw) and noncoronals (Kuw): Brent M., 25 [1997], Edmonton, Alberta, TS 654; Figure 5.13b Consolidation of /iw/ and /uw/ in front position: Fay M., 34 [1995], Lexington, KY, TS 283; Figure 5.13c Maintenance of /iw/ ~ /uw/ distinction: Matthew D., 45 [1996], Charlotte, NC, TS 483

/iw/ vowels of a speaker from Alberta. The mean for /Tuw/ is more than 2000 Hz, well front of the center mark of 1550 Hz, and there is no differentiation of /Tuw/ and /iw/. But the mean of Kuw in *roof*, *boots* etc. is well back of center, lower than 1400 Hz. This differentiation by 500 Hz is the phonetic realization of the regression coefficient of 480 Hz in Table 5.2. Figure 5.13b, the high back vowels of a speaker from Lexington, Kentucky, reveals a fully fronted system, where /iw/, /Tuw/ and /Kuw/ are indistinguishable in high front rounded position, some 900 Hz fronter than /uw/ before /l/. Figure 5.13c shows the high vowels of a speaker from Charlotte, North Carolina, who maintains the distinction between /iw/ and /uw/. The /iw/ class in *new*, *dew*, *Tuesday*, *Duke*, *shoes* is tightly clustered around a mean at 400, 2094 Hz, while /Tuw/ shows an equally tight cluster at 493, 1789 Hz. Both F1 and F2 differences are significant at the .001 level. The fact that /Tuw/ is only slightly front of center suggests that the distinction between /iw/ and /Tuw/ is maintained only by inhibiting the fronting of /Tuw/. In other words, the merger of /iw/ and /Tuw/ is correlated with the full fronting of /Tuw/.

Table 5.3 compares the means, age and coronal onset coefficients of /uw/ for eight major North American English dialects. The regional mean values show that the South and the Midland are the most advanced and the North the least advanced. The array of negative age coefficients indicates that all dialects except the Mid-Atlantic are engaged in change in progress in apparent time, but the size of the age gradient varies widely. Though the South is advanced in fronting, the age coefficient is quite low and, most notably, the coronal onset coefficient is only a small fraction of that found for other dialects. It is less than a third of the coefficient for the equally advanced Midland dialect, reflecting the Southern tendency to retain the /iw/ ~ /uw/ distinction.

The fully fronted /Kuw/ in Figure 5.13b reflects the general merger of /iw/ with /uw/ as a whole, even though /iw/ has no allophones in common with /Kuw/. The phonological effects of this merger are comparable to the phonological

Table 5.3   Regression analyses of F2 of /uw/ not before /l/ by region. All coefficients significant at p < .0001 level

	N	Mean F2(uw)	Age * 25	Coronal Onset
Midland	580	1713	−107	442
South	1,107	1703	−86	141
E. New England	116	1584	−244	456
Mid-Atlantic	190	1534		
Western Pennsylvania	161	1529	−119	338
West	468	1520	−76	362
Canada	521	1492	−155	469
North	1,062	1359	−83	514

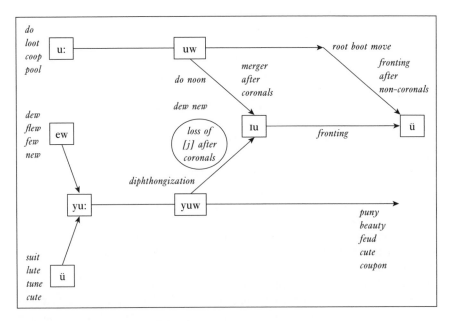

Figure 5.14   Development of /uw/

effect of the merger of /o/ and /oh/, and (in the discussion to follow) of the merger of /o/ and /ah/.

Figure 5.14 traces the history of these developments in a single overview, showing the origins of the /yuw/ class and its eventual merger with /uw/ in the course of the fronting process. As in the case of the low back merger, there is no external triggering event, but rather a series of interconnected changes across a long period. As with /oh/, historical accidents led to the formation of a highly skewed and marginal contrast of /iw/ versus /uw/. It is proposed here that the triggering event for the fronting of /uw/ is the collapse of the /iw/~/uw/ distinction. That distinction was the result of the loss of /y/ after coronals, one of the many deletions of the "peripheral phonemes" of modern English (Vachek 1964).[26] It is not likely that any further inquiry into the causes of the loss of this glide will illuminate our understanding of the fronting of /uw/ in North America.

5.6   The Northern Cities Shift

The Northern Cities Shift (NCS) was first described in 1972 in LYS, and its various stages have since been traced by a number of scholars (Labov 1991, Eckert 2000, Gordon 2001), as well as in the exploration of the principles of chain shifting in these volumes. Chapter 14 of ANAE shows that the Northern Cities Shift is the dominant

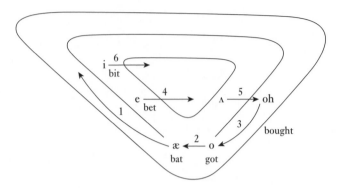

Figure 5.15   The Northern Cities Shift

vowel system of the Inland North, a territory of some 88,000 square miles, with approximately 34 million speakers. This rotation of short vowels is a remarkable development, given the relative stability of the English short vowel system from Old English up to the twentieth century.

Figure 5.15 reproduces the ordering of events in phonological space first presented in Figure 1.4. The events are clearly established, although some points of order are still open to question.[27] Let us consider the sequence by going backwards in time. The most recent event in Figure 5.15 is stage 6, the backing of /i/, which we take to be a later generalization of the backing of /e/. The latest stage in the main sequence is stage 5: the backing and rounding of /ʌ/ to the point that Inland North *bus* can sound like *boss* in other dialects. This seems to be a joint response to two preceding events: the increased margin of security in the back, caused by the lowering of /oh/, and a decrease in the margin of security, caused by the backward shift of /e/ towards the /ʌ/ region – so that Inland North *desk* sounds like *dusk* to speakers of other dialects. The lowering of /oh/ appears to be a response to the fronting of /o/, which in turn is generally accepted to be a response to the vacancy in the low front area created by the general raising and fronting of /æ/.

One causal link is missing from this account: what is responsible for the lowering and backing of /e/? As noted in the discussion of the Pittsburgh Shift in 5.3, the exit of a given vowel from a subsystem may attract two different neighboring vowels into the region vacated. In this case, early evidence indicates that /e/ first moved downward, into the low central area vacated by /æ/, at the same time that /o/ moved forward, creating a considerable overlap of /e/ and /o/ for many Inland North speakers (Labov and Baranowski 2006). Although this overlap has continued, the predominant tendency in the following decades was for /e/ to shift to the back, impinging on /ʌ/ (Eckert 2000).[28]

The current situation in the ANAE records of the 1990s was displayed in Figure 5.8, where the means for the Inland North (IN) are labeled against the background of nineteen other dialects. Here the IN mean for /æ/ (not including tokens before nasals) is higher and fronter than any of the other /æ/ means. A corresponding shift is seen in the IN mean for /o/, which is considerably fronter than any other. The diamond representing /e/ for IN is further back than in any other dialect, and the IN /ʌ/ is at the rear edge of the distribution for that vowel. We do not, however, see a marked lowering of /oh/ in this display.

In this account of the NCS the initial event is clearly the general raising of /æ/, marked "1" on Figure 5.15. The temporal evidence also favors this interpretation. The earliest records from the 1960s show both fronting of /o/ and raising of /æ/, but no evidence of the other sound changes (Fasold 1969, LYS). The geographic evidence for ordering is not as clear as in the Canadian Shift, since the complexity of the NCS requires that its geographic outlines be established by pairwise relations among its components.[29] Nevertheless, there seems little doubt that the general raising of /æ/ is the triggering event for the NCS. In the spirit of our current inquiry, we ask: what in turn triggered the raising of /æ/?

Although the generalized raising of short *a* is found throughout the Inland North, it is unique in the English-speaking world. No other dialect of English shows such a generalized tensing and raising, affecting even the function word *that* and polysyllables like *athletic* and *attitude*. All other dialects with short-*a* raising will differentiate prenasal vowels from others, but in the Inland North this difference is usually not significant. The unique character of this general raising emerges in Figure 5.16, based on an analysis of F1 of /æ/ in North America into four "natural

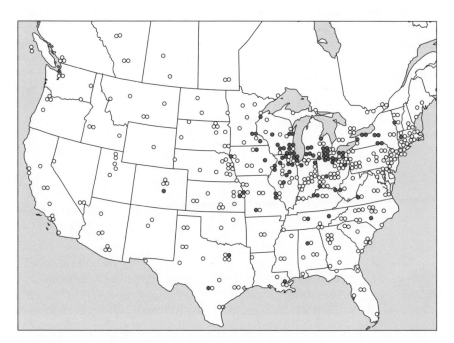

Figure 5.16   Natural break map for mean F1 of /æ/ (four ranges) showing range of 445 to 684 Hz (vowels before nasal consonants not included)

break" categories.[30] The black circles show the category with lowest F1 range, from 445 to 684 Hz. The natural break algorithm automatically isolates the Inland North, including all of the cities around the Great Lakes[31] and along the Erie Canal in New York State, along with the later extension along the Chicago–St Louis corridor and a small scattering of isolated speakers in the upper regions of the South. While /æ/ is raised and fronted in particular contexts by almost all speakers of North American English, a historical process in this particular area has eliminated all contextual conditions, in a process that may be represented as (8).

(8)   [+low, +ant] → [+tense]

The local character of this phenomenon, that is, its heavy concentration in the Inland North, shifts the inquiry to the identification of the people involved in this event and to the short-*a* tensing conditions in the dialects they spoke.

The ANAE maps of the NCS in Western New York State display a series of cities strung out on a line from east to west: Schenectady, Syracuse, Rochester, Buffalo.[32] They were founded as small villages by New England settlers in the eighteenth century and developed as major cities early in the nineteenth, when the Erie Canal was constructed (Figure 5.17). The Erie Canal realized an ambitious plan to open a waterway to the west, connecting New York City with the Great Lakes.[33] It was begun in 1817 and completed in 1825, with extraordinary economic consequences for Western New York State. Before the canal, the cost to ship one ton of goods from Buffalo to New York City was $100; using the canal, the same amount could be shipped for $10 (McKelvey 1949a). The great drop in cost of transportation prompted westward migration and the development of farmland throughout the Inland North.

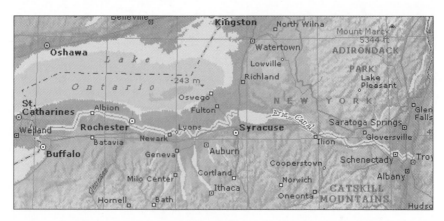

Figure 5.17   Cities on the Erie Canal (McKelvey 1949b). Reprinted by permission of Rochester Public Library

Fresh produce and vast quantities of wheat were shipped to the metropolitan areas of the East Coast, and consumer goods were shipped west (McKelvey 1949a and b). The consequences for urban growth were correspondingly great. At the end of the War of 1812 Rochester had a population of 331, largely of New England origin. The construction of the canal required large numbers of laborers, and a number of Irish immigrants arrived, forming the section of Rochester called Dublin. From 1820 to 1830, the population grew from 1,507 to 9,207 (McKelvey 1949a). The proportion of the population drawn from New England dropped steadily (10 percent in 1845, 5 percent in 1855) with the arrival of new immigrants from Great Britain, Ireland and Germany.

The major cities in New York State, with the exception of Binghamton and Elmira, are located along the trade route established by the Erie Canal from New York City to Albany, through Schenectady, Utica and Syracuse, to Rochester and Buffalo. Today nearly 80 percent of upstate New York's population is still to be found within 25 miles of the Erie Canal. Figure 5.18 shows that the growth of Rochester followed a logarithmic increase from 1820 to 1930. But this spectacular expansion was small compared to the growth of population in surrounding Monroe County and in the seven neighboring counties from 1810 to 1830, reaching a peak in 1850. This was the type of tenfold increase that is required to defeat the principle of first effective settlement (Zelinsky 1992): that the first group arriving in an

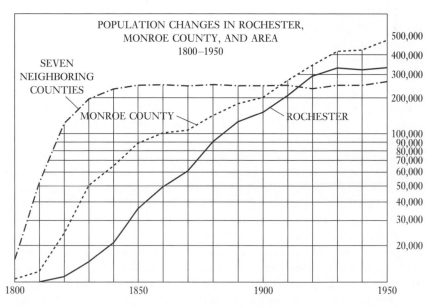

Figure 5.18 Growth of population in Western New York State, 1800–1950 (McKelvey 1949a). Reprinted by permission of Rochester Public Library

area sets the cultural pattern for those who arrive later. It represents the type of explosive growth that Herold (1990) documented in the coal-mining towns of Northeastern Pennsylvania as the trigger for the low back merger there. But the settlement of the Erie Canal and Inland North was a far larger social movement than the migration to the coal-mining towns in the Allegheny Plateau. A much greater and more diverse migration created the population of upstate New York, and involved at least four types of short-*a* systems.

1   *The nasal system*   There is general agreement that the original settlers of upstate New York were from New England. Current evidence on the short-*a* class in New England points to the dominance of the nasal system – that is, an allophonic tensing of all /æ/ before nasal consonants in both open and closed syllables, and nowhere else (ANAE, Chs 13, 16).

2   *The nasal system combined with the broad-a pattern*   Settlers from Eastern New England introduced the assignment of a variable set of short-*a* words to the broad-*a* class: *aunt, can't, half, past,* etc.

3   *The split short-a system*   It is evident that the main commercial traffic, freight and passenger, passed to and from New York City, whose new predominance as a port of entry coincided with the opening of the canal. The New York City short *a* is split into two phonemic classes, with tensing in syllables closed by voiced stops, voiceless fricatives and front nasals, along with many grammatical and lexical specifications (Trager 1930, 1934, 1942; Labov 1989b; ANAE, Ch. 13).

4   *The Celtic substrate*   We must also consider the sudden admixture of large numbers of speakers of Hiberno-English, where short *a* is normally low front or low central.

The end result of such dialect mixture is very often the formation of a *koine* (Trudgill 1986: 107–10) involving leveling (elimination of marked variants) and simplification. Three such patterns of simplification of these mixed short-*a* systems are to be found: (a) no tensing, as in Montreal or generally in Great Britain; (b) the nasal system; and (c) the general tensing of all short *a*, as in (8) above. This third option is what developed in New York State. Though we cannot be certain exactly when this linguistic development occurred, it seems most likely that it happened during the population explosion in the first third of the nineteenth century and before the system was exported to the Great Lakes region in the wake of continued westward expansion.

Figure 5.19 maps the westward extension of the Northern Cities Shift. The black symbols (and black isogloss) identify speakers who satisfy the UD criterion of the NCS: that is, /ʌ/ is further back than /o/(ANAE, Chs 11, 14).[34] For these speakers, the combined effects of stages 2 and 5 of the NCS have reversed the front–back relationship between /ʌ/ and /o/ that is found in other dialects. While /o/ moves to the front, /ʌ/ shifts to the back, so that the mean F2 of /ʌ/ is less than the

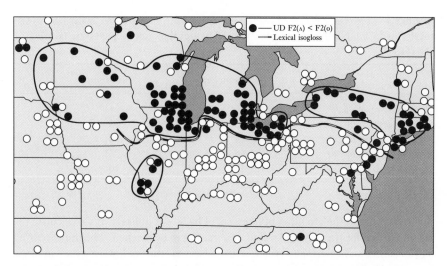

Figure 5.19 Extension of the Northern Cities Shift to the Great Lakes region of
the Inland North by the UD criterion. Black symbols and black isogloss identify speakers
for whom /ʌ/ is further back than /o/. The barred black-and-white isogloss is the lexical
line separating North from Midland based on DARE data

mean F2 of /o/. The black symbols are uniform throughout the Inland North as
defined here. Five black symbols appear to the southwest of this area, in the narrow
corridor leading from Chicago to St Louis – a diffusion of the NCS which will be
discussed in detail in Chapter 15. We also see a set of four grey symbols in the
Mid-Atlantic area to the east, a region with its own dynamic. Otherwise the distribution of the UD criterion is absolute: one of the cleanest divisions in North
American English dialectology.[35]

Furthermore, the Southern limit of the NCS coincides with the barred black-
and-white isogloss: the division between North and Midland, defined in Carver
(1987) on the basis of thirteen lexical oppositions (such as Northern *darning needle*
vs Midland *snake feeder*, *belly-flop* vs *belly-buster*, *stone boat* vs *mud boat*, *sawbuck* vs
trestle, *blat* vs *bawl*). The North–Midland line extends westward from New York
State, passes south of the Western Reserve in Ohio, runs close to the Northern
border of Indiana, and then turns south to include the Northern third of Illinois.

The lexical features that identify the North are largely rural terms, many of them
obsolete and unknown to city dwellers today. They reflect directly the agricultural
practices of the mid-nineteenth century, the period when the Inland North was
settled: clearing land, building stone walls and framing houses. But, as noted above,
the earliest evidence of the NCS sound changes dates from the 1960s. If the triggering linguistic event took place during the upstate New York population boom
of the first half of the nineteenth century, its effects must have lasted for a century

Table 5.4   Age coefficients for five elements of the NCS in regression analysis by vowel tokens for Inland North speakers [N = 63]. All figures show younger speakers favoring the change

	Coefficient	Probability
First formant of /æ/	–	–
Second formant of /o/	–12	< .05
Second formant of /oh/	–24	< .001
Second formant of /e/	68	< .001
Second formant of /ʌ/	17	< .10

before coming to the attention of linguists. This is not unlikely, if we calculate the time required for the present level of /æ/ raising to be reached. The initial tensing as /æ/ shifts to the peripheral track actually has the effect of lowering /æ/ in terms of higher F1,[36] and from studies of current sound changes in progress we can expect that the raising from low to upper mid position would take three generations.[37] The raising of /æ/ has reached its maximum in this area today, as shown by the age coefficients of Table 5.4, which is drawn from a regression analysis of vowels from sixty-three speakers in the Inland North (ANAE, Table 14.6). There is no correlation between age and the height (F1) of /æ/, even at the p < .10 level of significance. This indicates that the raising process has been active for some time and has reached its limiting value.

The specific hypothesis that is advanced here is that the triggering event for the general raising of /æ/ was the formation of a *koine* in Western New York State in the first half of the nineteenth century. This event was the result of a variety of contingent historical processes, so that further inquiry into its linguistic antecedents will not materially increase our understanding of the evolution of the Northern Cities Shift. That said, we continue to explore the dialectology of Western New England, the point of origin of the initial English-speaking settlement of the area, where many of the components of the NCS can be found in an incipient form (Boberg 2001). The match was struck by builders of the Erie Canal, but the timber that burned was grown in New England.

5.7   An Overview of Triggering Events

This chapter began with the proposition that a clear demonstration of the causal character of a chain shift required a bend in the chain of linguistic causality. It turned out that there were many such bends in the history of the sound changes in progress in North American English. They generally involve the removal of a vowel from one subsystem and its insertion into another. An improved understanding of the development of the complex English vowel system stems from the concept of the linguistic subsystem, in which the principles of chain shifting and maximum dispersion are defined (see Chapter 6). Mergers across subsystems play a particularly important role in these developments. Evidence for the reality of the subsystem concept is drawn both from phonological distribution and from phonetic differentiation, where the ability to distinguish phonetic from phonological effects is crucial.

Some of the triggering events encountered were linked with a chain of other triggering events, receding into the indefinite linguistic past with no obvious break in the chain of causality. The low back merger was linked to the eccentric composition of the long open-*o* word class, which has been a source of instability in English for many centuries. Two other cases showed sharp discontinuities in the succession of events. The fronting of /uw/ seems to have been triggered by the loss of the initial glide after coronal consonants in the oddly formed /yuw/ class; we pursued the consequences of that loss, but it did not seem fruitful to pursue its antecedents. Finally, the social and economic ferment centered on the building of the Erie Canal created sharp linguistic and social discontinuities, which triggered the revolutionary chain shifts of the Inland North in the twentieth century. We can of course probe into the mixed parentage of this new dialect, but it seems clear that a new linguistic world was born in Western New York State in the first third of the nineteenth century.

To some extent, these findings are conditioned by the complex character of the English vowel system with its sixteen phonemes, which is well out in the upper tail of the distribution of vowel inventories in the world's languages. Here the organization into subsystems plays a role that is not easily replicated in the more common-garden variety of five-vowel language. But other kinds of hierarchical organization into vowel subsystems are not difficult to find in languages with nasal vowels, glottalized vowels, creaky vowels, long and short vowels, or stressed and unstressed subsystems. Bradley (1969) describes elaborate chain shifts within and across glottal-tone and open-tone subsystems in Akha, a Lolo-Burmese language (Vol. 1, Ch. 5). Latvian dialects provide a dazzling array of chain shifts across ingliding, monophthongal, upgliding and short-vowel subsystems (ibid.). The chain shifts which characterize the early history of the British Celtic languages cross long and short, monophthongal and diphthongal subsystems (McCone 1996). Such hierarchical organization is of course even more common in consonantal systems.

The dialectology of the New World offers an attractive opportunity to study linguistic changes in progress. The events I have chronicled here are new sound changes, written on the tabula rasa of the frontier. As we follow their antecedents backwards in time, we encounter the dialectology and language contacts of the Old World, where layers of intersecting influence accumulate over the centuries. The record is blurred and many times overlaid, but it is worth deciphering. Tracing history as it is being made is exhilarating, but it is always helpful to know where we came from.

6

Governing Principles

6.1 The Constraints Problem

This chapter deals with the principles that constrain change in one direction or another. Given such a principle, we can predict, for a state A of the language, what state A' would be like if change should occur. In a formal grammar, this would be equivalent to distinguishing "possible" from "impossible" changes. Although many of these principles are strongly confirmed by rich bodies of data, they do not have such an absolute character. They refer to ways in which speech communities evolve, in which fundamental cognitive abilities interact both with physical capacities and with cultural practices. Given the right cultural configuration, there are very few general patterns that cannot be reversed. Our principles give us an understanding of what is normal, general and typical; but attempts to use them to define the impossible will inevitably stumble upon counterexamples.

Changes governed by such principles can be called "irreversible" or "unidirectional." I prefer the second, since it does not imply the absolute character signaled by "irreversibility." Unidirectional changes can reverse direction, if rarely, and these cases are of great interest in that they allow us to search for the special circumstances that permit things to go the other way.

Some of these governing principles were presented in LYS in 1972, and several were developed in detail in Parts B and C of Volume 1. Because this volume deals with change in progress, and changes in progress in most varieties of North American English are almost entirely phonetic and phonological, most of the governing principles will concern sound change. But in recent years the search for unidirectional principles of change has been particularly active in the study of grammaticalization (Heine and Kuteva 2005, Hopper and Traugott 2003, Haspelmath 2004). In addition to the unidirectional character of particular clines (main verb > tense/aspect/mood marker, nominal adposition > case), the unidirectional character of grammaticalization as a whole has been a major focus of attention. An entire volume has been devoted to this issue (Fischer et al. 2004; see in particular Ziegeler 2004).

The discussion in this volume is directed by what has been learned from research on linguistic change in progress, through real time or apparent time studies. Almost all of these changes are phonological, and the governing principles to be discussed here are phonological in character.

6.2   The (Ir)Reversibility of Mergers

Chapter 11 of Volume 1 presented the case for the irreversibility of mergers, a principle clearly stated in Garde's paper on Slavic inflections:

> A merger realized in one language and unknown in another is always the result of an innovation in the language where it exists. Innovations can create mergers, but cannot reverse them. If two words have become identical through a phonetic change, they can never be differentiated by phonetic means. (Garde 1961: 38–9)

The cognitive rationale for what I have called "Garde's principle" is quite clear. It rests upon the arbitrary character of the linguistic sign. The reversal of a merger is equivalent to relearning the original assignment of each lexical item, assigning the merged category to one of two arbitrary sets. Though it is clearly possible for individuals in close contact with the unmerged dialect to achieve this result by paying close attention to the speech of those around them, it does not seem likely that an entire speech community can do so.

The obverse of Garde's principle appears in studies of the acquisition of a phonemic split by second dialect learners. Chapter 18 of PLC, Vol. 1 reviewed Payne's study of the acquisition of the Philadelphia short-*a* system by children of out-of-state parents: only one of thirty-four children reproduced the core pattern. We interpreted this to mean that such lexical distributions, unlike simple phonetic output rules, had to be acquired from one's parents. Yet it is important to note that one child did acquire the Philadelphia pattern. As we examine other cases of change that reverses the expected direction, we will find that individual variation is a characteristic feature of the process.

Garde's principle does not need extensive support from a catalog of sound changes which follow it. There are a very large number of mergers in the historical record which have been known to go to completion without being reversed, and many sound changes have been traced which follow the unmerged-to-merged pathway. The mechanisms of the much smaller number of phonemic splits have been much discussed (secondary split through the loss of the Polivanov conditioning factor,[1] lexical borrowing), and spontaneous separation is not among these.[2] In testing the irreversibility of mergers, the first line of inquiry is to search for evidence on whether individual second dialect learners are able to acquire a distinction that is not present in their home dialect.

The /u/ ~ /ʌ/ contrast in Northern England has been the focus of much attention, since upward social mobility is associated with the ability to realize *put, bush, full, bull* as /u/ and *putt, but, gull, bulk* as /ʌ/. Sankoff (2004) reported on the acquisition of this distinction by two of the subjects in the *Seven Up!* series, who have been filmed every seven years since the age of 7. Seven-year-old Nicholas had a total merger; but at 35, after fourteen years spent in Wisconsin, he displayed unrounding in all but one token of *some* and one token of *much*. Seven-year-old Neil from Liverpool showed a mixed pattern; but, after exposure to other dialects in Scotland and London, he emerged as a consistent user of the distinction. Neither showed any evidence of hypercorrection. It appears that some adults can separate such large vocabulary sets;[3] the question remains as to whether an entire community can do so.

In the vowel systems of North American English, we find two cases that challenge Garde's principle.

6.2.1   The subset of vowels before /r/

The two cases of merger reversal to be considered next concern North American English vowels before /r/. These form a separate subset, distinct from the four vowel subsets of Chapter 1.[4] The initial position of Figure 6.1a shows the distinction of /ohr/ ~/ɔhr/ reflected in the opposition of *hoarse* and *horse, mourning* and *morning, cored* and *cord, ore* and *or*. This distinction was quite general in the North and in the South in the 1950s, but not the Midland (Kenyon and Knott 1953, Kurath and McDavid 1961). Map 8.2 of ANAE shows that speakers with the

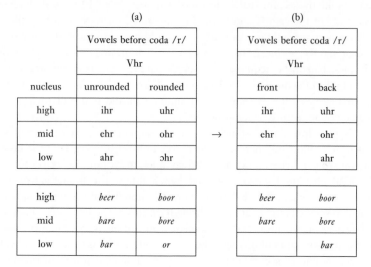

Figure 6.1   Vowels before /r/

distinction are to be found today only in a few scattered areas in Eastern New England, Southern Indiana and Illinois, South Carolina and the Gulf Coast. When this distinction collapses, the system is reorganized as a front/back system, conforming to that of the main vowel subsets of Figure 1.1, and Figure 6.1b is now the system for the great majority of speakers of North American English.

6.2.2   The reversal of the ahr/ɔhr merger in St Louis

The usual development in Figure 6.1 is not found everywhere in North America. A different pattern, which merges /ɔhr/ and /ahr/, while /ohr/ remains distinct, has been reported for three distinct areas: Utah (LYS, Bowie 2003), Eastern Texas (Bailey et al. 1991), and St Louis (Murray 1993, Majors 2004). Bowie's study of early Utah English shows that the merger was present among those born in mid-nineteenth century and that it gained in strength over the rest of the century. Earlier reports in Utah (Cook 1969, Lillie 1998) indicate that the merger is declining in favor of the distinction between /ahr/ and /ɔhr/ and the merger of /ɔhr/ and /ohr/. It is generally reported that the traditional St Louis dialect showed a firm merger of /ahr/ and /ɔhr/ (in mid back position rather than low central, as in the Texas reports). Many sources indicate that among younger speakers this is giving way to the norm for the surrounding territories: a separation of /ahr/ and /ɔhr/ and a merger of /ɔhr/ and /ohr/ (Murray 2002). We can examine the mechanism of such a reversal of merger through the acoustic analyses of the four ANAE speakers from St Louis whose vowel systems are charted in Figures 6.2–6.5. The Telsur interview was

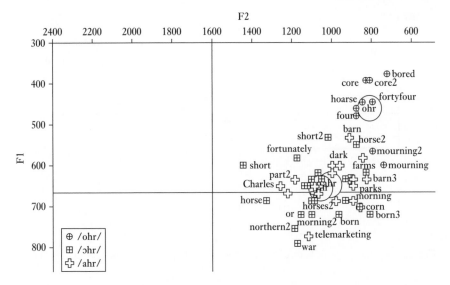

Figure 6.2   Back vowels before /r/ for Judy H., 57 [1994], St Louis, MO, TS 109

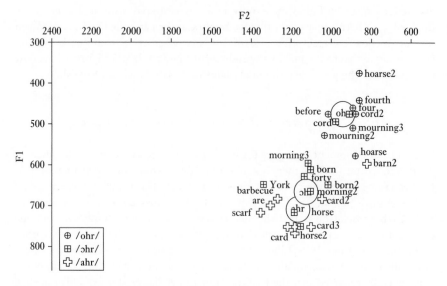

Figure 6.3   Back vowels before /r/ for Joyce H., 53 [1994], St Louis, MO, TS 167

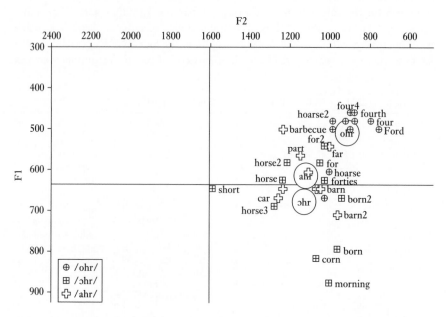

Figure 6.4   Back vowels before /r/ for Martin H., 48 [1994], St Louis, MO, TS 111

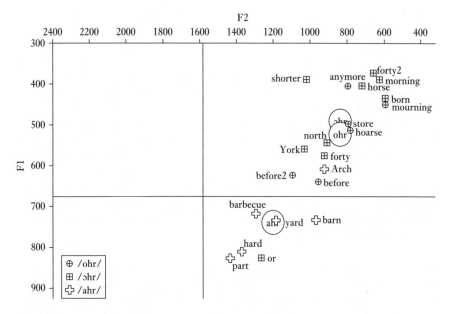

Figure 6.5 Back vowels before /r/ for Rose M., 38 [1994], St Louis, MO, TS 161

strongly focused on this area of the vowel system. *Hoarse* and *horse*, *mourning* and *morning*, *card* and *cord*, *barn* and *born* were elicited separately, and then pronounced and judged as minimal pairs.[5]

For the oldest speaker, Judy H. in Figure 6.2, the merger seems to be preserved with lexical fidelity. The /ohr/ cluster at the upper right overlaps the merged /ahr/ ~ /ɔhr/ distribution only for the two tokens of *mourning*, and these are well separated from the two tokens of *morning*, both from minimal pairs. The minimal pairs for *hoarse* ~ *horse* are also well separated. The merger of /ahr/ and /ɔhr/ is well attested by the relations of *barn* and *born*, where the two tokens of *barn* are higher than the two tokens of *born*.[6] In general, the elicited forms are concentrated in the peripheral area of the vowel space, as one would expect; but the clear separation of /ohr/ and merger of /ɔhr/ and /ahr/ are just as characteristic of the spontaneous forms as the elicited forms. In minimal pair tests, Judy H. judged that *hoarse* and *horse*, *mourning* and *morning* sounded different, and she heard *barn* and *born* as the same. The analyst's hearing confirmed this.

The same series of vowels is shown in Figure 6.3 for a second St Louis speaker, Joyce H., who is only four years younger. The clear merger of /ahr/ and /ɔhr/ and separation from /ohr/ is found. *Mourning* is included in the main /ohr/ group. However, the word *cord* plainly forms a part of the /ohr/ group, very far from the token of *card* at the bottom of the /ahr/ ~ /ɔhr/ distribution. In minimal pairs, Joyce H. agreed with Judy H. that /ohr/ and /ɔhr/ were different, but she heard /ahr/ and /ɔhr/ as "close," and the analyst agreed.

For the speaker Martin H., only five years younger, the vowel class distribution is preserved, but the distances are closer (Figure 6.4). The F1 difference between /ohr/ and /ɔhr/ is 200 Hz for the first two speakers, but only 160 Hz for Martin H. Martin's own judgment is that these two vowels are "close," while he still hears /ahr/ and /ɔhr/ as "the same."[7]

The youngest speaker in this series, Rose M., is only ten years junior to Martin H., but her Vhr system in Figure 6.5 is radically converted. /ohr/ and /ɔhr/ are now identified, both in her production and in her judgment, while /ahr/ is isolated in low position (mean F1 a good 250 Hz higher). There are remnants of the traditional St Louis pattern in the mid location of *arch* and, most strikingly, in the low position of *or*, an /ɔhr/ word.[8] Two of the nineteen words in Figure 6.5 are misassigned, which suggests (along with other examples) an error rate of about 10 percent in lexical identification.

This brief series of snapshots of the St Louis reversal was fortunately centered across the age range at which the change took place. The two older speakers confirm that the traditional St Louis system was consistent at one time, showing only occasional deviations from the identification of /ahr/ and /ɔhr/. The third speaker suggests the kind of phonetic approximation that Trudgill and Foxcroft (1978) identify as a mechanism of merger. The fourth speaker indicates the type of abrupt reorganization that Sankoff and Blondeau (2007) find in the shift of /r/ from apical to uvular in Montreal French. The inference from work on language change across the lifespan is that adults cannot make the radical readjustment of Figure 6.5. It seems most likely that Rose M. effected this change in her adolescent years or earlier.

The contrast between the fourth speaker and the first three leads us to believe that other reports of the reversal of the *card/cord* merger in St Louis are credible, *pace* Garde. The main argument for the unidirectionality of mergers is that reversal requires a word-by-word relearning, in other words a change that proceeds by lexical diffusion rather than by regular sound change. To the extent that the St Louis shift shows an approximation of /ohr/ and/ɔhr/, we can see regular sound change operating on the means of phonemic targets in an ongoing merger. But, to the extent that the separation of /ɔhr/ and /ahr/ shows lexical irregularities, we can recognize the mechanism of lexical diffusion. We must be alert to this issue in the next case of merger reversal.

6.2.3   The reversal of the fear/fair merger in Charleston

In a number of English dialects we find evidence of the merger of /ihr/ and /ehr/, so that *fear* and *fair*, *hear* and *hair*, *beer* and *bear* become homonyms: this happens in East Anglia (Trudgill 1974b), Newfoundland (Wells 1982), and New Zealand

(Gordon and Maclaglan 1989). The progress and mechanism of the ongoing New Zealand merger have been studied further in considerable detail (Holmes and Bell 1992, Maclaglan and Gordon 1996, Gordon et al. 2004, Hay et al. 2006, Shibata 2006), with findings quite consistent with Garde's principle. This merger has long been noted as a feature of the dialect of Charleston, South Carolina and its immediate environs (Primer 1888, O'Cain 1972, McDavid 1955, Kurath and McDavid 1961). Considerable variability is indicated in these earlier reports. Kurath and McDavid typically say that "*ear* sometimes rhymes with *care*" (1961: 22), and the merger is generally described as a relic feature, giving way to the distinction. If this case is relevant to the reversibility of mergers, it is important to know whether a total merger did exist at an earlier stage (see note 3).

Baranowski's study of the Charleston community, which involved 100 subjects in a socially stratified sample, devoted considerable attention to the /ihr/ ~ /ehr/ merger (2006, 2007). As prototypical of the older Charleston dialect, Baranowski took the speech of William McTeer, a sheriff from Beaufort, South Carolina, whom I interviewed in 1965. McTeer's /ihr/ and /ehr/ vowels are shown in Figure 6.6. The merger, in mid position, is evident, and the t-test table embedded in Figure 6.6 confirms the absence of any differentiation of the two vowels.

Baranowski's findings on minimal pair tests for the entire community is given in Figure 6.7, where complete merger is indicated by a level of 0 ("same" in production and perception) and consistent distinction by 2 ("different" in production and perception). Speakers whose ages fall into the two oldest decades are plainly merged, whereas those below 50 have a clear distinction, with a steep slope for those between

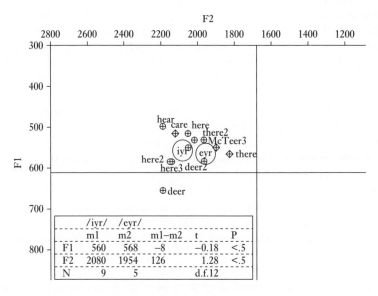

Figure 6.6 /ihr/ and /ehr/ vowels of William McTeer, Beaufort, SC [1965]

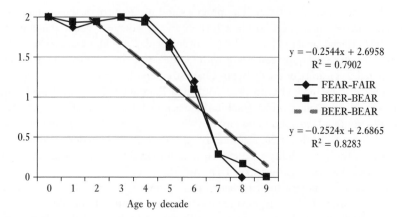

Figure 6.7   Reversal of the /ihr/ ~ /ehr/ merger as shown by two minimal pairs in Charleston, SC (Baranowski 2006, Fig. 6.25). Reprinted by permission of the University of Pennsylvania

50 and 79. There can be little doubt that the merger has been reversed. The broken line for *beer/bear* is a linear regression line for that pair. It is evident that the two pairs *fear/fair* and *beer/bear* follow identical s-shaped patterns of reversal. A logit transformation fits a straight line for both, with an r^2 greater than .99 (Baranowski 2007, Figures 6.26–6.27).

Baranowski's examination of individual speakers reveals several characteristics specific to the Charleston merger. Among the oldest speakers there is considerable variability. One 90-year-old woman has fully merged *beer* and *bear*, *fear* and *fair*, but makes a clear distinction between *here* and *hair* in spontaneous speech and minimal pair tests. The same pattern is repeated for an 85-year-old man, though others show a complete merger.

Across generations there is an abrupt change, which again suggests that children could grow up in a household with a solid /ihr/ ~ /ehr/ merger and arrive at adulthood with a clear distinction. Baranowski presents the case of an 82-year-old woman with no trace of a difference, while her 58-year-old daughter shows a merger for only one pair: *here* and *hair*.[9]

Charleston speakers also exhibit some degree of awareness of the opposition and its variability, rather than focusing on the phonetic position of one lexical item or the other. This appears in the remarkable exchange between Baranowski and a 42-year-old lower middle-class woman. The F1/F2 positions of the italicized words are indicated on Figure 6.8.

> *beer2* and *bear2*, [pauses, smiles] sound different to me, though some people think
> [...], OK *beer3* is something you drink and *bear4* is an animal, [but] some people if

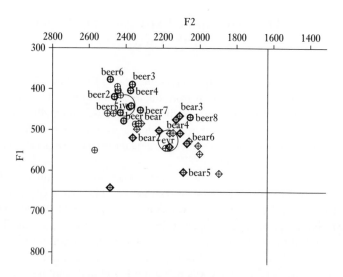

Figure 6.8 *Beer–bear* tokens of Kathy A., 42, Charleston, SC (Baranowski 2007, Figure 6.41). Reprinted by permission of Publications of the American Dialect Society

they hear me say *bear*3 they think I'm saying *beer*4. That happens all the time. [If you say what?] If I'm saying *beer*5, they think I'm saying [or if I say *bear*5, they think I'm saying] *beer*6, like the drink. [. . .] For some reason I know when I say *bear*6, they go b- – they think I'm talking about *beer*7 and I'm not talking about *beer*8. (Kathy A., 42, Charleston, SC)

The original minimal pairs, labeled simply *beer* and *bear*, were quite close. As the discussion of the distinction proceeded, the two targets were widely separated until the very last token, *beer*8, which was realized in the middle of the *bear* class.

Kathy A. shows a keen awareness of the issue, but on the whole one cannot say that the merger receives a strong social evaluation in this city. An unusual feature of this Charleston sound change is the absence of any social class or gender differences. None of Baranowski's regression analyses shows a trace of such effects. This is in contrast with other Charleston sound changes, like the fronting of /ow/, where the upper class is strongly in the lead. In that sense, the merger of /ihr/ and /ehr/ is not socially evaluated.

These two cases of the reversal of mergers would seem to have put a considerable dent in Garde's principle. Again, we find that the reversal of the merger is accompanied by a moderate degree of lexical variation. But before considering how the principle might be further modified, we can turn to the spatial aspect of the irreversibility of mergers – Herzog's corollary.

6.3   The Geographic Expansion of Mergers in North America

To the extent that mergers are irreversible, it follows that they will not contract geographically, but can only expand from one area to another. This is the logical basis of Herzog's corollary to Garde's principle, which was originally illustrated by the outcome of the meeting of two geographic waves of merger in the Yiddish of pre-war Northern Poland: four phonemes merging into one (Herzog 1965, Weinreich et al. 1968).

ANAE provides a geographic view of eight mergers in North American English. Three show rapid expansion, almost to completion. The extent of the merger of /iw/ and /uw/, in *dew* and *do*, etc., was shown in Figure 5.11 (based on ANAE, Map 8.3). Similar patterns are displayed by ANAE for the merger of /hw/ and /w/ in *which* and *witch* (ANAE, Map 8.1) and for the merger of /ohr/ and /ɔhr/ discussed above (ANAE, Map 8.2). For these three, the area of merger has expanded from a limited area in PEAS records of the mid-twentieth century – largely the Midland area – to cover most of the Eastern US, as well as the rest of the continent. There is no trace of any tendency to reverse these mergers.

The conditioned merger of /ey/, /e/, /æ/ before intervocalic /r/ in *Mary*, *merry*, *marry* covers most of the continent but appears to be fairly stable. The area from Providence to Philadelphia, where all three words are distinct in pronunciation, remains intact in this respect, and the surrounding Eastern Seaboard area preserves the distinction between *merry* and *marry* (ANAE, Map 8.4).[10]

6.3.1   The pin/pen merger

The merger of /i/ and /e/ before nasals has been widely reported for the Southern states (Brown 1990, Bailey 1997). Bailey and Ross (1992) report that the distinction was present for some speakers born before 1875.[11] ANAE finds the merger all but complete in the Southern region (as defined by the monophthongization of /ay/ before obstruents). Only twelve of 143 speakers showed a clear distinction in minimal pair tests using *pin* and *pen*, *him* and *hem*.[12] Figure 6.9 shows that the area of the *pin/pen* merger has expanded considerably beyond the South, extending to Oklahoma and Southern Kansas and reaching up to the Hoosier apex in central Indiana. Northern Florida is also included. In that new area of *pin/pen* merger expansion, only five out of forty-six speakers show a clear distinction of /i/ and /e/ before nasals. In Charleston, which shares few of the dialect features of the South, the *pin/pen* merger is in progress and is complete in the youngest generation.

Figure 6.10 shows the mean values for the production and perception of the merger of /in/ and /en/ in minimal pair tests across the major dialect areas of North America. Values range from 0 for consistent "same" to 2 for consistent "different."

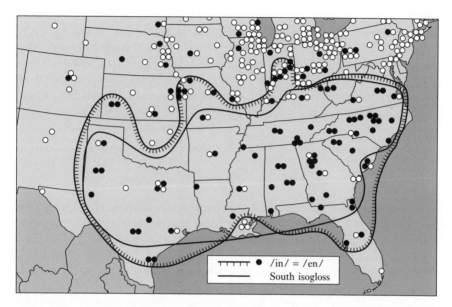

Figure 6.9 Expansion of merger of *pin* and *pen* beyond the South (ANAE, Map 9.5). *South isogloss* defines the South dialect region by monophthongization of /ay/ before obstruents. Solid circles: /in/ = /en/ in production of minimal pairs

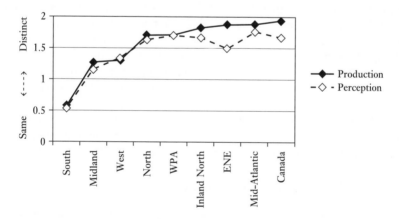

Figure 6.10 Mean values for minimal pair responses to the /in/ ~ /en/ contrast by region for production and perception. 0 = consistent "same" response; 2 = consistent "different" response

On the left, the South plainly has the most advanced and consistent form of the merger. Its two neighboring regions, the Midland and the West, show intermediate values which reflect the expansion of the merger. In Figure 6.10, the responses for production and perception are identical for those dialects affected by the merger, but perception shows slightly lower values for the four dialects that are most removed from the South, indicating a marginal awareness that *pin* and *pen* can be "the same." However, the *pin/pen* merger is not as socially marked as many other Southern features are. ANAE, Chapter 18 reports that elements of Southern phonology are receding in apparent time, some more than others. Unlike the Northern Cities Shift, the Southern Shift is inversely related to city size. The *pin/pen* merger, on the other hand, is directly correlated with city size (.42 per million on the 2-point scale, p < .0001).

6.3.2   Mergers before /l/

Two relatively new mergers have been reported in a series of sociolinguistic investigations in Utah, New Mexico and Texas: the merger of /i/ and /iy/ before /l/ in *fill* and *feel*; and the corresponding merger of the back vowels of /u/ and /uw/ in *full* and *fool* (LYS, Di Paolo 1988, Di Paolo and Faber 1990, Bailey 1997). The front vowel merger is primarily a Southern phenomenon, concentrated in those areas where the Southern Shift is most highly developed (ANAE, Map 9.7), while the back vowel merger is fully developed in Western Pennsylvania, where vocalization of final /l/ is also at its most extreme (ANAE, Map 9.6). Despite these differences in geographic location, the two mergers show strikingly similar distributions of minimal pair responses and, as Table 6.1 shows, they have almost identical profiles in apparent time. Regression analyses of both mergers across North America show an increase on the 2-point scale of more than 1 unit for every 25 years of age, indicating that the distinction is highly characteristic of older speakers and the merger of younger speakers. The merger of /il/ and /iyl/ is therefore quite independent of the Southern Shift, which is receding slightly in apparent time. Both mergers also show a sizable negative correlation with education.

Although we have no real-time data on the mergers before /l/, there is every reason to believe that they are expanding phenomena, at the opposite end of their life span from the almost completed mergers of /hw/ ~ /w/, /ohr/ ~ /ɔhr/ and /iw/ ~ /uw/.

Table 6.1   Regression coefficients for the merger of /i/ and /iy/, /u/ and /uw/ before /l/ in ANAE minimal pair data. Scale: 2 = distinct, 0 = same. p: * < .05, ** < .01, *** < .001

	/il ~ iyl/	/ul ~ uwl/
Age * 25 yrs	1.15**	1.12**
Education	0.468***	0.232*

6.3.3   The low back merger

The low back merger of /o/ and /oh/ represents the most substantial geographic division in North American English phonology, with many consequences for the rest of the phonological system. It is firmly documented from the 1930s for Eastern New England (LANE); from the 1940s for Eastern Pennsylvania (PEAS); and from the early 1970s for the West and Canada (Scargill and Warkentyne 1972, Terrell 1975). ANAE studied the low back merger through minimal and near-minimal pairs (*hot/caught; Don/dawn; sock/talk; dollar/taller*) well and through the acoustic measurement of distribution in spontaneous speech. Figure 6.11 shows the mean values for ANAE regions in both production and perception, in a display similar to Figure 6.10. North American dialects appear to fall into three groups. On the left are the four dialects that have traditionally been reported with the merger: Western Pennsylvania, Canada, the West and Eastern New England. In the middle are dialects in a transitional state, the Midland and the North outside of the Inland North, where /o/ and /oh/ are normally judged "close" in production and perception. At right are the three dialects with a phonological structure that resists the merger: the South, where /oh/ has a back upglide; the Inland North, where /o/ is strongly fronted; and the Mid-Atlantic region, where /oh/ is strongly raised. We also observe that the South is shifted down towards the transitional dialects. Again, the values for perception are slightly lower than those for production, except where the merger is the strongest.

Like most mergers, the low back merger of /o/ and /oh/ does not form a salient sociolinguistic variable. A series of regression analyses finds no significant effect for

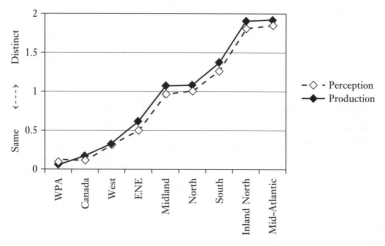

Figure 6.11   Mean values for minimal pair responses to the /o/ ~ /oh/ contrast by region for production and perception. 0 = consistent "same" response; 2 = consistent "different" response

Table 6.2   Significant regression coefficients for minimal pair responses to /o ~ oh/ opposition by region. Scale: 0–2. p: * < .05, ** < .01, *** < .001

	Midland	South	West
Age * 25 yrs	.23**	.29***	.15*
City population (in millions)		–.16*	
Education (years completed)		.06**	

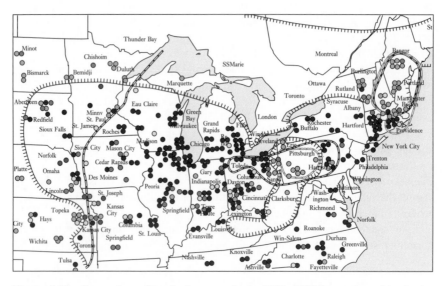

Figure 6.12   Comparison of low back merger in the 1950s (PEAS: grey barred isogloss); 1960s (OH68 survey: dark barred isogloss); and 1990s (ANAE: oriented isogloss) (ANAE, Map 9.3)

gender in any region and no effect of education or city size outside of the South (see Table 6.2). The South, however, is a different story. It shows a powerful positive age coefficient (consistent with Figure 6.11), indicating that younger speakers are the most likely to merge. As in the case of the *pin/ pen* merger, we observe that the bigger the city, the lower the value: the merger is an urban phenomenon. It is also associated with lower educational levels. These figures reflect the same retreat from salient Southern phonology in the big cities that we find for the Southern Shift and for the fronting of /uw/ before /l/ (ANAE, Chapter 18). In this case, the salient feature is the back upglide with /oh/. When it is abandoned, merger must follow, since the locations of /o/ and /oh/ are otherwise almost identical in F1/F2 position.

Our major concern here is with the stability or instability of the boundaries between the merged and the unmerged areas. Figure 6.12 is based on ANAE, Map 9.4, which superimposes the PEAS boundaries, the ANAE boundaries, and a study of the contrast of *hock* and *hawk* in the speech of long-distance telephone operators that I carried out in 1968 (OH68).[13]

Figure 6.12 shows that the merger was confined to Eastern New England in PEAS and OH68, but expanded to Western New England in the ANAE data of the 1990s. Furthermore, the merger had expanded to the east and to the west in Western Pennsylvania in OH68, and in ANAE it expanded further, to West Virginia. Irons (2007) reports further merger in Eastern Kentucky. The South generally shows a tendency to merger through the loss of the back upglide, as noted above (Feagin 1993). In the North Central states, one can observe a spread of the merger from Canada southward. However, there is one area on Figure 6.11 where the expected real-time pattern is reversed. If the merger is expanding from the West, the Western 1990s boundary for the low back merger should be located to the east of the 1960s boundary; but, on the contrary, it is located well to the west. There is a sizeable territory in Minnesota, South Dakota and Nebraska where the OH68 line is to the east of the ANAE boundary, and it appears that the low back merger has receded from the 1960s to the 1990s.

Is this reversal of the expected positions of the isoglosses an indication that the merger is being reversed in this area? If this is the case, we should find a reversal in apparent time, as in St Louis and Charleston. Table 6.3 shows the mean minimal pair ratings for the thirt-six Telsur subjects in the region where the OH68 isogloss lies to the east of the ANAE isogloss. As in Baranowski's data in Figure 6.7, consistent "different" ratings are assigned a value of 2, consistent "close" ratings, a value of 1, and consistent "same" ratings, a value of 0. Separate averages are given for perception (the speaker's judgment of "same" and "different") and production (the analyst's judgment of the speaker's productions). The thirty-six speakers are divided into three age groups. No significant difference appears between the 51–75 and 41–50 groups. However, the youngest age group, 18–30, has a lower mean value. T-tests show a probability of this difference being due to chance of .08 for perception and .01 for production. We can conclude, then, that the OH68 survey of telephone operators – whose local status was not as clearly defined as that of the Telsur subjects – did not succeed in locating the actual geographic boundary at the time. The merger appears to be moving forward in this border area, as in others.

The low back merger was the focus of five papers presented at the 2008 NWAV meeting in Philadelphia, and in all the cases discussed there were indications of

Table 6.3 Mean ratings on minimal pair test in area of Figure 6.12, where the OH68 isogloss is east of the ANAE isogloss

Age	Perception	Production
51–75	.84	1.16
31–49	.92	1.25
18–30	.61	.59**

merger expansion.[14] In Indianapolis, the characteristic "close" transitional stage of the Midland was found to be progressing further, towards merger by approximation (Fogle 2008). In Miami, a similar transitional stage displayed further progress towards complete merger among younger speakers (Doernberger and Cerny 2008). In Erie, Pennsylvania, Evanini (2009) finds that the shift to Midland alignment under Pittsburgh influence is accompanied by a fronted form of the merger, not present in PEAS but distinct phonetically from the merged phoneme of Pittsburgh.

The most substantial new study of the low back merger is that of Johnson (2010), who traced the boundary between the merged area of Southeastern Massachusetts and the area of distinction centered on Rhode Island, shown in Figure 6.13. Johnson first found an extraordinary stability of the boundary across generations, which raised some questions about the generality of Herzog's corollary.[15] However, when Johnson carried out deeper studies of family patterns in several cities, he found a sudden shift towards merger in the youngest generation of pre-adolescent children. Figure 6.14 shows such a pattern for the town of Seekonk (for location, see Figure 6.13), where there is considerable variation among adults. One can observe

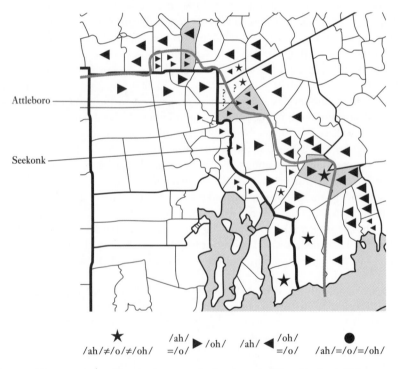

Figure 6.13   Boundary of low back merger in Southeastern New England (Johnson 2010, Figure 4.3). Reprinted by permission of the Publications of the American Dialect Society

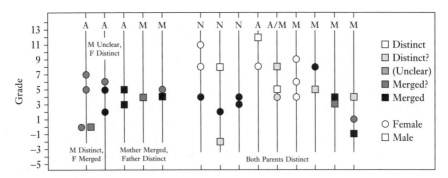

Figure 6.14 Development of the low back merger across generations in Seekonk (Johnson 2010, Fig. 6.5). N = North Seekonk; A = Central Seekonk; M = South Seekonk. Reprinted by permission of the Publications of the American Dialect Society

a shift to merged status for children in the elementary school grades, independent of gender or the parents' use of /o/ and /oh/. The town of Attleboro, just north of Seekonk, shows a similar shift. Though Johnson's regression analyses indicate some influence of the parental system on the eventual outcome, Figure 6.14 shows that the expansion of the low back merger is a community phenomenon that reaches children as they emerge from their initial family-centered language learning into the domain of peer-group influence.

These major shifts are taking place along the linguistic boundary and provide further support for Herzog's corollary. Although the boundary was stable for several generations, the changes now in progress are in the direction of the low back merger. Johnson also considers the possibility that some of the momentum towards merger is a general phenomenon, independent of geography; he finds some shift among speakers well within the state of Rhode Island. However, at community level none of these has as yet progressed as far as the movement towards merger displayed in Figure 6.14. Johnson gives considerable attention to the hypothesis that the impetus for change came from the movement of families from the merged Greater Boston area into the Seekonk-Attleboro area. His overall assessment is that there is only limited support for this idea. His Table 5.7 shows that the percentage of merged parents is much greater in South Attleboro than in Sekonk, yet the strongest impulse towards merger is found in the latter city. Furthermore, the percentage of inmigrant merged parents shows no increase among the younger children.

6.3.4 Reassessment of Garde's principle

The two counterexamples of St Louis and Charleston require a reassessment of the force of Garde's principle and, along with it, of Herzog's corollary. If we think of the boundary around the Charleston merger of /ihr/ and /ehr/, or around the one defining the St Louis merger of /ahr/ and /ɔhr/, it is clear that these isoglosses did not expand; instead they contracted to zero. How do these exceptions differ from the normal expansion of mergers?

The general pattern of North American English phonology is that regional dialects are becoming more diverse, but dialects associated with individual cities of moderate size are giving way to the regional dialect. The two cases of merger reversal that we have found here are associated with such a regional transformation of a city dialect. The reversal of the *card/cord* merger is part and parcel of the general replacement of the traditional St Louis dialect by an approximation to the Northern Cities Shift of the Inland North (see Chapter 15). Similarly, the reversal of the *fear/fair* merger is an integral component of the replacement of the traditional Charleston dialect by the regional Southeastern pattern (Baranowski 2007).[16]

The larger body of expanding mergers reviewed here is independent of any particular dialect. The contrasts of *which/witch, four/for* and *dew/do* were generally found throughout the North and the South, not associated with the phonology of an individual city. The *pin/pen* merger was associated with the Southern region as a whole, not with any particular city, and it has since expanded beyond the South. Although the mergers of *fill/feel* and *full/fool* showed some regional concentration in the ANAE maps, they have been reliably reported from many different regions. In fact the tendency for mergers to expand beyond regional boundaries is the basis for the ANAE policy (Ch. 11) of not using merger isoglosses to define North American English dialects.

The exceptions to Garde's principle can therefore be characterized as mergers that are associated and identified with a dialect in the process of replacement. This is not to underestimate the difficulty of separating a merged word class into two components, once their historical identity has been lost. The exploration of driving forces in Chapter 9 will attempt to deal with this problem.

There remains the problem of accounting for the fact that some urban dialects survive and others perish. The most prominent dialect associated with a single city is that of New York City. Despite the fact that the locally born white population who use this dialect has dropped to less than 50 percent of the city's total, there is little evidence of the dialect's decline or replacement. The dialect of the NYC Telsur subjects preserves its traditional features, as these were reported since the end of the nineteenth century.[17] The Philadelphia dialect, for which we have more detailed historical records, shows a similar stability in its basic structure: the short-*a* split, the back chain shift before /r/, the merger of /ohr/ and /uhr/, the near-merger of *ferry* and *furry*, the merger of *pal, pail* and *Powell*, the merger of *crown* and *crayon*. One of the sound changes traced in the 1970s – the raising and fronting of /aw/ – has begun to recede (PLC, Vol. 2; Conn 2005), but others have advanced further – the raising and fronting of (eyC), the backing and centralization of (ay0). The dialect of Boston has been strongly associated as a central focus of the Eastern New England region and there is no indication of its being replaced by some other regional pattern.[18]

Table 6.4 Metropolitan statistical areas and city population for seven cities

	City Size	MSA
New York	8,643,437	7,380,906
Philadelphia	1,585,577	4,952,929
Boston	574,283	3,263,060
St Louis	396,685	2,548,238
Pittsburgh	369,879	2,379,411
Cincinnati	364,040	1,597,352
Charleston	80,414	495,143

Population size appears to be a decisive factor in determining the survival of an urban dialect. Table 6.4 lists the 1990 populations of the seven cities discussed here and their associated Metropolitan Statistical Areas (MSAs). It appears that dialects of cities with populations of over half a million are stable, while those with smaller populations are not. The amount and type of "dialectal attrition" of these smaller cities varies from one case to another. The entire configuration of the Charleston dialect has been radically altered in recent decades (Baranowski 2007). Boberg and Strassel (2000) report that the specific short-*a* pattern of Cincinnati has been reversed in favor of the general Midland nasal pattern. St Louis has lost the most distinctive feature of its phonology, the merger of /ohr/ and /ɔhr/, and has imported most of the elements of the Northern Cities Shift from Chicago (Labov 2007). Among all these mid-sized cities, Pittsburgh shows the strongest tendency to maintain its local dialect. Its dominant stereotype, the monophthongization of /aw/, shows some attrition for those born after 1950 (Johnstone et al. 2002), but Pittsburgh also shows a new chain shift, specific to its phonology (Ch. 5 of this volume). As Johnstone et al. (2002) suggest, the high degree of local linguistic consciousness in Pittsburgh may be a supporting factor.

Though the major regional dialects continue to diverge, the general trend is towards the absorption of the smaller city dialects into their surrounding regional patterns. In this respect, the North American trend is similar to that described for many Western European dialects (Thelander 1980). The two cases of merger reversal that we have encountered here are a part of the mechanism of regional absorption.[19]

Three mechanisms have been identified for merger: phonetic approximation, lexical exchange, and sudden implosion of two categories into one (Trudgill and Foxcroft 1978, Herold 1990, 1997). The reverse process of splitting would seem to require lexical reorganization, and, so far, the lexical irregularities from St Louis and Charleston provide some evidence for a word-by-word relearning of the distinction. It is not likely that an entire generation of adults can do this. The limited amount of lexical variation in these cases suggests early contact with young speakers of the two-phoneme system by native speakers of the one-phoneme system. The critical number of inmigrant children for such a reversal is probably greater than the proportion needed to motivate the expansion of the low back merger (Yang 2009).

6.4   Principles Governing Chain Shifts

The development of governing principles of phonological change has taken its most substantial form in the domain of chain shifting, that is, in a series of changes that are causally linked in ways that preserve the number of distinctions (Martinet 1955; LYS; PLC, Vol. 1, Ch. 5). In this sense, chain shifts are the complement of the mergers discussed in section 6.3, which by definition reduce the number of distinctions. Yet many complex series of changes involve both mergers and chain shifts; as we will see, it is common for mergers to initiate, or follow from, chain shifts. Chapter 5 raised the question of how we distinguish chain shifts from parallel or generalized movement, and concluded that the causal character of chain shifts is most apparent when the changes involved are qualitatively different.

Given the recognition of a chain shift (1) with A as the *entering* element and with B as the *leaving* element,

(1)   A → B →

the temporal sequence is an essential issue. In a *drag chain*, B moves first; in a *push chain*, A moves first. If A and B moved simultaneously, this would be evidence of a generalized sound change – not of a chain shift in the sense of Chapter 5.

The existence of drag chains is generally accepted, but push chains remain a matter of controversy. In the view of sound change as an alteration in a set of binary rules (Halle 1962), a push chain is not possible: it would be equivalent to a merger. One possible governing principle for chain shifting would be that all chain shifts are drag shifts, which correspond to Martinet's concept of filling a hole in the pattern. Thus Martinet (1952) explains the Western Romance lenition of intervocalic stops as a push chain:

(2)   /pp tt kk/ → /ptk/ → /bdg/ → /βδγ/

(but see reservations in Cravens 2000 and 2002: 69 ff., where it is argued that voicing preceded degemination). In Volume 1, the Swedish Pattern 3 chain shift (Benediktsson 1970) was cited as evidence of a push chain – one initiated by the lengthening of short /a/ and the consequent backing and raising of /a:/ (see also Hock 1986: 157).

The issue as to whether push chains exist – and whether they are reasonably frequent – is an important one for our conception of the nature of sound change. Push chains presuppose that sound change takes place in a continuous phonological space in which margins of security may be diminished or expanded. The discussion of chain shifting principles to follow depends on the answer to this question, and it is therefore most relevant to ask what evidence has accumulated over the past decade and a half.

It is widely held that the Great Vowel Shift was a drag shift initiated by the diphthongization of the high vowels (Martinet 1955). But equal numbers of scholars agree with the argument of Luick (1903) in favor of a push chain, pointing out that the diphthongization of /u:/ did not occur when (in the North of England) /o/ was fronted rather than raised. In her article "The first push," Lutz (2004) finds evidence for an even earlier raising of /æ:/ and /ɔ:/ as initiating changes.

Some of the most productive work on sound change in progress has focused on the development of the New Zealand front vowel shift (3) (Woods 2000, Lau 2003, Gordon et al. 2004, Trudgill 2004, Langstrof 2006):

(3)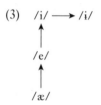

The Origins of New Zealand English (ONZE) project of Gordon et al. (2004) took advantage of recordings of early settlers made in 1948 by the New Zealand Broadcasting Service. It was established that the backing of /i/ to mid central position was a relatively late change. Studies of the earliest period (Woods 2000) and the middle period of the development of New Zealand English (Langstrof 2006) led to the conclusion that the shift was a push chain, in which the raising of /e/ preceded the backing of /i/. Langstrof further argued that the raising of /æ/ was the earliest stage in the process.

The generally accepted ordering of the Northern Cities Shift, as displayed in Figures 1.4 and 5.15, involves drag chain effects in stages 1–3, initiated by the general raising of /æ/. However, the ordering of stages 4 and 5 indicates that /e/ pushes backward towards /ʌ/ before /ʌ/ shifts further to the back. Chapter 6 of Volume 1 presented some evidence for a push chain on the basis of a limited number of speakers. The ANAE data set includes sixty-two speakers from the Inland North, where the NCS is active, with ages ranging from 14 to 78. Figure 6.15 shows the mean difference between the second formants of /e/ and /ʌ/ for four age levels within this group. If a drag shift were involved, the difference would increase from the beginning and close up at the end. But the figure shows the opposite tendency: the mean difference falls steadily from the oldest to the youngest group, which shows the smallest gap between the two vowels.[20] This is strong evidence of a push chain operating within the larger mechanism of the NCS.

The growing body of evidence for push chains supports the view that chain shifts, like mergers, operate within a phonological space of continuous dimensions. The F1/F2 diagrams which are generally used to display the progress of these mechanisms do not of course fully characterize the dimensions of this space. As we will see, duration is a prominent feature in the opposition and contrast of vowel

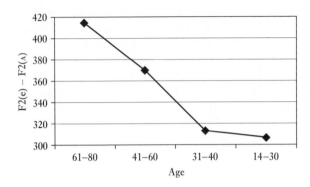

Figure 6.15   Mean differences of second formants of /e/ and /ʌ/ by age for 63 Telsur speakers in the Inland North

phonemes, along with rounding and dynamic directions of the trajectories that define the various vowel subsystems.

Given the possibility of both drag chains and push chains, a number of questions can be raised concerning the mechanism and nature of the causal link. The general theory that has been proposed here is that the shift of one vowel in response to the shift of another is a mechanical result of the language learning process (see PLC, Vol. 1, Ch. 20). Given the normal distribution of phonemes, with characteristic margins of security, outliers falling within the main distribution of a neighboring phoneme will not be recognized as consistently as other productions, and so will have less effect on the language learner's calculation of the mean. Figure 6.16a displays the situation. In Stage I, with normal margins of security, an outlying realization of phoneme B in the midst of phoneme A will have a finite tendency to be misunderstood as A, and to that extent will contribute less than others to the language learner's pool of tokens recognized as B. The resultant calculation will yield a target mean of, say, 1560 Hz. This is the normal conservative effect of neighbors on outliers, which contributes to the stability of a phonemic system. In Stage II of Figure 6.16a, phoneme A has shifted away, leaving a considerable gap. As a result, the same outlier is more likely to be recognized as a token of B and so will contribute to a shifted mean target of perhaps 1570 Hz. Stage III is the output of the language learner, who will aim at a target mean of 1570 Hz, with or without an outlier, and so will shift the main distribution to center on 1570 Hz.

Figure 6.16b is the corresponding mechanism of a push chain. Stage I represents the same stable beginning, with a single outlier of B in the A distribution. Stage II, however, is quite different from Stage II of the drag chain. The decreased margin of security between A and B leads to considerable overlap. Here some tokens of A are subject to decreased recognizability, namely those marked with circular outlines. As a result, the language learners of Stage II calculate a target mean somewhat higher than the actual mean of Stage I, say 1810 Hz in place of 1770.

The end result of successive repetitions of Stage II is seen in Stage III: a restoration of the normal margin of security, with a mean F2 of A 200 Hz greater than the mean F2 of B.

It should be apparent that the mechanism of a push chain is more complex than the mechanism of a drag chain in Figure 6.16a. But in this machinery there is no immediate answer as to why the circled tokens of A were recognized less frequently, but not so the adjacent tokens of B. If the overlap of A and B produced symmetrical results in terms of recognizability, we would see a symmetrical recoiling of the means of A and B to restore the situation found in Stage I. The preceding discussion

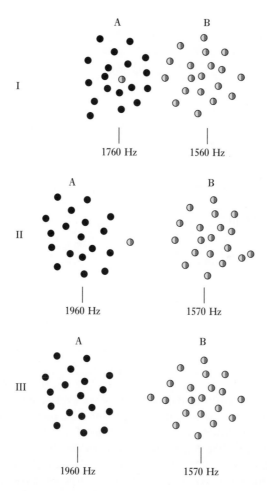

Figure 6.16a   Model of a drag chain showing the result of a shift away of a neighboring phoneme, which leaves a hole in the pattern

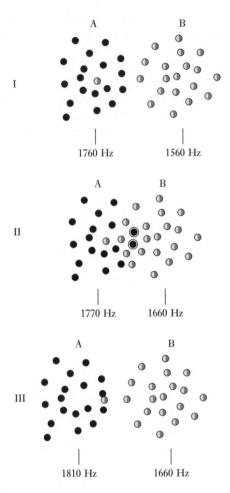

Figure 6.16b   Model of a push chain showing the result of a shift towards a neighboring phoneme, which results in an increased number of overlapping tokens

of the NCS indicates that this did not happen. An explanation for the continued asymmetry suggests that, in a push chain, the advanced tokens of B are marked as being more expected than the conservative tokens of A. This suggests a process of social marking that will be considered in greater detail in Chapter 9 on "driving forces."

In any case, the relative complexity of a push chain compared to a drag chain leads us to expect that drag chains would be more frequent in the historical record, and this seems to be the case.

6.5 Principles Governing Chain Shifting within Subsystems

The general principles of chain shifting were first put forward in 1972, in LYS, as the result of a general survey of chain shifts available in the historical record.

[1]   In chain shifts,

    a   long vowels rise;
    b   short vowels fall;
    c   back vowels move to the front.

Principle [1b] was divided into two cases: simple short vowels and the short nuclei of upgliding diphthongs. The classification of English vowels into "long" and "short" is not only based on their historical development, but on their phonotactic distribution, which persists unchanged in all modern-day dialects. As first discussed in Chapter 1, English short vowels cannot occur in stressed word-final position, no matter what sound changes affect their physical realization. To describe sound changes now in progress, it proved useful to adopt the tense/lax feature, which predicts the behavior of current vowels more closely than the short/long distinction. In the course of the Southern Shift (Figure 1.5), short front vowels become tense and the nuclei of long vowels become lax. These then follow the principles of chain shifting in [2]:

[2]   In chain shifts,

    a   tense nuclei rise;
    b   lax nuclei fall;
    c   back nuclei move to the front.

Although [2] is a useful reformulation, there is no generally agreed upon method or physical measurement that will decide whether any given vowel is tense or lax. It is well known that tense phonemes are opposed to lax partners on several physical dimensions. Tensing is accompanied by an increase in duration, by the development of inglides, and by the distribution of energy over time. The underlying assumption is that the production of tense vowels involves more muscular energy than that of lax vowels, but measures of muscular activity are not readily available for the detailed study of change in progress.[21] A more precise and practical measure is peripherality, defined as proximity to the outer envelope of distribution in two-formant space. For English and other modern West Germanic languages, one can define a phonological space with peripheral and nonperipheral tracks in both front and back areas of the vowel distribution. For these systems, we derive the principles in [3]:

[3]   In chain shifts,

> a   tense nuclei rise along a peripheral track;
> b   lax nuclei fall along a nonperipheral track.[22]

In Volume 1, this formulation was further developed in relation to articulatory position, where the front–back dimension coincides with the closed–open dimension, and a third principle is not required. Since the present volume will be concerned with the results of acoustic measurement on a large scale, the approach to the front–back movements will take a different direction.

The application of the concept of peripherality is particularly helpful in tracing changes in English diphthongs. In the historical record, tense and lax nuclei of diphthongs are not easily distinguished; but, in studies of changes in progress, acoustic measurements lead to a clear differentiation of diphthongal nuclei in terms of their distance from the outer limit of phonological space.

6.5.1   A redefinition of peripherality

Chapter 6 of Volume 1 developed the principles of chain shifting in a format most suitable for the acoustic exploration of sound change in progress, using the framework reproduced here as Figure 6.17a. Here peripherality is defined in terms of extreme values of F2. This was then extended to a framework in which extreme values of F1 were included as well, yielding the concentric framework of Figure 6.17b.

The question remains as to how much evidence there is for either of these definitions of peripherality as a constraint on chain shift movements. The individual vowel systems cited in LYS and in PLC, Volume 1 do not provide enough data to yield a decisive answer. Sufficient evidence is now available from the large data set of vowel measurements provided by ANAE. This comprises an acoustic analysis of 130,000 vowels from the systems of 439 speakers, aged 12 to 85, representing all the cities with a population of 50,000 and over in English-speaking North

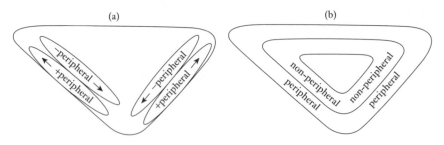

Figure 6.17   Two frameworks for a definition of peripherality in Volume 1; Figure 6.17a F2 only; Figure 6.17b F2 and F1

America. The individual systems are normalized with the log mean algorithm of Nearey (1977), which has proved successful in eliminating the differential effects of vocal tract length (ANAE, Ch. 6, pp. 39–40). Rather than attempt to plot the 130,000 tokens, or the mean values of each vowel for each speaker, Figure 6.18 plots the mean values of each vowel for the twenty-one dialects defined in Chapter 11 of ANAE.[23]

In Figure 6.18, an inner boundary separating peripheral and nonperipheral vowels is superimposed on the vowel distribution. The high and mid lax vowels are contained within the nonperipheral area. The means for /i/ (open circles) are clustered tightly in the upper left of the nonperipheral domain. The short /e/ means (open diamonds) are spread out on a path from upper mid to lower mid, all contained within the nonperipheral boundary. In the back portion of the nonperipheral area are located the means of their back counterparts, /u/ (solid circles) and /ʌ/ (solid upward triangles). The distinction between extreme and less extreme F1 values also serves to separate peripheral /uw/ from nonperipheral /u/ and peripheral /iy/ from nonperipheral /i/. The /uw/ symbols (solid circles with arrows pointing to the upper right) are spread out along the entire front–back dimension.[24]

On the other hand, the short or lax vowels /æ/ and /o/ are not distinguished by F1 values from /ah/, /oh/ or the nuclei of /ay/ and /aw/. All low vowels form

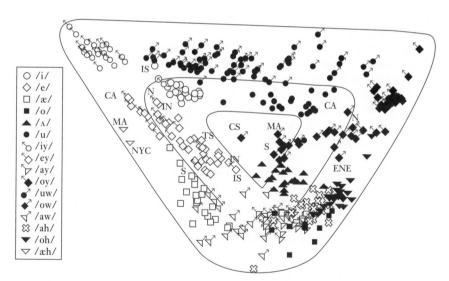

Figure 6.18 Peripheral and nonperipheral areas of the vowel system, redefined on ANAE data. Normalized vowel means of twenty-one ANAE dialects (N = 439) with nonperipheral tracks indicated. CA = Canada, CS = Charleston, ENE = Eastern New England, IN = Inland North, IS = Inland South, MA = Mid-Atlantic, N = North, S = South, TS = Texas South

an undifferentiated cluster on the F1 dimension and are separated only by F2. On the left, one can see an upward extension of /æ/ means along the peripheral path. Two extreme values of tense /æh/ (open downward triangles) represent the Mid-Atlantic (MA) and New York City (NYC) tense phonemes. The highest /æ/ (open squares) is labeled IN for Inland North: this is the generalized raising of /æ/ that defines the Northern Cities Shift. On the back portion of the peripheral track, one can observe the means for the three dialects that have tensed and raised /oh/ (solid downward triangles) and the tight cluster of /oy/ means (solid diamonds with forward arrow).

The utility of the peripheral/nonperipheral distinction is most evident in the word classes that cross the boundary. The symbols representing /ey/ (open diamonds with arrows to upper left) follow an elongated pattern from upper mid to lower mid, some on the peripheral track and others on the nonperipheral. The /ey/ means for Canada (CA) are the highest, and clearly peripheral. The /ey/ means for the North (N) and Inland North (IN) are almost as high, but are nonperipheral. The concept of nonperipherality has the greatest explanatory value in tracking the development of the Southern Shift (Vol. 1, Ch. 6; ANAE, Chs 11, 18). Once engaged in the Southern Shift, the Southern lax nucleus descends on the non-peripheral track. The /ey/ symbol marked "IS," the Inland South, is the leader in the development of the Southern Shift, and its position is very close to that of the backed and lowered /e/ marked "IN" (Inland North), descending by the same principle in the Northern Cities Shift. Following slightly behind, on the nonperipheral track, is "TS" for "Texas South."

The other facet of the Southern Shift is the tensing of the short vowels, which is again most extreme in the Inland South. The mean value of /i/ for the Inland South is indicated by the empty circle labeled "IS," located higher than any others and well across the boundary into the peripheral area.

Another vowel class that crosses the peripheral/nonperipheral boundary in Figure 6.18 is /ow/ (solid diamonds with arrows to the upper right). In the back peripheral track one can observe the means for the North (N) and Eastern New England (ENE), along with a group of other conservative dialects (see ANAE, Ch. 12). As /ow/ undergoes the process of fronting, the nuclei shift to the nonperiph-eral area and move steadily across to a central (Mid-Atlantic, South) and even front nonperipheral position (Charleston). Thus the fronting of /ow/ crosses the peripheral/nonperipheral boundary and is independent of principles [2] and [3]. This fronting of /ow/ is independent of any chain shifts, being essentially a parallel response to the fronting of /uw/.

In Figure 6.18 peripherality appears as a property of high and mid vowels, but not of low vowels. In the course of sound change, low vowels may rise to lower mid position and acquire peripherality, or they may fall to low position and lose this property. Another way to look at this process is to follow the lead of Stampe (1972) and Donegan (1978) in seeing peripherality as a means of increasing vowel color and distinctiveness, or, in their terms, of increasing chromaticity (see PLC,

Vol. 1, Ch. 6). On the other hand, the loss of peripherality entailed by a fall to low position leads to an increase in sonority.

6.5.2   The role of duration in low vowels

The differentiation of tense and lax vowels in low position is not dependent on F1 values or degrees of opening, but appears to involve other features, primarily duration. Labov and Baranowski (2006) studied the extensive overlap in low front position of short /e/ and /o/ in the Inland North. This overlap is the result of the response of both vowels to the gap in the pattern produced by the general raising of /æ/. Though there were many tokens occupying the same F1/F2 space, /e/ was significantly differentiated from /o/ by a mean difference in duration of 50 msec. Controlled experiments showed that 50 msec was a difference in duration sufficient to produce a radical change in recognition rates, longer values favoring /o/ and shorter values triggering a perceptive switch to /e/.

In the preceding chapter it was suggested that the NCS was initiated by a tensing of /æ/ and /o/, which was represented in Figure 5.15 as a shift from the [–peripheral] to the [+peripheral] track. This section has shown that peripherality does not distinguish low vowels, so that tensing of low vowels is most likely realized as an increase in duration.

Duration plays an even greater role in differentiating vowels in low position in Pittsburgh, where monophthongized /aw/ overlaps the F1/F2 space of /ʌ/. There is a sizable F1 difference between Pittsburgh /aw/ and Pittsburgh /ʌ/, but the durational differences are even greater. The mean duration of monophthongal /aw/ is 208 msec, whereas the mean duration of /ʌ/ is only 98 msec: this is a difference of six standard deviations, with no overlap between the shortest /aw/ and the longest /ʌ/.

The role of peripherality in the development of unidirectional changes in progress is a particular realization, in North American English, of the more general opposition of long and short vowels first presented in Chapter 5 of Volume 1. The essential point is that these governing principles of chain shifts operate only within subsystems and are triggered only when membership in a subsystem undergoes change.

6.5.3   The limitations of F2 perception and the instability of the peripheral/nonperipheral distinction

One of the most striking facts about the notation of dialectology is the disparity between the dimension of height and the dimension of fronting and backing. Many dialect atlases register as many as sixteen distinctions of height, using five or six alphabetic units like [i, ɪ, e, ɛ, æ] or [i, é, e, è, á, a], along with diacritics that indicate one level higher or one level lower. Whether or not one can achieve reliable agreement on sixteen distinctions, this corresponds roughly to the F1 range of 300 to 1000 Hz, or a discrimination of a little less than 50 Hz. On the other hand, dialect atlases and monographs rarely make more than three distinctions of fronting and backing, which correspond to an F2 range from 2800 to 600 Hz – a discrimination no less than 700 Hz. The rare use of fronting and backing diacritics yields no more than seven notational units, or a discrimination of differences of 300 Hz.

The use of logarithmic or Bark scales for fronting and backing reduces, but does not eliminate, this disparity between the two dimensions. Studies of just noticeable differences between isolated formants (Flanagan 1955) show F2 limens not much greater than F1 limens, but in connected speech the perceptibility of F2 differences is much less than for F1. The great majority of near-mergers, where people produce a difference they cannot recognize, concerns vowels that are differentiated only along F2 (Vol. 1, Ch. 12). This is characteristic of the near-merger of *source* and *sauce* in NYC (LYS), *fool* and *full* in Albuquerque (LYS) and Salt Lake City (Di Paolo 1988), and *ferry* and *furry* in Philadelphia (Labov et al. 1991). Chapter 13 of Volume 1 reviewed a number of paradoxical reports from the history of English and other languages, which could be resolved through the general observation that, whenever two phonemes are separated by an F2 distinction of less than 200 Hz, they will be perceived as "the same," but they may maintain separate histories in the speech community. Thus eighteenth-century *loin* and *line* were reported by contemporaneous observers to be "the same," but followed distinct paths in the centuries that followed.

Location on the peripheral or nonperipheral tracks will therefore distinguish the history and trajectories of vowels, but it is not a physical difference sufficient in itself to maintain a stable phonemic distinction.

6.5.4   Changes of subsystem in North American English

Chapter 9 of Volume 1 presented some general principles governing the shift of a vowel from one subsystem to another. The chapters to follow will trace the step-by-step progress of a number of English chain shifts, all initiated by a change of subsystem. It may be helpful to review the range of such changes and to consider whether they are unidirectional or bidirectional.

There are many different types of vocalic subsystems in the languages of the world, of which English has only a partial sampling. English has no nasal system, no creaky register, no glottal or ejective vowels, no tonal subsystems. The four subsystems that North American English does have are displayed in Figure 1.1, which is incorporated here in Figure 6.19. This is of course a phonemic display, located at a more abstract level of structure than the acoustic phonetic display of Figure 6.18. Each subsystem is organized into orthogonal discrete feature levels: [±high], [±low], [±front]. As pointed out in Chapter 9 of Volume 1, each subsystem assembles those units that are most subject to confusion in everyday speech. The

	SHORT		LONG					
			Upgliding				Ingliding	
			Front upgliding		Back upgliding			
	V		Vy		Vw		Vh	
nucleus	front	back	front	back	front	back	front	back
high	i	u	iy		iw	uw		
mid	e	ʌ	ey	oy		ow		oh
low	æ → o			ay		aw	æh	ah

Figure 6.19 Subsystems of North American English, with the Canadian Shift superposed

principles and mechanism of chain shifting developed in this chapter apply primarily within the V, Vy, Vw or Vh subsystem. In Figure 6.18, most of the Vy, Vw and Vh subsystems are located on the peripheral track, since the nuclei of their components are all peripheral. Although the nuclei of /ay/ are largely coincident with those of /ah/, it is not in danger of confusion with /ah/ as long as the front glide /y/ remains. However, some tokens of /ay/ will be confused with /ey/ and others with /oy/, even when these units are not engaged in change in progress.

The inglide which distinguishes Vh from V is not in fact as distinctive as the /y/ glide that marks Vy or the /w/ glide that marks Vw. This is the basis for the instability that was documented in the last chapter: in North American English, inglides alternate freely with short vowels. Thus the oppositions *bomb/balm*, *Tommy/balmy*, *have/halve* tend to collapse unless they are further reinforced.

The Canadian Shift, which was displayed in Figures 5.3 and 5.4, is superimposed upon the abstract vowel system of Figure 6.19. The merger of /o/ and /oh/ is shown by a unidirectional arrow from the V to the Vh subsystem. Thus the phoneme /oh/ has not become a member of the V subsystem, which occurs only in checked position, but rather the /o/ class has become an integral part of the /oh/ class, which has representatives in word-final (free) position (*law, flaw*). This development is integral to the consequential response in the V subsystem, which is now missing a low back member. In response, /æ/ shifts backward, following the mechanical operation of the drag chain discussed above. Consequently /e/ moves back and downward. In the various reports of the Canadian Shift (Clarke et al. 1995, De Decker and Mackenzie 2000, Boberg 2005, Hollett 2006, Hagiwara 2006, Roeder and Jarmasz 2009; see ANAE Ch. 15), there is considerable variation as to whether backing of lowering predominates.

It is interesting to note that all of the current changes of subsystem in North American English involve movement to the Vh subsystem:

a   Southern monophthongization of /ay/: /ay/ → /ah/;
b   Pittsburgh monophthongization of /aw/: /aw/ → /ah/;
c   the low back merger in Canada, the West, Western Pennsylvania, and Eastern New England: /o/ → /oh/;
d   Inland North general raising of /æ/: /æ/ → /æh/.[25]

These changes are all unidirectional, in the sense that no reverse sound change has been observed. There are no observations of unconditioned development of upglides from low monophthongs.[26]

So far the discussion has concerned unconditioned changes. For conditioned subsystems, such as vowels before /r/, it is even clearer that misunderstandings will be concentrated within the subsystem. The confusion of *far* and *for*, or *for* and *four*, is much more likely to occur than a mishearing of *four* for *phone*. Vowels before /r/ form a separate subsystem, as in Figure 6.1, because the phonetic influence of /r/ on the vowel is such that it is no longer obvious which vowel in the Vhr subsystem matches with which vowel in other subsystems – in other words, whether the vowel in *four* corresponds to the vowel in *flow* or to the vowel in *flaw*.

The back chain shift before /r/ is active in many areas of North America (ANAE, Chs 18, 19):

/ahr/ → /ohr/ → /uhr/
(*bar* → *bore* → *boor*)

It appears to be triggered by the merger of /ohr/ and /uhr/ rather than by an element leaving the Vhr subsystem.

With the vocalization of /r/, the Vhr system merges with the Vh system, with profound structural consequences (Labov 1966). Although the tide is now running in the other direction as far as /r/ is concerned, the ongoing vocalization of /l/ is currently active in many regions. It is producing new structural effects, namely a vocalic contrast in the Vw system of *go* [gɛo] versus *goal* [go:] in Pittsburgh, or the homonymy of *pal*, *pail* and *Powell* in Philadelphia, as reported in the last chapter.

6.6 How Well Do Governing Principles Govern?

We can judge the value of the principles developed so far in two distinct ways. On the one hand, we judge them by the proportion of the data they account for. ANAE provides data on twelve mergers in North American English, as shown in (4):[27]

(4) *Unconditioned*   *Conditioned*

	___ l	___ rC/#	___ rV	___ m/n
o ~ oh	i ~ iy	ih ~ eh	ey ~ e	i ~ e
hw ~ w	u ~ uw	oh ~ ɔh	e ~ æ	
iw ~ uw		ah ~ ɔh		
o ~ ah		uh ~ oh		

Two of these mergers have shown evidence of reversibility, which would seem to be a sizeable percentage of the total (two out of twelve). Another way of looking at the matter is to consider the massive geographic evidence for the expansion of mergers, which affects in one way or another all of the 326 cities studied by ANAE. In two communities we find a distinction expanding; in all we find at least some cases of mergers expanding.

When we consider the consistency of the principles of chain shifting, the evidence is even more favorable. In the original formulation of LYS, there appeared to be several counterexamples to the lowering of short vowels (for instance /e/ in New Zealand) and to the fronting of back vowels (for instance /e/ in the Northern Cities Shift). The formulation of [3] predicts that /e/ will fall along a nonperipheral track, and Figure 6.18 shows that this is what has happened to the mean position of /e/ in the Inland North: the diamond labeled "IN" has evidently lowered along the nonperipheral track.[28] From Langstrof's study of the raising of /e/ in the New Zealand chain shift (2006), we now know that this short vowel showed an increase in duration, indicating a shift to the tense class as it moved up along the peripheral track. As far as principle [3a] is concerned, there have never been counterexamples advanced to show tense vowels lowering in chain shifts.

A second way of evaluating general principles is the extent to which they can be accounted for by, and fit in with, our understanding of other principles of linguistic behavior. The unidirectionality of mergers scores high in this respect, since it is indissolubly linked to the arbitrary character of the linguistic sign and to every-thing we know about language learning ability. Chain shifting principles are another matter. Efforts to explain the principles in [3] are largely discursive and argumentative,[29] but do not yet connect with what we know of the mechanics of vowel production.

We may also ask of any general constraint whether it relates to the continued renewal and progress of change across generations. It is one thing to say that a merger tends to expand rather than contract, but it is quite another to say that it will do so. We have seen in this chapter that some boundaries of the low back merger have been stable for generations, while others are eroding rapidly. As a result of the tendency for mergers to expand, we abstain from using merger isoglosses to define regional boundaries. But there is nothing in this tendency that actually drives the merger.

It is even less likely that we can locate the driving force behind chain shifting in the general principles under [3]. Once a subsystem is disturbed through the loss or gain of a member, we can argue that the well-established tendency towards maximizing the distance among members of a subsystem will drive the chain shift along its destined path. But once again we must cite the opinion of Meillet (1921) that no universal principle can account for the fluctuating and sporadic course of sound change.

We will return to the problem of driving forces in Chapters 9 and 10. But before this we must examine more carefully the paths that lead to divergence. Given a triggering event and our understanding of the direction in which its consequences can flow, the crucial question remains: how do neighboring dialects take up different directions, and so become more and more different from each other?

7

Forks in the Road

7.1 The Concept of Forks in the Road

Chapter 1 divided the explanatory problems of linguistic change into two types. One is the existence of parallel developments after long separation – the problem confronted in comparing colonial Englishes of the Southern Hemisphere (Trudgill 2004). The other is the problem of explaining divergent developments in neighboring dialects that have never been separated – a common situation in North American dialectology. This chapter will examine cases of the second type and will attempt to characterize the common features of the forks in the road which lead to the increasing regional diversity of North American dialects.

Following the logic of Chapter 5, the identification of a triggering event is a terminal stage in the process of tracing, backwards in time, the linked series of changes that have affected a particular dialect. When we arrive at the triggering event, we are at the root of a branching process; otherwise all neighboring dialects would have followed the same causal path, and there would be no dialect diversity to deal with. If the triggering event turned out to be the geographic separation of two populations, there might be no problem to explain, for random variation and drift may very well account for the ensuing diversity. But the ANAE maps show sharp boundaries between speakers who have lived side by side for generations, in some cases even for centuries, with few physical or social barriers to communication. We have no reason to doubt the generality of Bloomfield's principle of accommodation, cited as [1] in Chapter 1. How, then, does it come about that neighboring dialects diverge rather than converge? This and the following chapter will put forward a general answer to this question, in the form of a two-stage model in which bidirectional changes are followed by unidirectional changes.

7.2   The Two-Stage Model of Dialect Divergence

Figure 7.1 displays this two-step model. The first stage, the development of bidirectional changes, depends on the existence of *forks in the road*, where an unstable linguistic situation may be resolved in one of two (or more) manners – often a choice that seems equiprobable, where small forces may lead the linguistic system to follow one route or the other. Such small forces may also induce one dialect to follow a different route from its neighbor. Given the unstable fluctuation of A and B in Figure 7.1, one group of speakers may adopt form A and the other form B.

Such equally balanced situations lead to bidirectional change, that is, to fluctuation in one direction or the other, often over considerable periods of time. The existence of a fork in the road does not in itself lead to divergence, since, under continual contact between the neighboring dialects, the principle of accommodation may lead to a resolution of the opposition in one direction or another, and to eventual convergence. Thus the dialect with form A may shift to B, or the dialect with form B may shift to A.

Lasting divergence occurs when the structural consequences of adopting A or B trigger further changes driven by the unidirectional principles of the last chapter, which are not easily reversed. In the domain of sound changes, these may be chain shifts, splits or mergers.

The upper half of Figure 7.1 will be instantiated and clarified in this chapter with examples of bidirectional changes ranging broadly over the history of English, from Old English to the current changes affecting North American English. The following chapter will deal with the developments in the lower half of Figure 7.1, where additional choice points will be found among unidirectional changes.

Two cases of fluctuating sound changes in the history of English will be examined in this chapter. They involve the pivot points in English vowel systems that largely determine the dynamics of North American English dialects: the low front short vowel /æ/ and the low back short vowel /o/. In both cases there is a wide range of phonetic realization: for /æ/, from [i:ə] to [a]; and, for /o/, from [u:ə] to [a]. In both cases phonemic oppositions are at issue: whether /æ/ is distinct from

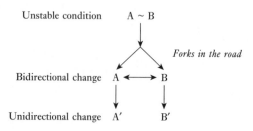

Figure 7.1   The two-stage model of divergence

/æh/; and whether /o/ is distinct from /oh/. The two situations appear at first glance to possess a striking front/back symmetry in both respects. But in actual fact front and back domains behave quite differently and have evolved in often divergent ways over the history of English.

7.3   The Fronting and Backing of Short *a*

The bidirectional changes to be considered here involve the alternation of a low front vowel [æ] with a low central vowel [a].

(1)

THE ORIGINAL FRONTING   The English language belongs to the West Germanic branch, which inherited the low back short vowel *a from Proto-Germanic. Old English, along with Old Frisian, fronted *a to *æ at a prehistoric stage ("Anglo-Frisian brightening"), but *æ then reverted to *a before back vowels. Thus Proto-West-Germanic *dag ("day") is realized in Old English as *dæg* (compare Old High German *tag*), but the plural is *dagas*; and Old English *fæder* ("father") corresponds to Old High German *fatar* and to Old Saxon *fadar*. Subsequent changes, as well as re-analyses and paradigmatic levelings, made *æ* and *a* distinctive phonemes.

MIDDLE ENGLISH BACKING   In late Old English and early Middle English, /æ/ shifted back to a low central [a], or even to back [ɑ], as shown by the change of spelling from æ to a. There was an extraordinary amount of dialect fluctuation, as explained by Wyld (1936: 110–12):

> The OE spelling *æ* remains in West Saxon and Northumbrian consistently, also in part of the Mercian area, while it is raised to *e* already in Early Kentish. [...] The Midland texts of the same date invariably have *a*. [...] After the beginning of the 14th century, pure Southern texts have *a* as well, to the extinction of the true Southern type. The Northern and Midland *a* type becomes the predominant, and finally the sole type apparently throughout the whole country [...].

EARLY MODERN ENGLISH FRONTING   The modern return to [æ] was again a slow process, marked by extensive dialect differentiation. Wyld summarizes this history as follows (ibid., 163–4):

> So far as the testimony of the Grammarians goes, the old back sound remained in the "best English" throughout the 16th century. It is certain, however, that the sound

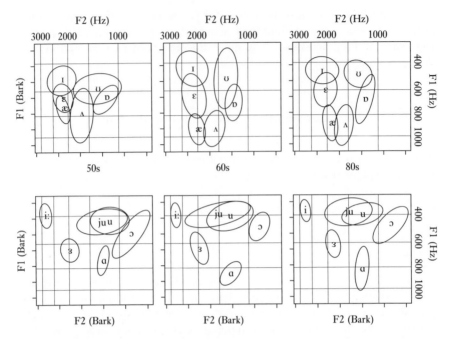

Figure 7.2   Backing of short *a* in Queen Elizabeth's short vowels (Harrington et al. 2000). Reprinted by permission of Cambridge University Press

had developed long before this. [...] A front pronunciation is pretty certain from Shakespeare's rhymes *scratch ~ wretch, neck ~ back*, both from *Venus and Adonis* [...] The fronted type seems to have been introduced slowly into the Standard Language, and was not fully accepted until towards the end of the 16th century [...] Once established, [æ] has remained unchanged.

RECENT BACKING IN THE UK   Wyld's finding that short-*a* has remained unchanged as [æ] was premature. In the conservative Received Pronunciation (RP) of his time, short-*a* was often reported as [ɛ], but the recent trend among educated speakers is a widespread backing from [ɛ] to [æˠ]. This appears clearly in the Harrington et al. (2000) study of changes in Queen Elizabeth's vowels in her birthday messages from the 1950s to the 1980s (Figure 7.2). The overlap of /æ/ and /e/ in the 1950s is replaced in the 1960s by /æ/ in low front position, with mean F2 of /æ/ lowering from about 2200 Hz in the 1950s to about 2000 Hz in the 1960s and to about 1900 Hz in the 1980s.

FLUCTUATION IN NORTH AMERICA   The variations in short-*a* realization reported above for the United Kingdom are reflected in an even wider range of short-*a* patterns in the United States. In the discussion of triggering events in Chapter 5, the Northern Cities Shift was linked to the formation of a short-*a koine* in Western New York State, the result of a mixture of radically different short-*a* systems during the population explosion associated with the building of the Erie Canal in the years 1817–25. Section 5.6 listed four such systems. One of these, the split short-*a* system of New York City, will not be considered here, for reasons to be developed in Chapter 15.[1]

The bidirectional changes considered here are the shift from a low front vowel to a mid or upper high fronted ingliding vowel, and vice versa:

(2)
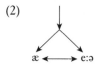

Figure 7.3 shows short-*a* distributions for three speakers from the New England area, which was the main source of westward migration to the Inland North. Figure 7.3a is the nasal system of Debbie T. of New Hampshire. Short *a* before nasal codas are well separated from all others, with no overlap in the two distributions. In contrast, the continuous short-*a* pattern of Elena D. in Figure 7.3b shows considerable overlap of oral and nasal codas. *Bad* is almost as high and front as *Dan*, and *bathroom* is close to *canvas*. The overall range is not as great as in Figure 7.3a, but many phonetic factors condition the position of a given token. Initial obstruent plus liquid produces the lowest and furthest back tokens, as in *black* and *slack*.

Among the New England short-*a* patterns one also finds some which appear to be precursors to the general raising of /æ/ in the Inland North. Figure 7.3c shows a general raising to lower mid position, with no tokens remaining in low front, but the separation between prenasal and preoral tokens is preserved. In fact this particular speaker, Phyllis P., is the only person outside of the Inland North who satisfies all the conditions of the NCS. Her short *a* is higher and fronter than her short *e*.[2] At the same time, Phyllis P. shows a solid merger of /o/ and /oh/, which is otherwise incompatible with the NCS. In this case the merger takes place in a strongly fronted position.

The continuous and raised nasal systems may be contrasted with short *a* in a fully developed NCS vowel system, as in Figure 7.3d. For Martha F. in Kenosha, Wisconsin, there is almost no difference in the distributions of prenasal and preoral tokens. Both types are intermixed in upper mid and lower mid position, with a small tendency for the prenasal tokens to be fronter.

An overall view of the range of short-*a* systems across New England and the Inland North appears in Figure 7.4, which plots the difference between the average F1 of preoral and prenasal tokens on the vertical axis, and the corresponding F2

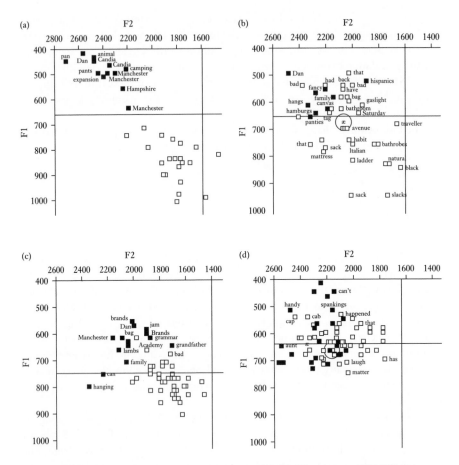

Figure 7.3a   Nasal short-*a* system of Deb T., 34 [1995], Manchester, NH, TS 726

Figure 7.3b   Continuous short-*a* system of Elena D., 70 [1995], Springfield, MA, TS 437

Figure 7.3c   Raised nasal short-*a* system of Phyllis P., 53 [1995], Rutland, VT, TS 434

Figure 7.3d   Raised short-*a* system of Martha F., 28 [1992], Kenosha, WI, TS 3

difference on the horizontal axis. New England speakers are displayed as open circles, and Inland North speakers as solid squares. The positions of the four speakers
of Figure 7.3 are labeled. Deb T. is located squarely in the midst of the nasal
system distribution, and Martha F. at the extreme of the Inland North, with minimal
differentiation of preoral and prenasal allophones. The continuous and raised nasal
systems are in the area of overlap.

When /æ/ remains in low front position, it is subject to backing to low central
position, as we have seen in the discussion in Chapter 5 (see also Chapter 8).

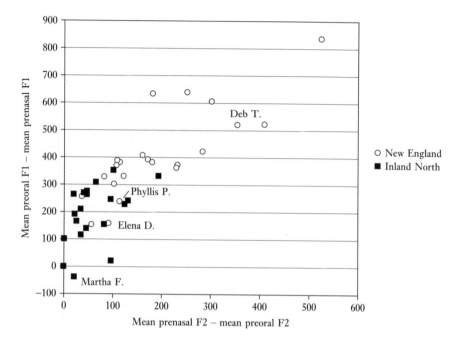

Figure 7.4 Differences between prenasal and preoral short-*a* tokens, as shown by mean differences in F2 and F1 for New England and Inland North speakers

7.4 Divergent Development of the /o/ ~ /oh/ Opposition

Chapter 5 traced two chain shifts – the Canadian Shift and the Pittsburgh Shift – to the creation of the highly skewed opposition of short *o* and long open *o* the result of a long series of historical accidents which were not intrinsically connected. This skewed opposition was the common inheritance of all North American English dialects, but not all dialects submitted to the subsequent merger. Chapter 11 of ANAE begins the classification of North American dialects by identifying three regions in which the merger of these classes is resisted: the Mid-Atlantic region, the Inland North and the South. The developments followed by these resistant regions involve several paths.

7.4.1   The unrounding of /o/

The first fork in the road is the rounded or unrounded realization of /o/, from [ɔ] to [ɒ] to [ɑ]. The rounded form of /o/ has long been dominant in Eastern New

England, a direct reflection of that dialect's predominantly Essex origins (Fischer 1989). The unrounding of /o/ was first observed in the United States by the spelling reformer Michael Barton (1830). Barton was born in 1798 in Dutchess County, New York, but traveled widely throughout New England and Montreal in teaching and promoting the phonetic alphabet he invented. Barton discovered that short *o* in his own New York State dialect did not conform to Noah Webster's description of short *o* as lower mid back rounded, but was rather an unrounded low vowel, more center than back. On the one hand, he found John Walker's scheme redundant "in making the sound of *o* in *not* and *a* in *far* to be different." He also argued with Burnap in Vermont that "the sounds of *a* in *all* and *o* in *of* were distinct." Barton's unrounded [ɑ] became the norm in the United States for the North, the Mid-Atlantic, the Midland and the West. When this unrounded [ɑ] merges with the /ah/ class of *father, spa, bra, pa, pajama* etc., it is best represented as /ah/, since the class as a whole includes stressed free vowels and is phonotactically distinct from the subset of short vowels.

However, the relation of [ɔ] to [ɑ] is not unidirectional.[3] Rounding of /a/, especially before nasals, is a widespread pattern. In many dialects of Old English, short *a* was spelled *o* before nasals, in *monn, begonn* etc. – a rounding that was later reversed as spellings reverted to *a*. Toon (1976) gives quantitative and lexical data on the change from *a* to *o* before nasals in West Saxon, and back to *a* with the decline of Mercian influence. Today the oscillation [ɒ] ~ [ɑ] is a common variable in English dialects, with [ɒ] as the dominant prestige form in RP and unrounded [ɑ] in local dialects such as that of Norwich (Trudgill 1972, 1974b). But Trudgill points out that the linguistic change moves in both directions. In Suffolk County the local form is rounded [ɒ], and Trudgill found that this phonetic realization was being increasingly imported into the Norfolk community by working-class men in close contact with the Suffolk norm. The low back merger of /o/ and /oh/ is realized as a lower mid back rounded vowel in many areas (New England, Western Pennsylvania, Canada).

The phonetic differentiation of /o/ and /oh/ as [ɑ] and [ɔ] is not, then, sufficient to inhibit the merger of these classes as a single low back vowel. The unrounding of /o/ is a fork in the road that may be retraced. For instance Dinkin's recent study of New York State (2009) shows that the unrounding of /o/ can be reversed, even when the Northern Cities Shift is operative. Younger speakers in Western New York State, born after 1960, show a distinct tendency to shift central /o/ to the back, a tendency that does not appear in the Western portion of the Inland North.

In spite of the general tendency of mergers to expand, the low back merger is not an immediate prospect for all North American English dialects. Chapter 11 of ANAE identified three regions of consistent resistance to this merger: the Mid-Atlantic, the Inland North and the South. In each of these regions different phonetic developments are involved.

Figure 7.5 shows the mean vowel values for the dialects involved in these developments: Providence, New York City and the Mid-Atlantic dialects (Philadelphia,

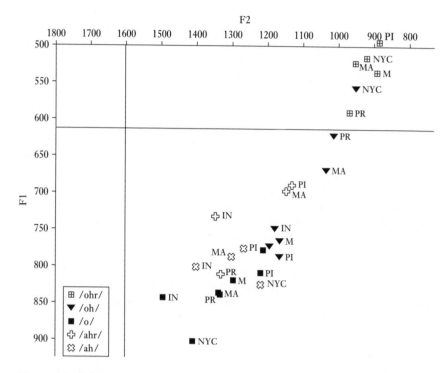

Figure 7.5 Raising of /oh/ in relation to /ohr/ and the low back vowels /o/, /ah/, /ahr/ for regional dialects of the Northeastern United States. IN = Inland North; M = Midland; MA = Mid-Atlantic; NYC = New York City; PI = Pittsburgh; PR = Providence

Wilmington, Baltimore). Within a narrow Mid-Atlantic corridor from Fall River, Massachusetts to Baltimore, /oh/ is raised to such a point that mean F1 is less than 700 Hz in the normalized ANAE grid. This upper mid rounded vowel (which actually becomes high in New York City) is much higher and backer than /ah/, the unrounded low back vowel resulting from the merger of /o/ with the class of *father*. As Figure 7.5 indicates, the backing and raising of /oh/ in New York City is associated with the parallel movement of /ohr/ in the back chain shift before /r/. Here /ohr/ rises to high position and merges with /uhr/, in *poor, moor* etc. (not shown in Figure 7.5).

(3) /ahr/ → /ohr/ → /uhr/
     /oh/ →

The backing and raising of /oh/ in this region is thus part of a systematic chain shift that follows the unidirectional principle that tense nuclei rise along peripheral tracks (3a of Chapter 6). In the Mid-Atlantic dialect area, /oh/ becomes closely associated with the nucleus of /ahr/, as indicated in Figure 7.5. In either case, the distance between /o/ and /oh/ is steadily increased as part of a unidirectional vowel shift, which is not easily reversed.

Figure 7.5 also shows the front position of /o/ for the Inland North (IN) – the aspect of the NCS which forestalls the low back merger of /o/ and /oh/. Here the enlargement of the distance between /o/ and /oh/ operates in a manner quite different from the Mid-Atlantic raising: /o/ moves strongly forward to fill the position formerly occupied by /æ/, and /oh/ shifts down and to the front behind it. Again, the movement of /o/ is not easily reversed, since it is locked into the larger context of the NCS.[4]

The third type of phonetic differentiation of /o/ and /oh/ occurs throughout the South. Unlike the Inland North and the Midland, the South shows no phonetic differentiation of the nuclei of these two classes, which are both low back vowels. Instead, a back upglide develops over most of the South for 20 to 100 percent of the /oh/ tokens (ANAE, Map 18.8). When the upglide is fully developed, the nucleus is slightly fronted and unrounded, a phonetic form that might be noted phonemically as /aw/. The consequences of this development will appear in the following chapter, which traces the further divergence of linguistic systems.

8

Divergence

Chapter 7 opened the discussion of divergence with the two-step model of Figure 7.1, and then focused on the bidirectional changes that make up the first half. The present chapter will focus on the second step in the model: the unidirectional changes that lead directly to divergence. The aim is to advance a general schema for divergence that may be useful for the study of change in other languages and in other societies.

8.1 Continuous and Discrete Boundaries

Divergence implies more than differentiation. Within a large territory there may be a continuous accumulation of small differences that result from the fact that a given change started in one area within the territory. The *Survey of English Dialects* (Orton and Dieth 1962–7) shows such a pattern as the result of the differential development of the Great Vowel Shift, which started in southeast England.[1] The divergence to be discussed here is of a more discrete type, the result of linguistic change moving in opposite directions on either side of a sharp boundary.

It must be observed that dialectologists often show very little confidence in the boundaries they draw. Typical is Carver's summary of his efforts to assemble the lexical evidence from the *Dictionary of American Regional English*:

> A map of language variation is merely a static representation of a phenomenon whose most salient characteristic is its fluidity. It is an almost seamless fabric covering the land. A person traveling southward from Superior, Wisconsin, to Mobile, Alabama, would be aware of the differing speech patterns but would not be able to say at what points along the route the changes occurred [...] What follows, then, is not the definitive description of regional dialects of America, because such a description is impossible. It is merely one attempt to seize the linguistic river as it flowed through. (Carver 1987: 19)

I quote this at length because it is so eloquent; similar statements on the continuous character of dialect boundaries are to be found throughout the literature (see also Chambers and Trudgill 1980; Kretzschmar 1992, Davis 2000). Some recent methods for dealing with dialect boundaries involve the mathematical description of continua (Heeringa and Nerbonne 2001), the typical result of the application of Bloomfield's principle of accommodation, as speakers mutually influence each other (see Ch. 1, [1]). Such continua may be stages in the process of dialect leveling that leads to general convergence.

The cases of divergence to be discussed here have a different character. They show sharp cleavages in the phonology of adjoining regions, with tight bundling of structurally related isoglosses.

8.2   The North/Midland Boundary

The deepest and most abrupt division in North American phonology is the boundary between the North and the Midland dialect regions, first delineated in the discussion of the westward extension of the Northern Cities Shift in Chapter 5. There we saw the coincidence of the lexical North/Midland boundary with one measure of the NCS, the UD criterion. In Figure 5.19 the North/Midland boundary, as defined by ANAE, coincided with the extension of the boundary between the North and the Midland, as defined by Kurath in the Eastern United States on lexical criteria (Kurath 1949). This lexical boundary is a cultural reflection of the settlement history of the region (see Figure 10.4).

The extent of divergence between the North and the Midland requires an assessment of the degrees of rotation of the set of vowels involved, as displayed in Figures 1.4 and 5.15. ANAE's exploration of geographic patterns found that relational criteria within the NCS gave more coherent measures of homogeneity and consistency than measures of individual sound changes. The four systematic measures used by ANAE are shown in Figure 8.1.

1   AE1   This criterion is the only one that does not involve the relations of two phonemes. It concerns the triggering event of the NCS: the general raising

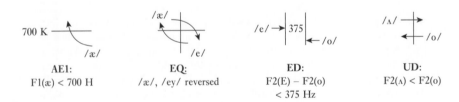

AE1:	EQ:	ED:	UD:
F1(æ) < 700 H	/æ/, /ey/ reversed	F2(E) − F2(o) < 375 Hz	F2(ʌ) < F2(o)

Figure 8.1   Four criteria for the advancement of the Northern Cities Shift

of /æ/. It is important to note here that this involves the mean of /æ/ only before oral consonants. While /æ/ is raised to upper mid position before nasal consonants in many dialects of North American English, a distinguishing feature of the Inland North is the minimal difference between oral and nasal submeans. The figure of 700 Hz yields maximum homogeneity for AE1 (.84).[2] In the normalized system used in ANAE, 700 Hz generally corresponds to the division between vowels perceived as high and vowels perceived as mid. The same value serves to distinguish the degrees of raising of the corresponding back vowel: the speakers who have mean F1 of /oh/ below 700 Hz are confined to a narrow belt along the East Coast, from Providence to Baltimore.

2   EQ   In conservative North American dialects, /e/ is higher and backer than /æ/, as in the positions of cardinal vowels in IPA charts. The general raising of /æ/ in the NCS is accompanied by a lowering and backing of /e/, so that their relative positions as measured by mean F1 and mean F2 are reversed.

3   ED   For most North American dialects, /e/ is a front vowel and /o/ is a back vowel. The mean F2 for /e/ for all dialects is 1927 Hz in the normalized system, and for /o/ 1302 Hz: a difference of 625 Hz. With the backing of /e/ and fronting of /o/, this separation shrinks. For the Inland North, the mean F2 values for /e/ and /o/ are respectively 1707 and 1491 Hz, a difference of only 216 Hz. The ED criterion that yields the greatest homogeneity (.87) is that, for assignment to the Inland North, this difference should be less than 375 Hz.

4   UD   For most North American dialects, /ʌ/ is located only slightly back of center, while /o/ – whether rounded or unrounded – is well to the back of center. In the NCS, /o/ shifts to the front, and /ʌ/ to the back. Maximum homogeneity (.87) and consistency (.85) are achieved by the criterion that /ʌ/ is further back than /o/.

Figure 8.2 shows the location of the means for the twenty-one North American dialects defined by ANAE for four NCS vowels, with the Inland North labeled. The extreme differentiation of the Inland North from all other dialects appears in the high front position of /æ/ (AE1), the backing of /e/ and fronting of /o/ (ED), and the backing of /ʌ/ (UD). One can also observe that /æ/ is higher and fronter than /e/ (EQ).

Figure 8.3 maps the Inland North with the four NCS isoglosses superimposed, adding AE1, EQ and ED to the UD isogloss of Figure 5.19. The lexical isogloss first seen in Figure 5.19 is also included. The four NCS isoglosses follow somewhat different paths to the east and west of the Inland North, but they coincide almost completely on the North/Midland boundary. The AE1 line dips south to include Fort Wayne in Indiana, and some variation appears in Northeastern Pennsylvania. Other than that, we have strict coincidence along this deep division, separating Inland from Midland cities.

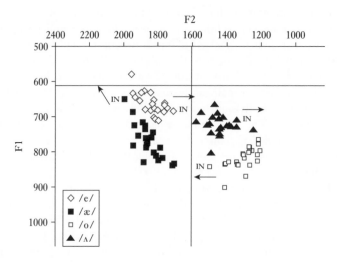

Figure 8.2 Position of Inland North means for four Northern Cities Shift vowels in relation to twenty other North American dialects. IN = Inland North

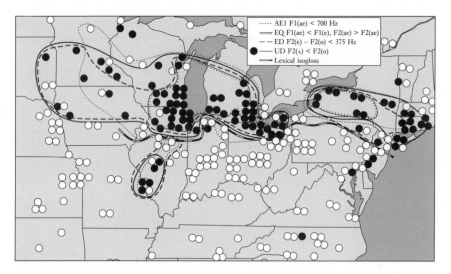

Figure 8.3 The coincidence of measures of the Northern Cities Shift along the North/Midland boundary

The city of Erie in the northwest corner of Pennsylvania deserves special comment. The lexical boundary plainly includes Erie within the North; but, of the NCS criteria, only ED includes Erie – and only by one of the two speakers.

Lexical and phonological data from the 1950s mark Erie as a consistently Northern city; it is the only community that has switched allegiance in the intervening period. Northern cities never show the low back merger in *cot* and *caught*. Erie has the merger, suggesting a pattern of Pittsburgh influence (ANAE: 205). The history and background of the eccentric behavior of Erie has been investigated in some detail by Evanini (2009).

The North/Midland boundary is linked to another deep division in North American English phonology: the fronting of /ow/. The fronting of the nucleus of /ow/ is strongly inhibited in the North and maximally promoted in the Midland (see Figure 10.3 and ANAE, Ch. 12). This correlation of the movements of /ow/ and /ʌ/ reflects an identification of the nuclei /o/ and /ʌ/ that holds for the entire Eastern half of the United States.

The divergence of the North and the Midland is seen most clearly in the development of /ʌ/ across age levels. In regression analyses on F2 of /ʌ/, the age coefficient is 1.37 for the North and −2.43 for the Midland, both significant at p < .05. That is, the younger the speaker is in the North, the further back the vowel: for every twenty-five years of decreasing age, one can expect F2 to be 34 Hz lower. In the Midland, the situation is the reverse: a speaker younger by twenty-five years will have an F2 greater by 53 Hz.[3]

Figure 8.4 is a scattergram of the relations of /ʌ/ and age in the Inland North and in the Midland. The horizontal axis shows the age of the speaker, the vertical

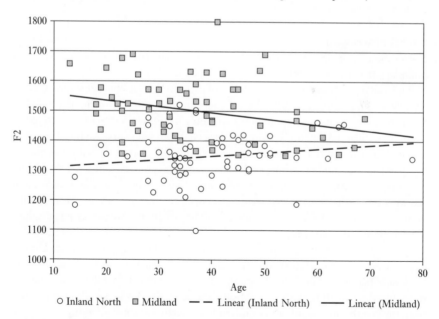

Figure 8.4 Divergence in the fronting and backing of /ʌ/ by age for the Inland North and the Midland

axis the F2 of /ʌ/. The lines show the general trends in the two regions. For the Inland North, the younger the speaker, the lower the F2 and the further back the vowel. For the Midland it is just the opposite: the younger the speaker, the higher the F2 and the fronter the vowel. No example of divergence more dramatic than this could be constructed. For the oldest speakers the two vowels are the same. For speakers aged 20 and under there is no overlap.

8.3   Communication across the North/Midland Boundary

Following Bloomfield's principle of density, first cited in Chapter 1 of Volume 2, one possible explanation of the sharp dialect differences across the North/Midland boundary is that this boundary is a natural product of discontinuities in the network of communication:

> The inhabitants of a settlement, village, or town [...] talk much more to each other than to persons who live elsewhere. When any innovation in the way of speaking spreads over a district, the limit of this spread is sure to be along some lines of weakness in the network of oral communication, and these lines of weakness, in so far as they are topographical lines, are the boundaries between towns, villages, and settlements. (Bloomfield 1933: 426).

Studies of average daily traffic flow show that this prediction holds for most of the dialect boundaries in the Eastern US, including that part of the North/Midland boundary that passes through Pennsylvania (Labov 1974).

This is demonstrated by recent studies of communication through a much larger data base. Thiemann et al. (2010) construct a proxy network for human mobility from the movements of 8.97 million banknotes in the United States, collected at the online bill-tracking study, wheresgeorgecom. The network, linking the 3,109 counties of the United States is defined by the flux matrix W whose elements w_{ij} quantify the number of bills exchanged between counties i and j per unit time. The major patterns of communication that emerge are shown in Figure 8.5. Here too we see that the cities of Western New York State communicate primarily with New York City, and the major connections from Chicago reach out equally into the North and the Midland.

Figure 8.6 shows the communication boundaries for the Northeastern United States from the national map constructed by Thiemann et al. on the basis of these bank note patterns. The Pennsylvania portion of the North/Midland boundary is reproduced again. But the larger Midland area in the Midwest is not separated from the North. Instead, minor boundaries run north and south, dividing the larger North/Midland areas into several east–west divisions, orthogonal to the North/Midland isogloss.

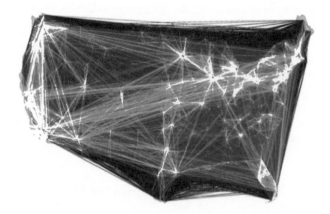

Figure 8.5 A proxy network for multi-scale human mobility, illustrating the flux *wij* of bank notes between 3,109 counties (Thiemann et al. 2010, Figure 1). Reproduced with the authors' permission

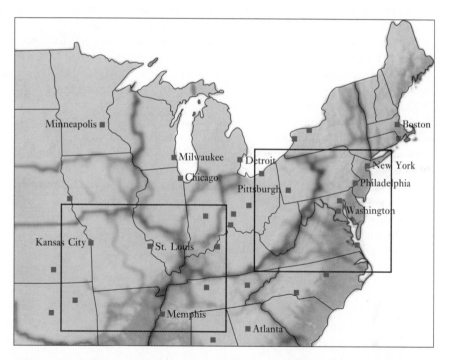

Figure 8.6 Effective subdivisions and borders in the Northeastern United States. Emergence of effective borders by linear superposition of all maps in the ensemble. Intensity encodes border significance (i.e. the fraction of maps that exhibit the border) (Thiemann et al. 2010, Figure 2). Reproduced with the authors' permission

We are therefore confronted with the situation first described in Chapter 1, [2b], and repeated below as [3]:

[3]   When two speech communities are in continuous communication, ling-
       uistic convergence is expected, and any degree of divergence requires an
       explanation.

What, then, is the mechanism that leads to such surprising divergence between neighboring areas?

8.4   The Two-Step Mechanism of Divergence

The previous chapter introduced the concept of a linguistic *fork in the road*: a choice between two directions of change that are equally likely to be selected in an unstable situation. Given this equally balanced choice, any number of small and accidental factors can lead to the initial differentiation. These choices are *bidirectional* and *reversible*: the same groups may move back and forth between them.

Chapter 7 showed that, in the history of English, the low vowels have been involved in many such unstable situations. The vowel /a/ has shifted back and forth phonetically more than once, from low front [æ] to central [a] and back again. Similarly, /o/ has shifted to /ɑ/ to [ɒ] and [ɔ] and back again many times.

Chapter 6 provided the theoretical basis for such instability. The low vowels are not marked for peripherality and are not subject to the imperatives of the principles of chain shifting. In this chapter the question of interest is how such a fluctuating situation can result in the permanent separation and the continued divergence of neighboring dialects. The two-step model put forward in Figure 7.1, reproduced here as Figure 8.7, states that such separation will occur when the bidirectional change is succeeded by a unidirectional change. In the phonological domain, uni-directional changes are of two types: chain shifts and mergers. I will first examine the merger of the low back vowels /o/ and /oh/, then return to the chain shifts that define the North/Midland boundary.

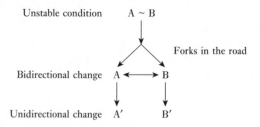

Figure 8.7   The two-step model of dialect divergence

8.5 Unidirectional Change: The Low Back Merger

The merger of long and short open *o* is the major unconditioned change taking place in the phonology of North American English, and it is one of the two major factors that differentiate North American dialects (Labov 1991). Chapter 5 projected the triggering event of this merger as a long series of historical accidents that led to the creation of the highly skewed and unstable long open-*o* class – a back rounded vowel, distinguished from short open *o* only by length.

One resolution of this unstable situation is the low back merger of /o/ and /oh/. As shown in Chapter 6, it is a solution that covers about 50 percent of the territory of English-speaking North America. The arrows in Figure 8.8 indicate the expansion of this merger from Eastern to Western New England, southwestward from Western Pennsylvania into West Virginia and Kentucky, southward from Canada into Minnesota, and eastward from the Southwest into Texas. The arrow in the lower section of New England corresponds to the most recent expansion in Southeastern Massachusetts reported in Johnson (2010). In addition, Dinkin (2009) finds that the low back merger is expanding into the Northern section of New York State adjacent to New England and is penetrating the areas of Eastern New York that are heavily influenced by the Northern Cities Shift. Given the general tendency for this merger to expand, one might conclude that it would ultimately eliminate divergence among dialects.

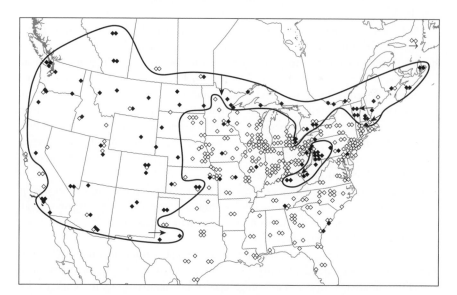

Figure 8.8 Expansion of the low back merger of /o/ and /oh/ in North America. Black tokens = merger in production and perception for all allophones. Arrows indicate direction of expansion in the second half of the twentieth century

8.6   Consequences of the Low Back Merger for the English Vowel System

8.6.1   The Canadian Shift

The low back merger is one possible outcome of a series of triggering events outlined in Chapter 5, but it is itself the triggering event for a variety of further consequences for the English vowel system. Figure 1.6 displayed the Canadian Shift, triggered by the low back merger. Like other initiating changes, the low back merger is a shift across subsystems (Figure 6.19): /o/ moves from the subsystem of short vowels to the subsystem of long and ingliding vowels. Merging with /oh/, it acquires allophones in free position, and so it is no longer a member of the short vowel subsystem. The loss of one of the six members in this subsystem then initiates a series of changes among the short vowels, following the principles discussed in Chapter 6, which govern movements within subsystems. The Canadian Shift is, then, a response to the impact of the low back merger on the short vowel subsystem: /æ/ moves back towards the position formerly occupied by /o/, and /e/ moves down towards the position formerly occupied by /æ/. In some accounts, /i/ shows a movement parallel to that of /e/.

8.6.2   The Pittsburgh Shift

In the two-step model of divergence, one or the other realization of a bidirectional change leads to a unidirectional change like the low back merger, and that merger has further consequences for the phonological system. The diversity of vowel systems is further developed by the options that follow. The mechanism of the chain shift depends upon the effect of the removal of /o/ from the subsystem of short vowels. But, as Figures 1.6 and 1.7 show, there are two possible consequences. The removal of the low back member will be followed by the shift of one neighbor, /æ/, or the other, /ʌ/. Chapter 5 has shown how this second option was taken up in the one area where the low back merger displays a discontinuous geographic distribution: Western Pennsylvania.

Figure 5.8 (reproduced here as Figure 8.9) is a plot of ANAE dialect means for the low vowels /æ/ and /ʌ/. The low position of Pittsburgh /ʌ/ compared to all other dialects is clearly indicated. On the other hand, Pittsburgh /æ/ shows none of the backing characteristics of Canadian /æ/.

The low back merger is evidently the conditioning event for the Pittsburgh Shift, just as it is for the Canadian Shift. Here, however, we have the same cause with two different effects. In the search for causes of linguistic change, it seems reasonable to expect that the same cause will have similar or comparable effects. Why is it that /ʌ/ moved instead of /æ/ into the empty space created by the back shift of /o/ and its merger with /oh/?

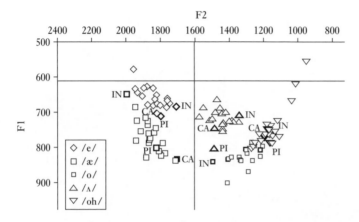

Figure 8.9 Mean positions of low vowels for twenty-one ANAE dialects, with Canadian Shift labeled for Canada [CA], Pittsburgh Shift labeled for Pittsburgh [PI] and Northern Cities Shift labeled for the Inland North [IN]

Among North American English sound changes there are other cases of two neighboring phonemes competing to fill the empty space in a pattern.[4] One might say that, in all these cases, the possibilities for either member in the pair fulfilling this role are equal, and it is a matter of chance which one was realized. But these choices are not equiprobable: as already noted, there are sixty communities which show evidence of the Canadian Shift, and only one city with the Pittsburgh Shift. We hypothesized above (Ch. 5, pp. 96–7) that the lowering of /ʌ/ in Pittsburgh was favored by its identification as the short counterpart of /ah/ – that is, of monophthongized /aw/. This monophthongization, a salient characteristic of the Pittsburgh dialect not found anywhere else in North America, thus acted as a second triggering event for the lowering of /ʌ/ rather than the backing of /æ/.

8.7 Resistance to the Low Back Merger

It was noted above that the end result of mergers might be a limitation rather than an increase in divergence. Since Herzog's corollary (Ch. 6) asserts that mergers will expand at the expense of distinctions, this phonological development in North American English might end in a situation where most of the continent is dominated by the low back merger. Indeed, many linguists feel that their great-grandchildren are destined to be integrated into this merger and into some of its consequences: the great majority would follow the Canadian Shift and a geographic minority would follow the Pittsburgh Shift. There is considerable support for this possibility. The Canadian Shift is quite uniform in Canada; but one may observe from Map 11.7

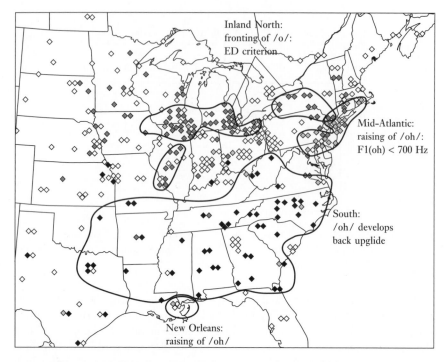

Figure 8.10   Areas of resistance to the low back merger in North America

of ANAE that ten of the 106 Telsur speakers in the West also satisfy the criteria for that shift (F2(o) < 1275, F2(æ) < 1825, F1(e) > 660). Though the Pittsburgh Shift is basically limited to its eponymous city, it shows some signs of expansion into West Virginia, along with the low back merger. Nevertheless there is some evidence that resistance to the low back merger is a fundamental characteristic of several large regions of the continent. The initial analysis of North American dialects in ANAE, Map 11.1 begins with a display of these regions; its salient features are extracted in Figure 8.10.

Among the bidirectional variables discussed in Chapter 7, the unstable relation of /o/ and /oh/ is accompanied by many fluctuations, and at any point this pair of vowels may be subject to the unidirectional process of merger. There are at this point three other processes that will make a merger much less likely, or forestall it altogether. They are all ways of increasing the phonetic distance between /o/ and /oh/.

1   The first of these processes is the raising of /oh/ to upper mid position. In a narrow strip of territory along the Eastern Seaboard, /oh/ is raised to a position with mean F1 less than 700 Hz.[5] This territory ranges from Providence, Rhode

Island to Baltimore, Maryland. In the early study of New York City (Labov 1966), raised /oh/ was subject to correction, but not as extensively as raised /æh/. In other parts of this Northeastern region, raised /oh/ is not a highly marked feature, but it is a salient identifier of the East Coast dialects for Westerners. The low back merger is not found in this territory.

There is no evidence as to when this raising was initiated. It is not mentioned in the earliest accounts of the New York City dialect (Babbitt 1896). In the 1960s, (oh) showed a slope in apparent time consistent with its increasing raising as a change in progress.

Raised /oh/ is found in only one section of the US outside of the Eastern Seaboard belt, and that is the city of New Orleans. The characteristic raised /oh/ of the New Orleans dialect is one of several pieces of evidence that point to extensive New York City influence. Though this influence could have taken many possible routes, the clearest documentation indicates extensive interaction and intermarriage alliances between New Orleans families and New York City cotton bankers in the nineteenth century (see Chapter 15).

2   An opposite form of the phonetic differentiation of /o/ and /oh/ is the fronting of /o/. This is reflected in Figure 8.1 as the ED criterion of the Northern Cities Shift: the reduction of the front–back difference between /e/ and /o/. As indicated in Figure 1.4, the fronting of /o/ is usually considered a second stage of the NCS, a response to the general raising of /æ/. Yet historically it must be linked to the prior step: the unrounding of [ɔ] to [ɑ] discussed in the last chapter. This unrounding extends beyond the Inland North: it is also found in the parts of the Eastern Seaboard belt where /oh/ is raised; in the Midland; in the North generally; and in the West.[6] The unrounding of /o/ may therefore be considered a precondition for the NCS (see the discussion of Michael Barton's discovery of this unrounding in Chapter 7). In any case, the further fronting of /o/, characteristic of the Inland North, seems to be required for resistance to the low back merger, since unrounded /o/ in the West does not inhibit this merger.

Chapter 6 found that low vowel shifts are not governed by unidirectional principles of chain shifting, since peripherality is not marked for low vowels. The bidirectional character of the movement of /o/ is further illuminated by the recent finding of Dinkin (2009) of a general backing of /o/ in New York State, both in areas fully dominated by the NCS and in fringe areas marginal to it. This phenomenon of backing appears to have occurred suddenly for those born in the 1960s. The backing of /o/ is accompanied by a weakening of the recognition of the /o/ ~ /oh/ distinction in minimal pairs in the fringe areas. Thus Dinkin finds that the resistance provided by the NCS to the low back merger is not as strong as the ANAE analysis asserts, and not as strong as that afforded by the raising of /oh/ on the East Coast. The backing of /o/ is not found in the larger Western part of the Inland North, where no influence of the NCS has been detected.

3   The Southern dialect region generally shows identical locations of /o/ and
     /oh/ in F1/F2 space, but differentiates /oh/ from /o/ by a glide in the high
     back direction, [ɔo], with the nucleus often unrounded to [ɑo]. Figure 8.10
     shows the distribution of this feature in the South, where diphthongization is
     largely coextensive with the defining Southern isogloss: the monophthongization
     of /ay/ before voiced obstruents (solid line in Figure 5.11).
         The unrounding of /oh/ to phonetic [ɑo] suggests a shift of phonemic nota-
     tion to /aw/. However, in Figure 1.1 the notation /aw/ is reserved for the
     back upgliding vowel, in *out, south, down*, etc. Throughout the Midland and
     the South, the nucleus of /aw/ is well front of center, as [æo] and [eɔ], especially
     before nasal consonants; by contrast, in the North this nucleus is located back
     of center, as [ɑo]. By itself, this phonetic differentiation would not normally
     furnish sufficient motivation for a shift of phonemic notation, but the linkage
     of the Southern unrounded [ɑo] for /oh/ and fronted [æo] for /aw/ does
     provide such a motivation, yielding the chain shift (1). While the shifts of
     subsystems we have been considering up until now involve additions to the
     long upgliding subsystem, this is a reverse process, which adds to the inventory
     of the Vw subsystem.

(1)   Southern Back Upglide Shift:
      /oh/ → /aw/ → /æw/

Despite its firm location in the chain shift (1), the back upglide is variable in the
extreme. As ANAE, Map 18.8 shows, the area where the back upglide occurs with
a frequency from 50 to 100 percent is only a little larger than the Inland South;
and, in much of the area shown here in Figure 8.10, it is present only 10–20 percent
of the time. For the five speakers in Atlanta, the Southern city with the most North
and Midland influence, the back upglide does not appear at all.
    Though the back upglide is a source of resistance to the low back merger, it is
not well enough entrenched to offer complete resistance. Feagin (1993) first reported
the low back merger among young upper middle-class speakers in Anniston,
Alabama; apparently this was a product of the complete abandonment of the back
upglide. Irons (2007) found an unexpected frequency of the low back merger in
Kentucky, and likewise attributed it to loss of the glide.
    In contrast, the phonetic adjustments of /oh/ and /o/ in the (Western) Inland
North and Mid-Atlantic areas offer consistent resistance to the low back merger.
The fronting of /o/ and the raising of /oh/ are variable, but no more than any
other change in progress. The mean values around which this variability is distributed are the parameters of interest. These are displayed in Figure 8.11, which shows
the mean values for /i/, /e/, /æ/, /o/, /ʌ/, /oh/ for each of the twenty-one
dialects and labels the items that are relevant to resistance to the low back
merger.

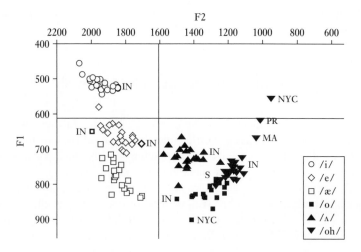

Figure 8.11   Resistance to the low back merger as shown by the distance between /o/ and /oh/ for the Inland North [IN], the South [S] and the dialects with raised /oh/: New York City [NYC], Mid-Atlantic [MA] and Providence [PR]

One can observe three degrees of raising of /oh/: in Mid-Atlantic to lower mid, in Providence to mid center, and in New York City, the most extreme, to lower high position. The great distance between NYC /oh/ and NYC /o/ is archetypical for that dialect. The /oh/ token labeled "IN" is at the upper end of the main /oh/ distribution.

The operation of the NCS is evident in the very front position of /o/ for the Inland North, the extreme position of Inland North /æ/, and the Inland North backing of both /i/ and /e/. On the other hand, there is no differentiation of /o/ and /oh/ for the South on the F1/F2 plane. The single label "S" indicates the mean value for both vowels, where F1 and F2 of /o/ and /oh/ coincide.

As a consequence of these phonetic shifts and rotations, the expected expansion of the low back merger has been blocked. Long-standing stability was the main finding in Johnson's study of the boundary between Eastern New England and Providence, as reviewed in the last chapter. This is what one would expect from the raised /oh/ of Providence. But the spread of the merger in the youngest generations and the backing of /o/ in New York State leave the long-term future of the low back merger an open question.

Although this volume is focused upon North American sound changes, it is relevant here to note that the raising of /oh/ is the basic mechanism operating in Southeastern England. While Received Pronunciation continues to differentiate

/oh/ from /o/ primarily by length, most popular dialects in that region raise /oh/ from lower mid [ɔ] towards cardinal [o].

8.8   Further Differentiation by Chain Shifts

In addition to the raising of /oh/ on the Eastern Seaboard, a further development along the back perimeter serves to differentiate these vowel systems from others. As /oh/ rises along the peripheral track beyond upper mid to high position in New York City, a parallel chain shift is engaged in the subset before /r/. Figure 8.12 shows schematically how vowels before /r/ rise, so that mean /ahr/ reaches the mid back position and mean /ohr/ rises to high position, merging with /uhr/. On the left is the New York City pattern, in which /oh/ rises to high position, in parallel with /ohr/ (Labov 1966). On the right, Philadelphia /oh/ is stable at mid position, and /ohr/ rises beyond it to the same merger with /uhr/.

Figure 8.13 traces the same process in individual speakers: one of the four ANAE subjects representing New York City above and one of the four subjects representing Philadelphia below. It is evident that the NYC /oh/ has reached high position, along with /ohr/ and /uhr/. One token of /uhr/ is embedded in the cluster of high vowels: the word *mature*, with F1 of 477 Hz and F2 of 821 Hz.

The raising of /ahr/ is considerably more advanced in Philadelphia, while /oh/ remains stable in mid position. We see that the nuclei of /ahr/ and /oh/ plainly coincide; this may contribute to the stability of /oh/ in Philadelphia. In the LVC study of the 1970s, /oh/ showed no significant coefficient in apparent time, but /ohr/ did (PLC, Vol. 2; Conn 2005). /ohr/ has now reached fully high position, as it has in New York City, merging with /uhr/. Since there is no trace of fronting of /u/ or /uw/ before /r/ in any North American dialect, it is inevitable that such a merger will take place if the mid vowel reaches high position.

The raising of /oh/ in the Northeastern coastal belt is thus accompanied by other movements along the back peripheral track, which carry these dialects further along their natural line of development.

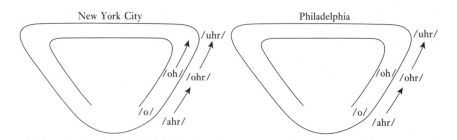

Figure 8.12   The Back Vowel Shift before /r/ in New York City and Philadelphia

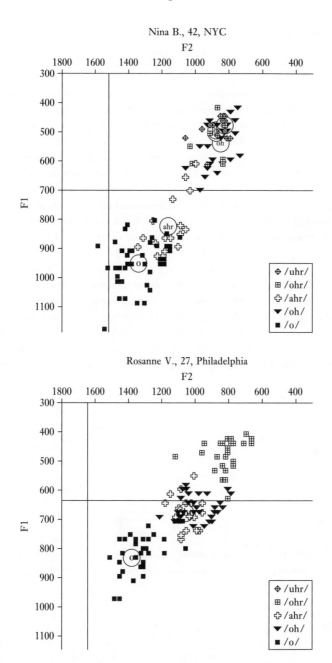

Figure 8.13 The Back Vowel Shift before /r/ in two individual speakers

8.9   A General View of Linguistic Divergence in North America

The various divergent developments that have been reviewed in this chapter are summarized in the single diagram of Figure 8.14. It considers the developments that spread from the unstable situation described in Chapter 5: the skewed opposition of /o/ and /oh/ in close approximation, in the nonperipheral and peripheral tracks of vowel space.[7] This opening scenario included a bidirectional shift: the unrounding or rounding of /o/. It was resolved in North American dialects by one of two options: on the left side of Figure 8.14, the unidirectional low back merger; on the right side, bidirectional shifts that increased the phonetic distance between /o/ and /oh/. Following the left-hand branch, we see dialects being further differentiated by one of two unidirectional shifts: the Canadian Shift or the Pittsburgh Shift.

The right-hand branch shows an even more complex differentiation. The phonetic distance between /o/ and /oh/ can be increased by one of three phonetic movements, all of which are bidirectional. The fronting of /o/ triggers one set of movements; the raising of /oh/ another; the addition of the back upglide a third. We know that the development of a back upglide can be followed by its loss, as demonstrated by the earlier history of English long open *o*, in Chapter 5, as well as by current developments in the South. These bidirectional shifts remain

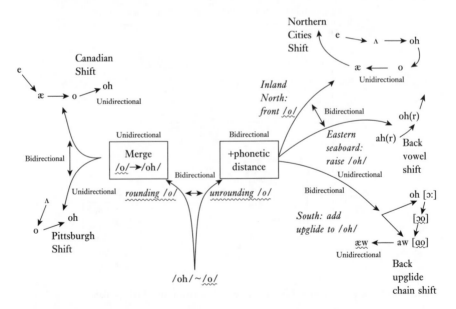

Figure 8.14   Development of divergence in North American English

bidirectional only until the vowels involved become engaged in chain shifts, as the nuclei move onto a peripheral track and become locked into the unidirectional mechanisms reviewed in Chapter 6.

The unidirectional character of chain shifts cannot be considered an absolute. As noted above, Dinkin (2009) finds a reversal of the fronting of /o/ in the Eastern portion of the Inland North. Lennig (1978) showed that the rotation of /a, o, u/ in vernacular Parisian French could be reversed, under social pressures from the upper middle class and as a structural consequence of the /a/ ~ /ɑ/ merger. ANAE finds that the Southern Shift is receding as a whole, in contrast to the other regional developments discussed here, and the attrition of the back upglide on /oh/ is one symptom of that recession. Nevertheless, chain shifts are not free to oscillate in either direction, since they are constrained by the governing principles reviewed in Chapter 6. Isolated sound changes are influenced by the same tendencies, but in a probabilistic manner that allows for considerably more fluctuation and more frequent exceptions.

The fundamental characteristic of the spreading tree of dialectal diversity is the alternation of bidirectional and unidirectional processes. If all sound changes were bidirectional, such divergence would not be expected between neighboring dialects, given Bloomfield's principle of accommodation. Nor would it be expected if, conversely, all changes were unidirectional, since every local region would be responding in the same way to basically the same constraints. Thus Figure 8.14 is an elaboration of Figure 8.7. The existence of forks in the road is a precondition for the permanent differentiation of A and B into A′ and B′.

9

Driving Forces

Up to this point we have considered the cognitive consequences of linguistic change in North America, the triggering events and governing principles that constrain the path of change, and the route by which neighboring dialects become increasingly different from each other. All of these factors are relevant to our effort to grasp the whys of linguistic change. Chapters 2–4 underlined the urgency of that quest in the light of the apparent dysfunctionality of change. As one answer to why, Chapter 5 allowed us to respond, "Here is how it started." Chapter 6 permitted us to explain why change proceeded in a given direction: because it could not go the other way. Chapters 7 and 8 explained how changes following the same governing principles could move neighboring dialects in different directions. The present chapter arrives at another, perhaps more basic sense of why: why as a search for motivating or efficient causes. What are the forces that drive the continuing process of language change?

Granted that the triggering events in Chapter 7 are particular accidents of history, the question remains whether continuing change may be the result of universal factors – a type of inherited but permanent instability. One such generally operating factor is the tendency to maximize dispersion within a subsystem, producing shifts in the direction that was originally determined by the unidirectional character of the triggering event (Martinet 1955, Liljencrants and Lindblom 1972, Lindblom 1988). A second factor is the principle of least effort, discussed briefly in Chapter 1. Although least effort is an important factor in processes of lenition (Bybee 2002), it is not immediately relevant to the vowel shifts and rotations that are characteristic of North American dialectal diversity, since these are realized in fully stressed syllables and frequently involve fortition – with increase of intensity, complexity and duration. A third such factor is the tendency to generalize changes across parallel members of the (sub)system, which is often seen as a form of rule simplification. The question is, then, whether such readjustment processes explain the phenomena, or whether there is evidence for additional factors to account for the tempo, direction and social distribution of change in progress.

General principles of this type would predict that sound change, once initiated, will move through the speech community in a uniform fashion.[1] It has been suggested that least effort affects one part of the population more than another (Kroch 1978), but this has not been demonstrated. In any case, it does not seem likely that the tendency to maximal dispersion, driven by the process of probability matching, would apply differently to children of different social groups

This point requires a reference to the observation of Meillet, which was first cited in Chapter 1 of Volume 1. Since language change is not uniform but essentially sporadic, it follows that no general principle can serve our present purpose of accounting for the driving forces of change:

> The only variable to which we can turn to account for linguistic change is social change, of which linguistic variations are only consequences [...] We must determine which social structure corresponds to a given linguistic structure, and how, in a general manner, changes in social structure are translated into changes in linguistic structure. (Meillet 1921: 16–17)

The sociolinguistic work of the past half century has identified a wide variety of social structures that correlate with a particular linguistic structure. We will examine each of these in turn, moving from the most clearly established to the most problematic ones.

9.1   The Importation of Norms

Change from above is clearly the result of social factors operating upon language. We usually recognize change from above by the fact that it involves high-prestige features, which spread downward from the social class of highest status. But this is not a sufficient criterion, because it is possible for the upper class to be an originating center of change within the system. Change from above (the linguistic system) implies that the new element is imported from some external language or dialect. Thus NYC (r) was imported from *r*-pronouncing dialects (Labov 1966); Montreal uvular (r) was imported from other dialects of Quebec and from European French (Sankoff and Blondeau 2007); and Arabic (q) was imported from classical Arabic into modern dialects (Abdel-Jawad 1987; Haeri 1996). Changes from above usually involve superficial and isolated features of language; they tell us little about the systematic forces that mold the history of dialect divergence, as outlined in the previous chapter.

9.2   Locality

A common reference point for the social motivation of language change is the Martha's Vineyard study of centralization as a marker of local identity (Labov 1963). Martha's Vineyard is a small speech community containing a number of smaller communities (Chilmark, Gay Head, Edgartown). The degree of centralization of /ay/ and /aw/ was correlated with positive or negative orientation towards permanent residence on the island. It is important to note that the reason for the general acceptance of the conclusion that local identity was a driving force was the existence of contrast within the community. Speakers with similar social characteristics differed in the degree of centralization to the extent that they differed in orientation towards their local site, Martha's Vineyard.[2] Hazen (2002) made a similar use of contrasting degrees of local identity in a study of the use of three variables by African–American youth in North Carolina, opposing "expanded" identity to local identity. The use of a linguistic form by a local speech community does not in itself show that the form in question is being used to mark or assert local identity, though this may be the case. To make local identity a meaningful factor in the motivation of a linguistic change, we need a correlation between degrees of local identity and the advancement of that change.

Local identity can of course be overt. Once a linguistic feature has risen to a sufficiently high level of social awareness and has become a stereotype, it may be subjected both to folklorization and to stigmatization. Johnstone et al. (2002) describe the high degree of public awareness of several features of the Pittsburgh dialect, such as the monophthongization of /aw/. New York City represents an extreme example of such unsystematic stigmatization (Labov 1966). Most middle-class speakers there consciously attempted to lower /æh/ and /oh/, in a lexically irregular fashion, while other aspects of the system, like the raising of /oy/, remained untouched. There can be no doubt that social forces can change language in this way, and the loss of the back upglide of /oh/ in the South, discussed in the last chapter, may be an example of this type. On the other hand, the low back merger and other mergers – the Northern Cities Shift, the Canadian Shift, the Pittsburgh Shift, and the Back Vowel Shift before /r/ – all take place well below the level of social awareness. Any effect of social identity will be unconscious, as in the case of Martha's Vineyard.

It is also possible that enhanced awareness may stabilize a dialect and preserve it from the effects of dialect leveling. Speakers of the Outer Banks dialect of Ocracoke, North Carolina and vicinity, long stereotyped as "hoi toiders" (LYS, Wolfram 1999), have received this kind of support from the research group at North Carolina State University (Wolfram 1994). This explicit appeal to local identity may result in language change; but it does not yield insight into the factors that created the dialect divergence to begin with.

9.3   Social Networks and Communities of Practice

The study of rural speech communities like Martha's Vineyard and Ocracoke may involve the linguistic patterns of several hundred people. In the search for the effect of social forces on language one may turn to even smaller social units: social

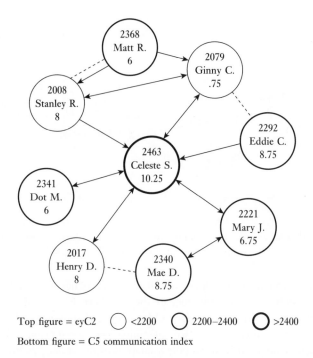

Figure 9.1 Flow of influence in the Clark Street social network in South Philadelphia. Arrows indicate those named in answer to the question "Where do your friends live?" Upper figure: mean F2 of /eyC/. Lower figure: Communication Index C5 (density of contacts within the neighborhood, combined with proportion of contacts outside the neighborhood). Dashed lines: family connections

networks (Moreno 1953) and communities of practice (Lave and Wenger 1991, Wenger 1998). Milroy and Milroy's study of Belfast found that participation in dense, multiplex networks preserved dialect features against the effects of dialect leveling, while weak ties to those outside the network promoted leveling effects (Milroy and Milroy 1978, Milroy 1980). Chapter 10 of Volume 2 applied the study of social networks to change from below in Philadelphia. The sociometric parameters were then correlated with the degree of advancement of the linguistic changes in progress. The C5 index identified the leaders of change as speakers who had the highest density of contacts within the neighborhood, in combination with the highest proportion of contacts outside of the neighborhood. The effect of weak ties here is not the same as in Belfast: instead of promoting a dialect leveling of the local vernacular, weak ties served as channels of influence for changes flowing to and from the broader community. Figure 9.1 displays a social network studied on Clark Street in South Philadelphia, an Italian upper working-class group of family and friends, where the central figure leads in both the C5 index and the raising of checked /ey/.

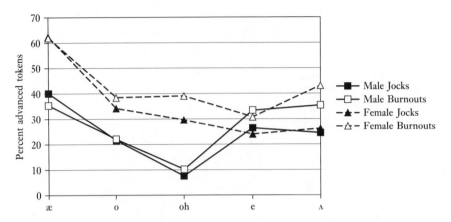

Figure 9.2   Percent advanced tokens for five stages of the Northern Cities Shift in a Detroit high school by group membership and gender (Eckert 2000)

The most thorough study of linguistic change in social networks is that of Eckert (2000), who studied the development of the Northern Cities Shift in suburban Detroit high schools. Figure 9.2, derived from Eckert's fine-grained study of the NCS, shows correlations with the two polar adolescent social groups (Jocks versus Burnouts) and gender. In Eckert's (1989) analysis of the social structure, *Burnouts* are youth who avoid and reject adult-dominated institutions and norms; in contrast, *Jocks* seek advancement and success by conforming to those norms, following the educational path to upward mobility.[3] The vertical axis plots the mean percent of tokens that were phonetically rated as advanced for each stage; the horizontal axis displays the five stages of the NCS as diagrammed in Figures 1.4 and 5.15.

Following the ordering of Figure 5.15, the most recent stages of the Northern Cities Shift are shown to the right: the backing of /e/ and /ʌ/. These are correlated with the high school social categories: the Burnouts show significantly greater values than the Jocks, while gender differences are not significant. But, for the three older stages, the situation is reversed: social category is not significant, but gender is a major differentiating factor.

Eckert interprets these data as evidence that sound change is driven among adolescents by its adoption by, and association with, a local community of practice. In the framework of Wenger (1998), the Burnout pattern involves the alignment of participation and reification. Members participate and learn from activities like cruising and smoking in the courtyard. The reification of membership in the community of practice is accomplished by such material facts as the style of jeans worn, in a pattern described in detail by Eckert. Extreme backing of /e/ and /ʌ/ may then be seen as a reification of community-of-practice membership and as a means of negotiating that membership. It is of course tacit rather than explicit knowledge. As such, it benefits from intense repetition.

In general, viewed as reification, a more abstract formulation will require more intense
and specific participation to remain meaningful, not less. (Wenger 1998: 67)

It follows that pressure to negotiate and maintain membership in a community of
practice like the Burnouts will lead to the further development of a sound change.
Eckert's analysis satisfies the requirement suggested above for valid evidence of a sound
change as a symbol of local identity, in that the backing of /ʌ/ is correlated with
degrees of membership in the community of practice. The subgroup of girls known
as "the burned-out Burnouts" displays an extreme pattern of "burned-out" behavior
and shows a value for the backing of /ʌ/ significantly higher than the level for female
Burnouts as a whole, which is indicated by the empty triangle at upper right.

The shift from social group to gender correlation exhibited in Figure 9.2 will be
referred to as "the Eckert progression." It is a finding of great importance, and we
will attempt to account for it at several points in this discussion of the driving forces
of linguistic change.

Ethnographic approaches to social variation go beyond the assignment of a class
label such as "Burnout" to a given variant. There is considerable emphasis on the
role of the individual as agent in negotiating his or her social status (Eckert 2000,
Mendoza-Denton 2008). The social meaning of variation lies in its value in the
negotiation of social membership. Chapter 1 of Eckert 2000 provides an informed
exposition of the subtle issues involved in the relations of the individual to the
group and a powerful argument for the individual as the basic unit of social variation. Much is to be learned from the study of individual variation, in seeing how
individuals make use of the complex structure of community variation to evoke
different social identities. To make the case strongly, we have to go beyond the
description of individual acts and observe how a person changes from one social
situation to another. Hindle's study of Carol Myers does just that (Hindle 1980;
see PLC, Vol. 2: 439–45). He mapped the vowel system of one Philadelphian,
Carol Meyers, as she moved from the travel agency office to dinner at home with
her family and then to a bridge game with her intimate friends. In Volume 2, Figure
13.9 showed regular style shifting from one context to another, and Figure 13.10
showed how the shift of (aw) from office to bridge game maps on to the change in
apparent time for the community as a whole.[4]

We must therefore recognize that individuals do use the style shifting of linguistic
variants to maximize their social status in a timely way. Given an individual's
manipulation of sociolinguistic variables, we may ask: can the overall direction of
language change in North American English be seen as the cumulative outcome of
individual acts of identity? As insightful as these views of individual variation may
be, the rest of this chapter will examine phenomena that are not easily accounted
for by the study of face-to-face interaction, which call for the recognition of larger
social forces operating outside of the individual's control.

Whether we adopt the construct of social network or community of practice, the
central question for this study of driving forces is to identify the pressures that

lead to incrementation within the group. Chapter 10 of Volume 2 discussed the "two-step flow of influence" model, which springs from the diffusion studies initiated by Katz and Lazarsfeld (1955). The central finding is that information and influence do not flow evenly to all members of a group, but primarily to a few *influentials* or *opinion leaders*, who then influence their peers, as in A:

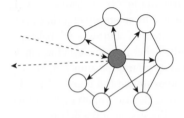

The coincidence of (A) with Figure 9.1 is evident. Celeste S. is the sociometric "star": her C5 index of 10.25 shows a considerable degree of influence coming from outside the group, as indicated in (A). It also suggests that, in order to pursue the driving forces of sound change, we must look beyond the local group, which responds to influence coming from the larger community. Although we have seen that sound change can be influenced by the results of face-to-face interaction, we have to look at the community as a whole and consider commonalities among people who are not in face-to-face contact. Modern society has created speech communities in which one will never be in immediate contact with more than a small fraction of the total. Yet we find in this larger speech community highly regular patterns of participation in change.

9.4   Socioeconomic Classes

Studies of large urban speech communities in the second half of the twentieth century have found regular patterns of social differentiation where the social category correlated with linguistic behavior is socioeconomic class (Labov 1966, 1980, Cedergren 1973, Trudgill 1974b, Weinberg 1974, Haeri 1996, Sankoff et al. 2001). To achieve a representative sample of the speech community, these studies interviewed individuals who were selected by a random or partly random process, which precluded their being in direct contact with each other. This often involves a stratified random sample, where the social groups of interest are given equal representation, independently of the proportion of the population they represent.[5] The characteristics that define speakers as belonging to such a social class group are not given by their interaction with each other, but by their similarity on general measures of power, status, wealth and symbolic capital. One advantage of studying such larger groups is that it gives access to the large-scale linguistic patterns that define the speech community as a whole, and ultimately the language. A disadvantage of the random sample of individuals is that it does not give us ready access to the family or local networks in which the dynamics of linguistic influence are played out.

The project on Linguistic Change and Variation in Philadelphia (LCV) was designed to combine studies of local interaction with the description of a large metropolitan speech community as a whole (see Vol. 2, Chs 3–12). This was done by a judgment sample of ten neighborhoods, stratified by their range of social class and ethnicity, extending from lower working-class Irish-dominated areas of Kensington to upper working-class, predominantly Italian areas of South Philadelphia, lower middle-class Jewish neighborhoods in Overbook, upper middle-class King of Prussia, and upper-class networks in Chestnut Hill. The neighborhood studies featured participant observation over three to four years, with many repeated recordings and group interactions. A random sample of the city as a whole was accomplished through a telephone survey of sixty speakers (Hindle 1978). The congruence of the results of the neighborhood study and telephone survey, with complementary sources of error, was taken as strong confirmation of the findings.

Figure 9.1 illustrated one result of the LCV's studies of interaction in local networks. The LCV project was designed to test a general hypothesis concerning the location of the leaders of linguistic change, shifting from the question of *why* language changes to *who* changes it. The curvilinear hypothesis that emerged from earlier studies (New York: Labov 1966; Panama City: Cedergren 1973; Norwich: Trudgill 1974b) holds that linguistic change from below is led by groups centrally located in the social spectrum. Figure 9.3 presents a larger-scale result for the same linguistic variable: the fronting and raising of /aw/ in *south*, *out*, *down*, *now*, etc. The variable extends from the conservative value [æo] to the advanced form [e:ɔ], with an F2 ranging from about 1500 Hz to 2500 Hz in the log-mean normalized system used here. Figure 9.3a shows the characteristic monotonic distribution across five age categories in apparent time.[6] Phonetic transcriptions published thirty years earlier show only conservative forms, a real-time differential that confirms the fact that we are dealing with change in progress.[7] Figure 9.3b displays the curvilinear distribution of (aw) across six socioeconomic classes.

There are two distinct problems of explanation involved here. One is to account for the incremental pattern of Figure 9.3a: why do younger speakers show regularly increasing values of the variable? The other is to account for the diffusion shown in Figure 9.3b: how does the change spread outward in a weaker form, from the leading group to groups increasingly distant on the social dimension? Most of the attention in sociolinguistic studies has been given to the second problem.

For both questions, it is reasonable to ask whether the driving forces are positive or negative. When linguistic changes rise to the level of social awareness, they are normally stigmatized and rejected; but that is not the case with (aw), which is rarely

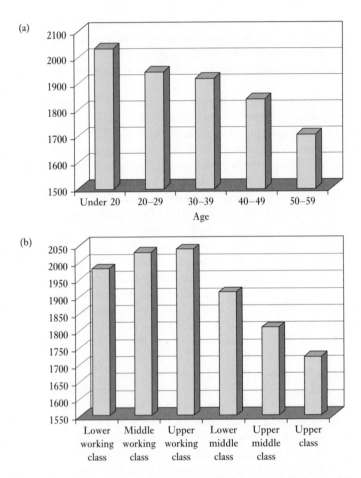

Figure 9.3   The curvilinear pattern of (aw) in the Philadelphia Neighborhood Study [N = 112]. Vertical axis shows expected values of F2 for each age range, calculated by adding age regression coefficients to the constant; Figure 9.3a Distribution in apparent time; Figure 9.3b Distribution by socioeconomic class

mentioned in direct discussion of the Philadelphia dialect.[8] The decline of the F2 values of /aw/ from the upper working class to the upper class might be seen as a retreat from a stigmatized local dialect, but that would not explain the upward slope from lower working class to upper working class.[9] Both the curvilinear pattern and the profile of the leaders of linguistic change in Chapter 12 of Volume 2 indicate that some part of the driving forces behind the diffusion involves positive forms of social motivation. Since most changes in progress lie far below the level of social awareness, it is generally agreed that these positive motivations are covert, although direct evidence for their existence is minimal.

9.5   Acts of Identity

At an earlier period, Sturtevant (1947) argued from general considerations that new linguistic forms are associated with the values and attributes of the originating group, and that speakers adopt those forms as an indication of their alignment with the group's values. He proposed that, in the course of change, one or the other linguistic variant is associated with a particular group as opposed to other groups, and when the social conflict is resolved the linguistic change goes to completion. Le Page and Tabouret-Keller (1985) developed a more elaborate description of this social process on the basis of their observations of language choice in Belize:

> The individual creates his systems of verbal behavior so as to resemble those common to the group or groups with which he wishes from time to time to be identified, to the extent that:
> (a)   he is able to identify those groups
> (b)   his motives are sufficiently clear-cut and powerful
> (c)   his *opportunities* for learning are adequate
> (d)   his ability to learn – that is, to change his habits where necessary – is unimpaired.

This approach to the motivation of linguistic change is explicitly formulated for choices made at a high degree of social awareness, like the use of Spanish or English Creole in Belize. Eckert and McConnell-Ginet (2003) produce a parallel argument for associating acts of identity with sociolinguistic variables:

> [W]ithin communities of practice, the continual modification of common ways of speaking provides a touchstone for the construction of forms of group identity – of the meaning of belonging to a group (as a certain kind of member). (p. 315)

The question is whether such acts of identity can be associated with linguistic variables which lie well below the horizon of conscious awareness. In Eckert's introduction to her high school study, she elaborates Wenger's concept of reification as an essential element in the interpretation of social symbols in general:

> The negotiation of the meaning of these symbols becomes overt only when aspects of meaning become reified [...] At that point, speakers can point to social meaning – they can identify others as jocks or burnouts, as elite or working class, educated or not, prissy or tough. (Eckert 2000: 43)

Our question is therefore an empirical one. Are the elements of the Northern Cities Shift reified for speakers and listeners in the Inland North? The subjective evaluation experiments carried out in New York City (Labov 1966, Ch. 12) and Philadelphia (PLC, Vol. 2, Ch. 7) have shown some degree of social evaluation on scales such as "job suitability" and "friendship." The NCS variables appear to be indicators rather than markers, with little style shifting associated with their social distribution (Ash 1999) and with no evidence of conscious awareness in the Inland North. It is possible that controlled experiments would detect the process of reification associated with the attribution of group identity.

9.5.1   Personal names and the ratchet principle

A different view of the role of individual choice can be derived from studies of another form of social behavior involved in rapid change: the choice of personal names. Lieberson (2000) assembles some of the massive data that show how this choice follows long-term trends, which run for 80 to 100 years in the same direction.[10] Lieberson's interest in the matter was stimulated by his own experience of making what he believed to be a carefully thought out choice of first name for his child, only to discover years later, as so many others do, that he had been unconsciously following community preference.[11]

Figure 9.4 plots endings of the fifty most common names for girls born in Illinois from 1918 to 1987. Names ending in -*a*, like *Rebecca*, *Eva* and *Julia*, have shown a steady increase over this period, along with names ending in -*ie* or -*y* like *Amy*, while the choice of names ending in -*n* (*Jane*) and -*s* (*Alice*, *Doris*, *Janice*) has declined.

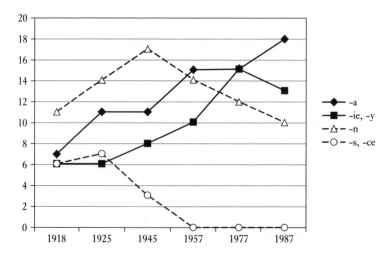

Figure 9.4   Endings of fifty most common girls' names in Illinois, 1918–87 (Lieberson 2000). Reprinted by permission of Yale University Press

While some sociologists have attributed the rise of fashions in personal names to conscious imitation of celebrities who carry those names, Lieberson shows that in almost every case the celebrity's name was already on the increase, responding to the social evaluation that was already present. As in the case of linguistic change, the mass media follow community change after some interval in time: they reflect change rather than generating it.

Lieberson argues that such long-term trends are the product of a structural factor, the "ratchet principle," which operates independently of other pressures in social life. When a feature of social behavior is recognized as "new," forms that shift further in that direction will be preferred as being in fashion, and older forms will be dispreferred as being out of fashion. The parallel between fashion in clothes and sound change is striking. Like vowels, skirts can only descend or rise within limits. Lieberson argues that, when that limit is reached, the change may be reversed, but the ratchet principle is not violated, since the reversal is accompanied by other changes. In sound change, [e:] may rise to a limiting height of [i:], but then it descends to [ɪy] and [əy] after diphthongizing.

Beside the governing principles set out in Chapter 6, the ratchet principle gives us another account for the unidirectional character of linguistic change. It shows us that systematic social change does not necessarily involve conscious choice, and that a wide variety of changes can be driven by a structural principle of great generality. But it does not define for us the linguistic correlate of "in fashion" or "out of fashion." Furthermore, the data on personal names reflect unconscious influence on conscious choices made by adults; they do not bear directly on the behavior of children in the process of forming and solidifying their linguistic systems. Data on personal names reflect regional trends, but they are not detailed enough to tell us whether members of all social groups are making the same choices or moving in the same direction.

9.6 The Relation of Social Classes in Apparent Time

A clearer view of the behavior of social classes in Philadelphia can be obtained by combining the information on age and social class in Figures 9.3a and b. Figure 9.5 is a scattergram showing the distribution of individual mean values for the fronting of /aw/ in Philadelphia by age and social class, on the basis of the same data that were used for Figure 9.3. The lines on Figure 9.5 are partial regression lines for individual social class groups, with slopes and intercepts calculated separately for each.[12]

The lower working class in Figure 9.5 shows no participation in the change, with a flat regression line. The solid dark regression line for the lower middle class shows the steepest slope, indicating the highest rate of change, while the upper working class (black dashed line) is just behind. The leading position of the lower middle class is therefore a characteristic of younger speakers: only in the age groups under 40 is the upper working class distinguished from the middle working class.

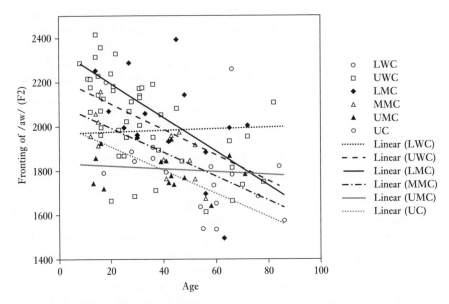

Figure 9.5 Scatterplot of the fronting of (aw) by age and socioeconomic class, with partial regression lines for social classes, from the Philadelphia Neighborhood Study [N = 112]. LWC = lower working class; UWC = upper working class; LMC = lower middle class; MMC = middle middle class; UMC = upper middle class; UC = upper class

The most striking and important feature of Figure 9.5 is the parallelism of the regression lines for the upper working class, lower middle class, middle middle class and upper class. The thirteen upper-class speakers (barred line) show a slope parallel to the slope of the leading group – the lower middle class. The correlation with age of the thirty-one upper working-class subjects is –.57; for the thirteen upper-class subjects, –.66. Both correlations are significant at p < .01. Whatever the cause of this remarkable phenomenon, the logic of Le Page and Tabouret-Keller does not apply here. Children of the Philadelphia upper class are specifically instructed that they are *not* middle class. It is not conceivable that they are motivated to adopt progressively fronter forms of /aw/ by the desire – conscious or unconscious – to be identified with the middle class or with the upper working class.

Figure 9.5 is not exceptional. The other Philadelphia variables show, even more consistently, parallel slopes for all social classes. Figure 9.6 is the corresponding display for the fronting of /ey/ in checked syllables (eyC), a new and vigorous change in the 1970s, which has continued through to the present (Conn 2005). All six social classes follow parallel lines, with the upper class matching exactly the slope of the leading group – the lower middle class.

These results raise serious obstacles to any proposal to explain sound change as a series of individual acts of identification with neighboring social groups.

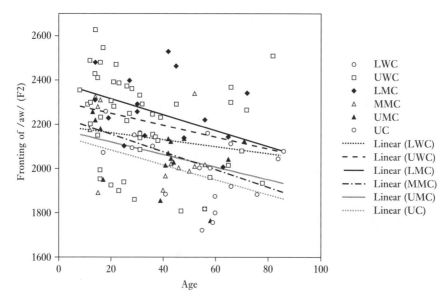

Figure 9.6 Scatterplot of the fronting of (eyC) by age and socioeconomic class, with partial regression lines for social classes, from the Philadelphia Neighborhood Study [N = 112]. LWC = lower working class; UWC = upper working class; LMC = lower middle class; UMC = upper middle class; UC = upper class

9.7 Gender as a Social Force

Sociolinguistic studies of the speech community have found that linguistic variation in the modern world is correlated with a small number of social variables: age, gender, social class, race/ethnicity, urban/rural status and location in social networks. While internal constraints on variation are typically independent of each other, it is normal to find strong interaction among the external factors. Typically, the differentiation of stable linguistic variables by gender varies across social classes. Linguistic changes from below show a somewhat simpler configuration: one or the other gender is usually in advance for all social classes (Labov 1990). In the great majority of cases, it is women who are ahead – usually by a full generation (Gauchat 1905, Hermann 1929; see PLC, Vol. 2, Chs 8–9).

The Eckert progression of Figure 9.2 resonates with the findings of Chapters 8, 9 and 11 of Volume 2 concerning the role of gender in the development of Philadelphia sound changes. Figure 9.7 illustrates the close association of gender differentiation with the progress of change. The mean differences between men and women rise and fall along with the rise and fall of age coefficients (here the absolute value of the age coefficient is multiplied by 20 for F1 and 30 for F2). On

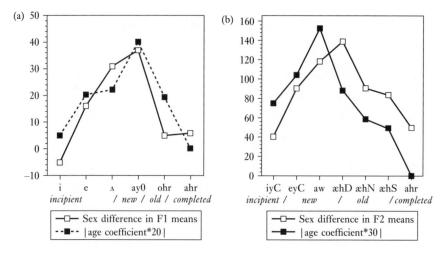

Figure 9.7 Mean gender differences and age coefficients for seven Philadelphia sound changes (PLC, Vol. 2, Figure 9.1); Figure 9.7a F1; Figure 9.7b F2

the left of each diagram there are incipient changes; in the center there are new and vigorous changes; and on the right there are completed changes. The Eckert progression of Figure 9.2 reflects the development shown in the left half of both of these diagrams. The newest changes have the least gender differentiation, while older, ongoing changes acquire progressively more marked gender differences until they reach a peak in the rate of change.

The degree of gender differentiation is not constant across age levels, as shown in Figure 9.8. In this figure, the vertical axis represents the expected value of F2, calculated for each gender by decade, from the constant and age coefficient. The dashed lines are regression lines drawn through the six decades for each gender. For women, it is practically a straight line (r^2 = .961), indicating that women advance steadily for each small unit of age. On the other hand, men show a poorer fit to the regression line, with r^2 of only .788.

This difference between men and women can be interpreted in terms of the asymmetry of language transmission (Labov 1990). Men of the oldest generation (Generation I) are not involved in the change. Those between 30 and 50 years of age (Generation II) are the first to have mothers affected by the fronting of /aw/, and show a sudden increment to a value equivalent to that of their mothers – that is, women from 50 to 70. From this point on, men are about a generation behind their mothers until the end of the process, when the gender difference shrinks. This pattern is duplicated for the other female-dominated new and vigorous change: the raising of checked /ey/.

The mechanism responsible for this pattern seems clear. We begin with the gender asymmetry of first language acquisition. The vast majority of language learners acquire

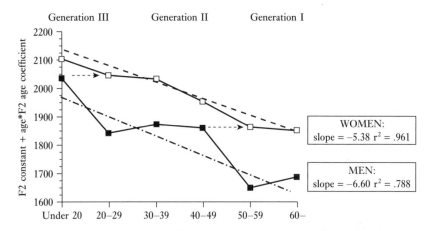

Figure 9.8 Fronting of (aw) by gender and age in the Philadelphia Neighborhood Study (PLC, Vol. 2, Figure 9.5). Dashed arrows indicate generational transmission

their first language from close contact with a female, not a male caretaker. In female-dominated changes, girls and young women advance the change following a logistic incrementation function (Vol. 2, Ch. 14), while males do not participate further in the change but remain at the base level they acquired from their mothers. After twenty to thirty years, the first children enter the speech community whose mothers were affected by the change, and boys as well as girls acquire that phonetic form in their first steps of language learning. Girls will increment their level of the variable throughout preadolescence, adolescence and (to some undetermined degree) early adulthood, while males remain, again, at the level of first acquisition. Throughout this process, males logically remain a generation behind females. The gap between males and females grows as females enter the period of logistic incrementation with the steepest slope. But, as the change comes closer to its limiting value, differences between males and females begin to shrink, as can be seen on the right in Figure 9.7.

Figure 9.9 shows the 2006 state of a simulated sound change that began in 1942, in which females increase their first acquired form of the change by a logistic increment, but males retain the level they first acquired in childhood. Male and female five-year olds both match the level of change of their 28-year-old mothers, but gender differences reach a maximum at the age of 17, when linguistic change more or less stabilizes. Males who first acquired the change as five-year olds from their 28-year-old mothers in 1965 are shown here as 41 years old in 2006.

The scenario of Figures 9.8–9.9 is replicated in the Wolf and Jiménez study (1979) of the devoicing of /dʒ/ in *calle* or *llama* in the Spanish of Buenos Aires. Figure 9.10 shows that men lag behind women by a full generation in this process. The female increment across ages is approximately linear, while the dashed arrows indicate how the male values correspond to the level of the last maternal generation.

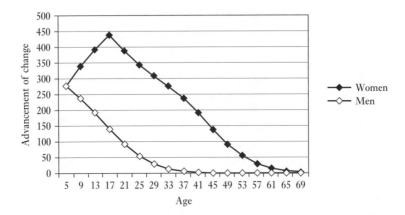

Figure 9.9 Gender differentiation in 2006 by age of a simulated sound change beginning in 1942, at four-year intervals (PLC, Vol. 2, Table 14.1)

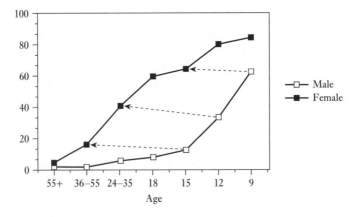

Figure 9.10 Percentage of the devoicing of /dʒ/ in Buenos Aires Spanish by age and gender [N = 12,898] (Wolf and Jiménez 1979, Table 5; see Figure 8.10 of PLC, Vol. 2)

This generational development explains the fact that women predominate in most linguistic changes from below. The same logic that will accelerate and bring to completion a female-dominated change will retard and even eliminate a male-dominated change. In the case of male-dominated changes, the second generation of males will not acquire advanced forms on first acquisition, but will instead begin at the low level of the mothers. Though these males may acquire some incremented forms from their peers, the progress of the change will inevitably be slower than for female-dominated changes, and may in fact be reversed and terminated at an early stage. Chapter 14 of Volume 2 develops these models in greater detail.

Given this differential pattern of gender for Philadelphia (aw) and (eyC), it would seem that the driving force is to be found among women, while men are reacting

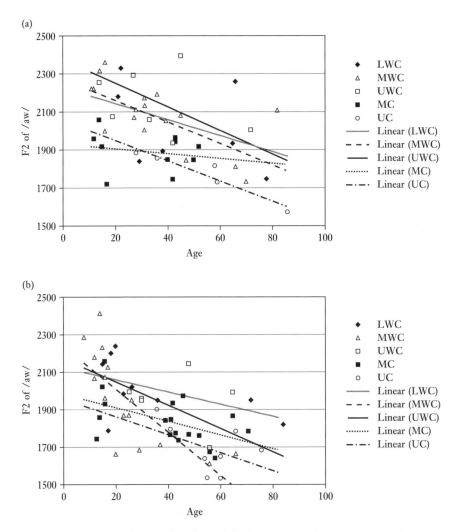

(a)

(b)

Figure 9.11a Scatterplot of the fronting of (eyC) by age and socioeconomic class for women from the Philadelphia Neighborhood Study [N = 53], with partial regression lines for social classes (class labels as in Figure 9.6)

Figure 9.11b Scatterplot of the fronting of (eyC) by age and socioeconomic class for men from the Philadelphia Neighborhood Study [N = 59], with partial regression lines for social classes (class labels as in Figure 9.6)

passively to the increment delivered at the time of first acquisition. If social class membership is a factor in this incrementation, we would then expect to find different patterns of social class response to the fronting of /eyC/ for men and women. But this is not the case. Figures 9.11a and 9.11b replicate the display of Figure 9.6

for men and women separately. The same parallel movement of social classes appears across age groups for the fifty-three women and fifty-nine men in the Philadelphia Neighborhood study. There is a somewhat greater variation in the regression lines for men, but the parallel behavior of the upper working class and upper class is perfectly preserved. The five upper-class women and the eight upper-class men follow the same pattern of fronting (and raising) of /aw/, and there is no difference among men and women in the tendency to move steadily in the same direction as the rest of the community. Whatever forces are driving sound change in Philadelphia, they are operating in the same way on both genders and on all social classes. If the "social meaning" that drives sound change were transmitted by intimate face-to-face interaction, the rate of change should diminish as the change spreads from the generating source.

This result is consistent with the "Constant Rate Hypothesis" that emerged from Kroch's studies of long-term syntactic change (1989). The various socioeconomic groups engage in the sound change at different levels, but they increment it at a constant rate. Males and females participate in the change at a roughly constant rate, but by virtue of a different mechanism within and across generations.

9.8   The Regional Dialect

We have seen that sound changes are diffused throughout the socioeconomic structure of a single metropolis at a constant rate. We will now consider a larger unit of social structure: the regional dialect.

Our initial understanding of complex chain shifts like the Northern Cities Shift was based on exploratory studies of a few large cities: Chicago, Detroit, Buffalo (LYS). The triggering event of the NCS, the raising of /æ/, appeared to follow the cascade model of diffusion from the largest city to the next largest city and so on down (Callary 1975). When ANAE was completed, the view we obtained of the NCS was quite different: a uniform distribution across a vast area, extending from Western New York State (Syracuse, Rochester, Buffalo) to Northern Ohio (Cleveland, Toledo), Michigan (Detroit, Flint, Grand Rapids, Kalamazoo), Northern Illinois (Chicago, Joliet, Peoria) and Southeastern Wisconsin (Kenosha, Madison, Milwaukee). This area is the *Inland North*, a conurbation of some 34,000,000 people across 88,000 square miles – the second greatest concentration of population in the United States. Chapter 5 has explored the triggering events that gave rise to the NCS. Chapter 8 has shown how the various stages of the NCS coincided at the North/Midland boundary; Figure 8.3 in particular displayed the striking divergence of the North and the Midland. Here we return to the NCS in pursuit of the driving forces responsible for the continued advance of this complex set of sound changes, now focusing upon the homogeneity of the region rather than its divergence from others.

Figure 8.3 displayed the AE1, EQ, ED and UD isoglosses that delimit the progress of the Northern Cities Shift, and identified the speakers that satisfy the

UD criterion. There is considerable variation in the Eastern and Western extent of these four isoglosses, but they coincide almost perfectly on the North/Midland boundary. The four criteria are intimately linked. We find, for example, that sixty of the seventy-one speakers within the ED isogloss also satisfy the UD criterion. The categorical nature of the North/Midland distinction is even more evident in the distribution of black and white symbols in Figure 8.3. Black symbols, indicating that /ʌ/ is further back than /o/, are almost uniform in the Inland North area, while the Midland and the South present a solid phalanx of white symbols.[13]

ANAE includes measures of homogeneity for each of the isoglosses concerned: the proportion of speakers within the isogloss area who display the sound change of interest. These figures are in the range of .84–.87 (Ch. 11, Appendix A). Since we are dealing with change in progress, we cannot expect complete homogeneity. ANAE subjects in their sixties and seventies are not likely to show the more advanced variants, except in the case of the general raising of /æ/, which seems to have reached a maximum. The uniformity which is of interest here is not the agreement of subjects within the city of Chicago, within the city of Detroit, or within the state of Michigan, but the identity of the NCS mechanism in all geographic subregions of the Inland North.

The uniformity of the Northern Cities Shift area makes it difficult to assign social motivation to local social networks or to local communities of practice. Speakers in Rochester are aware that they have a local accent; but they do not realize that the same local accent is to be found in Buffalo and Syracuse, and they have no idea that it is identical with the dialect of Chicago and Milwaukee. What social processes can account for the steadily rising levels of the NCS across this vast area?

The geographic uniformity of the Inland North does not mean that there is no social variation. With only one or two subjects for most communities, ANAE was not designed to test hypotheses on social differentiation.[14] However, a regression analysis was carried out to analyze the social variation that did exist among the seventy-one respondents located in the Inland North, examining age, gender, city size, occupation and education.[15] The significant effects are shown in Table 9.1. The parallels with the Eckert progression of Figure 9.2 are surprising, considering the fact that the Atlas is an instrument for examining geographic, not social, distribution.

The older stages of the change are registered in the first lines. As the oldest stage, AE1 is so close to completion that no significant age coefficient is found. Female gender is a strong and significant factor favoring the change. There is also a sizable positive correlation with the number of years of education completed.

The EQ measure combines an early and a late stage of the change.[16] A significant age coefficient appears, along with female gender, but no correlation with education. The ED criterion, again, combines a relatively early and a late stage of the change. It shows the strongest age coefficient, no gender effect, and no correlation with education.

Table 9.1 Regression coefficients for age, gender and education in Telsur speakers of the Inland North [N = 71] for four measures of the Northern Cities Shift. p values: * < .05, *** < .001. AE1: F1(æ) < 700 Hz; EQ: /æ/ higher and fronter than /e/; ED: F2(e) – F2(o) < 375 Hz; UD F2(ʌ) < F2(o). Positive figures indicate influences in the direction of the change in progress. Factors found not to be significant: city size, occupation

Criterion	Age *25 yrs	Female gender	Years of education
AE1		34*	8.6*
EQ	34*	26*	
ED	112***		
UD	37		–16*

The measure that reflects the most recent stage of the Northern Cities Shift is UD, which incorporates the backward shift of /ʌ/. Table 9.1 shows a small age coefficient (just below the .05 level of significance), no gender effect, but a strong negative correlation with education. This reflects the concentration of high school dropouts among those who satisfy the UD criterion. These adults were the Burnouts of Eckert's analysis: those who reject the institutional path to upward mobility through education.

9.9 Accounting for the Uniform Progress of the Northern Cities Shift

The geographic homogeneity of Figure 8.3 may be the result of the structural constraints on sound change outlined in Chapter 6. Given the triggering events of Chapter 5, these constraints dictate that change, if it occurs, will move in the same direction throughout the region. The gender coefficients of Figure 9.2 and in Table 9.1 may be accounted for by the general asymmetry of language transmission and acquisition, as discussed above. This still leaves open the search for the driving forces that animate the sound changes in a uniform way throughout the Inland North, but stop abruptly at the North/Midland and North/Canadian boundaries.[17] In consonance with Meillet's thinking, these forces cannot be universal, yet they must be broad enough to extend over the entire area. Most importantly, they must exert a uniform influence on people who are not engaged in face-to-face interaction.

Such zones of uniform influence are not confined to the Inland North. Fridland (2003) is a study of the weakening of the upglide of /ay/ in Memphis, considered as one aspect of the triggering event of the Southern Shift. The results show a common direction of change in the Euro-American and African–American communities, although the two are highly segregated.

African–Americans in Memphis appear to be moving toward forms which symbolize involvement in the Southern community and its associated heritage [. . .] While social unity was a part of the communities of practice explored by Eckert, I would expand her framework to suggest that these shared practices do not necessarily require individuals' social cohesion but merely require shared historical experience and a strongly circumscribing environment that places speakers in a similar social position relative to the external social world. (Fridland 2003: 296)

We will not attempt to explore the nature of this Southern heritage here, but it is in the spirit of a search for such larger frameworks that we pursue the explanations for the uniform direction of change throughout the Inland North.

Since the Eckert progression of Figure 9.2 appears to hold for the Inland North in general, we are driven to search for a set of social values associated with the sound changes that are more general than any local network can generate. Let us summarize the possibilities considered in this chapter.

1 *New versus old (the ratchet principle)*   This may indeed apply within the Inland North, though it has not yet been demonstrated that adolescents hear advanced forms as being "in fashion" and conservative forms as being "out of fashion." Such a demonstration would have to show that the backing of /ʌ/ is heard as "in fashion" in the Inland North, while directly across the Midland border the same sound would be heard as "out of fashion."

2 *Urban versus rural*   As the name "Northern Cities Shift" suggests, the advanced forms of the shift may be associated with the speech of the largest cities, and may be marked as *urban* as opposed to *small town* or *country*. This would be more plausible if it could be shown that the cascade or hierarchical model of diffusion applies to the NCS, where the changes are most advanced in the largest city, next most advanced in the next largest, and so on, going down.[18] This can be checked by entering the population of the city or the Metropolitan Statistical Area (MSA) into a regression analysis of the various measures of advancement. The finding is an important one. For the thirty Telsur cities of the Inland North, the result is uniformly negative: regression analyses reveal no effect of city size on the advancement of the NCS.

The absence of any relation between city size and the NCS is displayed in Figure 9.12, which plots the ED values of the sixty-three Telsur subjects against the natural logarithm of the speech community to which they belong. The regression line through these points is flat: r^2 shows that city size accounts for only .0095 percent of the variance in ED. The four Telsur speakers in the biggest city, Chicago, are labeled at the top, and the smallest of the big cities, Binghamton, at the bottom. This finding might of course apply only to the cities with a population over 50,000, which were sampled by Telsur. But we also have information on five towns of under 50,000, which are shown at the bottom of the diagram. These were the hometowns of subjects contacted in

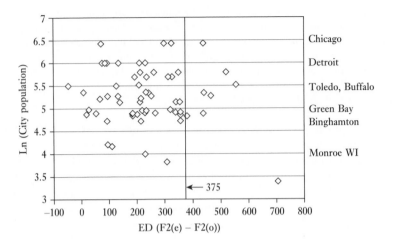

Figure 9.12 Scattergram of ED values of sixty-three subjects in the Inland North by log of city size

bigger cities, whose geographic history qualified them as representatives of the smaller community. Monroe, Wisconsin is labeled here. It is a town in south central Wisconsin, with a population of 10,241 in the year 2000. Four of the five small towns fall within the ED criterion of 375 Hz. Although further studies of small towns in the Inland North, like that of Gordon (2001), may show that these towns fall behind the big cities, the Atlas data give no indication of any relation between city size and the advancement of the NCS.[19]

If we turn to the North as a whole – the larger region that embraces the Inland North – the situation is quite different. The AE1 measure shows a significant effect of city size at the $p < .05$ level, and the EQ measure at $p < .01$.[20] However, this is simply a product of the fact that the big cities are concentrated in the Inland North. If we add location in the Inland North as an independent variable, this is always large and significant, and the effects of city size disappear – for the systemic criteria AE1 and EQ as well as for individual sound change measures. This does not necessarily imply that city size has no effect; the location and growth of large cities in the Inland North may be a part of the dynamic behind the NCS. But it does mean that the NCS displays a persistent uniformity across city sizes as well as across the geographic area of the Inland North.

Before turning away from a general correlation of the NCS with the element of city size, it should be noted that Eckert's study of four suburbs of Detroit leads her to the conclusion that "the newer changes have a very clear urban–suburban significance" (2000: 137) (these newer changes being the NCS (e) and (ʌ) backing). On the other hand, she notes that the older NCS changes "show a more variable geographic pattern" (2000: 136–7) and that "the greater variability of the older changes suggests that as changes lose stark geographic and age differences, and hence their value as an urban adolescent symbol, they become more fluid in the symbolic potential, showing greater local variability in use" (ibid., p. 137).

3   *Non-conformist versus conformist*   A third possible way of accounting for the uniformity of the NCS is to say that the social analysis of Eckert's *Jocks and Burnouts* applies not only to the suburbs of Detroit but equally to high schools throughout the Inland North, and that everywhere the most recent stages of the NCS are associated with a rejection of adult institutional norms. Logically, participation in an ongoing change is equivalent to a failure to conform to the norms of the older generation. Chapters 11–12 of Volume 2 developed the concept of nonconformity as a characteristic of leaders of linguistic change in Philadelphia. Close examination of the personal histories of the community leaders suggested that they may have acquired their advanced forms of Philadelphia sound changes through intimate contact with Burnout types in their adolescent years, and they may have preserved this social and linguistic style as they moved upward in the social system. Celeste S., the sociolinguistic and sociometric star of Figure 9.1, is a prototype of this pattern. To develop this concept further, we would have to follow a representative sample of adolescents from their high school years to their development in the adult community.[21]

Further studies along the abrupt North/Midland boundary may reinforce or reject these candidates for the driving forces that underly the uniformity of the NCS distribution in the Inland North. The next chapter will turn to the settlement history of the North and will explore the possibility that the uniform factor is an ideological pattern specific to this region and inherited from the founding population.

10

Yankee Cultural Imperialism and the Northern Cities Shift

Chapter 1 advanced the general principle that the community is conceptually and analytically prior to the individual; conversely, the behavior of the individual cannot be understood without a knowledge of the larger community that he or she belongs to.[1] This chapter is an endeavor to penetrate the structure of one very large community, the Inland North. A continuing problem is to account for its extraordinary homogeneity on the one hand and, on the other, to explain the sharp cleavage that separates it from neighboring speech communities, Chapters 6, 7, and 8 dealt with the internal development of North American sound changes, where neighboring systems are driven in opposite directions by unidirectional principles. Chapter 9 wrestled with efforts to identify the driving forces that animate these sound changes, and concluded without fixing on any one factor that was large enough to account for the scope of the phenomena. Here we will consider the historical and social setting in which the governing principles of sound change operate, and the possibility that the unconscious shifting of vowel systems is reinforced by long-standing ideological oppositions on a national scale.

10.1   The North/Midland Boundary

Figure 10.1 is a view of the Northeastern quadrant of the United States at night, from composite photographs taken by satellite in the 1970s. The photographs show the heat and light emitted from urban areas; the major cities involved in the Northern Cities Shift are labeled. The North/Midland line is shown in grey.

There are two questions of dialect geography to be resolved here: (1) Why is the North/Midland line located where it is? (2) Why do the cities of the Inland North all follow the Northern Cities Shift, while the dialects of Midland cities – Philadelphia, Pittsburgh, Columbus, Cincinnati, Indianapolis, St Louis – differ considerably from each other? These are matters of settlement history.

The boundary between the North and the Midland was first established by Kurath in 1949, and later extended through the Midwest by Shuy (1962), Allen (1964) and

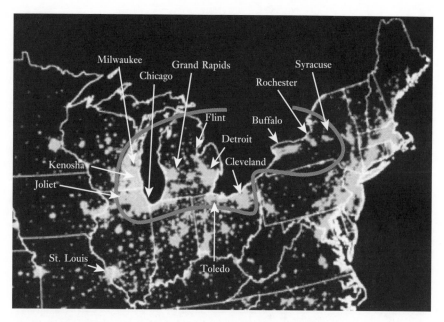

Figure 10.1 The US at night, from composite photographs taken by the US Air Force Defense Meteorological Satellite Program (DMSP) Operational Linescan System, with major cities of the Inland North labeled

Carver (1987). Figure 10.2 shows pairs of words used by Carver to define the North/Midland boundary (the ordering from east to west has no geographic significance). It is evident that most of them are rural and agricultural terms established during the earliest period of settlement in the nineteenth century. Many of them are now obsolete, or certainly not known to city dwellers: calls to livestock (sheep: *ko-day!* versus *sheepie!* or cow: *boss!* versus *sook!*); animal sounds (a calf's *blat* versus *bawl*); farm mechanics (*stone fence* versus *rock fence*, *sawbuck* versus *trestle*, *stone boat* versus *mud boat*).[2] The individual lexical isoglosses do not at all coincide as our phonological isoglosses do. Carver, who believed that all dialect differences formed seamless continua (see Chapter 8, p. 165), defined the various areas by the combined frequencies of Northern and Midland words.

Nevertheless, the line formed by the general trend of lexical oppositions is very close to that formed by the linked phonological features of the NCS and by other phonetic criteria as well. Chapter 8 (Figure 8.3) has demonstrated the coincidence of four measures of the NCS (AE1, EQ, ED, UD) with the lexical line. Figure 10.3 adds two other features of the North that are not connected with the NCS. One of these Northern delimiters is the ON isogloss (shown as a grey dotted line). It concerns the pronunciation (for those who distinguish /o/ and /oh/) of the vowel in the unique word *on*, which is /o/ in the North and /oh/ in the Midland (ANAE, Map 14.2). The second delimiter is the fronting of

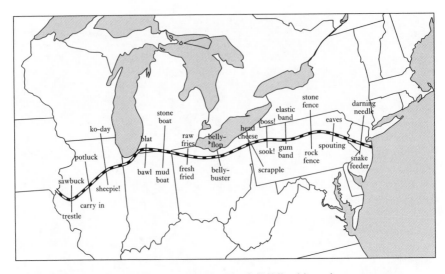

Figure 10.2 Lexical oppositions across the North/Midland boundary

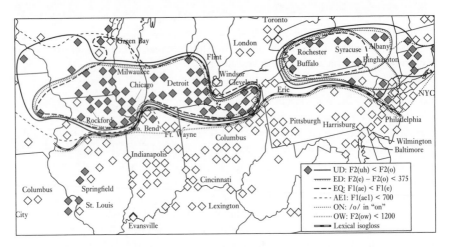

Figure 10.3 Coincidence of the North/Midland lexical isogloss with four measures of the NCS, the ON line and resistance to fronting of /ow/

/ow/, which separates the Midland, Mid-Atlantic and Southern regions from the North and New England. ANAE, Map 12.3 displays the isoglosses for F2 of /ow/ < 1100 Hz, < 1200, < 1300 and > 1400. The line of demarcation between the North and the Midland is the isogloss for F2 < 1200 Hz; as Figure 10.3 shows, this isogloss runs very close to the NCS bundle (the striated line running just below the lexical isogloss).

The North/Midland bundle is remarkably compact. As the last chapter noted, there are only two notable exceptions to the clean separation of cities into those with Northern phonology and those with Midland phonology:

- Northern Indiana: the line representing the general raising of short *a* in Indiana extends below Fort Wayne, which is otherwise a Midland city. The line for /ow/ < 1200 descends below both South Bend and Fort Wayne.
- the city of Erie in Northwestern Pennsylvania: this city lies outside of the Inland North as defined by the NCS, and so separates the Inland North into two discontinuous areas. Erie is not defined for the ON line, since /o/ and /oh/ are merged – a feature which separates Erie even more clearly from the Inland North. In Figure 10.3, Erie differs from the Midland only by the lack of /ow/ fronting and by its position on the lexical line. Evanini (2009) provides a detailed history of this development and sets the limits of Erie exceptionalism.

10.2   The History of the North/Midland Boundary

The location of the North/Midland boundary is clearly reflected in the settlement history of the region. Figure 10.4 is from Kniffen and Glassie's (1966) study of the diffusion of building methods. It shows three streams of westward migration: (1) the Northern migration from various areas in New England; (2) the Midland westward flow through Pennsylvania, moving south into the Appalachian area, then westward to lower Ohio, Indiana, Illinois and Iowa; and (3) the coastal South, moving inland up to the Piedmont area. The meeting ground of the Pennsylvania and New England stream shows a remarkable coincidence with the North/Midland linguistic boundary, and the area of the New England stream as it passes through New York corresponds quite closely with the Inland North of Figure 10.3.

To understand the great differences in dialect distribution in the North and Midland, it is necessary to follow the differences in patterns of westward migration. The New England stream was a community movement on a large scale, continuing the model of large-scale migration from England to the New World.

> Mass migrations were indeed congenial to the Puritan tradition. Whole parishes, parson and all, had sometimes migrated from Old England. Lois Kimball Mathews mentioned 22 colonies in Illinois alone, all of which originated in New England or in New York, most of them planted between 1830 and 1840. (Power 1953: 14)

> Entire communities of young New Englanders [...] emigrated to the area of New York west of the Adirondack and Catskill mountains [...]. (Carnes and Garrity 1996: 90)

The settling of Marietta, a Yankee enclave in Southeastern Ohio, is described by Holbrook (1950: 23):

Figure 10.4 Westward settlement streams as shown by building material (Kniffen and Glassie 1966, Figure 27). Copyright © 1966, reprinted by permission of the National Geographic Society

> The cabins and fort were hardly finished when the first families began to arrive. The women and children were in season to pick wild fruits and harvest the first vegetables the men had planted [...] Within a few months a school was being held, taught by Miss Bathsheba Rouse. There had been preaching from the very day the pioneers landed when Founding Father David Story had [...] thanked God for their safe passage and prompt arrival.

On the other hand, the settlement of the Midland was largely a movement of individual families.

> The Upland Southerners left behind a loose social structure of rural "neighborhoods" based on kinship; when Upland Southerners migrated – as individuals or in individual families – the neighborhood was left behind. (Frazer 1993: 630)

The originating areas of the settlement streams of Figure 10.4 match quite well the four "cultural hearths" posited by David Hackett Fischer (1989) as the source of American folkways. The New England stream continues the tradition of the Puritan migration from East Anglia to Massachusetts; the Pennsylvania stream expands the Quaker migration from the North Midlands to the Delaware Valley; the coastal South was originally settled by a movement of Cavalier society from the South of England to Virginia, and then to the Carolinas. Not shown so distinctly is the fourth movement, from the borderlands of England to the upland South. Much of the expansion in the Midland area from the Ohio River northward represents the movement of the Scots–Irish who came through Philadelphia and moved southward, first through the Appalachian area, then into the Midwest. The cultural conflict described by historians reflects the opposition between Yankees from New England and settlers from Fischer's "borderland" regions who migrated northward from the upland South.[3] In the discussion of cultural oppositions to follow, "Southerners" represent this upland Southern population, a culture quite distinct from the coastal or plantation South.[4]

These distinct patterns of migration of Yankees and upland Southerners are summarized in Fischer (1989: 813–14), from which Table 10.1 is extracted. This table shows preferred community type, typical house location, and persistence (percent of adults remaining in a community after ten years).[5] As noted above, Yankees moved as entire communities. They built towns and cities, established their houses along the populated roads and tended to stay put in the cities and towns they had built. Yankee communities maintained a strong emphasis on literacy; schools and colleges were among the first institutions built. In contrast, upland Southerners moved as single families or small groups, built houses in isolated rural locations and showed a strong tendency to move on before too long.

Table 10.1 includes Fischer's parameters for the Quaker cultural group, which expanded westward from Pennsylvania and Delaware into the Midland. The Quaker settlement pattern is intermediate in all three respects. They formed farm communities rather than towns, and built houses near their farms. The persistence of community populations was also intermediate. Since the nineteenth century, the cultural opposition across the North/Midland line has been perceived as a contrast of Yankee versus Upland South patterns, with less focus upon the Quaker heritage.

Table 10.1 Migration patterns of Yankees and upland Southerners

	Yankee	Upland South	Quaker
Settlement	Towns	Isolated clusters	Farm communities
House location	Roadside	Creek and spring	Corner-clusters
Persistence	75–96%	25–40%	40–60%

Source: David Hackett Fischer, *Albion's Seed: Four British Folkways in America*, Oxford: Oxford University Press, 1989, p. 814

This difference in settlement patterns had important linguistic consequences. In the North, children had continuous contact with other children speaking the same dialect. As this chapter and the last one show, an identical phonological system was transmitted intact from Western New York State to Wisconsin. The homogeneity of the Inland North is in marked contrast to the heterogeneity of the Midland cities. Philadelphia, Pittsburgh, Columbus, Cincinnati and St Louis each display different organizations of their vowel systems, while the vowel systems of Rochester, Syracuse, Buffalo, Cleveland, Detroit, Flint, Grand Rapids, Gary, Chicago, Kenosha, Milwaukee and Madison appear to be identical.

10.3   The Material Basis of the North/Midland Opposition

The settlement streams defined by Kniffen and Glassie (1966) in Figure 10.4 are based on geographic differences in cornering techniques in log cabin construction. The two most common types of cornering are shown in Figure 10.5. False cornering is the simplest and quickest, while V-notching, like dovetailing, is more effective in locking logs into place. Figure 10.6 shows, somewhat surprisingly, that V-notching was characteristic of the Midland, while false corner timbering prevailed in the North.

Kniffen and Glassie explain this situation in terms that accord well with Fischer's differentiation of settlement patterns:

> The predominance of the simpler methods of corner-timbering – square and saddle notching – over V notching and dovetailing in the Northern tier of states tends to support the conclusion that the migrating New Englanders, like the English of the Tidewater, regarded log construction as so temporary as to be unworthy of the skills they undoubtedly possessed as workers in wood. (Kniffen and Glassie 1966: 64)

False corner timbering   V-notching

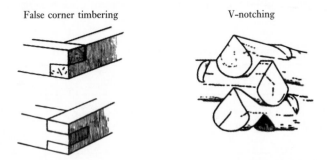

Figure 10.5   Two common types of log cabin corner construction (Kniffen and Glassie 1966). Copyright © 1966, reprinted by permission of the National Geographic Society

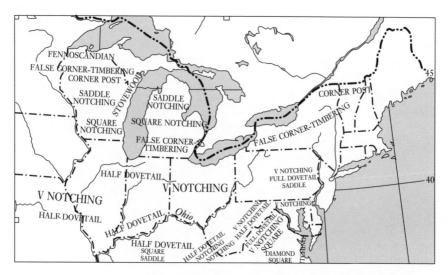

Figure 10.6 Types of corner construction in the North and Midland (Kniffen and Glassie 1966). Copyright © 1966, reprinted by permission of the National Geographic Society

In other words, Yankee settlers used simpler log cabin construction methods because they usually began work immediately on more permanent residences in their newly founded towns and cities.

Chapter 5 showed that the Northern settlement route was greatly facilitated by the completion of the Erie Canal in 1825. This led to the great expansion of New York City, which quickly surpassed Philadelphia as a port of entry and commerce, and to the rapid development of cities along the canal: Syracuse, Rochester and Buffalo. The effect on the east–west communication pattern was reflected in the situation of farmers in New York State who were located any distance from the canal. Wheat farmers in Cortland County (in south central New York) could not compete with wheat farmers in Ohio and Indiana, since the all-water voyage from the Great Lakes to the Hudson River cost less than a thirty-mile journey by road to the Canal.

Figure 10.7 shows the major transportation routes, including the main roads and canals, in the North and Midland regions in the period 1820–35. The general patterns of east–west communication are both the precondition and the consequence of the settlement routes of Figure 10.4. The canal era reached its peak in 1850, when water transportation gave way to the railroads.

In the North, railroads move westward around the Great Lakes to Chicago, and in the Midland, from Philadelphia to Pittsburgh and westward to Columbus, Indianapolis and St Louis. On the other hand, there is no major passenger traffic displayed here from Pittsburgh to Buffalo or from Columbus to Cleveland. This absence of north–south connections reflects and continues the patterns of migration and settlement that were established over two generations earlier, in the early 1800s.

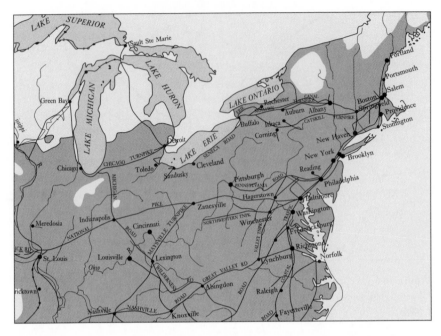

Figure 10.7 Major transportation routes in the North and the Midland, 1820–35 (from information supplied by W. H. Goetzmann, University of Texas; see the online map at http://www.lib.utexas.edu/maps/united_states/exploration_1820.jpg)

10.4 The Cultural Opposition of Yankees and Upland Southerners

Though on the whole the two streams of settlement were geographically distinct, there was a great deal of contact between Yankees and upland Southerners, and in many communities both groups were strongly represented. Much of our view of the Yankees comes from Midland historians (and linguists) who were deeply hostile to Yankee cultural style. The historian Richard L. Power displayed this antagonism in his 1953 study of Jefferson County in Southeastern Indiana, *Planting Corn Belt Culture: The Impress of the Upland Southerner and Yankee in the old Northwest*:

> [A]mong the new arrivals to Jefferson [County, Indiana] was a species of settler strikingly different in outlook from small [upland] southern farmers [...] these newcomers not only displayed a disgusting predilection for self-improvement schemes but were also fond of pointing out their virtues to those who took life at a less feverish pace [...] It was the Yankees who were described as yearning to constitute a social and cultural elite that would sponsor and support higher education, literary societies, and lecture courses, and follow their inclination to regulate the morals of the whole society. (Power 1953: 6)

Power carries his indictment of Yankee cultural style one step further:

> Taxed with being busybodies and meddlers, apologists own that the instinct for meddling, as divine as that of self-preservation, runs in the Yankee blood; that the typical New Englander was entirely unable, when there were wrongs to be corrected, to mind his own business. (Ibid., p. 6)

Thomas J. Morain examined the cultural characteristics of Yankees in a small town in Iowa. Even in his account of educational advancement, his resentment of the Yankee style is evident.

> One of the most distinguishing features of the Yankees of the nineteenth century had been their confidence that theirs was a superior vision and that America's future depended on their ability to impose their order on the life of the nation [...] They established thousands of public schools and private colleges, filled churches and lodge halls with committed believers, and codified their version of morality in the statute books. (Morain 1988: 256).

Morain essayed to codify Yankee cultural style under four headings of a "Yankee Confession":

* Life is a struggle, a test of will.
* The individual, not the government or any other social unit, is responsible for his or her own well-being.
* Success is a measure of character.
* The righteous are responsible for the welfare of the community.

To this, he adds the following:

> While conversion of the sinner to the higher path was the preferable means of reform, it was sometimes necessary to use the legal authority of the state by making immoral activities illegal. (Ibid., p. 45)

Yankee historians do not as a whole disagree with this analysis. Holbrook (1950) traced the Yankee pattern of emigration from New England through the orders that came back for Montpelier crackers and Gorton's codfish. He adds:

> [A]long with their crackers, their codfish, and their theology, they carried their peculiar ideas of government and managed, in spite of Kentucky statutes in Illinois, to impose their township system throughout the state [...] [T]hey did the same to or for Michigan, and also established the whipping post, in words taken from Vermont's original laws. When Wisconsin was carved out of Michigan, Yankees poured in so fast as to dominate politics, supplying eight of the state's first eighteen governors, and seven of its early United States senators. (Ibid., p. 16)

Yankee interference with Midland cultural patterns extended to language as well:

> At Greensburg in Southeastern Indiana, the Reverend J. R. Wheelock advised his Eastern sponsors that his wife had opened a school of 20 or 30 scholars in which she would use "the most approved N.E. school books," to be obtained by a local merchant from Philadelphia. "She makes defining a distinct branch of study and this gives her a very favorable oppy. of correcting the children and thro' them, the parents of 'a heap' of Kentuckyisms." (Power 1953: 114)

The Yankee's negative view of the upland Southerner was not confined to language. More explicitly, we read that in McLean County, Illinois, "the Northerner thought of the Southerner as a lean, lank, lazy creature, burrowing in a hut, and rioting in whiskey, dirt and ignorance" (*History of McLean County* 1879: 97).

Note that the term "Southerner" here refers to adherents of the upland South cultural pattern, who were in immediate contact with the Yankees. We do not find Yankee orators making the distinction between upland South or Backcountry and the coastal South. As the Civil War came to a close, the general denunciation of the South grew stronger. The prominent abolitionist preacher Henry Ward Beecher proclaimed:

> We are to have charge of this continent. The South has been proved, and has been found wanting. She is not worthy to bear rule. She has lost the scepter in our national government, she is to lose the scepter in the States themselves; and this continent is to be from this time forth governed by Northern men, with Northern ideas, and with a Northern gospel. (Beecher 1863)

10.5   Coincidence with Geographic Boundaries of Political Cultures

Figure 10.8 displays the geographic distribution of three political cultures of North America defined by Elazar (1972):

MORALISTIC   This group expects the government to help people achieve good lives. Governmental service is "public service." The community can intervene in private affairs if this serves communal goals.

INDIVIDUALISTIC   This group views government in utilitarian and individualist terms. Politics is a business like any other, which is dominated by "firms" (parties). Government should not interfere much in individuals' lives.

TRADITIONALISTIC   This group combines hierarchical views of society with ambivalence about "government-as-marketplace." Popular participation is scarcely important in comparison with elite participation. There is also a strong preference for maintaining the status quo, as evidenced by the South's general resistance to the civil rights movement.

It is immediately evident that the distribution of these three political cultures coincides with the dialect regions North, Midland and South. The characteristics of the moralistic group fit closely the Yankee traits described by the various historians cited above, and the individualistic group displays the opposition to Yankee reliance on control through governmental action, an opposition attributed to upland Southern inhabitants of the Midland.

Elazar recognizes that this distribution follows from the westward settlement patterns seen in Figures 10.4, 10.7 and 10.8. He traces the Northernmost pattern to the New England Yankee culture in ways that are consistent with the concept of "cultural hearth" developed by Fischer (1989). He also shows how the various inmigrant groups of the later nineteenth and twentieth century – German, Irish, Italian, Polish – adapted the cultural patterns of the earlier settlers, following the doctrine of first effective settlement (Zelinsky 1992). What is particularly important for our current analysis is that the geographic pattern in Figure 10.8 is based on a series of case studies of political behavior which are completely independent of the dialect data. Figure 10.9 displays the individual data points on which Figure 10.8 is founded.[6]

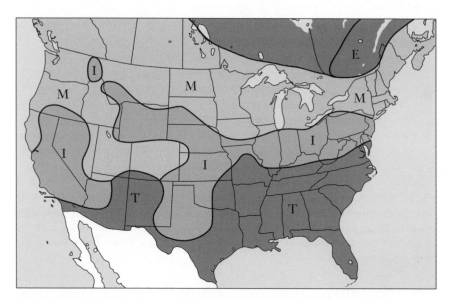

Figure 10.8 Distribution of political cultures in North America. M = Moralistic; I = Individualistic; T = traditional (Kilpinen 2010, based on Elazar 1972, Figure 11). Reprinted by permission of Pearson Education

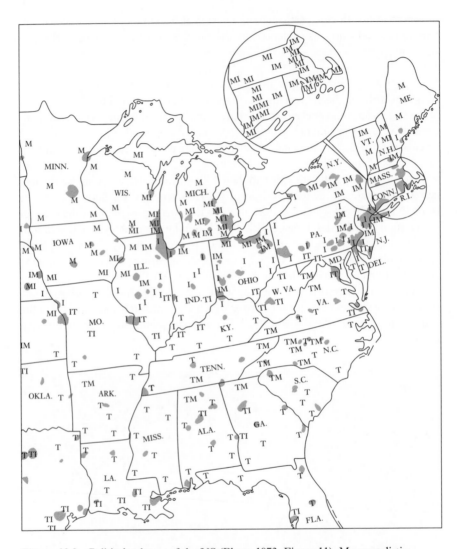

Figure 10.9   Political cultures of the US (Elazar 1972, Figure 11). M = moralistic; I = individualistic; T = traditional. Two letters juxtaposed indicate either a synthesis of two subcultures, or the existence of two separate subcultural communities in the same area, with the first dominant and the second secondary. Reprinted by permission of Pearson Education

Most obvious is the predominance of "I" in the Midland areas of Pennsylvania, Southern Ohio, Indiana and Southern Illinois. The "M" symbols are frequently combined with "I" in the North, but are rarely encountered south of the North/Midland line. The Chicago area shows an unexpected "I," as does Buffalo. But the great majority of Northern cities are marked by "M" symbols. It is interesting to see that Erie in northwest Pennsylvania, the only city that shifted its membership from the North to the Midland in the ANAE records, shows the characteristic Midland "I."

10.6   Red States, Blue States, and the Northern Dialect Region

The term "Yankee cultural imperialism," which I have used in this chapter heading, is taken from a chapter of that heading in Frazer's *Heartland English* (1993). Midland linguists have been particularly critical of John Kenyon's selection of Northern dialect patterns as the basis for standard broadcast English, as codified in the National Broadcasting Company pronunciation guide, and as a referent for the mythical "general American":[7]

> [W]e must learn what led to the establishment of Inland Northern as a prestige dialect in the Great Lakes region; we need to understand as well why scholars like Kenyon, George Phillip Krapp and Hans Kurath ... embraced the concept of Inland Northern as a General American." (Frazer 1993: 80)

Frazer's indignation extends to the political sphere:

> Perhaps the language of "Yankee cultural imperialism" was appropriate for a century of corporate expansion, leveraged buyouts, and American military intervention in the Philippines, Central America, the Caribbean, Vietnam, and the Middle East. (Ibid., p. 88)

This is a striking extension of a cultural critique to a political denunciation. Yankees are here identified with, and even held responsible for, the extreme right-wing politics of more recent times. One can see some rationale for this identification by observing the similarity between the cultural style of nineteenth-century Yankees and that of the New Christian Right in the twenty-first century. Both are marked by absolute certainty in their commitment to a moral position and by the promotion of legislation designed to ensure that everyone else conforms to that position.[8] Nevertheless, the geographic area we are dealing with, the Inland North and the Northern region surrounding it, along with the New England area from which the Northern settlement originated, is now recognized as the core of the Blue States – that is, the center of liberal political and ideological patterns in the United States.

Figure 10.10 shows the Blue States in terms of the 2004 election: those states colored grey voted for John Kerry on the Democratic ticket, and those colored white voted for George Bush on the Republican ticket. Superimposed on this map are two isoglosses. The solid isogloss is the Northern region, defined by conservative fronting

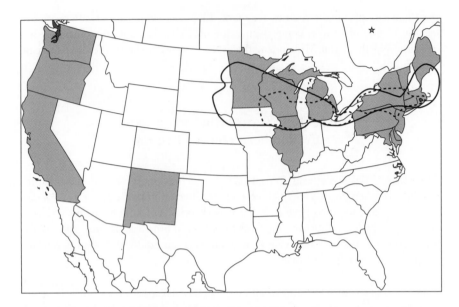

Figure 10.10   States voting Democratic in the 2004 election. Solid isogloss = the Northern region; dashed isogloss = the Inland North as defined by the UD criterion

of /ow/ (mean < 1200 Hz) and by the AWV criterion (which requires that the nucleus of /ay/ be fronter than the nucleus of /aw/). The dashed isogloss shows the Inland North defined by the UD criterion, as in Figures 5.19, 8.3 and 10.3.

The match between the Northern dialect region and the states voting Democratic is only a rough approximation of the relation of dialect areas to political stance, since dialect boundaries rarely follow state borders. A more precise view of this relation can be obtained by considering the vote county by county. Here maps are not as useful, since the rural areas dominate the geographical dimension, while our linguistic data are confined to cities of population over 50,000. The analysis to follow will take as units the counties in which the ANAE cities are embedded. In many cases the city is coextensive with the county; it is most often the county seat, and it always represents the largest part of the population in that county. The database is formed of seventy such counties in dialect regions on either side of the North/Midland boundary.[9]

10.7   Relation of Dialects to County Voting Patterns

The relation between the county voting patterns in 2004 and the North/Midland dialect opposition is displayed in Figure 10.11. The white circles, which represent

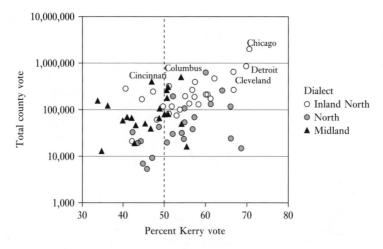

Figure 10.11   Percent county vote for Kerry by total county vote in the 2004 presidential election for counties in the Inland North, North and Midland dialect areas

Table 10.2   Democratic vs Republican county vote by dialect in the 2004 presidential election

	Inland North	North	Midland
Kerry majority	20	15	8
Bush majority	6	7	13

the Inland North counties, are shifted well to the right of the black triangles, which represent the Midland counties and fall as a whole to the left of the 50 percent Kerry voting line. The grey circles, which represent speech communities in the North outside of the Inland North, are also well to the left of the black triangles. Since on the whole these communities form smaller cities, they are located lower in the diagram.

Table 10.2 sums up this radical difference in the voting patterns of these two dialect areas. But it does not tell the whole story. Figure 10.11 indicates that population, as reflected in the total county vote, is a major factor in determining voting patterns. As we have seen, the Inland North has an especially large concentration of big cities, so that it is heavily urban compared to the North in general. Table 10.3 shows the results of two regression analyses of the data in Figure 10.11. The Midland is the residual group against which the North and the Inland North are compared. Analysis 1 shows that city size and the use of an Inland North or North dialect (as against the Midland dialect) are major contributors to the Kerry vote.

Table 10.3 Regression analyses of percent county vote for Kerry in 2004 presidential election by dialect groups, with and without total votes as an independent variable

Variable	Analysis 1		Analysis 2	
	Coeff	prob	Coeff	prob
Log county total vote (millions)	3.7	≤ .0001		
North dialect	10.7	≤ .0001	8.0	.0001
Inland North dialect	6.1	.0037	9.1	.0000

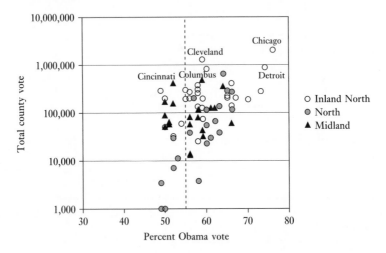

Figure 10.12 Percent county vote for Obama by total county vote in the 2008 presidential election, for counties in the Inland North, North and Midland dialect areas

At the level of 2004 county-by-county voting patterns, dialect areas coincide more precisely with Democratic preference than we observed at the state level, and we can now be sure that this is not an accidental phenomenon. Table 10.3 predicts that, in cities of comparable size on either side of the North/Midland boundary, like Columbus and Cleveland, we can expect a mean difference of about 6 percent in Democratic voting, which is enough to affect the state outcome (see Figure 10.11). But the second analysis in this table indicates that, if observers do not take city size into account, they will see an even larger difference. The voting pattern of the Inland North is a joint product of its urban character and the ideological background; the fact that big cities favor the Democrats is also the by-product of ideological history.

The political orientation represented by the Blue States/Red States geographic split was not notably different in the preceding election of 2000. Major shifts can be observed in the 2008 presidential election, as Figure 10.12 illustrates. Almost all Northern and Midland counties are advanced in the Democratic vote beyond the 50 percent level. The figure is compressed on the horizontal axis, indicating a

Table 10.4 Regression analysis of percent county vote for Obama in 2008 presidential election by dialect

Variable	Analysis 1		Analysis 2	
	Coef	prob	Coef	prob
Log county total vote (millions)	2.3	.0002		
Inland North dialect	2.8	.09	4.7	.01
North dialect	3.9	.026	2.5	.19

reduction in political orientation by city size. Table 10.4 is a regression analysis of the 2008 election comparable to Table 10.3 for 2004. The effect of population size is much reduced; but, when we do not take it into account in Analysis 2, the Inland North effect is magnified. An overall reduction in the polarization of the community is evident, but the correlation between dialect and voting pattern remains.

These results suggest the possibility of an association of ideological factors with the Inland North dialect. Such an association does not, of course, demonstrate a causal relation; but, in our search for the driving factors of change, it leads us to move beyond local factors, to consider a broader historical inquiry, with greater time depth. Chapter 5 showed that the Northern Cities Shift has its roots in the early part of the nineteenth century, though its full manifestation has become evident only in the second half of the twentieth. The ideological positions reflected in recent elections also have a long history.

10.8   The History of the Death Penalty

Another way of tracing the history of liberal political positions is through the status of the death penalty. This requires a return to the state as the differential unit. Figure 10.13 shows those states where the death penalty is not authorized for any crime, and the same two linguistic isoglosses are superimposed as in Figure 10.10. The association between the absence of the death penalty and the larger Northern dialect region (including North and Inland North areas) is notable. New York cannot be considered a strong exception within the Inland North, since most of its population is outside of the Inland North (14.5 million out of 19.3 million).

The history of the abolition of the death penalty is summarized in Table 10.5, which shows serial waves of abolition and restoration. The states with the earliest abolition are grouped to the left. In 1972, in the case *Furman* v *Georgia*, the US Supreme Court abolished the death penalty as constituting "cruel and unusual punishment." In the years that followed, all states except those listed in the last row of Table 10.5 passed legislation to re-instate the death penalty.[10]

Table 10.5 States with no death penalty, 1846–2008. √ = no death penalty. (√) = no death penalty except for treason. Grey areas: states within the Northern dialect region

	ME	RI	MI	WI	IA	MN	ND	SD	KS	NE	NM	TN	OR	WV	NY	VT	MA	NJ
1846–76	√	√	(√)	√	√													
1878–83	√	√	(√)	√														
1887	√	√	(√)	√														
1897–1915	√	√	(√)	√		√	(√)	√	√	√	√	√						
1916–39	√	√	(√)	√		√	(√)											
1957–69	√	√	(√)	√	√	√	(√)						√		(√)	(√)		
1972							√											
1973–2008	√	√	√	√	√	√	√							√	√	√	√	√

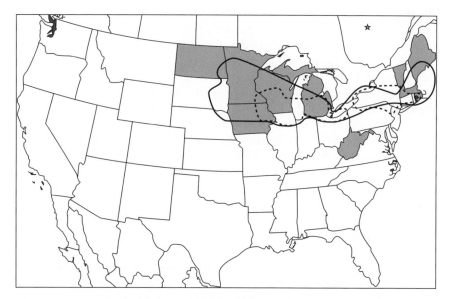

Figure 10.13   States with no death penalty in 2004. Solid isogloss = the Northern region; dashed isogloss = the Inland North as defined by the UD criterion

It is therefore clear that at least one ideological stance characteristic of the Blue States is not a recent development, but was active when the Northern dialect was first formed. We will now examine more closely that ideology and its formation, to see what other continuities and connections may exist.

10.9   Ideological Oppositions in the North

Thomas Morain's critical portrait of Yankee cultural style displayed a rhetorical bias which went beyond the Iowa community, embracing the Northern pattern more generally:

> Imbued with the notion that theirs was a superior vision, Yankees dutifully accepted their responsibility for the moral and intellectual life of the nation and set about to do what needed to be done, with or without an invitation from the uneducated, the undisciplined, the disinterested, or the unmotivated.
>
> Cultural uplift Yankee style also meant attacking sin and sloth. The initial settlement of Iowa coincided with three very active decades for American reform movements. Health fads, prison reform, women's rights, crusades for new standards of dress – the Northern states teemed with advocates of one cause or another.
>
> Most important among the reform movements of the day were the issues of abolition and temperance. (Morain 1988)

Phrases like "with or without an invitation," "sin and sloth," "health fads" and "teemed with" let us know that the author has judged Yankee activity to be unmotivated, excessive, somewhat comical and annoying. But when I first read the passage I was startled by the final phrase, "abolition and temperance." Whatever we may think about temperance, the abolition of slavery was not a trivial matter, to be classed with health fads, but an issue of utter seriousness. I turned to a number of other sources to trace the history of the Yankee orientation to the question of slavery. One of the most useful is Curtis Johnson's 1989 study of Cortland County in South Central New York State in the 1840s – the time and place where the triggering events of the Northern Cities Shift took place.

As noted in Chapter 5, the original settlers in Western New York State came mainly from New England. Johnson's study reports that 71 percent of the settlers in the 1790s came from New England; 19 percent from New York; and 10 percent from New Jersey and Pennsylvania (1989: 14–15). Like most other migrating peoples, the Yankees arriving in central New York formed their new society in the image of the communities they remembered (ibid., p. 21). However, there are a number of ways in which the westward expansion altered the structure of these communities.

One was the construction of the Erie Canal – which, as we have seen, brought in large populations from other areas, encouraged the development of big cities along the canal and altered agricultural markets for the rural areas. Chapter 5 has argued that the formation of a new *koine* was initiated by this vast population movement.

A second change was the great religious movement that converted Western New York State into the "burned-over district" (Cross 1950). This is the very area where the triggering event of the Northern Cities Shift took place (Chapter 5). Carnes and Garrity (1996) note that "[t]he restless settlers of the 'Burned-Over District' readily sought release in millennial and communitarian religion." The largely secular society of the 1790s was transformed by a series of religious revivals, which multiplied church membership: "In 1810 only one Cortland adult in 10 belonged to a church. By 1845, more than one fourth of the county's adults had joined a local congregation" (Johnson 1989: 39). This "Second Great Awakening" embodied a general shift, away from the stern Calvinist doctrine of predestination of the elect and towards an Arminian doctrine of free will, which opened the door to new standards of Christian conduct. There were violent disagreements on what those standards might be:

> Formalist evangelicals and nonevangelicals shared the conviction that the Christian mission went beyond individual salvation and involved religious endeavors that would benefit the larger community [. . .] In contrast, antiformalists doubted whether humans could change society. (Ibid., p. 68)

A more radical group than the formalists was the "Ultraists," who believed in total commitment to the eradication of individual, local and national sin (ibid., p. 113): this was an extreme form of Yankee devotion to social change. As the earlier quotation from Morain indicates, the two major evils identified in this program were alcohol and slavery. Prohibition and abolition formed the central political platform of the Ultraists.

All participants in the religious revival agreed in declaring that slavery was a sin; but there was radical disagreement on the political action implied. The Ultraists argued for a complete severance of relations with any church that tolerated slavery.

In his study of the "burned-over district" in New York State, Cross (1950: 224) shows that the community focused on slavery as the central moral issue:

> In February 1841, [an interdenominational convention] adopted a totally ultra-ist position, condemning the *Baptist Register* and all others who acknowledged evil without taking action, and concluded that "the abolition cause [. . .] must prevail before the halcyon day of millennial glory can dawn upon the world."

> No other section of the country would throughout the years before the Civil War prove to be so thoroughly and constantly sensitive to antislavery agitation. As the major issue of the century, furthermore, this crusade attracted more attention than others.

Moderate members of the congregation rejected the Ultraists as "fanatics." A long series of excommunications and church splinterings followed. A test case was the signing of the Liberty Party call for the abolition of slavery in 1841.[11] Johnson (1989) provides the data included in Table 10.6.

The most detailed study of the role of religion in politics before the Civil War is Carwardine (1993). Carwardine sees evangelical Protestantism[12] as the principal subculture in antebellum America. "The sheer numbers of evangelical Christians and their relative status in society gave them considerable political significance, whether they wished it or not" (ibid., p. xv).

Again, it appears that slavery was the central issue:

> It was from within this relatively small band of radical critics of slave society, particularly from the movement's orthodox evangelical wing, that the most determined efforts to politicize the slavery question emerged [. . .] Most respected the rights of slave states to jurisdiction within their own borders, but believed Congress could move against slavery wherever the federal government had jurisdiction. (Ibid., p. 135)

This moderate view was increasingly opposed to a more extreme position, which rejected any laws that permitted contact with, or tolerance of, slaveholders. "From the mid-1830s a number of abolitionists [. . .] moved further and further down the

Table 10.6   Signers of Liberty Party 1841 Call for Abolition of Slavery in Cortland County by religious orientation

	Members	Signers	Percent males
Formal	739	50	6.8
Antiformal	746	19	2.5
Ultraist	161	40	24.8

'no-human-government,' non-resistant, perfectonist, Christian–anarchist road" (ibid., p. 135), and a polarization of Northern and Southern evangelicals followed.

> By the later 1850s the idea of slavery as "good, and only good" had taken even deeper root in the South's churches. [. . .] A clear orthodoxy existed, centered on the propositions that slavery [. . .] was "justifiable in the sight of man and God"; that the system had yielded "untold and inconceivable blessings to the negro race." (Ibid., p. 286)

This opposition was not confined to the South. The central theme of this chapter emerges from Carwardine's account of the resistance to the Yankee political and cultural program on the part of those upland Southerners whose Midland viewpoint was presented earlier in this chapter. The Democratic Party's position was designed to appeal to

> lower-class rural folk, particularly but not exclusively in the rural South [. . .] who deeply resented the imperialism of the Yankee missionaries, their schemes for temperance, Sunday Schools and other reforms. (Ibid., pp. 111–12)

Carwardine finds that the Northern religious revival played a major role in the rise of the Republican Party in the 1850s and their victory in the 1860 presidential election:

> The emergence and ultimate success of the Republicans were dependent on a particular understanding of politics, one which evangelicals had played a major role in shaping. That political ethic was rooted in the moderate or "Arminianized" Calvinist theology of the Second Great Awakening, marked by an optimistic postmillennialism and an urgent appeal to disinterested action. (Ibid., p. 320)

This ideological movement was fully developed in the years leading up to the Civil War, and culminated in the abolition of slavery.

Next we will want to inquire into how these ideological questions intersected with national politics in the years that followed the Civil War. For this purpose I turn to Curtis Jensen's work, *The Winning of the Midwest: Social and Political Conflict 1888–1896* (1971). This is a study of the continuing ideological opposition in the Midwest, as it affected the outcome of national elections. Again, the split in church ideology plays a major role. Jensen sees religion as the fundamental source of political conflict in the Midwest. "The most revolutionary change in nineteenth century America was the conversion of the nation from a largely dechristianized land in 1789 to a stronghold of Protestantism by mid-century" (ibid., p. 62).

The opposition of formalists and antiformalists reappears as a division between "pietists" and "liturgicals," as it was expressed in struggles within many different denominations. Pietists were revivalists, emphasizing the experience of personal conversion and flatly rejecting ritualism. In contrast, "[l]iturgicals stressed the positive values of the institutionalized formalities of the old orthodoxies, whether Calvinist, Anglican, Lutheran, Catholic or Jewish" (ibid., p. 64). The political program

Table 10.7   Percentage of popular vote for the Republican Party in Indiana by county type and Yankee origin, 1880–96

County category	1880	1884	1886	1888	1890	1892	1894	1896
49 most rural	48	47	48	48	45	45	49	49
43 most urban	50	49	49	49	45	46	51	53
19 urban and Yankee	54	53	52	53	49	50	55	55
24 urban and non-Yankee	48	46	47	47	42	44	49	51
Statewide	49	48	49	49	45	46	50	51
Winner	Rep	Dem	Rep	Rep	Dem	Dem	Rep	Rep

Source: Richard Jensen, *The Winning of the Midwest: Social and Political Conflict, 1888–1896*, Chicago: University of Chicago Press, 1971

of the pietists echoed and continued the Yankee concerns we have documented. Pietists worked for "Sunday blue" laws, for the abolition of saloons and, before the Civil War, for a check to the growth of slavery, or even for its abolition. In the 1850s, American political parties re-aligned into an opposition between Republicans and Democrats, and "the great majority of [...] pietists entered the Republican Party, while the great majority of liturgicals became Democrats" (ibid., p. 69). In this political reshuffling Yankees were found on both sides of the fence, but they had a consistent leaning towards the Republican side, as a continuation of their pietistic orientation to social action. Table 10.7 shows the relation between Yankee origins and political orientation in late nineteenth-century Indiana. A "Yankee" county is defined as one in which migration had been predominantly from Northern states.[13] The counties that favored the Democrats were the 19 "urban and Yankee." The difference is not large – never more than 7 percent – but it is consistent across eight elections, and it was a critical factor during the long period when Republicans and Democrats were closely matched.

10.10   The Geographic Transformation

Given the Yankee evangelical, anti-slavery core of the Republican Party at the end of the nineteenth century, how do we account for the transformation that aligns the Yankee settlement and dialect area with the Democratic Blue States in Figure 10.10? There are some constant factors that continue to differentiate the two parties over time. From the outset, the Republican Party has identified itself with the interests of business, while the Democratic Party has claimed to represent the interests of the common man. Yet they have also been opposed on the issue of human rights for African–Americans. The major plank on which the Republican Party was founded, in 1854, was opposition to the extension of slavery, while the Democratic Party supported the right of states and territories to decide the issue. Table 10.8

Table 10.8 Presidential elections by four state groups of the Eastern US.
D = Democrat; R = Republican; (X) = one state deviant; / = 2+ states deviant;
S[outh] = TX, AR, LA, MS, AL, GA, FL, SC, NC, KY, TN, VA
M[idland] = MO, IL, IN, OH, WV, PA, DE, MD, NJ
N[ew] E[ngland] = ME, VT, NH, MA, RI, CT
N[orth] = NY, MI, WI, IA, MN

		S	M	NE	N	
1848	Fillmore	/	/	/	/	Whig vs. D
1852	Pierce	(D)	D	/	D	Republican Party formed
1856	Buchanan	D	(D)	R	R	
1860	Lincoln	D	(R)	R	R	
1864	Lincoln	S	(R)	R	R	S = Confederate States
1868–1876	Johnson/					Reconstruction
	Grant/Hayes					
1880	Garfield	D	/	R	R	
1884	Cleveland	D	/	(R)	(R)	
1888	Harrison	D	/	(R)	R	
1892	Cleveland	D	/	(R)	/	
1896	McKinley	D	(R)	R	R	
1900	McKinley	D	(R)	R	R	
1904	Roosevelt	D	R	R	R	
1908	Taft	D	R	R	R	
1912	Wilson	D	(D)	(D)	(D)	Progressive 3rd party
1916	Wilson	D	/	(R)	R	
1920	Harding	(D)	R	R	R	
1924	Coolidge	D	R	R	R	
1928	Hoover	/	R	R	R	S core D: AR, LA, MI, AL, GA, SC
1932	Roosevelt	D	/	(R)	D	NE core R: ME, VT, NH
1936	Roosevelt	D	D	/	D	NE core R: ME, VT
1940	Roosevelt	D	(D)	/	(D)	NE core R: ME, VT
1944	Roosevelt	D	/	/	/	NE core R: ME, VT
1948	Truman	/	/	(R)	/	States Rights: LA, MI, AL, SC
1952	Eisenhower	/	R	R	R	S core D: LA, MI, AL, GA, SC, NC
1956	Eisenhower	/	R	R	R	S core D: AR, MI, AL, GA, SC, NC
1960	Kennedy	/	/	/	/	Electors for Byrd in AL, MI
1964	Johnson	/	D	D	D	S core R: LA, MI, AL, GA, SC
1968	Nixon	W	/	/	/	Wallace (Ind): LA, AR, MI, AL, GA
1972	Nixon	R	R	(R)	R	
1976	Carter	(D)	/	/	/	R: VA
1980	Reagan	(R)	/	R	(R)	
1984	Reagan	R	R	R	(R)	
1988	Bush	R	(R)	/	(D)	
1992	Clinton	/	(D)	D	D	S core R: MI, AL, FL, SC, NC, VA
1996	Clinton	/	(D)	D	D	S core R: MI, AL, GA, SC, NC, VA
2000	Bush	R	/	(D)	D	NE core R: NH
2004	Bush	R	/	D	D	
2008	Obama	/	/	D	D	S core R: [TX], AK, LA, MI, AL, GA, SC

traces the distribution of voting results in national elections by the groups of states that approximate the major dialect divisions of the Eastern United States. The states taken to represent the North are limited to those whose territory falls mostly into the Northern dialect region – so that the upper third of Illinois and Ohio are not represented here, although they contain many Northern speakers. On the other hand, the states representing the South fall almost entirely within the defining isogloss of the Southern dialect region: monophthongization of /ay/ before voiced obstruents.

In Table 10.8 a clear-cut opposition between Northern and Southern states is indicated by means of the grey shading of the letters D and R. At the top of Table 10.6 is the Whig versus Democrat election of 1848, at a time before the Republican Party was formed, when the Democrats were not yet dominant in the South. Democratic control of the South began in the following election and continued without a break for ninety-two years – except for the period of Reconstruction after the war, when local Republican governments were supported by federal troops. Not even the Republican sweep of 1928 disturbed the Democratic monopoly of the six core Southern states. The series of "D" symbols in the Southern column comes to and end in the Truman election of 1948, when Southern opposition to the civil rights movement created a "states rights" third party. Against the tide of the Eisenhower landslides in the 1950s, the Democrats retained their dominant position in six Southern states. However, the electoral map splintered again in the crucial year of Kennedy's election, 1960, when all four state sections were divided.

In the years following Kennedy's election, the Southern vote switched sides. In the Democratic landslide of 1964 the South was divided, but the core Southern states were now Republican, not Democratic. In 1968, opposition to the civil rights movement gave these core states to George Wallace's American Independent Party. The following election, in 1972, was Nixon's Republican landslide, which won the South as well as the other sections. The last Democratic success in the South was achieved by a candidate from Georgia, Jimmy Carter, but from 1980 on the Republican Party has dominated the South. The South was divided in the Clinton victories of the 1990s, but here the Southern core states were Republican. In 2000 and 2004 one sees the crystallization of the Republican domination of the South in the face of an opposite and opposing Democratic block in the North.

The history of the Northern region can be read from the last column in Table 10.8. From 1856 on, the Northern states are solidly Republican, save for the disruption caused in 1912 by the election of the Progressive Party candidate, Theodore Roosevelt. This situation continued until the landslides of the New Deal era, from 1933 on. At that time, the core "rock-ribbed" Republican vote was not found in the Northern dialect region, but in the New England states of Maine and Vermont. Again, it was the 1960 Kennedy campaign that split all sections and marked the end of the Republican tradition in the Northern states. In the elections that followed up to 1992, the North swayed with the tide, voting mostly Republican

Table 10.9   Votes on original House of Representatives version of the Civil Rights Act of 1964

	Democrat		Republican	
	For	Against	For	Against
Southern	7	87	0	10
Northern	145	9	138	24

in Republican years, Democratic in Democratic years. The most recent sixteen years have shown a solid Democratic outcome in the Northern section, but only in 2000 and 2004 do we see clear opposition of a Democratic North and a Republican majority in the rest of the country. This is indicated by the grey shading of "D" and "R" in 2000–2004, with the positions of these two categories now reversed. The pattern is modified in the 2008 election – but maintained by Obama's lack of success in the core Southern states.

Table 10.8 shows that the crucial change in the orientation of the two parties occurred between the elections of 1964 and 1968, after Johnson shepherded the Civil Rights Act of 1964 through Congress. As shown in Table 10.9, the Republican Party was not opposed to this legislation: the vote split along regional lines, not party lines.

One of Johnson's most effective arguments was that passing this legislation was "the late president's most fitting memorial" (Beschloss 2007: 279). In fact, Kennedy was for a long time ambivalent in his support of the Civil Rights Act, which he postponed many times, mindful of losing the Southern vote that had elected him. In a recorded conversation with Louisiana Senator Russell Long,[14] Kennedy learned of an offer made by segregationists to commit their electoral votes in exchange for the abandonment of the civil rights legislation, as in the deal that led to the end of Reconstruction under Rutherford B. Hayes in 1876. Kennedy responded:

> But this isn't 1876. Because what happens is it will become the most publicized thing [...] everybody's looking, now what is this president promising this group and pretty soon you've got the Goddamndest mayhem.

Long suggested that "the Negro vote might be the key vote" and Kennedy intervened:

> At least I could count it [...] I think it's crazy for the South because this way I'm concerned about Georgia and Louisiana and these places, here's where we got a chance to carry them, but if I end up with no chance to carry them then I gotta go up north and try to do my business.

The 1964 election that followed showed the first switch of the core Southern states to the Republican column and the first Democratic vote in the North since Roosevelt; this was to lead to the current realignment of Red States versus Blue States. It appears that it was the political act of initiating the Civil Rights Act of 1964 and the Voting Rights Act of 1965 that brought about this realignment.

The common thread that unites this political and cultural history over 150 years is the attitudes of whites towards slavery and the unequal status of blacks and whites in the United States. In the nineteenth-century North, both abolitionists and moderates, both formalists and anti-formalists, both pietists and liturgicals shared the common articles of faith that all men were created equal and that slavery was a sin. A century and a half later, this ideology was the moving force that led to the correlation of the Inland North dialect and the political stance of the Blue States. While the cultural style of the Yankees may resemble that of modern-day right-wing Christian revivalists, the cultural content differed on the crucial dimension of race relations.

We cannot set aside the possibility that this continuation of Yankee ideology contributes to the momentum exhibited by the Northern Cities Shift on a broad scale across the Inland North. Though the NCS remains below the level of social awareness, it is possible that its speakers have (if unconsciously) come to associate this sound shift, over the past few generations, with the political and cultural outlook inherited from the Yankee settlers. Those associations have evolved over time with various social and demographic changes, and especially with the realignment of the two major parties in the 1960s. As long as these ideological differences persist, speakers may be more likely to align their productions towards those around them who share their own identity and world-view. And along the linguistic and cultural border, they may be less likely to accommodate to others whom they perceive as holding different or hostile views. If such accommodation is weakened by the ideological oppositions reviewed in this chapter, it might help to explain why the North–Midland boundary is the sharpest division in North American English dialectology, and why it has remained stable for almost a century.

11

Social Evaluation of the Northern Cities Shift

Chapter 9 traced the history of the Northern Cities Shift in the Inland North and Chapter 10 traced the political, religious and cultural history of that region. These joint histories raise the possibility that the continued influence of Yankee ideology contributes to the momentum of the Northern Cities Shift across the Inland North. Is there any evidence that the NCS, operating far below the level of social awareness, is identified unconsciously with a stance favoring the reduction of racial inequality and other liberal political positions?

Chapter 10 dealt with two such positions: attitudes towards slavery and racial inequality, and state-by-state resolution of the legality of the death penalty. One can identify a similar regional pattern on the issue of gun control. A CNN web site[1] provides information for each state on seven aspects of gun regulation: Child Access Prevention Law, Juvenile Possession Law, Juvenile Sale/Transfer Law, Permit to purchase, Registration of firearms, Licensing of owners, and Permit to carry. The following six states have legislation in five or more of these areas: Maine, New York, New Jersey, Michigan, Minnesota, Iowa. All but New Jersey fall in whole or in part within the Northern dialect region, as shown in Figures 10.9 and 10.13.

The overall stance of a state towards abortion may be assessed by many different measures.[2] One is the identification of states where no parental consent for minors is required. These are Massachusetts, Maine, New York and Wisconsin: all states within the North. Another measure is the existence of mandatory waiting periods. No waiting periods are required in the New England and Mid-Atlantic states as a whole, nor in the Mid-West, Illinois or Iowa. This is also true of most Western states and of Florida, so that the correspondence with the North is less precise.

In order to test the association of the North/Midland opposition with ideological positions, an experiment was designed in which subjects heard prototypical extracts of Northern Cities Shift and Midland speech and were asked to infer the speakers' probable stance for or against abortion, affirmative action and gun control.

11.1 The North/Midland Experiment 1

I first carried out this experiment in April 2000, at the University of Indiana in Bloomington. Extracts from two Telsur speakers were played to a group of ninety undergraduates. The first speaker was Sharon K. from Detroit, 37 years old in 1994, an advanced speaker of the NCS. The underlined words show generalized raising of /æ/, fronting of /o/, lowering of /oh/, and backing of /ʌ/.

(1) The – the way I <u>got</u> hired for this <u>one job</u> was really weird, 'cause I went in for a [...] secretarial position is what I went in for, and they had hired [...] ah – somebody else that didn't know anything, but it was a buyer's <u>daughter</u>, so then she <u>got</u> the <u>job</u>. And uh – they called me because I had <u>done</u> shipping and receiving as far as – the paper work, and they had <u>asked</u> me if I'd help out 'cause their – shipper had just had a heart <u>attack</u> and she wasn' comin' <u>back</u> for a while.

The second speaker was Mimi P. from Indianapolis, 45 in 1994, a characteristic speaker of the Midland dialect of that city. The underlined words show tensing of /æ/ before nasals but not in *that*, back position of /o/, fronting of /ʌ/ and /aw/.

(2) I read, <u>a-n-nd</u> like most women, I like to go <u>shopping</u> and play card games with <u>family</u> and friends and <u>that</u> kind of thing, <u>nothing</u> really exciting. We used to go <u>camping</u> quite a bit on the weekends, but our lives have shifted <u>enough</u> that we don't do that <u>much</u> right <u>now</u>, but uh that's <u>what</u> we do.

Figure 11.1 shows the Northern Cities Shift in the vowel system of Sharon K. The six means are connected to show the typical NCS pattern, with /æ/ raised and fronted beyond /e/, /e/ backed to align with the strongly fronted /o/, and /ʌ/ backed into the area of /oh/. Some of the key words from extract (1) are shown: the raised and fronted /æ/ in *back*; fronted /o/ as characterized by four pronunciations of *job*, very close to the mean of /e/.

Figure 11.2 shows the same vowels for Mimi P., the speaker of extract (2), with a characteristic Midland pattern. The mean of /æ/ is lower than /e/, which remains in front position, quite distant from /o/. Tokens of /ʌ/ edge forward to front of center and are quite distinct from /oh/ in the back. Some of the key words from extract (2) are shown. The range of /æ/ extends from high front (*family*) and upper mid front (*camping*) before nasals to low front (*that*) elsewhere. Short *o* in *shopping* is well back of center, though it is among the most forward in that distribution. In the /ʌ/ distribution, Mimi's *much* is in the center.

The student subjects at Bloomington were largely local: fifty-four of the ninety came from Indiana, and only ten from the North (nine from Chicago). Subjects

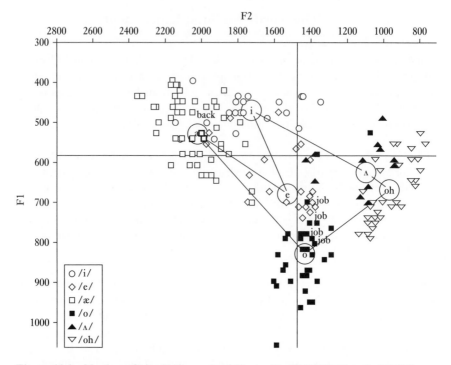

Figure 11.1 Northern Cities Shift vowels of Sharon K., 37 [1994], Detroit, TS 176

were asked to assign a city of origin to each speaker, and seventy-four of the ninety attempted to do so. Table 11.1 shows that they were surprisingly accurate: 78 percent of those who responded, correctly assigned the first speaker to the Inland North. These were evenly split between Chicago and Detroit. Since this speaker was in fact from Detroit, both responses are accurate: as we have seen, Chicago and Detroit are equivalent in their development of the Northern Cities Shift. In this sense, Michigan and Cleveland are equally correct responses. Three judges responded with Minnesota, correctly placing the speaker in the larger region of the North. Only twelve out of the seventy-four responses were wrong by placing the first speaker in the Midland or in the South.

There was less certainty concerning the second speaker, though she came from the same area as most of the subjects. Only fifty-four of the ninety tried to place her. Yet those who did so were quite accurate. Only seven made the gross error of assigning her to the Inland North, and twenty-eight accurately assigned her to Indianapolis. The twelve who assigned her to the neighboring Appalachian states erred in the other direction, but there is a solid basis of resemblance between Midland Indianapolis and the South.

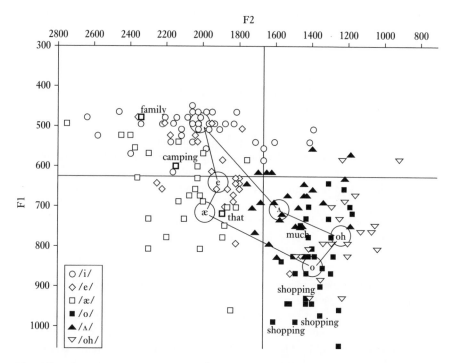

Figure 11.2 Northern Cities Shift vowels of Mimi P., 45 [2000], Indianapolis, TS 775

Table 11.1 Cities of origin assigned to the two speakers by student listeners at University of Indiana, Bloomington. Bold figures = correct dialect identification. [N = 90]

Speaker assigned to	Dialect area	Speaker 1 (Detroit)	Speaker 2 (Indianapolis)
Chicago	Inland North	**24**	3
Detroit	Inland North	**26**	3
Michigan	Inland North	**4**	
Cleveland	Inland North	1	
Minneapolis	North	3	
Ft Wayne, So. Bend	Transitional	1	
Indianapolis	Midland	6	**24**
Indiana	Midland	3	**4**
Other Midland	Midland	1	**12**
Kentucky, Tennessee	South	1	12
Atlanta	South		1
Denver	West	1	
TOTAL		71	59

Subjects were asked to evaluate each speaker on a seven-point Likert scale for four personal dimensions:

Intelligence	1 (moderate) to 7 (high)
Friendliness	1 (high) to 7 (low)
Education	1 (high) to 7 (low)
Trustworthiness	1 (low) to 7 (high)

The rating form continued with three political issues on which North and Midland speakers might be generally differentiated, following the data cited at the beginning of this chapter and in Chapter 10. The scale attributed the lowest number to the most liberal position, and the highest number to the opposition to that liberal position.

Abortion views	1 (pro-choice) to 7 (pro-life)
Affirmative action	1 (pro) to 7 (contra)
Gun control	1 (pro) to 7 (contra)

Subjects were then asked to rate the speaker on whether they sounded like someone "from your hometown."

No significant differences between the two speakers were found in ratings of intelligence, education or trustworthiness. The Indianapolis speaker was perceived as much more friendly ($t = 6.0$, $p < .0001$). No significant difference was found between the speakers' probable positions on abortion, but the Inland North speaker was significantly rated higher on support for affirmative action and even more so on gun control, as shown in Table 11.2.

A closer examination of these answers is provided in Figure 11.3. One can see that the largest single tendency is for subjects to give a neutral response at 4. Adding in those subjects who did not respond at all, one can see that the majority did not make any inferences about the speakers' political position from their dialect. The significant results come from a minority who reacted vigorously: in the case of affirmative action, they attributed strong support to the Detroit speaker, and, in the case of gun control, they projected strong opposition for the Indianapolis speaker.

The same pattern appears in the respondents' reactions on the abortion question in Figure 11.4. Although the overall results are not significant, the biggest difference

Table 11.2 Mean responses on political opinions attributed to Detroit and Indianapolis speakers by University of Indiana subjects

	Pro-choice	Pro-affirmative action	Pro gun control
Northern Cities Shift	4.41	3.98	3.71
Midland	4.56	4.38	4.25
Prob [t-test]	–	.02	.003

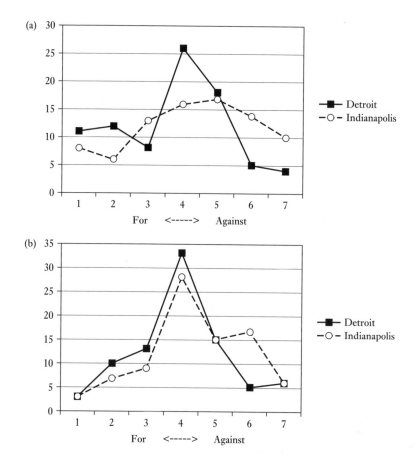

Figure 11.3 Number of responses, on a 7-point scale, for Detroit and Indianapolis speakers' projected position on affirmative action and gun control; Figure 11.3a Affirmative action; Figure 11.3b Gun control

between the two speakers was made by the twenty-seven subjects who attributed a strong pro-life position to the Indianapolis speaker (scale 6, 7) – whereas only seventeen attributed this position to the Detroit speaker.

These results are not as strong as those obtained in the subjective reaction tests conducted in New York City for the social evaluation of (r) (Labov 1966), in Harlem for (dh) (Labov 1972), or in Philadelphia for (æh) (PLC, Vol. 2, Ch. 6). They indicate that the majority of our Midland subjects are not sensitive to any social meaning that might be attributed to these radical differences in vowel organization, although there is a minority which does make such inferences. The results hold for the general population of ninety subjects. Regression analyses show no significant

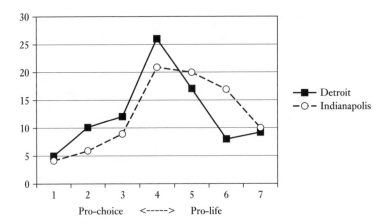

Figure 11.4 Number of responses, on a 7-point scale, for Detroit and Indianapolis speakers' projected position on abortion

effect of the subjects' origin or gender. Those who had the same origin as the speakers were not more inclined than others to say that the speakers sounded as if they came from their own hometown.

11.1.1   The effect of correct identification of dialect origins

This experiment was not as well controlled as some of the other subjective reaction tests mentioned, since the content of the two extracts was different in substance. For example, the mention of "camping" by the second speaker might have triggered the expectation that that speaker would be against gun control. The voice quality and speaking style of the two speakers differed. One way of distinguishing these general effects from the specific effect of the Northern Cities Shift is to examine the differences in response from those who placed correctly the dialect origins of the two speakers and those who did not. Any effect of the regional dialect on the listeners' attribution of ideological positions should be stronger for those who correctly identified the regional dialect of the speaker, and weaker for those who perceived the speaker as coming from some other area.[3]

Figure 11.5 shows the distribution of differences on the degree of support for affirmative action attributed to the two speakers. Here positive numbers indicate that the NCS speaker was given a lower score than the Midland speaker on the affirmative action item (since the scale was low for support and high for opposition). The solid bars represent the responses of the fifty-eight judges who correctly identified the NCS dialect of the speaker from Detroit.[4] The white bars represent the responses of the twenty-eight who did not do so, including those who gave no response to the dialect identification question. Again, we see that the modal value

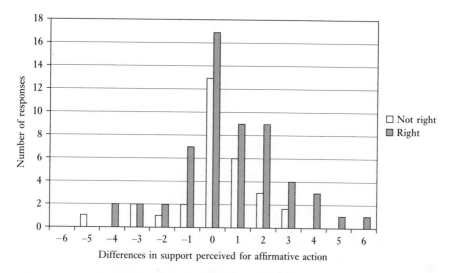

Figure 11.5 Differences in support perceived for affirmative action for those who did and did not correctly identify the dialect origin of the NCS speaker [Experiment 1, N = 85]

Table 11.3 Regression coefficients for differences in degrees of affirmative action support for the NCS and the Midland speaker as perceived by eighty-five listeners from the University of Indiana in Experiment 1

	Coefficient	Prob
Affirmative action support for NCS speaker	.78	> .0001
Listener's correct identification of NCS speaker	.67	.04
Pro-CHOICE support of listener	.16	.02
Support for gun control of listener	−.16	.07
Adjusted r² = 42.7 percent		

was to perceive no difference, for both groups of listeners. But all those who expected sizeable differences in affirmative action support – 3, 4, 5 units on the scale – correctly identified the NCS speaker.

When we enter the factor of correct identification into a regression analysis, the result of Table 11.3 appears. The stronger the support for affirmative action perceived for the NCS speaker, the greater the difference between the ratings of the two speakers: this is a normal effect. But a significant and equally large effect is the correct identification of the NCS speaker. This gives us some indication that the reactions of judges to the two speakers were a response to the dialect patterns rather than to other characteristics that differentiate them.

11.2   Conclusion

There is no doubt that language change may be local and reflect an immediate social motivation to reinforce local identity. But we have seen that language change in North America occurs on a much larger scale, where individual acts and motivations are irrelevant.

The results of this chapter, whatever their limitations, coincide with the large-scale political and ideological history found in Chapter 10. The correlations between the NCS and ideological factors do not imply an immediate causal relation between ideology and sound change. There are many other indirect relations that may hold between dialect differences and ideology. It is possible that the subjects of the experiment used the phonetic features to identify the urban origins of the speaker, and then drew inferences from a knowledge base that attributes certain qualities and ideological biases to inhabitants of the place in question. Or the speech forms themselves may be associated with these opinions. If that is the case, we have to consider that ideology can affect the development of sound change on a large scale. On the whole, the most convincing and demonstrable determinants of language change are structural and mechanical, but we must be alert to the possibility that ideology is a driving force behind change, as well as a barrier to its further expansion.

12

Endpoints

The study of linguistic change and variation focuses upon change in progress. But most changes are not in progress; they have gone to completion. It does not take much reflection to conclude that all but a few of the features of a given language are the result of completed changes. Those that are not are either universal features, which date back to the origin of language itself and have never changed, or features that are still in the process of change. All other invariant forms are the end result of change, the endpoints of the process that is the focus of these volumes. Over the course of time, continued change leads to rising levels of frequency of the incoming form, until some limit is reached and all speakers converge to that stable limit.

Many linguistic changes involve shifts in the frequency of a countable phenomenon. This is the case for the vocalization or restoration of English coda /r/, the shift of apical to uvular /r/ in Montreal French (Sankoff et al. 2001), or the loss of the French negative particle *ne* (Sankoff and Vincent 1977). The endpoint of such changes is 0 or 100, depending on what is being counted. In some cases it takes a very long time for the curve to reach its limiting value, but the limit is well defined.

In Montreal French, the ongoing change passes through a stage of sharp social stratification, with upper–class female speakers leading in the shift to uvular /r/. But the shift to uvular /r/ is so abrupt that adolescent children of parents with 100 percent apical /r/ will usually show 0 percent apical /r/. An equally abrupt transition may be seen in the restoration of consonantal /r/ in the South. The ANAE subjects include sixty-eight white speakers under 40 years of age in the Southern region; only two show any vocalization of coda /r/ (Figure 12.1). In 1972, O'Cain reported that the use of /r/ in Charleston was heavily weighted towards the lower social classes (p. 93), but in Baranowski's 2006 analysis age was the only significant factor (pp. 91ff). Such abrupt changes may obscure any social mechanism by which the changing pattern is transmitted.

In vowel changes which involve mergers, the limit is not an invariant quantity of the 0 or 100 percent type, but rather the loss of a significant distinction between two mean values. Again, this process can be quite abrupt, so that in Northeastern Pennsylvania Herold (1990) traced a complete transition across one generation, from a father with non-overlapping distributions of /o/ and /oh/ to his son, who

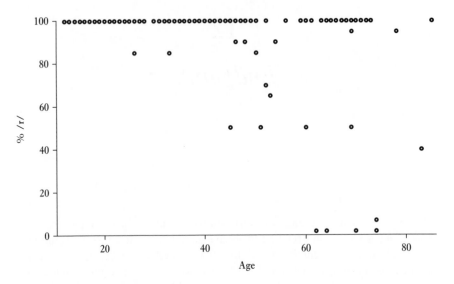

Figure 12.1 Vocalization of coda (r) among sixty-eight white ANAE subjects in
the South dialect region

showed a total merger of those two phonemes. Whether the ongoing merger is fast
or slow, the endpoint is clearly defined.

The situation is not so clear for the chain shifts that have been the major focus
of attention in these studies of change in progress. Some sound changes seem to
pass through what looks like an endless series of transformations: for instance, Latin
long ē has followed this trajectory in French: [ē] → [e⁽ⁱ⁾] → [ʌi] → [ɔi] → [oi] →
[ui] → [wi] → [we] → [wɛ] → [wa]; and Middle English ū has displayed an equally
dazzling array of intermediate stages, for instance [uː] → [ʊu] → [ʌu] → [au] →
[æu] → [ɛo] → [eɔ] in the present-day dialect of Philadelphia. These virtuoso
developments traverse the phonological space of several subsystems, routed by the
unidirectional pathways that lead from one subsystem to another (Vol. 1, Ch. 9).
Since these transitional movements are not yet fully understood, greater progress
might be made by examining endpoints within a particular subsystem. Given the
continuous character of the phonological space defined in Figure 6.17, it might
seem that the endpoints of raising on the peripheral track would be [i] and [u], and
that the endpoint of lowering on the nonperipheral track would be [a]. This turns
out not to be the case.

12.1   Skewness as an Index of Approach to Endpoint

Chapter 15 of Volume 2 introduced the study of skewing in the development of
linguistic change. Skewness is a measure of the left–right symmetry of the tails of

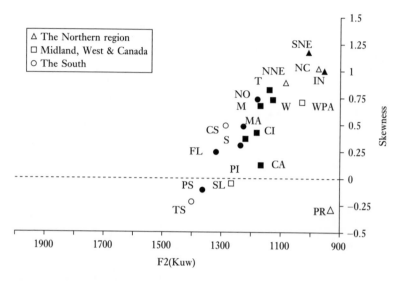

Figure 12.2 The development of skewing in the fronting of /Kuw/ for twenty-one North American English dialects (PLC, Vol. 2, Figure 15.14). Solid symbols represent negative age coefficients, indicating change in progress in apparent time

a distribution.[1] At the beginning of a sound change, the distribution of a vowel is strongly shifted in the direction of the new form and shows a long tail in that direction. As the change proceeds, more and more tokens are shifted in that direction, until symmetry is restored (zero skewness). As the change approaches an endpoint, the opposite direction of skewness develops, and a long tail appears in the direction of the more conservative forms. Finally, as the change comes to completion at the endpoint, symmetry is restored and skewness disappears again.

Figure 12.2 shows the development of skewing for the fronting of /Kuw/, the allophone of /uw/ after noncoronal consonants, for twenty-one North American English dialects as identified in the legend. The dialect abbreviations are:

CA	Canada	NNE	Northern	TS	Texas South
CI	Cincinnati		New England	SL	St Louis
CS	Charleston	NO	New Orleans	SNE	Southern
FL	Florida	PI	Pittsburgh		New England
IN	Inland	PR	Providence	W	West
M	Midland	PS	Piedmont South	WPA	Western
MA	Mid-Atlantic	S	South		Pennsylvania
NC	North Central	T	Transitional		

Conservative dialects, like Southern New England, are at the upper right of the distribution, with strong positive skewness and F2 mean values below 1000 Hz. The

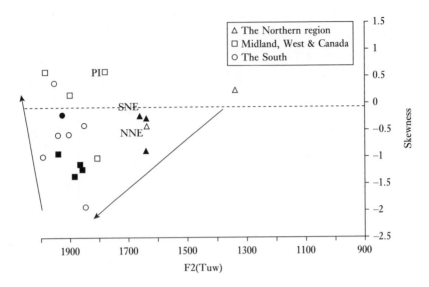

Figure 12.3 The development of skewing in the fronting of / Tuw/ for twenty-one North American English dialects (PLC, Vol. 2, Figure 15.16; dialect labels as in Figure 12.2). Solid symbols represent negative age coefficients, indicating change in progress in apparent time

most advanced dialect, the Texas South, is at lower left, almost at the normalized midpoint of 1550 Hz. The negative skewness approaching –.25 indicates that the long tail is now to the right, in the conservative direction. The fronting of / Kuw/ is a change strongly in progress for most dialects, as indicated by the negative age coefficients (solid symbols), and has not yet approached its endpoint. This progression of / Kuw/ shows a steady decline of skewness to zero and beyond, to small negative values. The regression coefficient on F2 for skewness is –.0017, with a probability less than .01.

Figure 12.3 gives the corresponding display for the more advanced allophone / Tuw/: the fronting of /uw/ after coronals. Chapter 5 laid out the series of linguistic events in which the fronting of / Tuw/ was triggered by the collapse of the /iw/ ~ /uw/ distinction after coronals – a fronting that was later generalized to produce the more moderate fronting of / Kuw/. The relation of fronting to skewness is more complex for / Tuw/ than for / Kuw/, since the overall trajectory of change passes through a period of increasingly negative skewness in the direction of change, returns to zero, develops skewing in the opposite direction and returns to zero again. We can trace this process by observing that the average skewness of the most conservative dialects (mean F2 of 1300–1800 Hz) is –0.16. For dialects with F2 means of 1800–1890 Hz, average skewness falls to –1.19. For the most advanced dialects, with F2 means over 1890 Hz, skewness rises again towards zero, with a mean value of –0.28.

The dialect with the most extreme fronting of /Tuw/ is the Inland South (see Figure 6.18), with mean F2 value of 1843 Hz in the log mean normalized formant space of ANAE. Since the mean value for the high front vowel /iy/ is 2032 Hz, the endpoint for fronting of /uw/ appears to be within 200 Hz of the central tendency of /iy/ – a limit determined by the margin of security for a stable distinction between these two major vowel classes. While /iy/ and /uw/ are also distinguished by the direction of the glide, extreme tokens of checked syllables frequently show minimal nucleus-glide differentiation. As noted in the Gating experiments of Chapter 4, the Birmingham realizations of *bouffed* and *bootlegger* show fronting of glides and their /uw/ is very often heard, in isolation, as /iy/.

The most extreme fronting of /ow/ in North America is produced by speakers of the Charleston dialect in their twenties (Baranowski 2007: 189). These speakers show a mean of about 1830 Hz, well front of the general center value of 1550 Hz, and around the same 200 Hz distance from the nucleus of the corresponding front upgliding vowel, /ey/, at 2053 Hz. But here the difference in the direction of glides is so extreme that there is no possibility of confusion in perception between the front upgliding and the back upgliding vowels. The limiting value for the fronting of /ow/ in Charleston may instead be the position of the back upgliding /aw/, which rises along the peripheral track as the nucleus of /ow/ fronts to the nonperipheral track.[2] In Philadelphia and other Southern dialects, the raised nucleus of /aw/ before and after nasals normally occupies a peripheral position, so that "Now I know" is heard as [nɛˤo aɪ nɛˀo].

12.2 Social Characteristics of Endpoints

The reduction of skewness to zero is a phonetic indication that a change is reaching an endpoint. On the vowel charts of an individual or a community, we can distinguish such stable distributions by their roughly spherical shape and compact character. Social distribution may also indicate the completion of a change. An endpoint in a sound change can be recognized when the affected phoneme is shifted markedly from the positions found in surrounding dialect regions and no variation by age, gender, social class, neighborhood or ethnicity can be detected within the community. It is of course possible that all members of the community have been moving this variable in lockstep and will continue to do so, but no such cases have so far been found in studies of the speech community.

The project on Linguistic Change and Variation in Philadelphia (LCV) provided the portrait of change in progress in the vowel system displayed in Figure 12.4. Each circle represents the mean value of a vowel for 112 speakers of the Neighborhood Study (Vol. 2, Ch. 5). The arrows drawn through the circles are vectors representing movement in apparent time. The heads of the arrows are the expected values for speakers who are 25 years younger than the mean for the population as a whole,

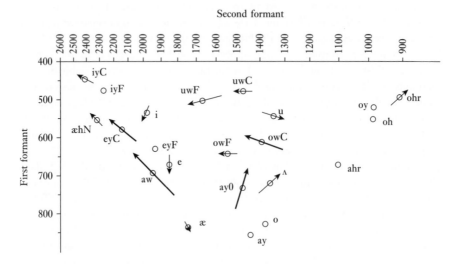

Figure 12.4   The Philadelphia vowel system in the early 1970s. Arrows represent significant age coefficients; the arrow head is the expected value for those 25 years younger than the mean, the arrow tail the expected value for those 25 years older than the mean

and the tails indicate the expected value for those who are 25 years older than the mean. The new and vigorous changes (aw), (eyC), (ay0) have the largest coefficients, with the weight of the lines signifying p < .001. The lightest and shortest arrows represent incipient changes, with p between .05 and .10. Mean circles with no arrows show no detectable movement in apparent time.

Some of the vowels that show no age coefficients are in phonetic positions typical of the initial position for North American English vowels, as described in Chapter 2 of ANAE. Short *o* is in low central position, along with the nucleus of /ay/ before voiced consonants and word-finally. But /ahr/ in *car*, *card*, *hard*, etc., is shifted from this initial low central position to a mid back location. This feature of the Philadelphia dialect is extraordinarily uniform. All Philadelphians whom we recorded said [kɔr] for *car*: male and female, young and old, upper class, lower middle class and working class. The pronunciation [kɑr] is simply not heard in the markets, bars or homes of Philadelphia. Though this mid back position of the phoneme /ahr/ is fully characteristic of Philadelphia, it is not a stereotype: it is never mentioned by outsiders and it never forms part of an imitation of the Philadelphia accent. It is not a marker: it does not shift from one style to another. Nor is it an indicator of gender, social class, neighborhood or ethnicity.

The shift of /ahr/ to mid back position is thus a model of a completed change, since we have every reason to believe that at some point it became rounded, backed, and raised from [ɑr] to [ɔr]. Following the logic of Weinreich, Labov and Herzog 1968,

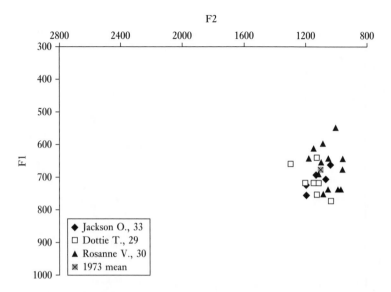

Figure 12.5   Distribution of /ahr/ for three Philadelphia Telsur speakers in 1996, compared to mean /ahr/ of LCV speakers in 1973

we can expect that it did operate as a linguistic variable across the trajectory of this raising process. Furthermore, it is locked into the Back Chain Shift before /r/ (Figure 1.8), described in ANAE for Philadelphia (p. 122), Pittsburgh (pp. 276–8) and the South (p. 245).

Figure 12.4 indicates some upward movement for /ohr/, the other member of this chain shift; and two other phonemes with /o/ nuclei have also moved towards upper high back position: /oy/ and /oh/. Since the backing and raising of /ahr/ is completed and the movement of /ohr/ is not, we can infer that the raising of /ahr/ along the peripheral track was the initiating event of the chain shift.

The three ANAE interviews in Philadelphia took place in 1996, twenty-three years after the LCV interviews that form the basis of Figure 12.4. Figure 12.5 plots all the /ahr/ words measured in the ANAE interviews against the grand mean of the 1973 data (indicated by X). It is evident that there has been no shift in the target of /ahr/; all new tokens are symmetrically clustered around the original mean.

Eight years after the Telsur interviews, Conn (2005) carried out a restudy of the Philadelphia vowel system, with sixty-five speakers drawn from a wide range of neighborhoods. His overall view of the system in apparent time, which corresponds to Figure 12.4, is displayed in Figure 12.6. The arrows indicate continued change in the same direction for the new and vigorous changes (eyC) and (ay0). The fronting of (uwF), re-analyzed in Figure 12.3 as (Tuw),[3] appears to have reached a maximum, while the set of /uw/ after noncoronal consonants, (Kuw), is moving forward vigorously, as it does in other US cities. On the other hand, the raising and fronting

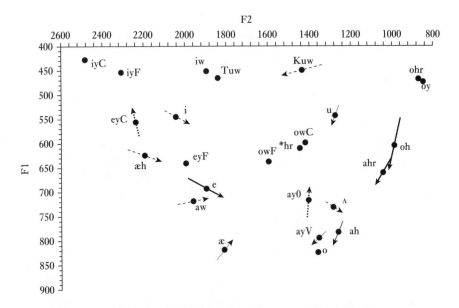

Figure 12.6   The Philadelphia vowel system in Conn's restudy of 2004 (Conn 2005, Figure 4.7). Arrows represent significant age coefficients; the arrow head is the expected value for those 25 years younger than the mean, the arrow tail the expected value for those 25 years older than the mean. Solid vectors: significant for both F1 and F2. Dashed vectors: significant for F1 or F2 only. Reprinted by permission of the University of Pennsylvania

of (aw) has apparently passed a maximum and is now receding. The incipient lowering of /e/ in Figure 12.4 has become a new and vigorous change in Figure 12.6, moving down and back. But the stable /ahr/ is receding slightly, along with /oh/, the category with which it is now identified (oh).

The structural constraints on vowel shifting relevant to this discussion of endpoints are of several different kinds:

1   chain shifting:

    a   the tendency to maximum dispersion within subsystems, triggered by the subtraction from, or addition to, that subsystem;

    b   the tendency for vowels to rise along peripheral tracks and to fall along nonperipheral tracks;

2   parallel shifting: the tendency to generalize vowel shifts to members of the same subsystem;

3   mergers: the tendency for mergers to expand at the expense of distinctions.

The maximal dispersion tendency will logically reach an endpoint when maximal dispersion is restored; this may be the case in the Southern Shift. Raising along the peripheral track will logically reach an endpoint when the nucleus reaches high position. This seems to be the case in the raising of /æh/ in the Northern Cities Shift. The fronting of the back vowels, common in North American English as well as in the history of several other languages, seems to reach a limit when the nuclei reach front nonperipheral position. In the Outer Banks of North Carolina – and also in Norwich, England, in Australia and in New Zealand – this fronting of the nucleus has been followed by a fronting of the glide (LYS: 135–44) and, in earlier periods of the history of English, by a loss of rounding and merger with front vowels. Nevertheless, the targets [ɪu] and [ɛo] seem to be reasonably stable endpoints in North American English. Finally, the logical endpoint of mergers is simply the loss of any distinction among the merging classes.

Another aspect of the endpoint question is the generalization of linguistic change to equal use by all members of a speech community. The social differentiation of sound change in progress can lead to stable social stratification, as in the case of negative concord or (ING) in English, *ne* deletion in French or aspiration and deletion of /s/ in Spanish and Portuguese. But more often the change goes to completion, affecting all members of the speech community equally. As we have seen, the oldest stratum of Philadelphia sound changes includes the backing and raising of /ahr/ in *car* or *card* to lower mid back position. At present there is no social differentiation of this feature: upper-class, middle-class and working-class Philadelphians have the same phonetic range, with no significant regression coefficients for age or gender. Consider also the Philadelphia lexical split of the short-*a* class into tense and lax members. The oldest working-class speakers and the oldest upper-class speakers share the same distribution: tense before voiceless fricatives and front nasals, except for irregular verbs and weakly stressed words; and tense before *mad, bad, glad* but lax for all other syllables closed by /d/ (*Dad, pad*, etc.).

It is often thought that speech communities can be subdivided without limit, so that cities can be divided into sections, which are in turn divided into neighborhoods, which are divided into blocks, which are divided into yet smaller networks. Empirical studies of the great cities – New York, Philadelphia, Montreal, Buenos Aires, Cairo – show that this is not so. Geographic neighborhoods within the city do differ, but only in so far as their linguistic differences reflect their social class composition. Though it may be difficult for New Yorkers to believe, *Brooklynese* is simply a label for working-class New York City speech (Labov 1966). It appears that a metropolis of more than one million inhabitants is indeed a geographically unified speech community, marked by uniformity of structure, general agreement in the evaluation of social variables, and social differentiation of both stable sociolinguistic variables and changes in progress. In many ways, this degree of uniformity is more difficult to account for than divergence. It still remains to be explained how the entire community reaches the same endpoints of linguistic change. Figures 9.5

and 9.6 show all Philadelphia social groups moving in the same direction, even though the changes involved were initially associated with social groups that could not reasonably be taken as reference groups for the entire community. How does such a situation come about, time and time again?

12.3   The Eckert Progression as the Product of Re-Analysis by Language Learners

The fundamental feature of the Eckert progression displayed in Figure 9.2 is that gender differentiation replaces social class differentiation over time – a process observed in the suburban Detroit high schools, in Philadelphia, and in the Inland North as a whole (Table 9.1).[4] It was observed in Philadelphia that the degree of gender differentiation rises and falls as one passes from incipient changes to new and vigorous changes, mid-range, almost completed and completed changes. It is not unreasonable to attribute the first part of this process to a general tendency for first-language learners to reinterpret social class differences as gender differences. We have also seen how the gender asymmetry in language transmission logically leads to the observed predominance of female leadership in linguistic change (Labov 1990, PLC, Vol. 2, Chs 13–14). Female-dominated changes will be accelerated in transmission, as women pass on to their children a relatively advanced form of the change. On the other hand, male-dominated changes will progress less vigorously, since the predominantly female caretakers will be transmitting less advanced forms of these variables to their children. The question before us is to account for the origin of gender bias in language change.

The proposal put forward here is that this bias results from the re-analysis of social class differences as gender differences by first-language learners. Children acquire a knowledge of gender differentiation much earlier in life than they acquire knowledge of social differences. At an early stage in their third year of life, children recognize that people are divided into two major categories, male and female; and they can label pictures of each verbally (Kohlberg 1966, Weinraub et al. 1984). At 31 months, most children can say whether they are male or female, and by the end of the third year they show awareness of the fact that some activities and behaviors are associated more with one sex than another. On the other hand, most children's experiences with social class differences begin considerably later. A child's first contacts with people of different social backgrounds will normally occur as s/he leaves the home environment for daycare or school. I am suggesting here that, when children do come across class differences in language, they have a tendency to reinterpret those differences according to categories they already know, which are, to them, the most salient and familiar ones – in other words they will tend to attribute such differences to gender roles. By the logic outlined above, this tendency will be accelerated when the newer forms are heard from (and associated with) females, and it will proceed at a slower pace when they are associated with male linguistic behavior.

It is not suggested that gender differences are transmitted from parents to their children in first-language learning. The evidence of Figures 9.8 and 9.9 indicates that little boys do not learn the pattern of their fathers, but begin where their mothers are – so that, in each successive generation, males show an upward trend. They do not adopt their Philadelphian mothers' forms of /aw/ in *house*, *mouth*, *south* as typical female forms, but rather as the community norm. This suggests a second general tendency: to reinterpret the initial caretaker's norms as the general norm of the community rather than as specifically female behavior.

The fact that most changes go to completion indicates that the outcome of the Eckert progression is not stable. Gender differentiation does not continue indefinitely. On the contrary, the difference between males and females disappears as the change continues. Thus Conn (2005) found that the predominance of males in the centralization of (ay0) in Philadelphia, so prominent in 1976, had disappeared by 2005.

In Figure 9.8, females seem to show an asymptotic approach to some limiting value of the change. These limiting values are the endpoints that are the focus of this chapter. The differences between male and female speakers disappear as the change nears such an endpoint. In sum, endpoints of vowel changes are found:

a   for mergers, in the complete loss of distinction between the merging classes;
b   for chain shifts, in the re-establishment of maximal dispersion in the subsystems that were disturbed by the triggering event;
c   for parallel shifts, at the limit of the phonological space occupied by the subsystem affected.

In cases (b) and (c), change seems to stop when the margin of security with a neighboring phoneme is roughly 200 Hz in the F2 dimension and 100 Hz in the F1 dimension. It is also important to note that some chain shifts are combined with mergers. Some terminate in mergers, as in the Back Chain Shift before /r/, where /uhr/ has no possibility of shifting to a fronter position. Others are initiated by mergers – like the Canadian Shift and the Pittsburgh Shift, both triggered by the low back merger of /o/ and /oh/. In both cases the shift reaches an endpoint when margins of security for unmerged members approach this limiting value.

Part C

The Unit of Linguistic Change

13

Words Floating on the Surface of Sound Change

One of the central questions of the mechanism of linguistic change concerns the unit of change: is it sounds or words that change? In recent decades it has been demonstrated that some changes proceed by lexical diffusion (Wang and Cheng 1977, Phillips 1980, Labov 1989b, Shen 1990, Krishnamurti 1998), whereby change proceeds gradually through the lexicon by the more or less arbitrary selection of individual words. In most such cases, there is a correlation of word frequency with order of selection (Fidelholtz 1975, Hooper 1976, Phillips 1984). Nevertheless, for most historical and comparative linguists the regularity of sound change is the basic working principle, and the finding that a given change follows a regular Neogrammarian path is not a publishable result.

Though there has been some critical reaction to evidence for lexical diffusion (Pulleyblank 1978, PLC, Vol. 1), there has not yet been any systematic effort among contemporary researchers in dialectology and linguistic variation to demonstrate the regularity of sound change in which the basic unit of change is the phoneme. ANAE provides a data set that renders such an exploration feasible: measurements of 130,000 stressed vowels, representing the speech of 439 subjects in 205 cities. This yields a wide range of words to examine; for example there are 610 different words in the 8,314 tokens of /ow/.

This chapter examines three changes in progress which appear to be candidates for regular Neogrammarian change. We will examine the fronting of /uw/ in all of North America; the fronting of /ow/ in the Midland and the South; and the general raising of /æ/ in the Inland North. Multiple regression will be used to determine the relative influence of phonetic environment, contextual style, social factors, lexical identity and word frequency as determined in the Brown corpus (Kucera and Francis 1967).

13.1   The Issues Reviewed

The principle of the regularity of sound change, as discussed in PLC, Volume 1, Chapter 15, is encapsulated in the original statement of the Neogrammarians: "Every sound change, inasmuch as it occurs mechanically, takes place according to laws that admit no exception" (Osthoff and Brugmann 1878) – and in the structural interpretation of this position by Bloomfield:

> Sound-change is merely a change in the speakers' manner of producing phonemes and accordingly, affects a phoneme at every occurrence, regardless of the nature of any particular linguistic form in which the phoneme happens to occur [. . .] The whole assumption can be briefly put into the words: *phonemes change*. (Bloomfield 1933: 353–4)

Yet other scholars – primarily Romance dialectologists – insisted on the word as the fundamental unit of change, as exemplified in the slogan "Chaque mot a son histoire" (see Malkiel 1967, PLC, Vol. 1: 472–4).

In recent times, the primacy of the word has been reemphasized by Wang and his associates: "We hold that words change their pronunciations by discrete, perceptual increments (i.e., phonetically abrupt) but severally at a time (i.e., lexically gradual)" (Cheng and Wang 1977: 150). Labov (1981) recognized the existence of both types of change, and attempted to resolve the controversy by defining the conditions under which each type was to be found. It was proposed that regular sound change is the result of a gradual transformation of a single phonetic feature of a phoneme in a continuous phonetic space, and that lexical diffusion is the result of the abrupt substitution of one phoneme for another in words that contain that phoneme. Nonetheless, proponents of lexical diffusion have continued to insist that the word is the fundamental unit in all sound changes, and that regularity is to be found only in the outcome (the endpoints of the last chapter). "The lexically gradual view of sound change is incompatible, in principle, with the structuralist way of looking at sound change" (Chen and Wang 1975: 257).

To make the definition of lexical diffusion more testable, the concept of "word" needs to be specified. It is not likely that the word is the basic unit in play, since we do not find cases where different inflectional forms are selected in sound change. Thus Labov (1989b), Roberts and Labov (1995), and Brody (2009) find that in the lexical diffusion of short *a* in Philadelphia, *planet* is selected for tensing in the subset before intervocalic nasals. In New York City, *avenue* is the only item where short *a* is tensed before intervocalic voiced fricatives. There has never been any indication that the plural forms *planets* or *avenues* behave differently from the singular, though singular and plural forms are different words. It appears that, when we find that change is proceeding by lexical diffusion, the unit of selection is the stem – that is, the root with all its derivational affixes, before the addition of inflectional suffixes.[1]

A second issue for lexical diffusion is the unspecified nature of the selection of such stems. Lexical diffusion through the vocabulary cannot be predictable and systematic: if it is, then the basis of that selection is the mechanism of change, not lexical diffusion. To be identified as lexical diffusion, the process of selection must have an arbitrary and unpredictable character. Phonetic constraints on stem selection may be present in this process, but they are not determinative. The same may be said for grammatical constraints like function word status or morphological composition, and for analogical patterns as well.

Frequency (of stem or lemma) is almost always associated with lexical diffusion, and indeed the presence of frequency effects is often taken as a test for lexical diffusion (Bybee 2002, Phillips 2006, Dinkin 2008). Nevertheless, frequency effects, when they do occur, do not predict which stems will be selected next, but rather establish only the probability of selection.

Finally, it is argued that the selection of particular words may be influenced by the need to preserve meaning (Gilliéron 1918). This is in direct opposition to the Neogrammarian view that sound change is a mechanical phonetic process uninfluenced by semantics or the desire of speakers to communicate. Many demonstrations of such meaning preserving events have been put forward and indeed cited at length by Bloomfield, though it has never been quite demonstrated whether such lexical adjustments occurred in the course of the sound change or after it was completed.

In contrast, regular sound change is projected as affecting every word in which the given sound occurs in the specified phonetic environment, irrespective of frequency, meaning or grammatical status.

The evidence for the basic unit of sound change – the stem or the phoneme – is asymmetrical in terms of scholarly citations. All recent papers on the topic that come to my attention are reports of lexical diffusion. Conversely, no proponent of lexical diffusion has found evidence of regular sound change. This would seem to be decisive, were it not for the consideration, noted in the first paragraph of this chapter, that the historical and comparative linguists who work on the assumption of regularity do not write papers confirming this assumption, even when all members of a given word class show the same behavior. No one body of historical evidence examined to date has been lexically rich enough to provide a decisive demonstration of one or the other viewpoint. For this reason, it seems reasonable to make use of the massive evidence of ANAE to explore this question.

13.2   The Fronting of /uw/

Map 13.1 of ANAE shows that the fronting of /uw/ after coronals (*too, two, do, noon, suit,* etc.) is characteristic of all North American English dialects, in that the mean F2 value of the nucleus is higher than 1550 Hz, the grand mean in the

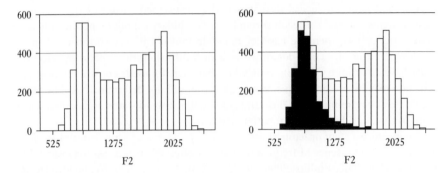

Figure 13.1 Distribution of second formant of /uw/ for all North American English dialects [N = 7,036]. Left: all tokens. Right: black = tokens before /l/s

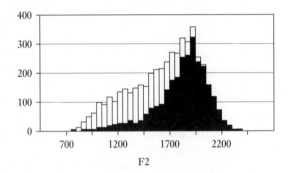

Figure 13.2 Distribution of F2 of /uw/ not before /l/ for all North American English dialects [N = 4,721]. Black = coronal onsets [Tuw]. (Mean = 1811 Hz.)

logmean normalized system. The few exceptions to this pattern are found in Minnesota, Southern Wisconsin, Northern New Jersey, Eastern New England and a scattering of eight speakers in the Inland North. Fronting of /uw/ after noncoronals (*roof, move, boot,* etc.) is more regionally delimited, as shown in ANAE, Map 12.2. These vowels are front of center only in the Midland and the South, and are well to the back (< 1200 Hz) in the North and New England. The West and Canada show an intermediate pattern.

Figure 13.1 displays the second formant distribution of all /uw/ in the ANAE data. The bimodal distribution on the left might appear at first sight to be evidence that only some lexical items are being selected and others are not. But this pattern is entirely a product of the major phonetic constraint, the effect of a following /l/. In Figure 13.2, which shows the distribution for all /uw/ not before /l/, the bimodal effect disappears. We do note a skewing to the left, a phenomenon that played an important role in the discussion of endpoints in Chapter 11.

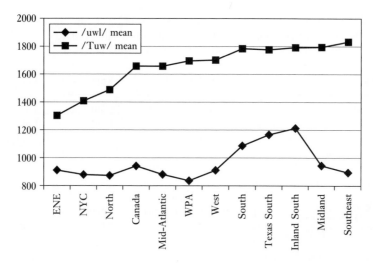

Figure 13.3   Second formant of /uw/ after coronals and /uw/ before /l/ by dialect region

Figure 13.3 charts the effect of a following lateral in retarding the fronting of /uw/ for twelve dialect regions. The upper line shows the mean value of /Tuw/, the allophone after coronal onsets, which ranges from around 1300 Hz for Eastern New England to just above 1800 Hz for the Midland and the southeast (the Southern perimeter). The lower line shows that, for 9 of the 12 regions, the F2 of /uw/ before /l/ is well below 1000 Hz. It rises slightly above that limit for the three dialects defined as members of the South by monophthongization of /ay/ before voiced obstruents.[2]

Table 13.1 examines the full range of phonetic features that influence the fronting of /uw/ as a whole. The first column of Table 13.1, Run 1, shows the result of a multiple regression analysis that accounts for a very large part of the variance – over two thirds, with adjusted r^2 at 68.5 percent. This analysis is the result of many trials aimed at achieving the maximum explanation of variance by phonetic effects alone, yielding a uniform and stable set of regression coefficients. All effects selected here show a probability of $p \leq .0001$.

The largest single effect, as one would expect, is the negative impact of a following lateral (−570 Hz). In this analysis there is only one other coda effect: the positive factor associated with final (that is, open) position, as in *do, two, too,* etc.

There are eight coefficients associated with the form of the onset, listed from the most positive to the most negative. In this detailed phonetic analysis, the large positive effect of coronal onset noted in Chapter 5 is broken up into a few positive effects and many large negative effects of noncoronal features. An initial /st/ cluster

Table 13.1   Significant regression coefficients (p < .01) of F2 of /uw/ in ANAE data.
Run 1: Phonological factors only. Run 2: Social and stylistic factors added.
Run 3: Lexical items added (N > 25). Runs 4, 5: Random split of Run 3

Variable	Run 1	Run 2	Run 3	Run 4 (odd)	Run 5 (even)
N	6,955	6,955	6,578	3,501	3,454
Constant	1,698	1,710	1,721	1,755	1,693
Adj r^2	68.5%	72.5%	72.5%	71.8%	73.5%
Coda					
Free	90	109	103	94	113
Lateral	−570	−569	−569	−556	−581
Onset					
/st/	271	249	244	299	185
Nasal	98	93	87	116	59
/d/	72	50	47	52	43
NonCor_NonCor	−135	−132	−130	−135	−127
Velar	−137	−132	−142	−127	−157
Labial stop	−185	−71	−74	−79	−69
Lateral	−159	−165	−179	−170	−187
Labial	−185	−194	−201	−204	−198
/h/	−249	−255	−268	−272	−262
Social					
South		189	188	192	182
Attention to speech		8	7	4	10
Age * 25 yrs		−57	−56	−78	−376
Lexical					
zoo			−172		−243
Vancouver			−148	−156	

(as in *stoop*) has the greatest influence on favoring the fronting process; it is followed by nasal onsets and by the voiced apical stop /d/. Progressively greater negative effects are shown for velars, labial stops (*pool, boot*), laterals, labials generally; and the most negative effect on F2 raising is initial /h/. The negative effect of labials is consistent with the low locus of labial consonantal transitions (*ca* 800 Hz). The joint effect of labials and velars is registered by the factor "NonCor_NonCor," which indicates that neither onset nor coda is coronal (that is, both are labial, velar or zero).

Among the onset effects, the favoring of /st/ and /d/ conforms to the relatively high locus of coronal transitions (*ca* 2800 Hz). Several onset influences are not so clearly predictable, for example the surprisingly large negative effect of an initial /h/ (represented primarily by *who, hoot, hoop* and *Hoover*).[3] The coefficient for

/st/ onsets is not obviously a phonological effect, since it is almost entirely repre-sented by the word *stoop*.

Run 2 adds three social and stylistic influences on the fronting of /uw/. The effects are significant, again, at the p < .0001 level, but their total contribution to explaining the variation is relatively small: r^2 rises by only 4 percent. Still, the fronting of /uw/ is plainly a change in progress in apparent time, with a negative coefficient of –57 Hz for every twenty-five years of age. Across three generations the shift is considerable: /uw/ is projected to show an F2 mean 114 Hz greater for Generation III than for Generation I.

The factor "Attention to speech" is realized by stylistic ratings on the following well-known scale, used to classify the degree of formality within a sociolinguistic interview:

1   casual speech
2   careful speech
3   group
4   elicited
5   reading text
6   word lists
7   minimal pairs

It is interesting to note that the fronting of /uw/, which is occurring well below the surface of conscious attention, is favored when attention is directed to pronun-ciation, as in the minimal pairs *dew* and *do*.[4]

The third social factor is the speaker's location in the South (as defined by the monophthongization of /ay/ before voiced obstruents and word-finally – see ANAE, Chapter 18). This is a strongly positive effect, registering the fact that the fronting of /uw/ is more advanced in the South than in the Midland, Mid-Atlantic, or peripheral areas of the southeast.

The addition of social and stylistic factors in Run 2 produces no change in the phonological factors, which retain their significance at the level of p < .0001 and show only slight quantitative shifts. This result confirms the general finding that internal constraints on a sound change are normally independent of social and stylistic factors.

What will happen if we now take into account the lexical identities of the tokens and the frequency of those lexical items? If the sound change does select words one at a time, the phonological constraints should shrink or disappear, and be replaced by lexical identities. To answer this question, the stressed /uw/ words that occurred more than twenty-five times in the ANAE corpus (set thirty-one in all) were each added as a separate factor in the regression analysis of Table 13.1. The result is reported as Run 3, which shows only coefficients with a significance level of p < .01. Two of the thirty-one appear as significant effects at the p < .01 level: *zoo* (N = 25) and *Vancouver* (N = 28). None of the effects of Runs 1 and 2 disappear. There are only small fluctuations in the numbers, and the significance level of p < .0001 remains for all except "Attention to speech," which drops to p < .01.

It is possible that the negative effect of *zoo* reflects the combined phonetic effects of onset /z/ and free position, but such a phonetic definition is indistinguishable from lexical identity. Similarly, the negative coefficient for *Vancouver* may be the result of the complex syllabic construction of this word. Since there are no other words that satisfy this description, the issue of lexical versus phonetic motivation is here moot.

As noted above, lexical frequency is a major factor in those cases where lexical diffusion has been clearly established. However, the frequency of words in the ANAE data set cannot be related directly to frequency in the language as a whole, since many of the key words were concentrated by elicitation, using techniques like the semantic differential ("What's the difference between a *pond* and a *pool?*"). Frequencies in the Brown corpus were therefore added as a factor in Run 3.[5] In this run, Brown frequency was not a factor at any level of significance.

The addition of this lexical information does not raise the amount of variance accounted for. The adjusted r^2 remains at 72.5 percent. We conclude that lexical identity has not added any substantial amount of explanation of the manner in which this sound change proceeds.

Another way to test the robustness or importance of regression effects is to split the data set and see which effects are maintained, indicating how completely they penetrate the data. Runs 4 and 5 of Table 13.1 give the results of a division that is independent of the lexical and phonological distribution. Run 4 shows results for all items spoken by speakers whose subject numbers are odd, and Run 5 for all those whose subject numbers are even.[6] The effects from Run 3 that are preserved in each split half are shown in the final two columns. Robust effects are those that are preserved in both Runs 4 and 5 (normally at the p < .00001 level, but minimally at the p < .01 level).

The ten phonological effects are preserved in both halves at the p < .0001 level, with only small differences in the numerical values of the coefficients. The three social factors recur in both halves, with very little change. But neither of the lexical effects is found in both halves of the data.

Figure 13.4 shows the mean F2 values for the thirty-one words with frequency greater than twenty-five, which were tested for significance in Table 13.1. Those with lateral codas are grouped at the lower left. One can recognize slight phonetic effects within this group; the one item with an apical onset, *tool*, has the highest F2. But it is a good 224 Hz lower than *coop*, the least fronted word in the other two sets. The main body of words is most neatly divided into those with coronal onsets and noncoronal onsets, although the more detailed analysis of Table 13.1 uncovered more explanatory factors.

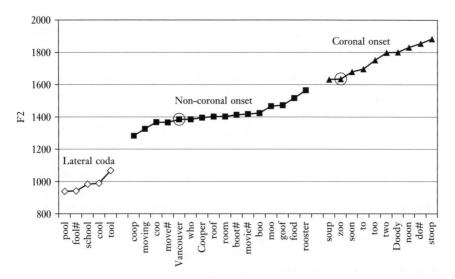

Figure 13.4 Mean F2 values for the thirty-one /uw/ words which occur more than twenty-five times in the ANAE data. Circled items show significant lexical effects in Run 3. # indicates stems with more than one inflectional form

The two circled items, *Vancouver* and *zoo*, are among the least frequent in the data set, and it is not likely that they represent linguistically significant events within the sound change. They emerge from an initial analysis in which all thirty-one items are retained without regard to their significance, with the following distribution:

p < .0001	p < .001	p < .01	p < .05	p > .05
school	*Vancouver*	*Cooper*	*5 items*	*15 items*
	zoo	*movie*		
		noon		
		tool		
		cool		

As the nonsignificant items are removed from the model, the probabilities of the remaining items decline, ultimately leading to the result of Run 3. Throughout this process the phonological and social factors remain stable, while the estimates of the lexical coefficients fluctuate noticeably. In another analysis in which coronal onset was substituted for the labial and velar onset factors, different lexical items emerged – *noon* and *coop* – and then disappeared in the split-half test.

Reviewing the evidence of Table 13.1 and of Figures 13.1–13.4, we can answer the question, "Does the fronting of /uw/ spread through the lexicon one word at a time?" The answer is, clearly, "No." All words which are not followed by an /l/ are selected to participate in the fronting process, and the rate of fronting is influenced primarily by their phonetic environment. Are there significant lexical effects on the fronting process? There is an indication of some kind of lexical differentiation, as a slight modification of forces that are fundamentally phonological.

13.3   The Fronting of /ow/

We can now apply the same techniques and the same logic to a parallel sound change: the fronting of /ow/ in North American English. This process differs in geographic range from the fronting of /uw/ in that it is basically confined to the Midland, the Mid-Atlantic region, the South and the peripheral southeast, a configuration named in ANAE as 'the Southeastern superregion' (Figure 13.5).

Figure 13.6 shows the distribution of the mean values of F2 for the 3,658 words measured for the Southeastern superregion. The bimodal configuration of Figure 13.1 does not emerge, but the strong effect of a following lateral is evident for /ow/ as for /uw/.

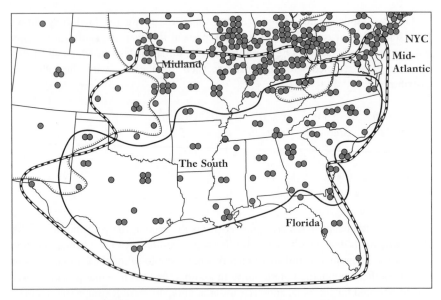

Figure 13.5 The Southeastern superregion, as indicated by the barred isogloss, including the Midland, the Mid-Atlantic region, the South and the peripheral areas outside the South proper (ANAE, Map 11.11)

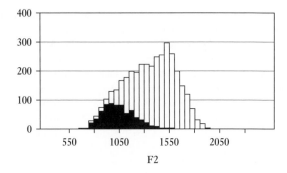

Figure 13.6 Distribution of /ow/ vowels for the Southeastern superregion [N = 3,658]. Vowels before /l/ are shown in black

Table 13.2 follows the analytic procedure of Table 13.1, applied to the fronting of /ow/ in the Southeastern superregion. Run 1 examines the twelve phonological influences on F2 for all coefficients whose t-test probability is less than .01 (in fact, p ≤ .0001 for all). The amount of variance accounted for by phonology is 50.8 percent, somewhat less than for /uw/, since there is more regional variation for /ow/ even within the Southeastern region. Again, the largest single effect is that of a following lateral, −394 Hz. Free position favors the advancement of the /ow/ nucleus, while a following labial, velar, or nasal all retard it, with a somewhat smaller effect of following syllables.

Turning to the onset conditions, we note immediately considerable reduction in the negative effect of noncoronals, a major feature in the fronting of /uw/.[7] As with the coda, the absence of any consonant favors fronting, as does the presence of an apical nasal. Four onset features retard fronting at about the same level: onset glottal /h/, lateral, stop plus lateral, and labial. All of these are expected results of consonantal articulation, traceable to tongue movements and transition shapes in the acoustic signal. However, the size of the negative effect of initial /h/, which is about twice that of other effects, is again surprising, since /h/ as a voiceless vowel should have no coarticulatory influence on a following vowel (see note 3).

Run 2 of Table 13.2 adds the significant social effects, which are somewhat different from those encountered in the case of /uw/. There is a female advantage of 40 Hz. The stylistic component is here the reverse of the one for /uw/. It is represented by the same scale of attention paid to speech from 1 to 7, where increasing attention is registered by higher numbers. The effect is −9, so that the difference between the main body of spontaneous speech (level 2) and minimal pairs (level 7) would be −45 Hz.

Finally we note that the fronting of /ow/ in the Southeastern superregion is advancing in apparent time more slowly than /uw/, at a rate of −16 Hz per 25 years of age, as compared to −57 Hz for /uw/. Again, the contribution of social factors

Table 13.2 Significant regression coefficients (p < .01) of F2 of /ow/ in the Southeastern superregion. Run 1: Phonological factors only. Run 2: Social and stylistic factors added. Run 3: 35 lexical items added. Runs 4 and 5: Random split of Run 3a

Variable	Run 1	Run 2	Run 3	Run 3a	Run 4 (odd)	Run 5 (even)
N	3,658	3,658	3,658	3,658	1,669	1,989
Constant	1,523	1,559	1,570	1,558	1,631	1,523
Adj r^2	50.8%	51.6%	52.2%	52.3%	56.0%	50.4%
Coda						
None	95	95	91	58	76	65
Polysyllabic	−53	−50	−54	−47	−104	−42
Velar	−67	−55	−57	−92		−108
Labial	−89	−85	−83	−86	−50	−111
Nasal	−110	−114	−105	−103	−104	−94
Lateral	−394	−387	−388	−377	−371	−390
Onset						
None	89	87	86	76	65	96
Apical nasal	82	78	99	106	82	130
Glottal	−101	−117	−99	−93	−123	−100
Lateral	−111	−75	−121	−103	−121	−71
Stop/lateral	−118	−124	−129	−114	−146	−98
Labial	−138	−142	−142	−134	−137	−144
Social						
Attention		−9	−10	−10	−20	
Female		40	40	39	72	
Age * 25 yrs		−16	−17	−17	−43	
Lexical						
Frequency			*−.02			
going			−253	−304	−211	−455
ocean				128	173	
doe				110		
coke				70		*77
know				57		*75
go#				53		77
goat				*61		
pole				*−65		

* p < .05

is small compared to that of phonological factors: the percentage of variance accounted for increases by only 0.9 percent.

The main focus of this examination is the /ow/ lexicon and its possible influence on the fronting of the nucleus. Figure 13.7 compares the ANAE /ow/ vocabulary to the /uw/ vocabulary by the frequency of these words in the Brown corpus.

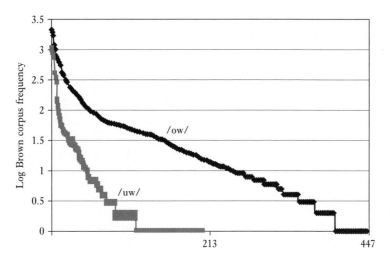

Figure 13.7   Distribution of /uw/ and /ow/ tokens in the ANAE database by Brown corpus frequency

There are twice as many items in the /ow/ set as in the /uw/ set, and a much higher range of frequencies. The total number of vowels measured by ANAE is not so much greater than for /uw/ (8,813 versus 6,578), but it is evident that the /ow/ vocabulary makes up a much larger component of the English text.

To estimate the extent of lexical diffusion in the fronting of /ow/, Run 3 of Table 13.2 considered thirty-two stems with frequency greater than twenty-five in the ANAE database. These are displayed in Table 13.3, with frequencies in the entire ANAE database and in the Southeastern superregion. They are grouped into eight items with /l/ codas, eight with coronal onsets and sixteen with neither of these features.

None of these thirty-two items appears in Run 3 of Table 13.2 as a significant effect at the p < .01 level. However, one inflectional form of the go# stem, *going*, significantly retards fronting. There are eleven tokens in the Southeastern data, with a mean F2 value of 1170 Hz, while the word *go* with no inflection has a mean F2 of 1548 Hz. Frequency in the Brown corpus is a marginally significant effect in this run at p < .05 (such marginal probabilities are indicated with an asterisk in the table). The effect of −.02 is half as large as that registered in Run 3 of Table 13.1, but here it is negative: frequency disfavors the fronting of /ow/ instead of favoring it.

So far, the criterion for a significant effect has been p < .01, since a search of more than twenty items is likely to produce at least one .05 effect by chance. If we relax this criterion and permit .05 effects to remain, we obtain the result of Run 3a, with seven additional lexical items, five at the p < .01 level and two at the p < .05 level. It is important to note that these are additive effects, which do not replace any of the previous findings. Comparison of the phonological and social

Table 13.3 Frequencies of thirty-two /ow/ stems entered into regression analysis in Run 3 of Table 13.2 for all ANAE data and the Southeastern superregion. # indicates a stem with several inflectional forms

Noncoronal onset			Coronal onset			Prelateral		
Word	All	SE	Word	All	SE	Word	All	SE
home#	695	284	no	348	163	cold#	270	115
go#	398	176	soda	406	148	bowl#	202	100
coat#	398	165	toast#	253	102	goal	137	67
both	218	96	sofa#	231	93	old#	209	88
coke	136	91	know#	199	97	pole#	82	45
boat#	213	109	doe	37	21	gold	60	29
most	153	77	donut#	83	20	Polish	59	23
goat#	179	88	notice#	60	22	fold#	47	25
phone#	107	38						
road#	77	38						
mostly	47	22						
over	63	21						
ago	37	18						
Minnesota	57	15						
ocean	27	13						
coast#	61	10						

variables for Runs 2 and 3 shows only small changes; in no case are phonological effects replaced by lexical effects. The amount of additional variance explained is very small: r^2 rises by only 0.1 percent.

Figure 13.8 displays the mean F2 values of thirty high frequency /ow/ words in the Telsur data. Unlike the distribution of /uw/ words in Figure 13.4, there are here only two separate ranges: vowels before /l/ and all others. The seven circled symbols are those with coefficients listed in Run 3a. There is a concentration in the upper end of the main sequence, all positive coefficients, indicating that the lexical items are slightly ahead of what their segmental structure would predict. The one item in the prelateral group, *pole*, shows the opposite tendency to be further back than its phonology would predict.

Runs 4 and 5 follow the technique, used in Table 13.1, of splitting Run 3a into those speakers with even and with odd subject numbers, in order to determine which constraints are retained in both halves of the data set. Only one of the twelve phonological effects fails to recur in both halves: the negative effect of a velar coda. None of the three social factors survives in the even half of the data set. Finally, none of the seven marginal lexical items that were added in Run 3a

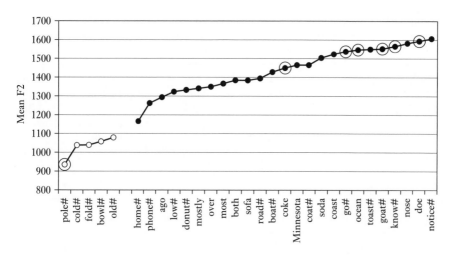

Figure 13.8   Mean F2 values of all /ow/ words submitted to regression analysis in Run 3. Open symbols = vowels before /l/. Circled symbols = words with positive coefficients, p < .05

is selected as significant in both halves of the data, which demonstrates that, as for /uw/, the lexical effects which appear in regression analyses for /ow/ are tenuous at best.

13.4   Homonyms

Homonyms are key elements in the search for lexical diffusion. One of the early arguments for lexical development was the split of tones for homonymous words in the Chinese dialect of Chaozhou (Cheng and Wang 1977). Two of the most frequent /ow/ words in the ANAE data are *know* and *no*, and in the /uw/ data set we can examine *two* and *too*.[8] These pairs were analyzed in the Philadelphia data of Tables 16.6 and 16.7 in PLC, Vol. 1, and no significant difference emerged. Since the ANAE data set is about ten times larger, we may be able to detect a difference. In fact, Table 13.4 shows that *no* and *two* are significantly different in the advancement of F2.

Figure 13.9 is a scattergram of all tokens of *no* and *know* in F1/F2 space. For most of the area, the two words are strongly overlapped. But one can observe a heavy concentration of *no* in the lower left corner of the diagram, where few tokens of *know* are to be found. These are the affective, emphatic tokens of the negative, which are more open and fronter than ordinary words. They suggest that prosodic rather than lexical factors are responsible for these small effects.

Table 13.4 Comparison of F2 for two homonymous pairs in all ANAE data

	know	*no*	*two*	*too*
N	179	348	825	346
Mean	1409	1497	1801	1752
Standard deviation	239	214	260	265
t-test	t = 4.327, df = 525,		t = 2.93, df = 1,169,	
	p < .0001		p < .01	

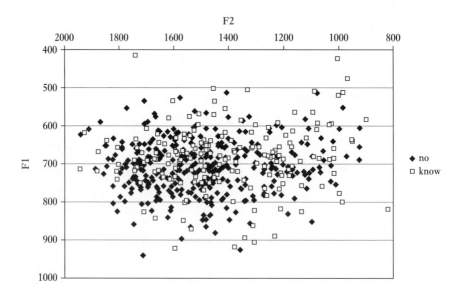

Figure 13.9 Distribution of *no* and *know* tokens in all ANAE data

13.5   The Raising and Fronting of /æ/ in the Inland North

The third examination of the extent of lexical differentiation in sound change focuses on the raising and fronting of /æ/ in the Inland North. The general raising of /æ/ is a good candidate for a regular Neogrammarian sound change. In contrast with the short-*a* split in New York City and in the Mid-Atlantic region, this raising has shown no evidence of grammatical or lexical conditioning (Fasold 1969, LYS 1972, Callary 1975). It has been proposed as the triggering event of the Northern

Table 13.5 Significant regression coefficients (p < .01) of the raising of /æ/ along the front diagonal in the Inland North. Run 1: phonological factors only. Run 2: social and stylistic factors added. Run 3: thirty-five lexical items added. Runs 4 and 5: random split of Run 3

Variable	Run 1	Run 2	Run 3	Run 4 (odd)	Run 5 (even)
N	2,672	2,672	2,672	1,516	1,156
Constant	2,403	21,952	1,512	1,606	2,076
Adj r^2	18.0%	23.0%	23.1%	19.8%	30.9%
Coda					
Nasal	127	129	130	146	111
Nasal cluster	50	54	53	59	
Coda complexity	−19	−10	−11	−13	−70
Following syllable	−72	−61	−66	−55	−76
Onset					
Apical	82	105	104	118	100
Labial	40	39	38	39	31
Lateral	−53	−56	−56		−68
/s/	−34	−46	−46	−39	−47
/b/	−64	−74	−73	−85	−53
Glottal	64	72	67	73	77
Social					
Attention to speech		28	27	17	38
Female		37	36		78
Age * 25 yrs		35	33		76
City size (in millions)		11	11		22
Lexical					
unhappy			31		

Cities Shift in the many studies of that phenomenon (LYS 1972, Eckert 2000, Gordon 2000, 2001, Murray 2002, Jones 2003). Throughout, the NCS has shown fine-grained phonetic conditioning characteristic of Neogrammarian change. None of these studies has searched specifically for lexical effects on this process, so it is not possible to affirm that they do not exist until this has been done.

Table 13.5 registers the analysis of the raising and fronting of /æ/ in the Inland North. In this case, both F2 and F1 are involved in the measure of movement along the front diagonal:

$$D = \sqrt{(2 * F1)^2 + F2^2}$$

Run 1 found ten phonological constraints on the raising process at the p < .01 level of significance. The well-known nasal effect is the largest, even though the

Table 13.6 Frequencies of 25 /æ/ stems entered into regression analysis of Run 3 in Table 13.5 for all ANAE data and Inland North region

Nasal	ALL	IN	Voiced stop	ALL	IN	Fricative	ALL	IN	Voiceless stop	ALL	IN
pants	368	52	bag	733	147	half	179	15	Saturday	418	63
Dan	277	35	bad	813	110	last	140	15	sack	544	111
pancakes	163	23	tag	393	73	have	248	36	back	518	67
ham	251	33	sad	464	84	has	137	36	hat	335	43
man	82	19	mad	294	77				accent	233	26
Spanish	204	25	dad	222	36				jacket	211	26
family	221	25							unhappy	197	26
									black	162	11

distinguishing feature of this general raising in the Inland North is the relatively small difference between nasal and oral environments. In addition, there is an additional effect of nasal clusters, as in *pants* or *hand*. On the other hand, the existence of any kind of complex coda has a small negative effect on raising. Considerably larger is the retarding action of one or more following syllables, as in *family* or *Spanish*. The onset effects show a favoring influence of initial apicals, as reported in previous studies, and a negative influence of laterals. Labials are intermediate, with a lower positive coefficient than apicals. Not previously reported is a set of specific onset conditions: a negative influence of initial /b/ (as opposed to other labials), of /s/ (as opposed to other apicals), and the same favoring effect of initial /h/ that appeared in previous tables.

Although these phonological constraints are sizable and mostly significant at the p < .0001 level, the total amount of variance explained is not large, only 18 percent. Run 2, which includes social and stylistic factors, adds 5 percent more.

As with the fronting of /uw/, greater attention paid to speech leads to more raising.[9] Female speakers are ahead of males, as previous reports indicated. However, the age coefficient indicates some recession of /æ/, while ANAE reports no age effect for F1 (ANAE, Table 14.6). City size is a small but significant factor: cities with greater population than another by one million will be eleven units further along the diagonal. Again, we note only slight changes in the size of the phonological coefficients with the addition of social factors, since the latter are normally independent of internal constraints.

Run 3 makes the critical addition of the twenty-five lexical items listed in Table 13.6. These are stems with more than eighty tokens in the ANAE lexicon as a whole, and more than fifteen in the Inland North. They represent all the major classes of segmental environments, including /æ/ before nasals, voiced stops, fricatives and voiceless stops. The end result shown in the Run 3 column is that only one word survives the demand for p < .01 significance: *unhappy*. If we relax this criterion as we did in Run 3a of Table 13.2, and allow a limit of p < .05, then four more words appear in the list: *black*, *has*, *Saturday* and *pants*.[10] The random character of these lexical selections may reflect the arbitrary character of lexical diffusion, but it is more likely that they represent statistical fluctuation. Once again, we see that adding a rich store of lexical items to the statistical model has no effect upon the factors established without them in Runs 1 and 2. Finally, we note that the split-half criterion for robustness, reported in Runs 4 and 5, eliminates this one remaining word from both halves. The four social and stylistic factors all fail to appear in one half or the other, but eight of the ten phonological factors are stable under this test.

13.6   Overview

The inquiries of this chapter have examined the extent of lexical differentiation in three sound shifts that affect large areas of North American English. The investigation has used quantitative methods to define the nature of this participation and found that, in each case, there is a small number of word stems that are significantly ahead of, or behind, what would be predicted by their segmental makeup. Unlike the major phonological effects, they are not robust enough to survive the split-half test. If we were to expand the data base to ten times the current size, we can suppose that many more such small lexical effects would appear, but in most cases we would be unable to resolve the difference between fine-grained phonetic and lexical description. Only in the case of frequent homonyms like *no* and *know* is it possible to demonstrate the influence of lexical identity.

13.7   Participation in Sound Change

It seems possible that some words differ in the extent of their participation in the ongoing sound changes, adding a very small amount to our understanding of the sources of variation. However, the fundamental issue to be resolved is whether the process of sound change selects words or stems one at a time, or phonologically defined units. The regression analyses of Tables 13.1, 13.2 and 13.5 treat the entire distribution of phonemes as continuous ranges. However, all the evidence points towards a discrete rule that fronts non-low vowels that are not followed by a liquid /l/ or /r/:

[1]   [–low] → [–back] / __~ [+cons, +voc]

Table 13.7 Regression analysis of all tokens of /ow/ in the Southeastern superregion before /l/ and other. All: Run 3 of Table 13.2

Variable	Prelateral	Other	All
N	1,558	2,909	3,658
Constant	926	1,578	1,570
Adj r²	9.9%	36.1%	52.2%
Coda			
None		57	91
Velar		−60	−57
Polysyllabic		−76	−54
Labial		−77	−86
Nasal		−115	−105
Onset			
Coronal	56		
None		113	86
Apical nasal		73	99
Glottal		−116	−99
Lateral		−133	−121
Stop/lateral		−145	−129
Labial		−181	−134
Social			
Attention to speech			−10
Female	−26	66	40
Age * 25 yrs	57	−43	−17
Lexical			
ocean		146	128
Pole	−60		

This rule will produce the overall break between the main body of /uw/ and /ow/, and the residual vowels before /l/ not affected by the sound change.

Table 13.7 shows separate regression analyses for /ow/ vowels before /l/ and all others. In the first column, it is evident that most phonological constraints do not apply to the vowels not affected by the sound change. The coda constraints are irrelevant by definition, and most onset constraints are missing, with only a small influence of coronal articulation. The social effects before /l/ are reversed: female gender and younger age favor backer forms of /owl/. On the other hand, constraints on the main body of /ow/ tokens, shown in the second column, are unaffected by the absence of the prelateral group, except for the lexical set. Of the five words added in Run 3a of Table 13.2, *ocean* proves to be significant for the nonlateral set and *pole* for the lateral set, with about the same values.

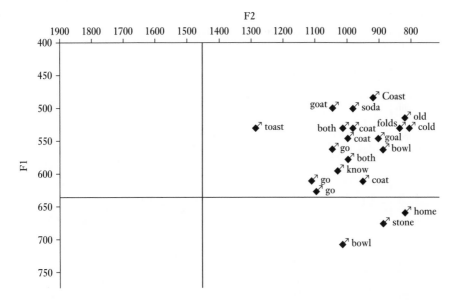

Figure 13.10 Conservative position of /ow/ in the vowel system of Alex S., 42 [1996], Providence, RI, TS 474 (double scale)

A closer view of this process can be obtained by comparing the /ow/ vowels of speakers with different degrees of advancement. Figure 13.10 is an expanded view of the conservative, unfronted pattern in the speech of a 42-year-old man from Providence, Rhode Island. Only the word *toast* is somewhat fronted; the rest are well below 1200 Hz in the F2 dimension, with a mean of less than 1000 Hz. It can also be observed that /ow/ before /l/ is backer than other allophones: thus *old*, *cold*, *bowl*, *fold*, *cold* are closer to the back periphery than the remaining tokens, with the exception of *home*.

Figure 13.11 shows a moderate degree of fronting in the speech of a 32-year-old woman from Cleveland, Ohio. The distribution is now bimodal. Ten /ow/ nuclei have F2 above 1200 Hz, but vowels before /l/ remain below 100 Hz, along with two tokens of *home*.

In Figure 13.12, the difference between prelateral and other tokens has become a gulf of 400 Hz. This is a arche typical Midland pattern, in this case of a 37-year-old woman from Columbus, Ohio. We see that the process of fronting fails categorically to apply to /ow/ before /l/. It makes no difference whether we are dealing with a common word like *gold* (Brown frequency 52) or a less common word like *colt* (frequency 18). No words before /l/ are selected, and no words not before /l/ fail to be selected.

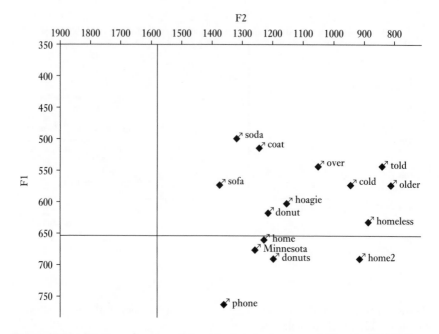

Figure 13.11   Moderate fronting of /ow/ in the vowel system of Alice R., 32 [1994], Cleveland, OH, TS 110

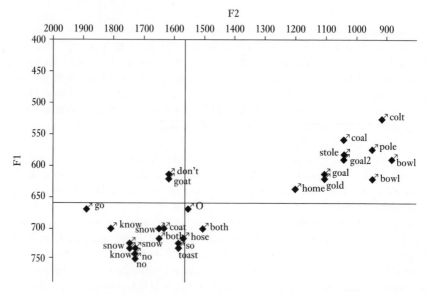

Figure 13.12   Advanced fronting of /ow/ in the vowel system of Danica L., 37 [1999], Columbus, OH, TS 737 (double scale)

Table 13.8   Mean F1 and F2 values of /ow/ words with onset /h/ and coda /m/

	N	F1	F2
/ow/ not before /l/	5,950	616	1304
All /owl/	2,576	575	1010
home	775	669	1068
Oklahoma	14	589	1045
homebody, etc.	28	641	1037
Omaha	10	655	1119
hoe	26	621	1233

Not quite. One word not before /l/ remains in back position in this figure: *home*. Though this is slightly fronter than the prelateral words, it appears to be a part of the unfronted distribution. The back position of *home* is evident in Figure 13.11, and is a repeated pattern throughout the Telsur vowel charts (see ANAE, Figures 12.13, 12.14). It seems that *home* is not selected by the rule in [1], which might have to be modified to exclude this and perhaps other lexical items.

However, it is also possible that the behavior of the vowel of *home* is predictable from its phonetic environment. In Table 13.7 we see that an initial /h/ has a coefficient of −116, and a following labial has one of −77. The combination of the two might well produce the effect seen in Figure 13.12. Here again, we may have a moot situation in which lexical identity and phonetic motivation cannot be distinguished.

Fortunately, we can attack the problematic status of *home* in a different way. There is another word in the ANAE corpus in which initial /h/ precedes and /m/ follows a stressed /ow/ vowel, and that is *Oklahoma*. As indicated in Table 13.8, there are fourteen tokens of this word in the data set. The words *home* and *Oklahoma* share nothing but the phonetic environment of /ow/.

Table 13.8 shows the mean F1/F2 values of the relevant words. Besides *home* and *Oklahoma*, we have a few derived forms like *homely* and *homeless*, and compounds like *homebody, homemaker, homestead, homework* – twenty-eight in all. To illustrate the effect of a following /m/ without initial /h/, I have included *Omaha*. The effect of initial /h/ without coda /m/ can be assessed with *hoe*.

Figure 13.13 displays the mean values of Table 13.8. It is evident that *home* and its derivatives are aligned with /ow/ before /l/ on the F2 dimension, but so is *Oklahoma*. *Omaha* is slightly fronter than this, but *hoe* is much fronter – only 71 Hz less than the mean for nonlateral /ow/.

If phonetic factors are indeed wholly responsible for the back position of *home*, it follows that the influence of a following /m/ is greater than the figures in Table 13.7 would lead us to predict. In fact, if we add an interactive factor of "Coda: Labial nasal" to Table 13.7, it contributes to the explanatory power of the model, with a

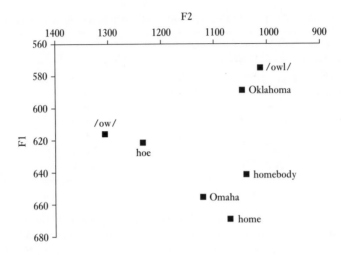

Figure 13.13   Mean values of words relevant to the *home* problem

coefficient of -79 and $p < .01$. The more general factor "Coda: Nasal" declines from -115 to -96, and "Coda: Labial" from -76 to -60. The expected value of F2 for *home* is then derived as follows:

[2]   Constant + Coda: Nasal + Coda: Labial + Coda: Labial nasal + Onset: Glottal
      1519   + (-70) + (-89) + (-79) + (-69) = 1212

The combined effect of labial and nasal features in the coda thus brings the prediction for /ow/ in this context close to the 1200 Hz line, which marks the limiting boundary of the unfronted allophones. The F2 value of 1068 for *home* in Table 13.8 is still lower, but the close grouping of *home*, *homebody* (*homeless*, etc.) and *Oklahoma* makes it seem most probable that this is the result of phonetic rather than lexical factors.

13.8   The Modular Separation of Phonological and Social Factors

Throughout this analysis it has been evident that, whatever lexical effects are found in the three sound changes studied, they are independent of the phonological and social factors. Addition of lexical items in the regression analysis did not affect the significance, direction or size of the phonological and social factors. This is not

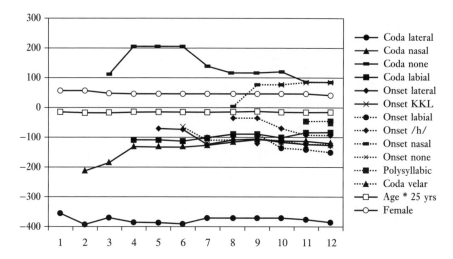

Figure 13.14   Progressive addition of phonological factors for /ow/ for the Southeastern superregion, with social factors included

what would be expected if the lexical and social information were stored in association with phonological information in the same set of memories. It also indicates that lexical differentiation (say, of *no* versus *know*) will be implemented at a different stage of production from that which realizes the phonemes /now/.

Such independence or modularity has been found to be characteristic of internal structural versus social and stylistic factors in previous studies (D. Sankoff and Labov 1979; Weiner and Labov 1983). The lexical influences we have detected in this chapter are too small and unstable to demonstrate this independence as clearly as if we had been studying a true case of lexical diffusion, such as the tensing of short *a* in Philadelphia. We do, however, obtain a clear view of the independence of phonological and social factors in these data, as displayed in the successive runs in Tables 13.1, 13.2 and 13.5.

The modularity of internal and external factors is displayed more directly in Table 13.9 and in Figure 13.14. Here the phonological factors that influence the fronting of /ow/ are added serially, beginning with the largest and proceeding to the smallest – the basic operation of stepwise regression. The two main social factors, age and gender, are maintained throughout. The amount of variation explained rises from 34.6 percent to 51.6 percent. As each new phonological factor is added, we observe changes in one or more other phonological factors. For example, when "Coda: Nasal" is added in Run 2 at a value of –212, the negative value of "Coda: Lateral" increases from –356 to –395. When "Coda: Labial" is added in Run 4 at –112, the value of "Coda: None" (free syllables) jumps from 109 to 207. This is equivalent to saying: "Free position favors fronting; but, if we now take into account

Table 13.9 Progressive addition of phonological factors for /ow/ for the Southeastern superregion, with social factors included

Run	1	2	3	4	5	6	7	8	9	10	11	12
Adjusted r	34.6	42.7	44.8	46.5	46.7	46.9	49.5	50.0	50.1	50.9	51.4	51.6
Coda: Lateral	−356	−395	−371	−387	−389	−391	−372	−371	−371	−373	−377	−388
Coda nasal		−212	−184	−129	−131	−132	−123	−109	−109	−103	−111	−115
Coda none			109	207	206	207	139	116	116	123	84	85
Coda labial				−112	−113	−115	−104	−93	−93	−101	−80	−86
Onset Lateral					−68	−71	−130	−120	−120	−120	−126	−118
Onset KKL						−63	−121	−111	−111	−112	−123	−124
Onset labial							−102	−92	−92	−135	−144	−142
Onset /h/								−35	−35	−68	−87	−95
Onset nasal									77	77	78	78
Onset none										77	78	88
Polysyllabic											−48	−50
Coda velar												−56
Age * 25 yrs	−16	−17	−17	−15	−15	−16	−17	−16	−16	−17	−16	−17
Female	55	54	47	46	46	46	46	46	46	45	43	41

that some of the low values of checked forms have prelabial lowering, then the effect of free position must be even greater to predict the observed values." Major shifts of this type can be observed throughout the twelve runs, even for the smaller effects at the end. The negative effect of onset /h/, added first at −35, increases to −95 as more small constraints are added.

On the other hand, the two social factors, indicated with open symbols, remain constant, with only slight fluctuations throughout the twelve runs. The negative factor "Age * 25 years" enters at −16, and nowhere does it rise above −17 or fall below −15.

13.9   Conclusion

These results confirm the view of sound change as a phonetically driven process that affects all words in a phonologically defined set. The close study of these regular sound changes in progress reveals them to be just as Paul, Leskien, Osthoff, Brugmann, Saussure and Bloomfield described them. When we engage the data directly, there are tantalizing glimpses of lexical peculiarities. But these are not the stable, robust parameters of phonetics and phonology. They hover at the edges of statistical significance, appear and disappear with changes in the analysis or sample size, and rarely repeat themselves. Some of this fluctuating behavior can be attributed to the arbitrary nature of the linguistic sign, but on the whole they seem to be statistical accidents.

That is not to say that all sound changes proceed like this. Part C of Volume 1 documented the solid case for changes that proceed word by word. Further progress is being made on defining the conditions that lead to lexical diffusion. Fruehwald (2007) argues that what was thought to be a regular sound change, namely Canadian raising of /ay/ in Philadelphia, is now showing unmistakable signs of lexical diffusion, probably as a result of the opacity of the *rider* ∼ *writer* merger. We continue to trace lexical diffusion in the short-*a* tensing of Philadelphia, where tensing before /l/ has moved towards completion while tensing before intervocalic /n/ has retreated to a single lexical item, *planet* (Brody 2009).

The most likely hypothesis is that regular sound change is the unmarked case. As with any negative demonstration, establishing the absence of lexical diffusion is a difficult undertaking, and in principle it will never be completed. The lexical identities that we have been pursuing are epiphenomena; they will not stay still long enough to be captured and labeled. But, to the extent that they do exist, they seem to represent influences on a late stage of production, a fine-tuning of the output of well-established rules, constraints and categories. This implies the existence of several cycles in the process of speech production, where the influence of stored memories and affective associations is exerted on an unmarked output. Thus the output of *home* in [2] may be further determined by social and stylistic parameters that come into play at a different level of linguistic organization from that engaged in the mobilization of phonemic categories.

Sound change is defined here as a shift of targets within the continuous parameters of phonological space. It is opposed to changes in the membership of phonological categories at a higher level of abstraction. It is also opposed to fluctuations that respond to frequency and lexical identity. But, as we have seen in previous chapters, sound change is not isolated from the rest of the phonological system. Sound change is governed by the intricate interplay of systemic relations within and across subsystems and by the functional economy of the system as a whole.

14

The Binding Force in Segmental Phonology

The units of linguistic change that we have focused on so far are segmental phonemes whose targeted means shift in a continuous acoustic space. A segmental phoneme of this type, like the /ow/ of Chapter 13, is a paradigmatic assembly of the vowels in *go*, *boat*, *boats*, *hope*, *low*, *stone*, etc. Throughout the discussion, it was apparent that the vowel in *go* behaved differently from the one in *road*, but this was attributed to coarticulation with the segmental environment. At the end it appeared that, as the fronting of /ow/ advanced, the subset of *bowl*, *old*, *cold*, etc. was discretely separated from all others. The set of vowels influenced by the change included all /ow/ except those before /l/, but there was no suggestion that the prelateral phoneme was no longer an allophone of /ow/. The unit of change in this case was thus something less than a segmental phoneme. This chapter considers situations where the effects of coarticulation are strong enough to disrupt the unity of a phoneme and searches for evidence of a binding force that resists such disruption.

Table 1.1, reproduced here as Table 14.1, shows the notation used for North American English vowels in this volume, with key words that serve to identify the word classes involved. It represents an initial position from which all North American dialect patterns can be derived. The sixth short vowel, represented here as the original /o/ in *pot*, serves as a useful point of reference in considering North American English as a whole. As discussed in Chapter 7, this vowel was unrounded to a low back or central vowel [ɑ] in most North American dialects, but it remains [ɔ] in Eastern New England, Canada and Western Pennsylvania. For these dialects and for the West, the checked /o/ has merged with /oh/, while in others it merges with /ah/, becoming an integral part of one or the other long ingliding vowel.[1] Note also that, although the great majority of speakers no longer distinguish /iw/ from /uw/ – so that *lute* rhymes with *loot* and *suit* rhymes with *boot* – those who still preserve this distinction are enough to justify the retention of this fourth member of the back upgliding subset as /iw/.

This binary representation of English vowels serves a number of functions:

a   It captures the major phonotactic regularity of the North American English vowel system: that all words terminate in consonants or glides. Conversely,

Table 14.1   North American English vowels in the ANAE notation

nucleus	SHORT		LONG					
			Upgliding				Ingliding	
			Front upgliding		Back upgliding			
	V		Vy		Vw		Vh	
	front	back	front	back	front	back	front	back
high	i	u	iy		iw	uw		
mid	e	ʌ	ey	oy		ow		oh
low	æ	o		ay		aw	æh	ah
high	*bit*	*put*	*beat*		*suit*	*boot*		
mid	*bet*	*but*	*bait*	*boy*		*boat*		*bought*
low	*bat*	*pot*		*bite*		*bout*	*salve*	*father*

no stressed words end with a vowel. No matter what sound changes take place in any given North American dialect, there are no dialects with short stressed vowels at the ends of words.[2]

b   It defines the subsystems in which chain shifting operates to obtain maximum dispersion of the elements (Chapter 5).
c   It predicts the direction of those changes that involve parallel movement and nucleus–glide differentiation.
d   It shows the initial position from which North American dialects can be generated by retracing the sound changes of the nineteenth and twentieth centuries.

Though Table 14.1 represents each segment as a unit, the structure is easily decomposed into features that identify each vowel. Thus the short vowels can be rewritten as in (1):

(1)

	i	e	æ	u	ʌ	o
vocalic	+	+	+	+	+	+
consonantal	−	−	−	−	−	−
high	+	−	−	+	−	−
low	−	−	+	−	−	+
anterior	+	+	+	−	−	−

while the long vowels, each one having two morae, are represented as in (2):

(2)		iy	ey	ay	oy	iw	uw	ow	aw	æh	ah	oh
	vocalic	+ −	+ −	+ −	+ −	+ −	+ −	+ −	+ −	+ −	+ −	+ −
	consonantal	− −	− −	− −	− −	− −	− −	− −	− −	− −	− −	− −
	high	+ +	− +	− +	− +	+ +	+ +	− +	− +	− −	− −	− −
	low	− −	− −	+ −	− −	− −	− −	− −	+ −	+ −	+ −	− −
	anterior	+ +	+ +	− +	− +	+ −	− −	− −	− −	+ −	− −	− −

It will be observed that the short vowel /o/ in (1) and the nucleus /a/ of long vowels in (2) have the same feature sets. In this initial system they are distinguished by the redundant feature [+round], and /o/ is represented phonetically as [ɔ]. The situation is inherently unstable, as developed in Chapter 5: /o/ merges with /oh/, with /ah/ or with both.

These features, or others that are homologous with them, have been used by phonologists since Jakobson and Halle (1956) and Chomsky and Halle (1968). In one sense, they merely capture the hierarchical headings of Figure 14.1, reducing them to a binary format. Since the arrays of (1) are also elements of (2), it may be asked whether these six vectors form the basic units of sound change. This cannot be the case, since we have seen that, in the Southern Shift, /e/ and /i/ move in the opposite direction from the first morae of /ey/ and /iy/, and in Pittsburgh /o/ moves back while the first mora of /ow/ moves forward. In many dialects, the /a/ nucleus in /aw/ moves in the opposite direction from the /a/ in /ay/. The elements on which sound change seems to operate are the single morae of the short vowels, when they occur without a following glide, and the combinations of two morae, vowel and glide, as the paired features of (2).

If the units of change were only these single mora and two morae combinations, then all sound changes would be unconditioned. All instances of a single or paired feature would be selected to participate in a given change, depending to a greater or lesser extent on the neighboring features. This appears to be the case with the major chain shifts we have studied: the Northern Cities Shift, the Southern Shift, the Canadian Shift and the Pittsburgh Shift. But even more common are conditioned sound changes, where the effects of coarticulation split a phoneme into two discrete allophones. Figures 13.10–13.12 provided a graphic view of this process in the fronting of /ow/. In the nasal short-*a* system, all vowels followed by a [+nasal] feature are raised to high front position, while all others remain at low front (see Figure 5.7 for Pittsburgh; Figure 7.3 for Manchester, New Hampshire; and generally ANAE, Ch. 13). In Philadelphia, /ey/ in checked position has been rising steadily to high position for the past fifty years, while /ey/ in free position remains at lower mid (PLC, Vol. 2; Conn 2005). The fronting of /uw/ involves not only the splitting off of the prelateral allophones but, for most speakers, a clear separation of vowels after coronals from others (Figure 5.13a, ANAE, Map 12.2).

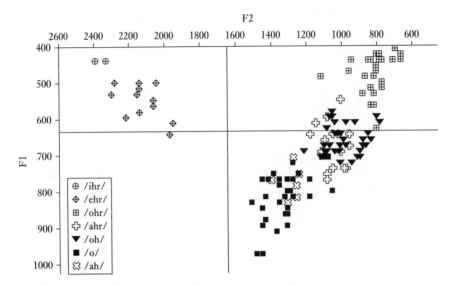

Figure 14.1   Identification of the nucleus of /oh/ with the nucleus of /ahr/ in the vowel system of Rose V., 30 [1996], Philadelphia, TS 587

In general, chain shifting maintains the unity of the segmental phoneme, while conditioned sound changes exhibit the disruptive effects of coarticulation. Given the extreme results of the nasal short-*a* system, where the two allophones are at opposite ends of phonological space, the evidence for the integrity of the phoneme is essentially that of complementary distribution: the sound [iə] before nasals fits the hole in the distribution of [æ] in the phoneme /æ/, which never occurs before nasals. Yet, when *Ann* is indistinguishable from *Ian*, one might be tempted to posit a phoneme /ih/ comprising *idea, Ian, theater, Leah, Sophia, Ann, family* and *camera*, since there are no alternations uniting [æ] and [iə].[3]

Among the conditioning effects of sound change in English, one of the most extreme is the lowering and backing of vowels after obstruent/liquid onsets, as in *grip, dress* and *black*.[4] This is responsible for one of the best known exceptions to regular sound change in the history of English. When Middle English (ME) ɛ: in *knead* rose to merge with ME e: in *need*, several representatives of the lowest allophones were so low that they were re-analyzed as members of the ME æ: phoneme, as it rose to [ɛ:] and finally to [e:] and [eɪ]. These words were *great, break* and *drain* (see PLC, Vol. 1: 297–8 for a more complete account). The same phenomenon appeared in the raising of ME ɔ: to o:, where one word was left behind: *broad*. Today this is the one exception to the phonics rule that the vowel pair *oa* stands for the phoneme /ow/: it is separated from its original cohort and is now merged with /oh/. A similar series of disruptions in the ME o: class led to the exceptional merger with /ʌ/ of the two words *flood* and *blood*.

Indeed, coarticulation can do more than disrupt a few words; it can rotate a subset of allophones so completely that their original identities are lost. This has clearly happened in French, where the four or five nasal vowels are not easily matched with oral counterparts. Such disruption has also happened in North American English dialects, where a fifth vocalic subsystem before tautosyllabic /r/ must be recognized, as in Table 14.2. Here the feature [±round] can be used to distinguish from back what would otherwise be central. The distinction between /ohr/ and /ɔhr/ is irretrievably lost for most North Americans, for whom there are only six members of this subset. The front vowels /ihr/ and /ehr/ can more or less be identified with /iy/ and /ey/, but /ʌhr/ cannot easily be matched with any of the short vowels that were originally distinct in *fir, her, world, fur*. In the back, /ohr/ is midway between /oh/ and /ow/ in most dialects. While /ahr/ is associated with /ah/ in some dialects, in others the Back Chain Shift before /r/ leads to an identification of the nucleus of /ahr/ with /oh/. Figure 14.1 shows this re-identification in the vowel system of a 30-year-old woman from Philadelphia. While /ah/ remains in the same region as /o/, the Back Chain Shift carries /ahr/ to mid position, so that it occupies the same region as the black triangles of /oh/. Thus the Vhr subsystem has rotated in a manner independent of the Vh subsystem.

The recognition of a subsystem of English vowels before /r/ is equivalent to recognizing that the combination Vhr is a unit of linguistic change distinct from Vh. This raises the question as to whether there are other such subsystems, in which the coarticulatory effect of the defining environment overrides the identities of the more general categories. A likely possibility for present-day North American English is a prenasal subsystem of short vowels which we might label VN, shown as Table 14.3. Here the following nasal consonant serves as a differentiating environment, much as /w/ or /y/ does for the upgliding vowels. We know that some items within this set are highly confusable, given the frequency of the merger of /i/ and /e/ before /n/. The test for the linguistic significance of such a subsystem is whether or not we observe allophonic chain shifting within it.

Table 14.2 The subsystem Vhr in North American English

Ingliding Vhr			
	front	back	
		unrounded	rounded
high	/ihr/ *fear*		/uhr/ *moor*
mid	/her/ *fair*	/ʌhr/ *fur*	/ohr/ *four*
low		/ahr/ *far*	/ɔhr/ *for*

Table 14.3 Hypothetical subsystem VN of short vowels before nasals

Prenasal VN		
	front	back
high	/iN/ *pin, him*	
mid	/eN/ *pen, hem*	/ʌN/ *pun, hum*
low	/æN/ *pan, ham*	/oN/ *pond, tom*

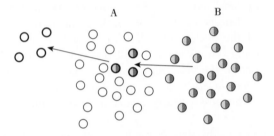

Figure 14.2 Allophonic chain shifting. Allophones of phoneme A (heavy outline) shift to front and corresponding allophones of phoneme B shift to overlap main distribution of A

The concept of allophonic chain shifting is illustrated in Figure 14.2, a modification of the original chain shifting pattern of Figure 6.16. Here the symbols with heavy outlines correspond to the shifted allophone, for example short *a* before nasals. If the prenasal allophones of phoneme A move up and away from the main distribution, then the margin of security of the prenasal allophones of B is increased. Following the argument of Chapter 6, prenasal outliers of B in the midst of the main A distribution would not then be confused with A, since the prenasal allophones of A are not in that area. The end result would be the type of allophonic chain shifting illustrated in Figure 14.2.

14.1   Is There Allophonic Chain Shifting before Nasals?

The VN subsystem is a good test case of allophonic chain shifting, since all North American English dialects show some tendency to the raising and fronting of /æ/ before nasals.[5] The general question to be posed is whether or not /oN/ will respond to the raising and fronting of /æN/ by shifting forward.

Figure 14.3 tests this question in a display of the first two stages of the Northern Cities Shift, as seen in the vowel system of a woman from Detroit. The highlighted

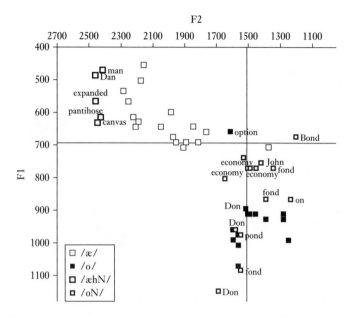

Figure 14.3   Advanced Stages 1 and 2 of the NCS for Libby R., 42 [1994], Detroit, TS 125. Highlighted symbols: prenasal vowels

Table 14.4   Mean values for prenasal and other /æ/ and /o/ for Libby R. ** denotes a difference significant at p < .01

	F1		F2	
Coda	+nas	−nas	+nas	−nas
/æ/	578	623	2305**	2044
/o/	878	913	1459	1482

/æ/ tokens before nasals are higher and/or fronter than others. Though this difference is relatively small in the Northern Cities Shift, Table 14.4 shows that F2 for prenasal /æ/ is significantly higher than for other tokens, at the p < .01 level. This pattern is not replicated in the /o/ distribution. Prenasal tokens are scattered among others, and there are no significant differences among the means. This situation is similar for all Inland North speakers. Although the general correlation between the fronting of /æ/ and the fronting of /o/ is quite high (.66) – this correlation does not extend to the prenasal allophones. No cases of allophonic chain shifting have been found in the Inland North.

While the differentiation of prenasal and other /æ/ is minimal in the Inland North, it is maximized in speakers from New England, the Midland and the West

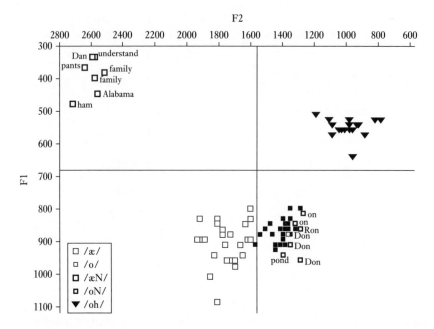

Figure 14.4   Prenasal /æ/ and /o/ of Debora L., 37 [1996], Providence, RI, TS 469

who exhibit the nasal short-*a* system. Figure 14.4 shows the /æ/ and /o/ tokens for a speaker from Providence, RI, with a nasal short-*a* system. The complete and dramatic separation of the prenasal /æ/ tokens is not matched by a corresponding front shift of the prenasal /o/ tokens. On the contrary, the /oN/ tokens – *on*, *Ron*, *don*, *pond* – occupy the back part of the /o/ distribution. The widely separated /oh/ is added to emphasize that the back position of /o/ is in no way connected to a low back merger. The absence of allophonic chain shifting is quite general for speakers with a nasal system. There are no speakers in the Telsur data set who shift prenasal /o/ tokens into the low front area when this area is occupied by /æ/ tokens before oral consonants. Furthermore, there is no correlation between the F2 of /æ/ and F2 of /o/ for the 96 Telsur speakers with a nasal system: r^2 is .06.

These individual demonstrations can be followed by a view of the overall relations of the means of the vowels involved. Figure 14.5 compares the oral and nasal allophones of /æ/ and /o/ for forty-two speakers in the Inland North who have a generalized raising of /æ/ and for ninety-six speakers in North America with a nasal short-*a* system. Those with the nasal system have a mean value for /o/ before nasals that is significantly backer than before oral consonants ($t = 16.3$, $p < .0001$). For the Inland North group with the general raising of /æ/, there is no significant difference between oral and nasal allophones.

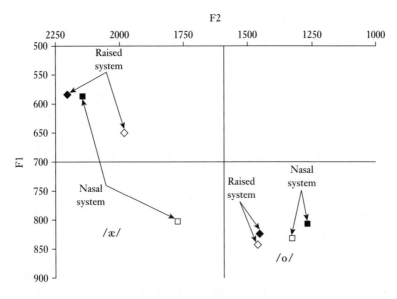

Figure 14.5   Relation of oral and nasal allophones of /æ/ and /o/ for forty-two speakers of the Northern Cities Shift with general raising of /æ/ and ninety-six speakers with a nasal short-*a* system. Solid symbols: vowels before nasal consonants

14.2   Allophonic Chain Shifting in the Southern Shift?

The Southern Shift provides the clearest example of chain shifting as distinguished from generalized sound change. This section will examine the possibility of allophonic chain shifting before voiced and voiceless finals in this process.

The triggering event of the Southern Shift is the monophthongization of /ay/, which is followed by the descent of the nucleus of /ey/ along the nonperipheral track, with more advanced tokens overlapping the monophthongal /ay/ area. As pointed out in Chapter 5, the concatenation of these two events cannot be explained as a form of parallel movement or rule generalization. No generalization of monophthongization or of lowering can account for the sequence. There are two different types of events, as shown in Table 14.5: the removal of /ay/ from the subsystem of front upgliding vowels; and the readjustment of the remaining elements. In the abstract representation in Table 14.5, two kinds of readjustment might take place: either /oy/ or /ey/ might fall to the position formerly occupied by /ay/. At this point, the general principles of chain shifting developed in Chapter 6 come into play: lax nuclei fall along the nonperipheral path, and tense nuclei rise along the peripheral path. The more concrete representation of Figure 6.18 shows the mean /oy/ for all dialects with a nucleus firmly located on the back peripheral path (solid diamonds with upper left arrow). On the other hand, the mean /ey/ for a number of dialects is seen at

Table 14.5   The Southern Shift across the Vy and h subsystems

	SHORT		LONG					
			Upgliding				Ingliding	
			Front upgliding		Back upgliding			
	V		Vy		Vw		Vh	
nucleus	front	back	front	back	front	back	front	back
high	i	u	iy		iw	uw		
mid	e	ʌ	ey	oy		ow		oh
low	æ	o		ay		aw	æh	ah

various stages of descent along the nonperipheral path, with the Inland South [IS] in the lead. This is the acoustic image of the discrete feature shifting of Table 14.5.

We can now investigate the consequences of the allophonic distribution of monophthongization. Figure 14.6 shows the outer limit of the South, defined as the region where /ay/ is monophthongized to some degree before obstruents.[6] Within the South there is often a sharp difference between monophthongization before

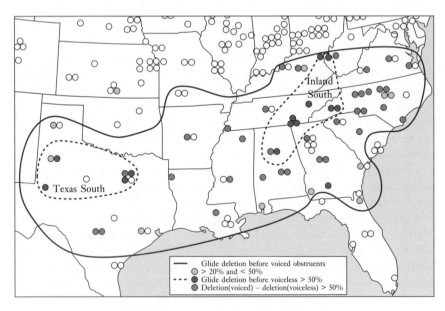

Figure 14.6   Monophthongization of /ay/ before voiceless obstruents and elsewhere in the South

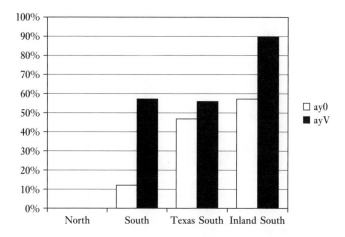

Figure 14.7 Differentiation of monophthongization of (ay0) and (ayV) in three regions of the South: Inland South, Texas South and the South outside of these two areas

voiceless obstruents (ay0) and monophthongization before voiced consonants and final (ayV).[7] This is not true for the speakers designated by empty symbols, who have a frequency of monophthongization of (ayV) less than 20 percent, or for the light grey symbols, with monophthongization of (ayV) more than 20 percent but less than 50 percent. Nor is it true for the across-the-board types – the thirteen speakers indicated by dark grey symbols, for whom monophthongization of both (ay0) and (ayV) are more than 50 percent.[8] These speakers are concentrated in the Inland South (the Appalachian area) and the Texas South.

For the majority of the forty-nine Southern speakers indicated by medium grey symbols, the difference between (ayV) and (ay0) is more than 50 percent (N = 34). The overall differentiation of the two allophones is displayed in Figure 14.7.

The basic relationship behind the chain shift is shown in Figure 14.8, which plots the mean values of /ey/ and /ay/ for twenty-one North American dialects. The Inland South mean for /ey/ is shifted strongly towards the /ay/ distribution, and, as Figure 14.7 shows, it is the Inland South that comes closest to the complete monophthongization of /ay/.

Within the Southern region as a whole, individual speakers show the same relationship, displayed in the scattergram of Figure 14.9. The trendline shows that, for each 10 percent increase in the monophthongization of (ayV), one adds 6.3 Hz to the expected value of F1 of (ey): that is, /ey/ lowers as monophthongization of /ayV/ increases. The relationship is significant, accounting for 27 percent of the variance. Now the question to be addressed is whether the difference in the monophthongization of the two allophones of /ay/ is reflected in a parallel shift of the corresponding allophones of /ey/.

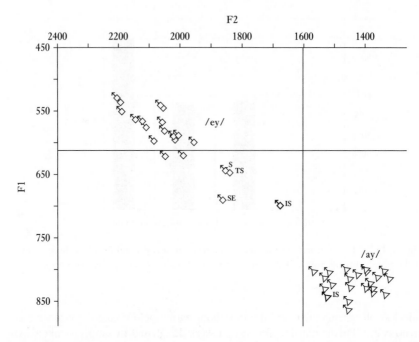

Figure 14.8 Mean positions of /ey/ and /ay/ for twenty-one North American dialects. IS = Inland South; TS = Texas South; S = South; SE = Southeastern areas not included in the South (Charleston, Florida...)

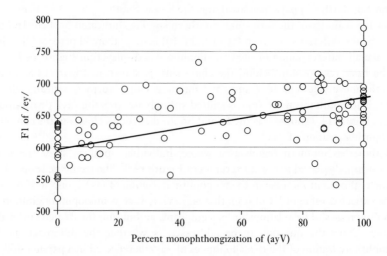

Figure 14.9 F1 of /ey/ against monophthongization of (ayV) for all speakers in the South

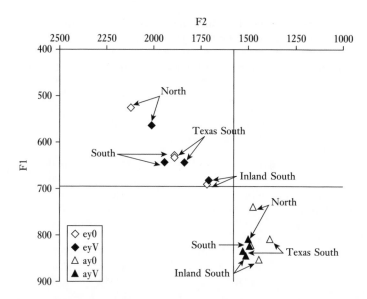

Figure 14.10 Mean values of /ay/ and /ey/ before voiceless consonants and elsewhere for the North, South, Texas South and Inland South

Allophonic chain shifting would be realized as a lower position for /ey/ in pre-voiced and final position (eyV), and as a higher position for /ey/ before voiceless consonants (ey0). Figure 14.10 plots the mean values of these allophones of /ey/, as well as the positions of (ay0) and (ayV) for the various Southern dialects. If allophonic chain shifting were taking place, we would expect to find distinct (ey0) and (eyV), corresponding to a difference in monophthongization for (ay0) and (ayV), for the South generally – but not so much for the Texas South or the Inland South dialects, where that difference is diminished. No such pattern appears in Figure 14.10: the F1/F2 positions for (ey0) and (eyV) are not significantly different for any region of the South.

Figure 14.10 does show a differentiation of (eyV) and (ey0) for the North. This is parallel to the "Canadian raising" of /ay/, which is characteristic of the North and North Central regions (Eckert 2000, ANAE, Map 13.10). This parallelism has not been noted in previous descriptions of the Northern dialect area. It can be considered either as allophonic chain shifting or as a case of generalized movement, as suggested at the beginning of this chapter.

The mean values on which this diagram is based are displayed in Table 14.6. The first section of the table compares the possible differentiation of (ey0) and (eyV) for the speakers with the most extreme monophthongization in the South: the seventeen subjects with 100 percent (ayV). No significant difference between (ey0) and (eyV) is found for either F1 or F2. The second section presents the results

Table 14.6 Means and standard deviations for F1 and F2 of /ay/ and /ey/ before
voiceless consonants and elsewhere for the South and the North

	F1 (Hz)	F1 Stdev	F2 (Hz)	F2 Stdev	N
South: (ayV) = 100%					
(ey0)	679	66	1738	196	89
(eyV)	673	77	1709	209	297
Prob	0.5		0.24		
t	0.67		1.16		
South: (ayV) − (ay0) > 50%					
(ey0)	651	64	1827	199	192
(eyV)	656	79	1797	218	571
Prob	0.56		0.09		
t	0.58		1.68		
North					
(ey0)	526	70	2122	202	573
(eyV)	565	75	2014	200	1,307
Prob	< .0001		< .0001		
t	9.7		10.7		
(ay0)	738	90	1475	184	473
(ayV)	809	94	1503	144	1,215
Prob	< .0001		< .001		
t	10.6		3.3		

for the subset of Southern speakers who are most likely to show allophonic chain
shifting: those who show the greatest difference between (ay0) and (ayV). Again,
we find no difference in the mean values of (ey0) and (eyV).

The last two sections of Table 14.6 show the mean values of the /ay/ and /ey/
allophones in the North. The F1 difference between (ay0) and (ayV) is 71 Hz,
which is above the 60 Hz criterion adopted for Canadian raising in ANAE,
Map 13.10. The F1 difference between (ey0) and (eyV) is 39 Hz: it is smaller, but
also significant at the $p < .0001$ level. This parallel allophony indicates the potential
for a disruption of the unity of the phoneme; but it is hardly noticeable, both to
native speakers and to phoneticians. It is quite remote from the disruption produced
by the migration of (ayV) into the long and ingliding subsystem, which opposes
white [waɪt] to *wide* [wa:d]. It is more akin to the Philadelphia raising of checked
/eyC/ discussed in Chapter 2, by which the vowels in *paid* and *main* overlap with
the vowels in *peed* and *mean*, while the free allophones remain in lower mid position. In the North the two phonemes move upward before voiceless consonants
without any overlap, a movement that does not threaten to disrupt either phonemic
unity.

14.3   The Binding Force

Much of this chapter concerns the coarticulatory disruption of phonemes – as an accomplished fact, as in the case of *great*, *break* and *drain*, or in the English subsystem before /r/; or as an unrealized possibility, as in the nasal subsystem or the Southern Shift. The unrealized possibilities are in fact the great majority. The binding force which counters these disruptive forces is strong enough to ensure the long-term identity of most phonemes. Its effects may be seen in two general tendencies that we observe in the course of the linguistic changes studied here. The absence of allophonic chain shifting has a positive consequence: we observe that a phoneme responds to the movement of a neighboring phoneme only when all the allophones of the latter have vacated the neighboring space.

In cases of lexical diffusion, where change proceeds word by word, the binding force is overridden from the outset, and a restoration of the original phoneme can be accomplished only by external factors. In the course of a regular conditioned sound change, the integrity of a phoneme may be threatened, and extreme allophones may be reinterpreted as, and merged with, other phonemes. Yet most historical word classes are preserved over time in the process of reintegration that has been documented at many points in previous chapters: the reassembly of (Tuw) and (Kuw) examined in Chapter 5; the parallel integration of (ow) in the most advanced stages of fronting seen in Chapter 12; and the general raising of /æ/ in the Northern Cities Shift. Despite some losses and disruptions, it can be recognized that a phoneme is more than a collection of allophones; it is rather an entity that responds to historical processes in a unified manner. This observation gives support to the linguistic construction of categories based on complementary distribution and aligns linguistic change with other evidence for the psychological reality of the phoneme.

Part D
Transmission and Diffusion

15

The Diffusion of Language from Place to Place

Most of this volume and the two preceding have dealt with linguistic change from below in the sense defined in Labov (1966): the gradual development of the linguistic system in the speech community, driven by factors internal to that community. Yet relations between speech communities are present in the background throughout and sometimes emerge to take center stage. Chapter 9 examined the social and linguistic conditions that lead to the divergence of neighboring dialects and the overall dispersion of linguistic systems in North America. The discussion of triggering events in Chapter 5 included a case of massive population movement and mixture in the genesis of the Northern Cities Shift in Western New York State. This chapter will confront some of the principles governing changes that are the result of dialect contact, introducing a distinction between transmission within the speech community and diffusion across communities.

15.1   Family-Tree and Wave Models of Change

Throughout the history of linguistics, two models of linguistic change have coexisted in an uneasy relationship. The family-tree model has been the principal guide and major output of the comparative method. Yet all linguists agree that there are some situations where the effects of a wave model must be recognized, registering the influence of distinct terminal nodes of the tree on one another. Such wave effects are seen most clearly in communities with extended periods of bilingualism; in the formation of pidgins and creoles; and in the major *Sprachbund* areas in which features spread across languages in ways unrelated to place on the family tree. Contact effects may appear as inextricably embedded in the reconstruction of normal linguistic development. Ringe, Warnow and Taylor (2002; hereafter RWT) present their current best tree for Indo-European as Figure 15.1, with the Germanic languages branching from the major node which includes Balto-Slavic (Old Church Slavonic, Lithuanian, etc.) and Indo-Iranian (Vedic, Avestan, etc.). Yet, as suggested by the

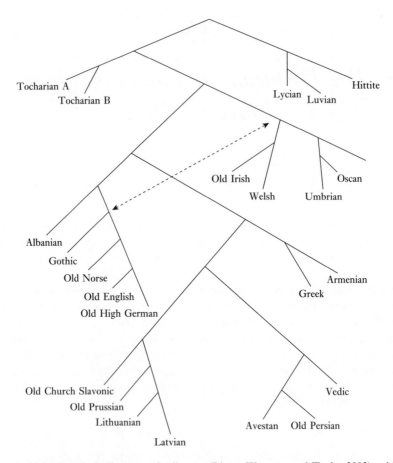

Figure 15.1 Best Indo-European family tree (Ringe, Warnow, and Taylor 2002), with indication of shared characteristics of Germanic with Italo-Celtic branch

dashed arrow (my addition to the diagram), Germanic shares many characters with the Italo-Celtic branch, which split much earlier from the main Indo-European community. The authors find that this situation reveals the modification of the family-tree descent characters by later contact:

> This split distribution of character states leads naturally to the hypothesis that Germanic was originally a near sister of Balto-Slavic and Indo-Iranian [...] that at a very early date it lost contact with its more easterly sisters and came into close contact with the languages to the west; and that that contact episode led to extensive vocabulary borrowing at a period before the occurrence in any of the languages of any distinctive sound changes that would have rendered the borrowings detectable. (RWT, p. 111)

This is of course only one of innumerable findings on the effect of language contact, from Schmidt (1871) through Weinreich (1968) and beyond. Bloomfield's discussion of the limitations of the family-tree model includes a diagram with this very example of Italic influence on Germanic, adapted from Schrader's original (Bloomfield 1933: 316). I cite RWT here because the contact problem is foregrounded in one of the most recent and sophisticated developments of the family-tree model for the most studied of all language families: Indo-European. It would seem, then, that any general view of language descent must be prepared to integrate the two models of language change. This chapter will argue that the two models involve linguistic processes that are quite different in their mechanism and effects, the results of different types of language learning.

15.2   Defining Transmission and Diffusion

We begin with the concept of *linguistic descent*, the basic concept that underlies the family-tree model. Bloomfield's chapter on the comparative method states the conditions under which we can recognize one language as a later stage of another (1933: 316ff.). Hoenigswald (1960) also devotes a chapter to the formal definition of mother, daughter, and sister relations. The formulation of linguistic descent given by RWT (p. 63) goes beyond the relationship of the linguistic forms, and introduces the social process of linguistic acquisition that will be a main focus of this chapter:

> A language (or dialect) Y at a given time is said to be descended from language (or dialect) X of an earlier time if and only if X developed into Y by an unbroken sequence of instances of native-language acquisition by children.[1]

This unbroken sequence of native-language acquisition by children is here termed linguistic *transmission*. The continuity of dialects and languages across time is the result of the ability of children to replicate faithfully the form of the older generation's language, in all of its structural detail and complexity, with consequent preservation of the distances between the nodes of the family tree. But linguistic descent can be preserved even when this replication is imperfect, that is, when language changes. This is the normal type of internal language change; it is termed "change from below" or change from within the system, as opposed to "change from above" or the importation of elements from other systems (Labov 1966).[2] Change from below may involve the systematic interaction of social, cognitive or physiological factors, which is responsible for the increasing distances between the nodes over time. Such internal changes are generated by the process of *increment-ation*, in which successive cohorts and generations of children advance the change beyond the level of their caretakers and role models, and in the same direction, over many generations (see Vol. 1, Ch. 14). Incrementation begins with the faithful transmission of the adult system, including variable elements with their linguistic and social constraints (Labov 1989a, Roberts 1993). These variable elements are then advanced further in the direction indicated by the inherited age vectors.[3] Children's incrementation of the change may take the form of increases in frequency, extent, scope or specificity of a variable.[4]

When entire communities move, they carry with them the agents of transmission and incrementation. Describing the development of new colonial dialects, Trudgill argues that

> most of the complicated work leading to the eventual establishment of a new, single norm will be carried out by children under the age of eight [. . .] hence the deterministic nature of the process, and the similarity of outcomes from similar mixtures. (2004: 28)

As noted above, analyses within the family-tree model regularly report the effect of changes that diminish the distances between nodes of the family tree. This may happen spontaneously, when parallel branches converge through independently motivated changes; but more often it is the result of contact between the speech communities involved and the transfer of features from one to the other. This transfer across branches of the family tree is here designated linguistic *diffusion*.

The process of comparative reconstruction normally employs the family-tree model and treats contact or "wave model" effects as disturbing elements that limit the precision of the reconstruction. What RWT makes explicit is here assumed: that transmission is the fundamental mechanism by which linguistic diversity is created and maintained, and that diffusion is of secondary importance. However, the wave model first proposed by Schmidt (1871) does provide an alternative version, in which diffusion is the main mechanism of linguistic change. This process of diffusion first creates a continuous web of linguistic similarities and differences. In Bloomfield's summary:

> Schmidt showed that special resemblances can be found for any two branches of I[ndo]-E[uropean], and that these special resemblances are most numerous in the case of branches which lie geographically nearest each other. Different linguistic changes may spread, like waves, over a speech-area, and each change may be carried out over a part of the area that does not coincide with the part covered by an earlier change. The result of successive waves will be a network of isoglosses. Adjacent districts will resemble each other most; in whatever direction one travels, differences will increase with distance, as one crosses more and more isogloss-lines. (Bloomfield 1933: 316)

How, then, are the discontinuities between languages created in this model? They are the result of a secondary process in which speakers of one particular dialect gain a form of ascendancy – political, economic or cultural – and the ensuing expansion of this dialect wipes out the intermediate forms of the original continuum. Thus the divergence of branches in the present sense is the result of the elimination of diversity through dialect leveling. This notion of a basic dialect continuum accords well with the principle of density that Bloomfield introduces in his chapter on dialect geography. Bloomfield does not adopt Schmidt's alternative explanation of diversity, but rather withdraws to a view of the family-tree model as an ideal pattern that is never realized in reality without rejecting the idea itself: "The comparative method [...] would work accurately for absolutely uniform speech-communities and sudden, sharp cleavages" (ibid., p. 318).

The following sections will argue that the primary source of diversity is the transmission (and incrementation) of change within the speech community, and that diffusion is a secondary process of a very different character. Such a clear dichotomy between transmission and diffusion is dependent upon the concept of a speech community with well-defined limits, a common structural base and a unified set of sociolinguistic norms. Although for many scholars, including dialectologists, speech communities form continua without clear boundaries between them (Carver 1987, Heeringa and Nerbonne 2001), we find that the best studied communities in the Eastern United States are discretely separated from their hinterland. New York City turned out to be a geographic unity defined by a common structural base (Labov 1966), as is shown on the one hand by the match between the department store study and the study of the Lower East Side, and, on the other, by the sharp contrast between out-of-towners and native New Yorkers. So, too, was Philadelphia, where the geographically random telephone survey matched the long-term study of ten neighborhoods, and the oldest upper-class Philadelphian matched the oldest working-class Philadelphian in the specifics of the complex short-*a* split that defines the community (Labov 1989b; PLC, Vol. 2). As Chapter 9 showed, an even more startling uniformity and deeper divisions between speech communities are found by ANAE. The extraordinarily homogeneous vowel system of the Inland North is sharply separated from the Canadian system to the north and the Midland system to the south, with a tight bundling of a dozen structural isoglosses.

This discussion of transmission and diffusion will draw from such well-defined communities and from the highly structured patterns that define them. The nature of the inquiry may depend in part on the difference between dialectology in North America and studies in Western Europe (Auer and Hinskens 1996, Trudgill 1996, Kerswill 2004). In European studies the contrast between transmission and diffusion is less prominent, since the main phenomena involve the transfer of well-known features of older and well-established dialects. We do not find there many reports of changes from below that depend upon transmission through incrementation, as in the new sound changes of North America. A second difference has to do with the degree of involvement with linguistic structure. Most discussions of dialect continua deal with lexical isoglosses, lexical incidence, or unconnected phonetic variables, where the distinction between transmission and diffusion may not be so clear. The argument to be advanced below is dependent upon more abstract phenomena: linguistic changes that involve grammatical conditioning, word boundaries, and the systemic relations that drive chain shifting.

15.3   Structural Diffusion

In discussions of the linguistic consequences of language contact, the question of structural borrowing regularly comes to the fore. There is no question about structural transmission within the community: if structures were not transmitted across generations, there would be no continuity in language. The issue is entirely about what can happen in diffusion across communities.

RWT argue for a strong linguistic constraint against structural diffusion. They state that the essential condition for the family-tree model is that morphosyntactic structures are faithfully transmitted across generations and are *not* transferred from language to language in normal linguistic development. Thomason and Kaufman (1988) contend that social factors can override linguistic constraints, discounting the impact of any structural factors. Moravcsik (1978) proposes five general principles that delimit the extent of borrowing; but Campbell (1993) offers a critical overview of the validity of such constraints. Hock and Joseph note that "structural elements usually do not diffuse through borrowing" (1996: 14), but are the cumulative results of changes in pronunciation and lexical borrowing. Winford concludes that "[t]he case for direct borrowing of structure in any of these [bilingual] situations has yet to be proved" (2003: 64).

In a meticulous review of the literature on structural borrowing, Sankoff (2002: 658) concludes that the notion of a "cline of borrowability" must be upheld:

> Though most language contact situations lead to unidirectional, rather than bidirectional linguistic results, conditioned by the social circumstances, it is also the case that linguistic structure overwhelmingly conditions the linguistic outcomes. Morphology and syntax are clearly the domains of linguistic structure least susceptible to the influence of contact, and this statistical generalization is not vitiated by a few exceptional cases.

Close investigations of some cases of structural borrowing have shown that they are actually consequences of lexical borrowing: "On the other hand, lexicon is clearly the most readily borrowable element, and borrowing lexicon can lead to structural changes at every level of linguistic structure" (ibid.).

The borrowing of preposition-final constructions into Prince Edward Island French, carefully studied by King (2000), is cited by RWT in support of their position that structural borrowing has proved to be an illusion in the few cases which have been studied in sufficient sociolinguistic detail. If this is the case, the contrast between transmission and diffusion is absolute. One copies everything; the other is limited to the most superficial aspects of language, words and sounds.[5] However, it seems unlikely that the actual situation is so abruptly polarized. Joseph (2000) presents convincing cases of the diffusion of syntactic structures across the languages of the Balkans. The spread of the construction Verb-"not"-Verb may be based on a common lexicalized model with the verb "want," but there is no such evidence in the replacement of infinitival complementation by finite forms.[6] In any case, contributors to this debate agree – with the exception of Thomason and Kaufman – that there are structural limitations on what types of linguistic patterns can be transmitted across languages.

15.4   Accounting for the Difference between Transmission and Diffusion

It is proposed here that the contrast between the transmission of change within speech communities and the diffusion of change across communities is the result of two different kinds of language learning. On the one hand, transmission is the product of the acquisition of language by young children. On the other hand, the limitations on diffusion are the result of the fact that most language contact takes place among adults. It follows that structural patterns are not as likely to be diffused, because adults do not learn and reproduce linguistic forms, rules and constraints with the accuracy and speed that children display.

This hypothesis is informed by recent studies that have greatly refined our understanding of the extent of those changes in language learning ability that take place at the end of the critical period (see the recent reviews of Newport 1990 and Scovel 2000). The period of decline in language learning ability extends from roughly 9 to 17 years of age. The experiments of Johnson and Newport (1989) showed that subjects who had acquired a second language after 17 years of age could not reproduce the syntactic judgments of native speakers. Oyama (1973) and Payne (1976) showed that children who arrived in a speech community after the age of 9 did not acquire the local phonological pattern with any degree of precision. However, many recent studies show that adults do have the capacity to change their linguistic systems to a significant degree after this critical period (Sankoff 2004). Real-time replications consistently show some adult movement in the direction of the change (Vol. 1, Ch. 4). A real-time re-study of Montreal French (Sankoff et al. 2001, Sankoff and Blondeau 2007) found a quantitative shift of apical to uvular /r/ for about a third of the adult speakers. At the same time, it was observed that no adults showed the total conversion to uvular /r/ that was characteristic of many pre-adolescents.

15.5   Diffusion in Dialect Geography

Evidence for the differentiation of family-tree and wave models may be drawn from dialect geography, which provides simultaneous records of both diffusion and transmission. The differentiation of regional dialects yields a fine-grained model of family-tree evolution. Dialect geography also focuses our attention upon diffusion, since the distribution of features across contiguous dialects leads to the inference that some have spread in a wave-like process of diffusion from one dialect to another (Trudgill 1974a, Bailey et al. 1993, Wolfram and Schilling-Estes 2003). With the advent of quantitative studies in the 1960s, this process of diffusion could be examined in some detail.

15.5.1   The diffusion of (æ) in Norway

Striking examples of diffusion are found in Trudgill's study of the Norwegian dialects of the Brunlanes Peninsula (1974a). Figures 15.2a and b show the progress of the lowering of /æ/ over two generations. The numbers on the map represent a scale of lowering from 0 to 500. They indicate both incrementation of the variable in the cities that are the points of origin and the geographic diffusion from them to the next largest cities – and ultimately to the small villages of the countryside.

The data from Figure 15.2 were originally used to support the gravity model of diffusion, in which the influence of one city on another is proportional to their population sizes and is inversely related to the square of the distance between them.[7] But they also illustrate the striking difference between the two types of language change: incrementation in urban speech communities and diffusion across the countryside. In Figure 15.2a, the towns of Larvik and Stavern have values above 240 for the oldest generation of speakers, over 60 years old; in Figure 15.2b, the middle generation of speakers in those cities shows values of over 280. This increase in the magnitude of the lowering process points to incrementation as the generating process in the city of origin.[8]

Figure 15.2 also illustrates the opposite process: the steady decline of the variable as one moves away from the city centers to the inland rural area, where values under 200 are found. Viewed as a process of diffusion from the city centers, this decline can be seen as a wave of continuous weakening as each new level of the variable (æ) diffuses outward. It is also possible to see Figure 15.2 as an array of incrementing regions, where each surrounding area exhibits incrementation at its own level, and the only difference between the big city and the small town is the time at which the process was initiated.

This issue cannot be resolved solely on the basis of the data from Brunlanes, which are presented as an output phonetic process with no structural conditions or consequences. More complex data, to follow from North American English, will make it possible to distinguish parallel development from diffusion. But, given the urban influence indicated in Figure 15.2, we can expect a certain degree of weakening of ongoing change in outlying areas, since the expanding forms are copied from adults who are at a relatively conservative level to begin with, and acquired by

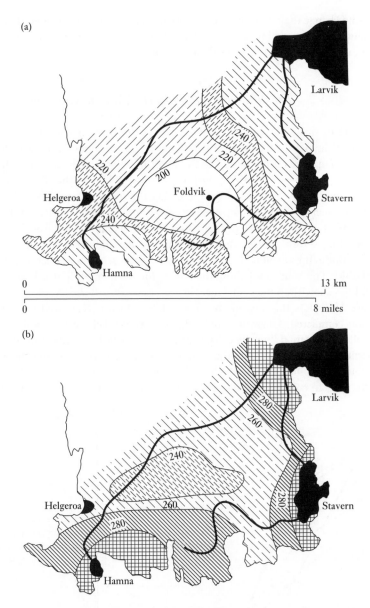

Figure 15.2 Lowering of /æ/ on the Brunlanes Peninsula (Trudgill 1974a, Maps 7, 8);
Figure 15.2a Speakers 70 years of age and older; Figure 15.2b Speakers 25–69 years of
age. Reprinted by permission of Cambridge University Press

adults who change their own speech in a sporadic and inaccurate manner. The next case shows how a sociolinguistic variable diffusing from an urban center can be dramatically reinterpreted in an outlying community.

15.5.2   The diffusion of (an) from Tehran to Ghazvin

The nature of this adult contact is illustrated in the study of the urban Persian dialect of Tehran by Modaressi (1978). One of the sociolinguistic variables he studied was (an), the raising of /a/ to [o:] and [u:] before nasals, as in the shift of name of the capital city from [tehra:n] to [tehru:n]. This variable shows regular social stratification in Tehran, where the higher the social status of a speaker, the lower the frequency of (an) raising. Modaressi also studied the small city of Ghazvin, ancient capital of the province of that name, located about 150 km from Tehran.

Figure 15.3 shows percent raising of (an) by age and style for Tehran and Ghazvin. Both cities exhibit sharp stylistic stratification and a regular advance of the variable. The solid lines show the values for Tehran, and, at a lower level, dashed lines show the values for Ghazvin.

Figure 15.4 plots this variable by social class, which is registered by years of education completed. Ghazvin is only slightly behind Tehran for speakers with some college education, but the difference increases with lower educational levels. Furthermore, the two communities show opposite directions of sociolinguistic stratification: the more education the citizens of Tehran have, the less they raise /an/ to [u:n]. In contrast, the more education citizens of Ghazvin have, the more

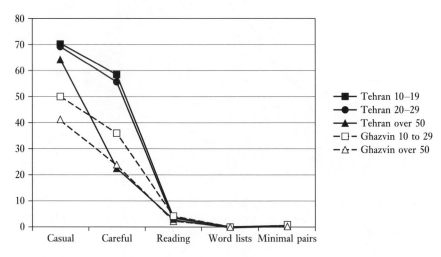

Figure 15.3   Percent raising of (an) by age and style in the Persian of Tehran and Ghazvin

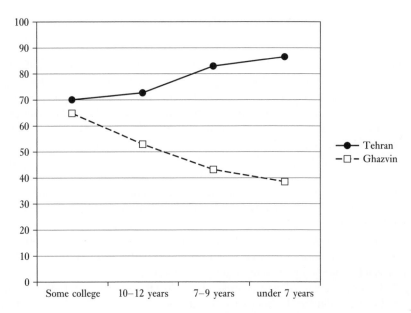

Figure 15.4 Percent raising of (an) by education in the Persian of Tehran and Ghazvin

they raise /an/. This result makes sense only if we infer that the contact between Tehran and Ghazvin occurs primarily among more educated adults and that the variable spreads downward in Ghazvin, at a progressively lower rate through a network of adult contacts. While the original adoption of the Tehran raising of (an) was a matter of speaker-internal accommodation (Trudgill 1986, Ch. 1; Joseph 2000), the speaker-external spread through the Ghazvin community follows a reverse pattern of social prestige among adults.

This is not to say that incrementation will not also take place among children in Ghazvin. But they will have inherited the new variable through the filter of adult diffusion, along with the social evaluation particular to Ghazvin. These examples from dialect geography support the notion that the diffusion of linguistic variables from place to place is carried forward by adults, from whom we expect less advanced rather than more advanced forms of the variables. One odd result of this diffusion is that, in Ghazvin, casual speech favors the forms that are most common among the highest-prestige speakers – a sociolinguistic anomaly.

The lowering of (æ) in Norway and the raising of (an) in Iran are typical of the many phonetic output rules that we find in studies of sound change in progress. In order to pursue the question of whether structural features can be diffused, we need to consider more complex patterns than the unconditioned lowering of /æ/ or raising of /a/ before nasals. The diffusion of the grammatically conditioned short-*a* split of New York City provides such a case.

15.6   The Diffusion of the NYC Short-*a* System

Almost all dialects of North American English show a raising and fronting of some members of the historical short-*a* class (ANAE, Ch. 13).[9] Phonetic conditioning is always present, in some cases as a continuum, in others as a discrete division into *tense* and *lax* distributions.[10] In some cases the tense and lax classes are phonetically predictable by simple rules; in others they are not. There are five basic types of distribution:

a   *The nasal system*   All short *a* before the front nasal consonants /n/ and /m/ are tense (*ham, hammock, man, manage, span, Spanish*), while all others are lax.

b   *Raised short* a   All words with historical short *a* are tense. Found only in the Inland North.

c   *Continuous short-*a *raising*   Short-*a* words are variably tensed, with vowels before nasal codas leading and vowels before voiceless stops and after obstruent liquid onsets (*glass, brag*) remaining in low front position.

d   *Southern breaking*   Short *a* is broken into a low front nucleus, palatal glide and following inglide in the Southern dialect area.

e   *Split short-*a *systems*   In New York City and the Mid-Atlantic region, the distribution of tense and lax vowels is governed by a complex of phonological, grammatical, stylistic and lexical conditions.

One form of the type (e) distribution is specific to New York City and its immediate environs, and was first described by Babbitt in 1896.[11] Babbitt reported that older speakers used the tense variant for the New England broad-*a* class, while younger speakers appear to have had the modern system as first described by Trager (1930, 1934, 1942) on the basis of his Newark, New Jersey speech pattern.[12] The older and the newer systems agree in tensing (in closed syllables) before some front nasal clusters and all front voiceless fricatives; but the newer system expands to include all front nasals, all voiceless fricatives and all voiced stops in coda position, as indicated in Figure 15.5. While both systems have tense *can't, dance, half, bath, pass, past*, the new system adds *man, stand, cash, cab, mad, badge, flag*. The degree of raising and fronting is a strong sociolinguistic marker, and New Yorkers frequently lower their tense vowels in careful speech. But the distribution into tense and lax classes is not socially evaluated and is uniformly distributed in the spontaneous speech of community members, to the extent that it is not disturbed by the effects of formal observation (Labov 1966).

To this phonetic conditioning a number of specific conditions are added:

1   *Function word constraint*   Function words with simple codas (*an, I can, had*) are lax, while corresponding content words are tense (*tin can, hand, add*). *Can't*, with a complex coda, also remains tense. This preserves the contrast

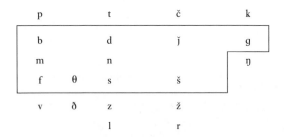

Figure 15.5 Codas that condition tensing of short *a* in New York City

of tense *can't* versus lax *can* in environments where the /t/ is elided or neutralized.

2 *Open syllable constraint* Short *a* is lax in open syllables, yielding tense *ham, plan, cash* but lax *hammer, planet, cashew*.

3 *Inflectional boundary closing* Syllables are closed by inflectional boundaries, so that tense forms include *planning* as well as *plan, staffer* as well as *staff*.

4 *Variable items* Considerable variation is found before voiced affricates and fricatives, in closed syllables (*jazz*) and in open ones (*imagine, magic*).

5 *Initial condition* Initial short *a* before codas that normally produce tensing are lax (*aspirin, asterisk*), except for the most common words (*ask, after*).

6 *Abbreviations* Abbreviated personal names are often lax (*Cass, Babs*).

7 *Lexical exceptions* There are a number of lexical exceptions: for example *avenue* is normally tense, in contrast to lax *average, savage, gavel*.

8 *Learned words* Many learned or late learned words with short *a* in tense environments are lax: *alas, carafe*.

Given the lexically specific conditions (4–7), it would seem necessary to analyze this pattern as a phonemic split. However, Kiparsky (1988) argued from the standpoint of lexical phonology that the patterns of change in progress within the community indicated the presence of a lexically and grammatically conditioned rule. To decide the issue, more information is needed than we now have available on how the pattern is learned. Chapter 18 of Volume 1 discussed the relation between the Philadelphia and the NYC split of short *a*. The similarity between the two systems was underlined by the fact that New Yorkers had greater success in learning the lexically determined aspects of the Philadelphia pattern than in learning the more rule-governed aspects.

At this point in the discussion, the tense class will be referred to as /æh/ and the lax class as /æ/, without deciding how these classes are generated or stored. Figure 15.6 shows the characteristic distribution of tense /æh/ and lax /æ/ for an ANAE speaker from New York City recorded in 1996. Nancy B. was then 65 years old, a homemaker and secretary of Italian–American background. Only two members

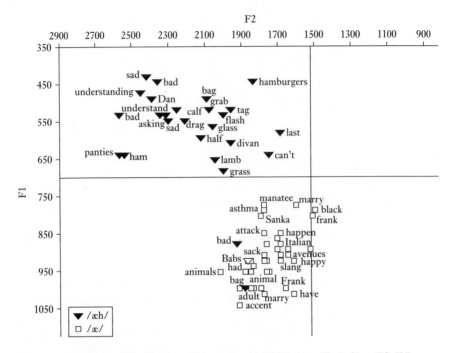

Figure 15.6 Short-*a* distribution of Nancy B., 65 [1996], New York City, TS 495

of the tense class (one each of *bad*, *bag*) were corrected to the lax class during the interview. Otherwise we observe a clear separation between the two classes. The tense /æh/ class includes short *a* in closed syllables before voiced stops (*sad*, *bad*, *bag*, *tag*, *drag*), front nasals (*ham*, *understanding*, *hamburgers*, *can't* and *divan*), and voiceless fricatives (*calf*, *flash*, *glass*, *last*, *grass*). In the lax category are corresponding words with short *a* in open syllables (*animal(s)*, *manatee*), function words (*have*, *am*, *had*), and environments that are always lax (*happen*, *attack*, *black*), including before velar nasals (*Frank*, *slang*, *Sanka*).

The dialect of New York City is confined to the city itself and to several neighboring cities in Northeastern New Jersey (Weehawken, Hoboken, Jersey City, Newark).[13] The NYC short-*a* distribution is uniform throughout this area and, as far as we know, has been stable through most of the twentieth century. It is clear that the New York City short-*a* system is very far from whatever beginnings it had as a simple, phonetically determined sound change. This system has developed the lexical and morphological irregularities characteristic of many late stages of change (Janda and Joseph 2001). It therefore gives us an opportunity to see what happens to this complex structure when it diffuses to other communities.

ANAE shows that the New York City pattern was diffused to four other communities, along the paths shown in Figure 15.7.

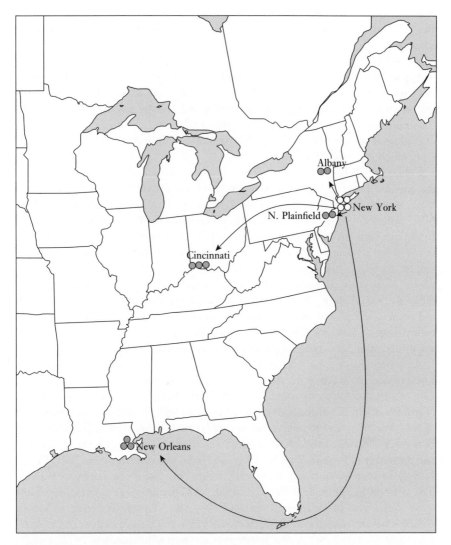

Figure 15.7   Diffusion of the New York City short-*a* pattern to four other speech communities

15.6.1   Diffusion to Northern New Jersey

I was born in Rutherford, New Jersey: a small residential *r*-pronouncing town studded with Dutch farmhouses, just outside of the New York City speech community. Though the local dialect that I acquired was *r*-pronouncing, the short-*a* system generally conformed to the descriptions of the NYC short-*a* system given above.[14] But there was a striking difference in the absence of the function word constraint. A very common utterance among residents of this Northern New Jersey area was "Did you say C–A–N or C–A–N–T?," since the vowel is tense in both words and the /t/ is often neutralized before a following apical obstruent (as in "I can't tell you"). Tense vowels are found in *am, an, and* as well. I originally cited this as an example of how the advance of sound change can override functional constraints; but, from the perspective of the present study, it appears as an instance of the loss of structural detail in the diffusion of the NYC short-*a* system to dialects with which it is in contact.

Cohen (1970) is a detailed study of short-*a* systems in New York City and in the adjacent areas of Northern New Jersey. He finds that the area closest to New York, Bergen County (between the Hackensack and Hudson Rivers), replicated the NYC features outlined above, with no more variation than we find in the city itself. In the area between the Hackensack and Passaic Rivers, including Rutherford, there is a striking tendency to lose the functional constraint before nasals, so that *can, am, an, and* are tense. Variable tensing is found in open syllable word types like *planet, fashionable*. Beyond the Passaic River, the short-*a* systems are radically different from that of New York City. ANAE interviews carried out in the 1990s in Passaic and Paterson show a uniform nasal system, with tensing before and only before nasal consonants. This gives us some indication of what may have preceded the diffusion of New York City influence into Bergen County.

Although the original ANAE design was aimed at cities of 50,000 or more, it was extended to study a number of small towns in the area between New York City and Philadelphia. Two speakers from North Plainfield, NJ were interviewed. North Plainfield is a residential community of 20,000, located 28 miles southwest of New York City and 18 miles southwest of Newark, the nearest full representative of the NYC dialect. One ANAE subject was Alex O., an 81-year-old retired tool and die maker of Russian/Polish background, who was interviewed in 2001. Figure 15.8 shows that his short-*a* system clearly follows the basic New York City pattern. The symbols in Figure 15.8 are cued to the NYC pattern; grey triangles represent tense /æh/ and black squares represent lax /æ/. Vowels are tense in closed syllables before voiced stops (*cab, bad, glad*) and voiceless fricatives (*bath, math, glass, past, rash, Alaska*). A few words that are normally tensed in NYC, mostly polysyllables, are found in the lax class: *mash, candidate, mansions*.[15] An important item here is lax *bag;* words with final /g/ are uniformly lax outside of NYC. As in NYC, inflectional boundaries close the syllable (*banning*). The open syllable constraint is partially intact, with lax *Canada* but tense *classics*.[16] The lexical exception *avenue* is tense, as in NYC. The crucial difference from NYC is the absence of the functional constraint before nasals, as shown in the tense positions of *am* and the auxiliary *can* along with the noun *can*. (However, *had* is lax.)

The second North Plainfield speaker studied is a younger man, Michael O., a consultant in criminology of Irish background, 58 years old in 2001 and not related

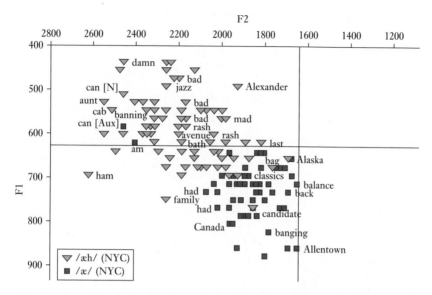

Figure 15.8   Short-*a* system of Alex O., 81 [2001], North Plainfield, NJ, TS 815

to Alex O. Michael O. preserves the NYC system in its basic outlines before front nasals, voiced stops and voiceless fricatives, but with further loss of structural detail. In his speech we observe the tensing of *am* and auxiliary *can* at the same phonetic position as in Alex O.'s speech; but his *had* is also tense. On the other hand, the lexical exception *avenue* is lax. The open syllable constraint is weaker: *camera, damage, Janet, planet, Spanish, Catholic* are tense, but *manage* and *castle* are lax.

In these cases and in those to follow, we recognize the influence of the NYC system by its complex and unusual conditioning of tensing before front nasals, voiced stops and voiceless fricatives – a feature found only in NYC and in communities that have a history of contact with NYC. A number of lexical and phonetic details may or may not be copied with the basic phonetic pattern. Most subject to loss through diffusion are the open syllable constraint and the function word constraint.

15.6.2   Diffusion to Albany

Albany was actually settled before New York City. Established by Henry Hudson in 1609, it was the second permanent settlement in the colonies which would later become the United States. It had a long and separate history, during and after the Dutch period. But the construction of the Erie Canal from 1810 to 1827 led to a steady flow of population from New York City to Albany and westward. It is not

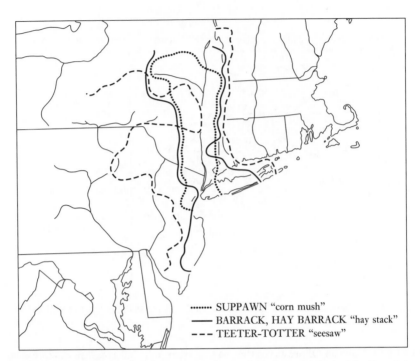

Figure 15.9   The Hudson Valley as a dialect area (Kurath 1949, Figure 13). Copyright © 1949, reprinted by permission of the University of Michigan Press

surprising, then, to find a number of lexical maps from the *Word Geography* of Kurath (1949) that display an affiliation between New York City and the Hudson River valley. Figure 15.9 traces the distribution of three vocabulary items that are common to the NYC region and the Hudson Valley: the words *suppawn* for "corn meal," *barrack* for "hay cock" and *teeter-totter* for "seesaw." Of these, *teeter-totter* is most likely to survive in New York City today; it was used regularly by Lower East Side subjects in 1963 (Labov 1966).

The short-*a* distributions in New York State outside of the Hudson Valley do not resemble the New York City system. Most of these cities have type (b), the wholesale raising of short *a* characteristic of the Inland North. New England is dominated by the type (a) nasal pattern. But, in Albany, the two ANAE speakers exhibit a striking resemblance to the NYC pattern – the situation illustrated in Figure 15.10: the short-*a* distribution of John E.[17]

Anyone familiar with New York City phonology will recognize Albany as a close relative. The back vowel /oh/ in *law* and *coffee* not only is raised to upper mid back position, but also shows the type of rounding ("pursing") specific to New York City. The tensed short *a* has a strongly fronted nucleus, which rises to upper mid and lower high position. As in New York, the tense set is a complex configuration

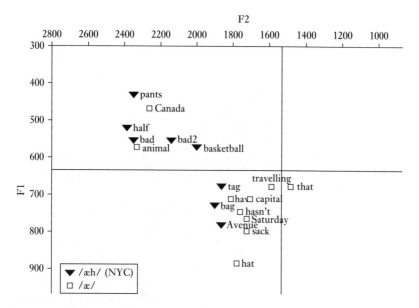

Figure 15.10   Short-*a* tokens of John E., 46 [1995], Albany, NY, TS 353

of voiced stops, voiceless fricatives and front nasals. However, a close examination of the specifics of the Albany system reveals some marked departures from NYC.

As in Figure 15.8, the symbols in Figure 15.10 are keyed to the tense/lax classes of NYC. Empty squares in the upper left region and solid triangles in the lower right denote deviations from the NYC system. As in NYC, short *a* before voiced stops and voiceless fricatives is tense (*bad, half, basketball*). But Albany shows the loss of the open syllable constraint: two tokens each of *Canada* and *animal* are clearly tensed. As in North Plainfield, short *a* before /g/ is lax: *tag* and *bag*. The word *avenue*, which normally has a tense vowel in NYC, is lax here.

The diffusion northward of the short-*a* system to Albany represents a transportation of the general phonetic basis for the NYC split, but not a faithful copy. The opposition of closed versus open syllables is lost and, with it, the grammatical opposition between tense *planning* and lax *planet*. What remains is the separation of the tokens into a bimodal distribution of allophones determined by the unusual phonetic constraints that are found in NYC: voiced stops (with the exception of /g/) and voiceless fricatives, along with front nasals.

Dinkin's exploration of dialect boundaries in upstate New York State (2009) yields a richer picture of the diffusion of NYC features into the Hudson Valley. Figure 15.11 shows the vowel system of a 53-year-old retired retail worker from Poughkeepsie, a city halfway up the Hudson Valley between New York City and Albany. Again, the phonetic pattern of the NYC system is reproduced, with its

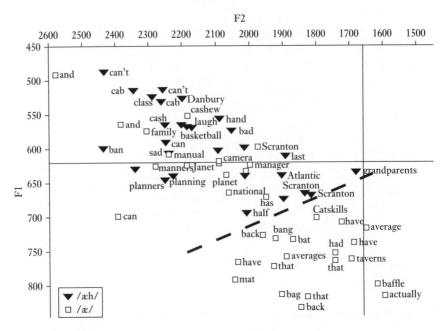

Figure 15.11 Short-*a* vowels of Louie R., 53 [2009], Poughkeepsie, NY (Dinkin 2009). Reprinted by permission of the University of Pennsylvania

tense short *a* before front nasals, voiceless fricatives (*laugh, cash, last, basketball*) and voiced stops (*cab, bad*). Again, among the voiced stops, /g/ is excepted from tensing (lax *bag*). The function word constraint is weakened: *can, and, has* are among the tense vowels, though *have* and *had* are lax. The open syllable constraint is also missing: *national, cashew, family, camera, planet, manner* are all tense.

15.6.3 Diffusion to Cincinnati

The city of Cincinnati is represented by four speakers in the ANAE database; three are analyzed acoustically. Figure 15.12 shows the characteristic short-*a* system as displayed in the productions of a 58-year-old woman, Lucia M., a former teacher of Irish/German background, who was then working as an accountant at a savings-and-loan firm. One can observe a division into tense and lax sets, which is characteristic of NYC. The tense set includes short *a* before front nasals (*ham, aunt, chance, divan*), voiced stops (*mad, sad, dad*) and voiceless fricatives (*cash, hashbrowns*). Boberg and Strassel (2000) noted the resemblance between the Cincinnati and NYC short-*a* patterns; they interviewed fifteen more subjects, paying considerable attention to short *a* (see also ANAE, Ch. 19).

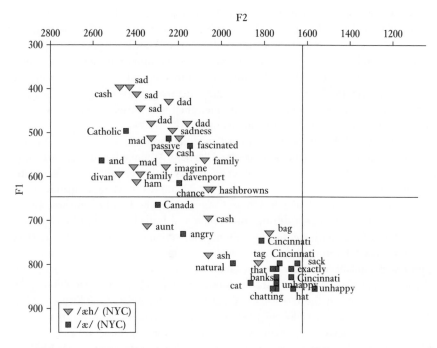

Figure 15.12   Short-*a* system of Lucia M., 58 [1994], Cincinnati, OH, TS 120

We find in Cincinnati the same type of deviations from the NYC pattern as in North Plainfield and Albany, shown in Figure 15.12 as dark squares among the grey triangles. The open syllable constraint is consistently violated, as shown in tense *Catholic*, *passive*, *fascinated*, *davenport* and *Canada*. In addition, the function word *and* is found in the tense group, reflecting the loss of the grammatical constraint. Among the lax tokens, the only clear exception to the NYC pattern is vowels before /g/.

Our first task is to account for the resemblance between NYC and Cincinnati in historical terms – in the original settlement pattern or by later contact. Cincinnati lies squarely in the Midland area, which was generally populated by a settlement stream that passed through Philadelphia, Western Pennsylvania and Kentucky. But, while the Mid-Atlantic region of Baltimore, Wilmington and Philadelphia limits tensing before voiced stops to only three words (*mad*, *bad*, *glad*), Cincinnati has general tensing before all voiced stops except /g/. While the Mid-Atlantic region limits tensing to codas with front voiceless fricatives, Cincinnati resembles NYC in tensing before palatal /š/ as well. It should also be noted that the five oldest Cincinnati subjects interviewed by Boberg and Strassel had uniform tensing before voiced fricatives – an environment that is variable in NYC.[18]

We are fortunate in having very detailed accounts of the settlement of Cincinnati. From 1943 to 1963, the Historical and Philosophical Society of Ohio published a *Bulletin* with contributions from many local scholars. We will consider this evidence on the settlement history of the Cincinnati speech community in some detail, since it gives us an intimate view of the process of diffusion and bears crucially on the relation between the New York City and the Cincinnati short-*a* patterns. The great majority of the settlers whose origins are identified were raised in New Jersey, not far from the North Plainfield area just considered.

The history of the city now known as Cincinnati began in 1787, when Congress opened to settlement the land between the Allegheny Mountains and the Mississippi River (Shepard 1949). Several prominent veterans of the Revolutionary War made the first purchase of land near the mouth of the Miami River. Major Benjamin Stites was a native of Scotch Plains in Union County, NJ, who first became acquainted with the Cincinnati region during the French and Indian wars, and he conveyed his enthusiasm for settlement to Judge John Cleves Symmes. Symmes was a native of New York who moved to New Jersey at the age of 28. He and his associates purchased 330,000 acres between the Great Miami and Little Miami Rivers. With Symmes's party was Ephraim Kibby, a hunter, road builder and Indian fighter who afterwards served in the territorial legislatures; his birthplace was listed as New Jersey in 1754 (although Sjodahl 1964 argues that he came to New Jersey to enlist in the 4th New Jersey Regiment from his family home in Somers, Connecticut). Shortly afterwards, a party of twenty-six settlers headed by Stites arrived.[19] His children Benjamin Jr, Elijah and Hezekiah were all prominent in the early history of the area; Benjamin Jr's wife is said to have been the first white woman in Cincinnati.

Among the early settlers, the Burnet family had great influence in the first half of the nineteenth century (Stevens 1952). Dr William Burnet (1730–91) was a native of New Jersey born of Scottish parents, a member of the Continental Congress and Surgeon General during the Revolutionary War. One of his sons, William, went to Cincinnati in 1789 but returned in 1791. In 1796 two other sons, Jacob and George, moved to Cincinnati; they both became lawyers and took part in the territorial government of Ohio. Burnet's youngest son Isaac went to Cincinnati in 1804, studied law with Jacob and married a woman from a Cumberland County, PA family. He became the county prosecuting attorney and was succeeded by another New Jersey man, Joseph Crane. Isaac Burnet and Joseph Crane then opened the Dayton Manufacturing Company together with two other businessmen, one from New Jersey, the other from Rhode Island. Isaac Burnet was elected mayor of Cincinnati in 1819, and served for twelve years.

At a meeting of the Cincinnati Pioneer Association in 1844, it was noted that the oldest pioneer present was William Dennison, born in New Jersey. A monument to another prominent early pioneer, Daniel Drake, shows that he was born in 1785 in Essex County, NJ (Blankenhorn 1950). A study of the Old Stone Episcopal Church centered around Reverend John Collins, who came to Cincinnati in 1802 from Gloucester County, NJ.

In 1957, Shepard discovered a trunk full of letters in the attic of a house in North Bend, a suburb of Cincinnati. Written by a neighbor who had left the farming district of New Jersey, they were addressed to relatives back in New Jersey, describing in alluring terms the new tract of land purchased by Judge Symmes (Shepard 1957).

The view that emerges of the linguistic formation of the Cincinnati dialect is clear. From its founding in 1788 to at least the middle of the nineteenth century, Cincinnati society was dominated by people from central New Jersey. Settlers were drawn from many other areas as well, like Rhode Island, Connecticut and Pennsylvania, but a typical board of directors had three of four members from New Jersey. The great majority of the community leaders identified in these historical notes came from the area of New Jersey which now has the short-*a* system of Figure 15.8.

This was not a community migration of 10,000 to 20,000 people, typical of the New England migrations discussed in Chapter 10. People moved as individuals or in small groups, occasionally returning, and often married outside of their groups of common origin. At least for the earliest period, the NYC short-*a* system was transmitted from adults to other adults, contacting settlers from other dialect regions in their new home: a case we would have to classify as diffusion rather than transmission. The situation is made more complex by the local origins of the settlers. Some of the New Jersey migrants may have come from communities that maintained the NYC system intact. Others may have had the modified system we saw in North Plainfield, and hence they may have been the agents of a second diffusion. In any case, Cincinnati children of the first quarter of the nineteenth century absorbed from their parents the simplified form of the NYC system described here. The diffusion was effective: with its New Jersey origins and continued contact with the home communities, the Cincinnati dialect resisted leveling with other Midland dialects to the end of the twentieth century.

This second diffusion has created a further distance from the original NYC pattern. The open syllable constraint is practically gone in the Cincinnati version, as well as the grammatical constraint. Furthermore, two phonetic parameters have been generalized. Voiced fricative codas lead here to tensing much more consistently than in New Jersey or New York. As we have seen elsewhere, the constraint against tensing before velars is extended from nasal to oral consonants – that is, to /g/.

At this point we have to consider the possibility that the short-*a* systems of Plainfield, Albany and Cincinnati represent an original stage of the NYC pattern, which was faithfully transmitted to New Jersey and Albany and then perhaps less faithfully westward, while the features that now distinguish NYC – particularly the grammatical constraint – are later developments. This would correspond to the version of the wave model elaborated by Wolfram and Schilling-Estes (2003).

The earliest account we have of the NYC short-*a* system is Babbitt (1896). Our present argument assumes that, one century earlier, the NYC system was similar to what it is now. If our speculations on the earlier history of the NYC short-*a* system are correct, this system had its origins in the British broad-*a* system at a time when the British vowel was fronted (Ferguson 1975; PLC, Vol. 1), and it has undergone considerable change from that point on. The grammatical constraint would be one such innovation. On the other hand, the open syllable constraint is shared by all versions of the British broad-*a* system and by the NYC system. The question then remains: is there any evidence that the grammatical constraint does date back to the time of the Revolutionary War? Though we have no direct evidence, indirect evidence characteristic of the comparative method stems from the fact that the dialects of Philadelphia, Reading, Wilmington and Baltimore – clearly cognate with NYC in having the phonemic split of short *a* – share this constraint. The function words *can*, *am*, *an* are also lax in the Mid-Atlantic short-*a* systems.[20] The likelihood that these are independent innovations is not very great, considering the fact that no other case has been reported in North America or in Britain across the wide variety of short-*a* developments. As we have seen, the changes that have taken place are rather in the other direction: that of the shift of short *a* in function words from lax to tense.[21] We therefore proceed with the most likely scenario, that the British broad-*a* class was transformed early on in the formation of the American English of the two major cities of the Mid-Atlantic region through the common innovation of a constraint on function words, an innovation that has been faithfully transmitted within these speech communities but not diffused to others.

The next case shows a resemblance to New York City in a broader range of phonetic phenomena; with evidence of commercial relationships that led to intimate social intercourse with New York City during the nineteenth century.

15.6.4   Diffusion to New Orleans

Though the city of New Orleans is located in the Southern United States, it has long been recognized that its dialect is quite different from that of other cities in the South. ANAE defines the South as a dialect region by the monophthongization of /ay/ before voiced obstruents – the initiating stage of the Southern Shift. Such monophthongization is found only marginally in New Orleans. There are no traces of the second and third stages of the Southern Shift, which involve the reversal of the relative positions of the short vowels and front upgliding vowels. Still, New Orleans does fall within the larger Southeastern superregion, characterized by the fronting of /ow/ and resistance to the low back merger (ANAE, Map 11.11).

Many observers have noted a resemblance between the speech of New Orleans and that of New York City. For example Liebling (1961) remarks:

> There is a New Orleans city accent [...] associated with downtown New Orleans, particularly with the German and Irish Third Ward, that is hard to distinguish from the accent of Hoboken, Jersey City, and Astoria, Long Island, where the Al Smith inflection, extinct in Manhattan, has taken refuge.

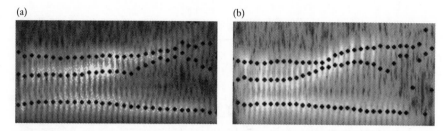

Figure 15.13 LPC analysis of pronunciation of vowel nuclei of (a) *first* and (b) *pers(on)* by Sybil P., 69 [1996], New Orleans, LA, TS611

Like most public observers of city dialects, Liebling interprets working-class metropolitan accents as geographic subdivisions. But the perception of similarity between New York City and New Orleans is based on reality. It is well known that New Orleans has the palatalized form of the *r*-less mid central vowel [əɪ] in *work*, *thirty*, etc., which forms the main stereotype of older New York City speech. Labov (1966) reports that this stigmatized *r*-less feature was rapidly disappearing among younger speakers. However, close attention to the *r*-colored form used by many New Yorkers today reveals a continuing trace of palatalization. Figure 15.13 displays this phonetic characteristic of New Orleans in two mid central vowel nuclei as pronounced by one of the oldest ANAE speakers from New Orleans: Sybil P., 69, of German/Italian background. In Figure 15.13a the vowel in *first* shows a steady state for 101 msec, with F2 at about 1373 Hz. F2 then rises abruptly, for 44 msec, to a peak of 1964 Hz. At the same time it comes into close proximity with F3, producing the auditory effect of a palatalized [r]. In Figure 15.13b a similar pattern is followed in the first syllable of *person*, though the conjunction of F2 and F3 is not maintained for as long.

A palatalized mid central vowel is also characteristic of areas of South Carolina and Eastern Georgia (Kurath and McDavid 1961), and can be found in the Gulf States (Pederson et al. 1986). In New Orleans, it appears in conjunction with many Northern phonetic features. One phonetic characteristic rarely found in the South is the use of stops for interdental fricatives, widely recognized as a feature of New York City working-class speech.[22] Sybil P. uses initial stops in *Thursday* and *thirties*. (It should be noted that Sybil P. had worked as a secretary in a bank and cannot be considered a lower-class speaker.)

When we turn to the short-*a* system, the parallels between New Orleans and New York City become even more striking. Figure 15.14 displays the short-*a* distribution of Sybil P. The solid triangles and empty squares superimpose the NYC system on the New Orleans system, so that similarities and differences are immediately visible. Three black triangles appear in the lax distribution: *Dan*, *grandparents*, *after*.[23] In the tense distribution, we find short *a* before front nasals; voiced stops /b/ and /d/ (*bad*, *sad*, *crab*, *Crabtree*); and voiceless fricatives (*asked*,

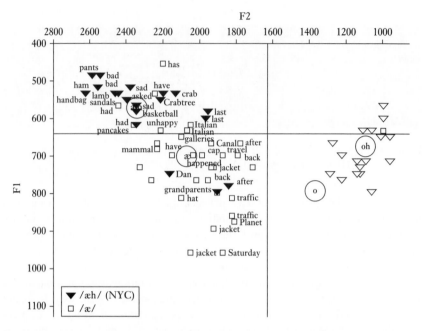

Figure 15.14   Short-*a* distribution of Sybil P., 69 [1996], New Orleans, LA, TS 611

basketball, last). The general constraint excluding function words is absent: *has, have* and *had* are all tense. This also suggests that, as in Cincinnati, the distribution has been generalized to include the voiced fricatives /v/ and /z/. On the other hand, the constraint against tensing in open syllables is present here, as shown by lax *mammal, planet, travel, traffic.*

New Orleans displays another feature that is uncommon in the South: the raising of /oh/ in *law, cost, hawk*, etc. to mid and lower high back position. ANAE, Chapter 18.4 shows that, for most Southern speakers, the nucleus of /oh/ is in the same position as /o/ in *cop* or *rock* and is distinguished by a back upglide. Outside of New Orleans, /oh/ raised to upper mid position is found in a continuous belt of East Coast cities ranging from Southeastern Connecticut to New York City (and Albany), Philadelphia and Baltimore. Figure 15.14 also shows the clear separation of /o/ and /oh/. The mean F1 of /oh/ is 677 Hz, comparable to the raised /oh/ of the Mid-Atlantic, which is defined by the criterion F1(oh) < 700.

A younger New Orleans ANAE subject is Elizabeth G., who was 38 years old when interviewed in 1996.[24] Again, the distribution of tense vowels matches the NYC system, including short *a* before front nasals, voiced stops (*dad, bad, sad, grabbing*) and voiceless fricatives (*ask, grass, glass, master, past*). Again, the class of function words is tense and not lax (*have*). The status of the open syllable constraint is severely weakened. The word *internationally* is clearly tense, and *ceramic* is in an intermediate position. On the other hand, *Canada* and *catholic* are definitely in the lax set.

As further evidence of the weakness of the open syllable constraint in New Orleans, one may consider the speech of Dr John (Mac Rebennack), a prominent representative of the New Orleans musical tradition, who grew up in the Third Ward of the city during the middle of the twentieth century. In a broadcast of March 16, 2005, Dr John showed the following pattern in the distribution of tense and lax short *a*.[25]

tense (closed syllable)	*answer, fancy, hand, bad, dad*
tense (open syllable)	*piano (2), classical, daddy, fascinate [2], Manny*
lax (closed syllable)	*that, cats, fact, that's, at*
lax (open syllable)	*Allen*

Dr John's tensing pattern includes front nasals, voiced stops and voiceless fricatives, as in New York City, but open syllable words are treated in the same way as words with closed syllables.

In New Orleans, as in Cincinnati, the local pattern is receding. Two other New Orleans speakers analyzed acoustically are 38 and 44 years old; both show the nasal short-*a* system typical of the South, as in Shreveport and Baton Rouge.

The history of New Orleans points to repeated and extensive connections with New York City. While Cincinnati was an industrial rival of New York in the middle of the nineteenth century, the city of New Orleans had intimate and complementary relations, as the port of shipment for the cotton trade financed by New York bankers. This aspect of the history of New Orleans is described by McNabb and Madère (1983, Ch. 3, p. 1):

> From 1803 until 1861, New Orleans' population increased from 8,000 to nearly 170,000 [...] By 1830, New Orleans was America's third largest city, behind New York and Baltimore [...] During the Pre-Civil War period, a scarcity of capital in New Orleans forced seekers of large-scale investment to look to New York, London, or Paris.

Berger (1980: 137) summarizes the evidence for close relations between New Orleans and New York City in the middle of the nineteenth century:

> In the ante-bellum period, roughly between 1820 and 1860, financial, commercial and social relations between the city and the South were at fever pitch: New York banks underwrote the plantation economy, cotton was shipped routinely from New Orleans, Charleston, Savannah and Mobile to be trans-shipped to England, and Southern planters regularly combined business with pleasure in the Big Apple of the 1800s.

He goes on to cite the judgment of Foner (1941) as to the predominance of New York influence on the New Orleans economy: "Down to the outbreak of the Civil

War, New York dominated every single phase of the cotton trade from plantation to market."

Berger's aim was to buttress the case for the derivation of the NYC palatalized mid central vowel from New Orleans; this is the opposite direction of influence from the one proposed here for the short-*a* pattern.[26] The gravity model and the historical facts argue rather for a greater direction of influence from the larger city. We find many descriptions of commercial and social relations between New Orleans and New York in the five-volume history of *The Old Merchants of New York City* by John Scoville (1870); the typical pattern involves movement of New Yorkers to New Orleans. In Scoville's Chapter 3, we read that Walter Barrett took a letter of credit for one million dollars to New Orleans by way of Wheeling, hoping to outstrip his competitors in buying up that year's cotton crop (p. 26). It is reported that the founder of the great New York mercantile firm of E. K. Collins & Son had a house in New Orleans (p. 141). Among the oldest commercial firms of New York City was Brown Brothers & Co., who established in 1842 a branch in New Orleans under the name of Samuel Nicholson, "who had been many years their clerk" (p. 187). Bradish Johnson, head of the firm of Johnson & Lazarus, had a brother Henry who was located on a plantation in New Orleans. When Henry died, he left the plantation to Bradish, who proceeded to New Orleans and established more favorable conditions for the 250 slaves, many of whom were able to purchase their own freedom (p. 185). In Scoville's description of the prominent Seixas merchant clan, founded by Benjamin Seixas in 1780, we read: "Madison [Seixas] is in New Orleans, and a partner in the large firm of Glidden and Seixas" (Scoville 1870, Vol. II: 127).

Among the bankers closely tied to New Orleans there were many representatives of the large Sephardic Jewish families (Lazarus, Seixas). Scoville frequently underlines the importance of the Jews in early nineteenth-century New York:

> The Israelite merchants were few then [1790], but now they have increased in this city beyond any comparison. There are 80,000 Israelites in the city. It is the high standard of excellence of the old Israelite merchants of 1800 that has made this race occupy the proud position it does now in this city. (Ibid.)

We can see how intimate the relations were between the Jewish population of the two cities by examining Korn's history *The Early Jews of New Orleans* (1969), which deals with social and business relations from 1718 to 1812. References to New York City are found on 55 pages – a larger number than for any other city.[27]

Following the publication of ANAE, I received a letter from Mr Herman S. Kohlmeyer Jr, Senior Vice President of the investment firm A. G. Edwards, who described himself as "the last person in New Orleans who still makes his living from the cotton trade." His account leaves no doubt that Jewish merchants with strong New York City connections played a formative role in the upper-class speech of New Orleans:

I am the great-grandson of some of our top cotton merchants [...] as is my closest friend. They were all German Jewish immigrants who came over in the 1830–1860 era [...] I remember very well friends of my father's generation who talked about how hard they "woiked" before they went home to their house on "Foist" Street. That was very much our upper class speech, as much with the Christians and with the Jews.[28]

The detailed linguistic resemblances between New York City and New Orleans involve both of the pivot points that have been found to determine the main directions of development of North American English dialects: the status of short *o* as an integral phoneme, distinct from long open *o*, and the status of short *a* (Labov 1991). As in New York, the New Orleans raised /oh/ ensures the separate status of short *o* as the phoneme /o/.[29] As in New York, New Orleans divides short *a* into two distinct classes, separating tense vowels before front nasals, voiced stops and fricatives in closed syllables from voiceless stops and liquids. However, the New Orleans configuration is only superficially similar to that of New York: it is a phonetically conditioned set of allophones rather than a grammatically and lexically specified distribution.

15.6.5   The common pattern

In the four cases of diffusion of the New York City short-*a* pattern presented above, phonetic conditioning by the following segment is the common thread, though the phonetic pattern is not perfectly transmitted. As Dinkin (2009) points out, the diffusing pattern tends to regularize and simplify. While NYC differentiates the voiced velar stop /g/ from the nasal velar /ŋ/, /æ/ regularly becomes lax before /g/ as the system spreads geographically. Tensing before voiceless fricatives is sometimes generalized by extension to tensing before voiced fricatives. But the most regular differences are found at a more abstract level. The function word constraint is lost: with few exceptions, *can, am, and, have, has, had* are tense, though they are always lax in NYC. The second major difference is the loss of the constraint against tensing in open syllables, which is quite general – though not complete – in New Orleans. It might seem at first glance that this represents the loss of a phonological constraint. But, on reflection, it may be seen as the loss of the effect of inflectional boundaries in closing the syllable. When short *a* is tensed in all open syllables, there is no longer a difference between [Cardinal] /mænɪŋ/ and /mæhn#ɪŋ/ [the pumps], or between monomorphemic /bænər/ and /bæhn#ər/, a person who bans. The adults who adopted the NYC system did not observe that tense /mæhn#ɪŋ/, /bæhn#ər/, /pæhs#ɪŋ/, /pæhs#ər/ were bimorphemic, while /mænɪŋ/, /bænər/, /kæsəl/, /bæfəl/ are not. Accordingly, they generalized the tensing of bimorphemic words to all words of this phonetic shape. This is consistent with the proposition that the main agents in diffusion are adults, who are less likely to observe and replicate abstract features of language structure.

15.7   The Transmission and Diffusion of
Mergers and Splits

The argument so far has not considered the type of structural diffusion that is most frequent and prominent in historical linguistics and dialectology, namely mergers. Herzog's corollary of Garde's Principle (Herzog 1965; PLC, Vol. 1) states that mergers expand geographically at the expense of distinctions; there is massive empirical evidence of such expansion.[30] Though the adoption of a merger is not conventionally considered to be structural borrowing, it must be viewed as such, since the recipient dialect loses one of its categories in adopting the structure of the expanding dialect. Up to this point we have been arguing that adults do not easily acquire new structural categories; but the evidence so far does not bear on the loss of a category.

Herold's proposal concerning the diffusion of a merger argues that speakers of a two-phoneme system, coming in contact with a one-phoneme system, find that the contrast is not useful and so cease to attend to it (1990, 1997). Chapter 2 of this volume provides some evidence to support this asymmetric mechanism. There is ample evidence that merger in perception precedes merger in production (Di Paolo 1988, ANAE, Ch. 9), and near-mergers give us a static view of such a situation (Labov et al. 1991; PLC, Vol. 1, Ch. 12). But this does not tell us how a merger in the adult speaker's perception would be transmitted to the speaker's children. There are indeed numerous cases of a contrast strongly maintained among adults but solidly merged in the speech of their children. Herold (1990) provides a detailed view of a parent with a clear, non-overlapping distinction between /o/ and /oh/ and a son with total merger.

Chapter 6 referred to Johnson's 2010 study of the geographic boundary of the low back merger in Eastern Massachusetts (Figure 6.13). Across three older generations, the boundary was stable: the Eastern New England merger showed no signs of expanding towards the Rhode Island border. But in two small towns, Sekonk and Attleboro, Johnson found children in the fourth to sixth grade shifting to the merger, including some whose parents both made the distinction (Figure 6.14). He attributes the change to the inmigration of commuting families from the Boston area. Yang (2009) provides a calculation which shows that a moderate proportion of inmigrant children with the merger (21.7 percent) can trigger the acquisition of the merger by children of parents who have the distinction.

The transfer of linguistic patterns from parent to child is not limited by the relative complexity of what is being transmitted. The continuity of the New York City split short-*a* system from 1896 to the present and the uniformity of the Mid-Atlantic short-*a* system in Philadelphia, Reading, Wilmington and Baltimore indicate that such patterns can be faithfully transmitted across generations through children's language learning abilities. However, there is evidence that a pattern of this complexity cannot be learned as a second dialect, even by children. These volumes have cited several times the results of Payne's study of the acquisition of the Philadelphia dialect by children of out-of-state parents in King of Prussia (1976, 1980). She found that children under 10 years of age acquired the phonetic variables of the Philadelphia system after only a few years in King of Prussia, but only one of thirty-four children of out-of-state parents acquired the lexical and grammatical conditioning of the short-*a* system. For our present purposes, it is relevant to recall the degrees of approximation to the Philadelphia system exhibited by children of out-of-state parents (PLC, Vol. 1, Ch. 18). This is parallel to what we have seen happening in North Plainfield, Albany, Cincinnati and New Orleans: diffusion of the phonetic conditioning of the NYC system, without its lexical, grammatical or syllabic conditioning. In this complex case, children who must learn the system from their peers rather than from their parents will not achieve the precise acquisition of the system that is characteristic of normal parent-to-child transmission.

This conclusion is consistent with the fact that the distinction between transmission and diffusion is maximal in the case of splits. The converse of Garde's Principle is that splits are rarely reversed. Britain's (1997) account of the complexities of the /u/ ~ /ʌ/ split in the Fens shows the irregular result of a rare case of expansion of a split, where the two-phoneme system is favored by social prestige. The constraint on learning a new phonemic contrast applies equally to studies of the children of inmigrant parents. Trudgill examined the ability of twenty adults born in Norwich to reproduce the local distinction between the vowel classes of *own* [ʌun] and *goal* [gu:l]. Ten whose parents were born in Norwich did so; the ten whose parents were born elsewhere did not (Trudgill 1986: 35–6).

This confirms the position of RWT that an *unbroken* sequence of parent-to-child transmission is required to maintain complex patterns of phonetic, grammatical and lexical specification like the NYC short-*a* pattern. Therefore, if speakers from other dialect areas enter the community in large numbers, their children will dilute the uniformity of the original pattern. Although the Mid-Atlantic dialects are quite stable at present, there is some indication of such a weakening. Lexical diffusion of open syllable words before /n/ has been observed since 1980 (Labov 1989b, Roberts and Labov 1995); some neighborhoods report general tensing before /l/ (Banuazizi and Lipson 1998); some inmigrant groups do not show the Philadelphia pattern even in the second generation (Friesner and Dinkin 2006) and still other neighborhoods show shifting to the default nasal system, as in certain small towns of Southern New Jersey (Ash 2002). In a study of twelve white New Yorkers, Becker and Wong (2009) found the traditional NYC pattern among older and middle-aged speakers – but not among speakers 18 to 32 years old, who seem to be shifting to the default nasal system.

To examine more closely the difference between transmission by children and diffusion by adults, we turn to a complex phonological change, which is free of such lexical and grammatical specification: the Northern Cities Shift. The structural complexity involved here has to do with the intricate interrelations among vowels as they evolve in chain shifts within and across subsystems (Martinet 1955, Moulton 1960).

15.8   Diffusion of the Northern Cities Shift

The Northern Cities Shift, first described in this volume in Figure 1.4, has been
a point of reference in many of the preceding chapters. Figure 15.15 shows in detail
how the NCS is realized in the vowel system of Kitty R. of Chicago in 1993, when
she was interviewed at the age of 56. The general raising of /æ/ to upper mid
position is marked by the solid black squares, and the fronting of /o/ by the small
empty squares, with five tokens well front of center. Diamonds indicate the backing of /e/ with a mean F2 of 1864 Hz, only 320 Hz higher than the F2 of /o/
(1544 Hz). /ʌ/ is shifted well to the back, overlapping /oh/, which has not
lowered extensively.

The geographic distribution of the NCS was displayed in Figures 8.3, 10.1 and
10.3. Figure 15.16 displays the area dominated by the NCS by means of the ED
structural criterion, as it was first defined in Figure 8.1. In this map, grey circles
indicate speakers for whom the difference between the mean F2 of /e/ and the

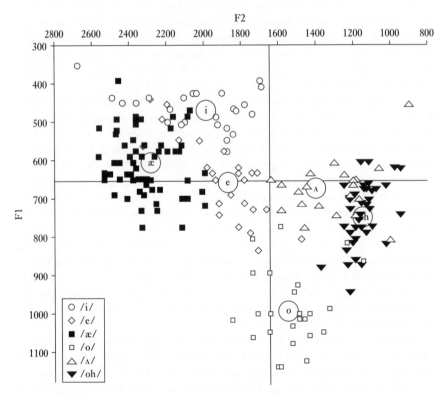

Figure 15.15   The Northern Cities Shift in the vowel system of Kitty R., 56 [1993],
Chicago, IL, TS 66

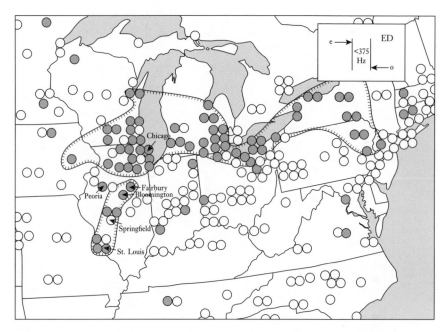

Figure 15.16   The ED measure of the advance of the Northern Cities Shift in the Inland North and the St Louis corridor. Grey symbols: F2(e) – F2(o) < 375 Hz

mean F2 of /o/ is less than 375 Hz. The figure adds an isogloss circumscribing the St Louis corridor, a stream of NCS features extending from Chicago to St Louis, which appeared in Figures 8.3 and 10.3 and is the more direct focus of this section.

The most striking feature of the Northern Cities Shift relevant to this study of transmission and diffusion is the uniformity of the pattern over the very large area of Figures 10.3 and 15.16. The history of westward settlement must be taken into account in order to understand this uniformity. The earliest records we have of the chain shift of /æ/, /o/ and /oh/ date from the 1960s. Chapter 5 argued that the initiating event of the NCS took place a hundred years earlier, during the construction of the Erie Canal in Western New York State. A koineization of various complex short-*a* systems to the simple general tensing of /æ/ seems to have occurred when workers and migrants from all over the northeast were integrated into the rapidly expanding cities of Rochester, Syracuse and Buffalo. The unrounding and centralization of /o/ had already taken place in Western New England (ANAE, Ch. 16). The westward migration of entire communities, described in Chapter 10, set the conditions under which the chain shift was transmitted faithfully across the Inland North as far as Wisconsin.

The linguistic boundary separating the Inland North and Midland vowel patterns is the sharpest and deepest division in North American English phonology

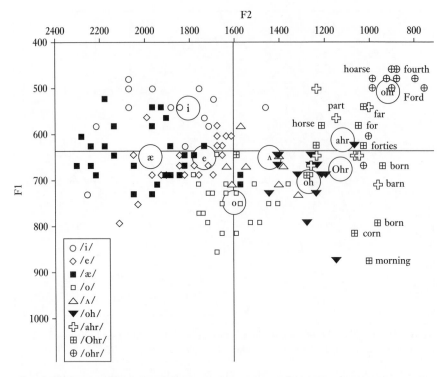

Figure 15.17   Northern Cities Shift and merger of /ɔhr/ and /ahr/ for Martin H., 48 [1994], St Louis, MO, TS 111. (On this chart, /Ohr/ = /ɔhr/)

(Figure 10.3). The isogloss bundle that separates these two areas combines five measures of the progress of the NCS, the Southern limit of Canadian raising of /ay/, and the Southern limit of dialects with /aw/ backer than /ay/ (ANAE, Ch. 11). Figure 15.16 shows that the front–back approximation of /e/ and /o/ is quite generally absent in the Midland region, except for St Louis and nearby communities. The city of St Louis, located as it is squarely in Midland territory, has recently developed many of the elements of the NCS. This city has long been known to display a mixture of Northern, Midland and Southern features (Murray 1993, 2002), but recent decades have witnessed a strong shift to Northern phonology. The characteristic St Louis merger of /ahr/ and /ɔhr/ in *are* and *or*, *card* and *cord*, *barn* and *born*, etc., has all but disappeared among younger speakers, who display instead the general merger of *or* and *ore*, *cord* and *cored*, along with a clear separation of this class from /ahr/ in *are* and *card* (Majors 2004).

   Figure 15.17 shows the St Louis vowel pattern in the system of Marvin H., who was interviewed in 1994, at the age of 48.[31] We observe on the one hand the traditional back merger before /r/. At the upper right, one can see, tightly clustered, the traditional /ohr/ class (*hoarse, four, Ford*). In mid position is the class of /ɔhr/ (*for, born, horse, corn, morning*) alongside /ahr/ (in *part, far*, and *barn*). The distinction

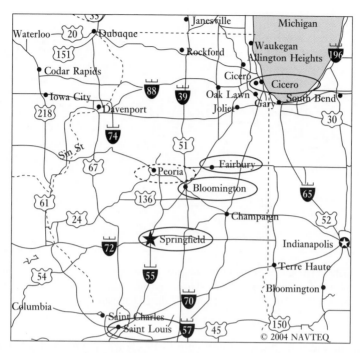

Figure 15.18   The corridor along Route I-55 from St Louis to Chicago

between *hoarse* and *horse*, *four* and *for* is well maintained, as well as the merger of *for* and *far*, *born* and *barn*. At the same time, the distribution of the NCS vowels matches the Chicago pattern of Figure 15.16 quite well. All /æ/ tokens are raised to mid position, /o/ is well fronted and /e/ is backed close to the midline. The difference between the second formants of /e/ and /o/ is only 134 Hz. /ʌ/ is moderately back, and some tokens of /oh/ are quite low. It is apparent that Marvin H. has combined the traditional St Louis pattern with the Northern Cities Shift.

This recent development in St Louis is not an independent phenomenon, distinct from the chain shift in the Inland North. Many ANAE maps show diffusion of NCS features along a narrow corridor extending from Chicago to St Louis along Route I-55 (Figure 15.18). This is the route of travel and interchange between Chicago and St Louis, and, for many citizens of St Louis, it is the most common highway to follow as they leave their home city. I-55 from Chicago to St Louis coincides with the Eastern end of Route 66, the westward highway that is so deeply embedded in American folklore. The ANAE data for this corridor are based on speakers from three cities along the interstate highway (Fairbury, Bloomington, Springfield), along with four speakers from St Louis.[32]

In Figure 15.16, fifty-nine out of the sixty-seven speakers within the Inland North isogloss satisfy the ED criterion, a *homogeneity* of .88. A similar proportion of speakers in the St Louis corridor do so: seven out of nine.

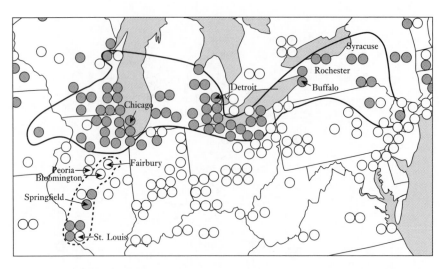

Figure 15.19   The UD measure of the advance of the Northern Cities Shift in the Inland North and the St Louis corridor. Grey symbols = UD measure: F2(ʌ) < F2(o). Solid isogloss = the Inland North as defined by the ED measure

A second measure, displayed in Figure 15.19, shows even more clearly how the St Louis corridor is differentiated from its Midland neighbors. Stage 2 of the NCS, the fronting of /o/, and stage 5, the backing of /ʌ/, have the effect of reversing the relative front–back positions of these two vowels by comparison with neighboring dialects. As defined in Chapter 8, the UD criterion defines the progress of the NCS: speakers involved in this chain shift are those for whom /ʌ/ is further back than /o/ (grey circles on Figure 15.19). Of all the measures of of the NCS, presented in Chapter 8, this one yields the sharpest differentiation between the Inland North and the Midland. Homogeneity within the Inland North is even greater than for the ED measure: sixty-five out of sixty-seven subjects in the Inland North satisfy the UD criterion, or .94. The almost total absence of grey symbols in the Midland area of Figure 15.19 contrasts with the five grey symbols in the St Louis corridor. Though this corridor is represented in ANAE by only four cities and nine speakers, the probability that this feature occurs in the corridor by chance is less than 1 in 1,000.[33] On the other hand, UD marking is significantly less frequent here than in the Inland North: only five of the nine speakers in the St Louis corridor are marked with grey symbols.[34]

Figures 15.16 and 15.19 illustrate the diffusion of the NCS along I-55 from Chicago to St Louis. However, it appears that the NCS along this corridor is not the same linguistic phenomenon as that found in the Inland North. There is good reason to believe that the systematic chain shift mechanism, triggered by the general raising of short *a*, is not driving the shift in the St Louis corridor.

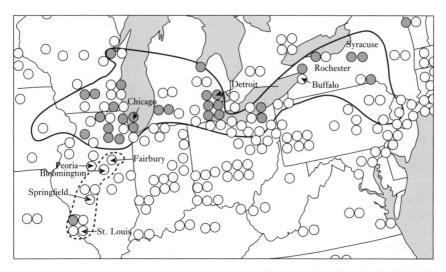

Figure 15.20   Speakers who meet all criteria of the Northern Cities Shift: AE1, O2, EQ, ED, and UD. Solid isogloss = the Inland North as defined by the ED measure

Figure 15.20 is a map of the same region, displaying speakers for whom the NCS is complete, in other words speakers who show all the relevant criteria. In addition to the ED and UD criteria, these include:

AE1: general raising of /æ/ in non-nasal environments, F1(æ) < 700 Hz
O2: fronting of /o/ to center, F2(o) < 1500 Hz
EQ: reversal of the relative height and fronting of /e/ and /æ/:
   F1(e) > F1(æ) and F2(e) < F2(æ).

Figure 15.20 shows that only twenty-eight of the sixty-seven Inland North speakers meet this strict criterion – or 42 percent. Sixteen of the twenty-eight are located in the largest cities: Detroit, Rochester, Syracuse, Chicago. On the other hand, the St Louis corridor contains only one such speaker, Martin H. in Figure 15.17 – and there are no others outside of the Inland North.

The other eight speakers in the St Louis corridor show an approximation to the NCS rather than the complete pattern of Figure 5.15. Five speakers in the corridor meet the AE1 criterion; but only two are marked for O2 and only one for EQ. The inference to be drawn is that the new vowel patterns of St Louis are not a locally evolved and transmitted structural consequence of the general raising of short *a*, but rather the result of the borrowing of individual elements of the NCS from the Inland North region centered on Chicago.

The geographic distribution of the various stages of the NCS in the Inland North and along the St Louis corridor makes it clear that there is much more variation

Table 15.1 Stages of the Northern Cities Shift found in nine speakers from Northern Illinois and in nine speakers from the St Louis corridor – with ages, rank ordering, and correlation of age with rank

Northern Illinois	AE1	O2	EQ	ED	UD	Age	Rank
Sterling IL	√	√	√	√	√	34	1
Elgin IL (1)	√	√	√	√	√	19	1
Elgin IL (2)	√	√	√	√	√	42	1
Joliet IL	√	√	√	√	√	30	1
Rockford IL (1)		√	√	√	√	37	2
Belvidere IL	√		√	√	√	33	2
Hammond IN	√	√	√			45	3
Rockford IL (2)	√				√	65	4
Lena IL	√					47	5
r-correlation							.74
age coefficient						.	.08*
St Louis Corridor							
St Louis MO (1)	√	√	√	√	√	48	1
St Louis MO (2)	√	√		√	√	57	2
Springfield IL AK	√			√	√	60	3
Fairbury IL	√			√		25	4
Bloomington	√			√		27	4
Springfield IL (1)				√		32	5
Springfield IL (2)					√	67	5
St Louis MO (3)					√	53	5
St Louis MO (4)				√		38	5
r-correlation							−0.21
age coefficient							n.s.

in the corridor. St Louis speakers are generally in advance of the speakers from the smaller cities along Route I-55. This would not seem to be much different from the view of diffusion obtained in the Brunlanes Peninsula by Trudgill (1974a) in Figure 15.2. In the "cascade" model displayed there, change moves from the largest city to the next largest, and so on down, rather than moving steadily across the geographic landscape as in the contagion model (Bailey et al. 1993). But the progress of the NCS in the St Louis corridor, including St Louis itself, is marked by irregularity in both structure and age distribution.

To the extent that the NCS is the result of the incrementation of sound changes by successive generations of children, we should find a clear relationship between age and the advancement of the shift. The ANAE study of the NCS in the Inland North as a whole shows significant age coefficients at the .01 level for the raising of /æ/, the fronting of /o/, the backing of /e/ and the backing of /ʌ/ (ANAE, Ch. 14). Table 15.1 compares the nine subjects of the St Louis corridor with nine speakers from Northern Illinois who are located within the Inland North. Check marks indicate whether a given speaker satisfies the criterion for five systematic measures of the NCS (AE1, O2, EQ, ED, UD). It is apparent that the shift is more advanced in Northern Illinois, but the crucial question is the trajectory of the change in apparent time. In the right hand column, each speaker is ranked for degree of advancement within his or her region by the number of criteria satisfied, and this ranking is then correlated with the age of the speaker. While the speakers from Northern Illinois show a sizable r-correlation of .74 with age, a small negative correlation of $-.21$ appears for the St Louis corridor. A regression coefficient for age on ranking of .08, significant at the .05 level, is found for Northern Illinois, indicating that a difference of fifty years between two speakers would project to a shift of four units in the rankings. No significant regression coefficient is found for the St Louis corridor.

This result suggests that the advancement of the NCS in the St Louis corridor is not the result of incrementation by children within the speech community, but rather the result of the influence of the Inland North speech pattern on adults. The conversion of the St Louis system to that of the Inland North may eventually lead to the participation of young children in the process and to further incrementation within the community, but the present situation seems to reflect a slower and less regular shift among adults – the result of diffusion along the corridor.

Martin H. appeared in Figure 15.20 as the only ANAE subject from St Louis to represent the NCS fully. A more characteristic view of how the NCS is realized in St Louis may be obtained from Figure 15.21, which plots the vowel system of

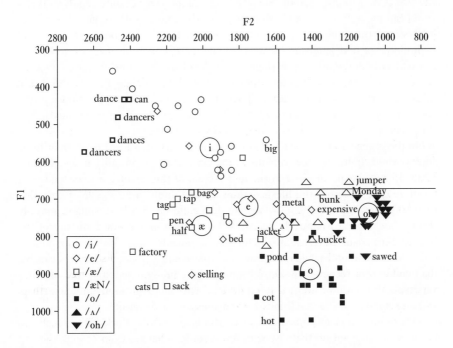

Figure 15.21   NCS vowels of Rose M., 38 [1994], St Louis, MO, TS 161

Rose M., the fourth St Louis speaker of Table 15.1.[35] Only one of the NCS movements is vigorously represented: /e/ moves down (*bed*, *selling*) and back (*metal*, *expensive*). There are traces of the other shifts: /ʌ/ has moved back to a moderate degree and, as a result, there is considerable overlap between /e/ and /ʌ/. Two tokens of short *o* have moved front of center (*pond*, *hot*), but the general /o/ mean, 1405 Hz, is well back of the normalized general F2 mean of 1590 Hz. The most striking deviation from the NCS pattern is the behavior of /æ/. Instead of a general movement to upper mid position, Rose M. shows the nasal system characteristic of the Midland: only the allophones of /æ/ before nasals move to mid front position (*dance*, *dancers*, *can*). The majority of the /æ/ tokens remain in low front position, even though a few /o/ tokens cross the center line.

15.9 The Social Context of Transmission and Diffusion

Our studies of the spread of the New York City short-*a* system and of the Northern Cities Chain Shift have allowed us to differentiate the diffusion of linguistic change across communities from the transmission of sound change within the speech community. At the outset, it was argued that change from below is driven by the continuous process of incrementation by children, who reproduce in full and advance their parents' system. Such incrementation can be quite rapid, so that a vowel can move from low to high position in the course of three generations; yet it preserves the integrity of the system, acquired with the speed, accuracy and faithfulness of first-language learners. In the incrementation of change, children learn to talk differently from their parents and in the same direction in each successive generation. This can happen only if children align the variants heard in the community with the vector of age: that is, they grasp the relationship: the younger the speaker, the more advanced the change. In such interrelated chain shifts as the NCS, the various elements advance together.

On the other hand, contact across communities involves learning, primarily by adults, who acquire the new variants of the originating community in a somewhat diluted form. As summarized in the first section of this chapter, recent studies of language change across the lifespan show us that adults are capable of changing their language, but at a much slower rate than children. Adult learning is not only slower, but it is also relatively coarse: it loses much of the fine structure of the linguistic system being transmitted. Our results coincide with evidence from numerous studies of second language acquisition that adult learners are far less capable than children of recognizing and reproducing the fine-grained structure of social variation. We can now address the question: what kinds of population structures and movements set the conditions for transmission or diffusion?

This inquiry first examined the short-*a* system of New York City, which has been transmitted within that city with few recorded changes from 1896 to the end of the twentieth century. The geographic uniformity of the NYC speech community, from Queens and the Bronx to Jersey City and Newark, suggests the uniform conditions under which an unbroken sequence of parent-to-child transmission can take place. The fact that the original population absorbed very large numbers of European immigrants, yet still maintained this continuity, is a tribute to the force of the doctrine of first effective settlement (Zelinsky 1992). It also shows that the concept of "unbroken sequence" does not imply that all transmission is necessarily within the nuclear family. Second-generation children of non-native speakers are capable of disregarding their parents' non-native features from such an early age that they become first dialect speakers of the local vernacular (Labov 1976). In contrast, it appears that children of native speakers of other dialects cannot match this performance (Payne 1976).[36]

The Inland North is a much larger territory, encompassing 88,000 square miles and some 34 million people. How can we account for the uniformity of the vowel system and its directions of age throughout this vast area? The settlement history of this region associates this uniformity with the migration of intact communities westward, in which entire cohorts of children, parents, kin and communal groups moved together. In his history of the westward migration, Richard Lyle Power points out that

> [m]ass migrations were indeed congenial to the Puritan tradition. Whole parishes, parson and all, had sometimes migrated from Old England. Lois Kimball Mathews mentioned 22 colonies in Illinois alone, all of which originated in New England or in New York, most of them planted between 1830 and 1840. (1953: 14)

The Yankee migration to the Inland North continued the cultural pattern of New England settlement, described by Fischer (1989) as a largely urban movement with a stronger emphasis on the nuclear family than is found in competing traditions.[37] New England folkways were transmitted intact in the course of these migrations (Fischer 1989, Frazer 1993, Carnes and Garrity 1996, Chapter 10 of this volume). Uniform transmission is favored by the two measures of stability in the community of New England settlers provided by Fischer (1989): high persistence[38] (75–96 percent) and low internal migration (pp. 814–15). We can attribute the uniformity of the phonology of the Inland North to the continuity of transmission within the inmigrating families and communities over the past century and a half, in which sound changes are steadily incremented by child language learners. This is the social structure that supports linguistic transmission over many generations.

From the account of the initiating conditions for the NCS in Western New York State, we know that this westward migration also absorbed substantial numbers of speakers of other dialects. While the NCS is a system of mutually interacting dependencies of some complexity, it does not have the grammatical and lexical intricacy of split short-*a* systems, and the social conditions for intact transmission may not be as stringent.

The uniformity of the vowel systems in cities of the Inland North may be contrasted with the great variety of systems found in the Midland. Widely differing patterns and directions of change are to be found in Philadelphia, Pittsburgh, Columbus, Cincinnati, Indianapolis and St Louis (ANAE, Ch. 19). Midland linguistic heterogeneity may be correlated with a pattern of westward migration that contrasts with the Yankee pattern just described. The initial Quaker settlers moving westward from Philadelphia placed a strong emphasis on the creation of farm communities, while the other component of Midland settlement – the back-country population of the upland South – created even smaller units of isolated households. Fischer gives only moderate levels of persistence for Quaker populations (40–60 percent), and low levels for the upland South (25–40 percent).

Nevertheless, large Midland cities did form, as various combinations of trade and travel brought populations together from various areas. The structure of the traditional St Louis dialect differentiates it from all other Midland cities. It is the result, not of large-scale migration from any one region, but of a mixture of Southern, Midland and Northern speakers in the second half of the nineteenth century (Frazer 1978; Murray 1993, 2002). It is undoubtedly the Northern component that distinguishes St Louis from the surrounding area. Frazer (1978) finds that St Louis and the adjoining counties of Illinois form a speech island in regard to eight Northern lexical items[39] and to several features of pronunciation that mark the area as Northern, as opposed to South Midland: (1) /aw/ in *south* or *down* is not fronted; (2) /iw/ in *dew*, etc. is not fronted; (3) /oh/ does not have a back upglide; (4) /ay/ is not monophthongal before resonants; and (5) the front short vowels are not ingliding. None of these are elements of the NCS, but together they suggest that St Louis would be receptive to a chain shift that originated in the Northern phonological system.[40]

Frazer (1978) points to ideological factors that reinforced the effect of Northern dialect features on speakers in St Louis, particularly those of German origin. The Yankee anti-slavery ideology was attractive to the Germans of St Louis, who shifted from the Democratic to the Republican Party in the election of 1860.[41] We can therefore project a receptivity to Northern influence from a period well before the development of the NCS in the middle of the twentieth century. But the diffusion to St Louis of the uniform, communally created Inland North dialect was not accomplished by a communal migration. Rather, we must suppose continued contact through the movement of adults, largely commercial, along the corridor now centered on Route I-55.[42] This is the social context that is associated with a partial transfer of the structure being borrowed.

The diffusion of specific linguistic structures is one of many changes that spring from adult language contact. Trudgill (1986) describes the various scenarios of dialect leveling (the elimination of marked variants), simplification, and their combination in koineization. Such cases represent more radical losses of structural features than those we have dealt with here. The diffusion of the short-*a* pattern or of the NCS implies the expansion of marked forms into an environment that is receptive to them and does not require radical deletions or reversals to accommodate them. All of these contact phenomena share the common marks of adult language learning: the loss of linguistic configurations that are reliably transmitted only by the child language learner.

15.10 Prospectus

This chapter began with the observation that both family-tree models and wave models are needed to account for the history of, and relations within, language families. Family trees are generated by the transmission of changes internal to the system of the speech community, while the wave model reflects the effects of diffusion through language or dialect contact. We then considered the general consensus of a strong constraint against the diffusion of abstract linguistic structures in language contact. The main thrust of this chapter is to advance an explanation for this difference by attributing internal developments to generational learning – the incrementation of change in an unbroken sequence of parent-to-child transmission – and by assigning the major effects of diffusion to the results of extra-generational learning by adults. If this is the case, it follows that the results of language contact will be less regular and less governed by structural constraints than the internal changes that are the major mechanism of linguistic diversification in the family-tree model. The difference will still be a matter of degree, since recent studies of language change across the lifespan have shown that adults do participate in ongoing change, though more sporadically and at a much lower rate than children.

When linguistic forms are diffused through contact among single adults or individual families, less regular transmission can be expected. The cases studied here suggest the basic reason why structural borrowing is rare: the adults who are the borrowing agents do not faithfully reproduce the structural patterns in the system from which they are borrowing.

The main body of this chapter applies this thinking to the study of dialect diffusion, focusing on two cases found in the ANAE data. There is evidence that the complex short-*a* tensing system of New York City has diffused outward to at least four different areas. The resulting systems resemble that of New York City in its superficial outline – the phonetic conditioning of tensing by the following segment – but differ from the original model in the absence of grammatical conditioning, in the open syllable constraint and in specific lexical exceptions. The Northern Cities Shift developed simultaneously in all areas of the Inland North. The chain-shifting mechanism operates with a high degree of consistency, linking the movements of six vowels in an overall rotation. But the transmission of the NCS along the St Louis corridor produces a more irregular result, indicating that the individual sound changes are diffusing individually rather than as a systematic whole.

16

The Diffusion of Language from Group to Group

The preceding chapter dealt with the diffusion of linguistic structures from place to place. The speech communities described so far – New York, Albany, Cincinnati, New Orleans, St Louis – are formed by the population defined in American society as the white mainstream. They are geographical unities, differentiated internally by social class, but separated sharply from the African–American and Latino populations in the same cities. Most American cities include three major communal groups, in the sense defined in Blanc's 1964 study of communal dialects of Baghdad (in that case, Jewish, Christian and Muslim). Since contacts between such communal groups are primarily among adults, we can expect the same loss of structure that was observed in geographic diffusion when linguistic patterns spread from one group to the other.

16.1 Diffusion to the AAVE Community

We can begin this inquiry with a general review of studies of the influence of surrounding dialects on African–American Vernacular English (AAVE). While the speech of African–Americans in the United States covers a wide range of grammatical and phonological features that may be called "African–American English," the specific dialect designated AAVE refers to the geographically uniform grammar found in low-income areas of high residential segregation. Baugh (1983) defines AAVE as the speech of African–Americans who live with, work with and speak with other African–Americans. There is considerable phonological variation within AAVE (Myhill 1988). The uniformity mentioned here refers to the nation-wide uniformity of AAVE grammar: primarily, to its morphosyntactic and morphological features and to the tense/mood/aspect system (for NYC, see Labov et al. 1968, Labov 1972, Labov 1998; for Washington, see Fasold 1972; for Los Angeles, see Baugh 1983; for Philadelphia, see Labov and Harris 1986, Ash and Myhill 1986; for Bay Area, see Mitchell-Kernan 1969, Rickford et al. 1991, Rickford 1999, Rickford and Rafal 1996; for Texas, see Bailey 1993, Cukor-Avila 1995). Undoubtedly some regional

Table 16.1 Indices of dominance for five ethnic groups in Philadelphia, from 1850 to 1970 (proportion of a person's census tract that consists of the same group)

	1850	1880	1930	1940	1950	1960	1970
Blacks	11	12	35	45	56	72	74
Irish		34	8			5	3
German	25	11	5	3			
Italian		38				23	21
Polish		20				9	8

Source: T. Hershberg, A tale of three cities: Black, immigrants and opportunity bin Philadelphia. 1850–1880, 1930, 1970. In T. Hershberg (ed.), *Philadelphia: Work, Space, Family and Group Experience in the Nineteenth Century*, New York: Oxford University Press, 1981, pp. 461–95, Table 8

variation will eventually be found in AAVE grammar, but so far only small quantitative differences have been reported. The national uniformity of AAVE grammar remains a mystery to be solved, which goes beyond the scope of this volume.

The various studies of the pronunciation of African–American English carried out since 1964 offer an opportunity to examine the process of diffusion across communal groups that inhabit the same cities but are separated from each other by sharp residential boundaries. While residential segregation for most ethnic groups declines over time in the US, segregation of blacks and whites has undergone a steady increase up to the very high degree reached in the 1980s and has remained stable ever since (Hershberg 1981, Massey and Denton 1993). Table 16.1 shows this progression for the index of dominance in Philadelphia. While the Irish, German, Italian and Polish groups show a regular decrease in segregation, the African–American group rises steadily across the decades. Residential segregation is the primary condition responsible for the recent divergence of AAVE from other dialects, as is seen in the exponential rise in features such as habitual *be*, or in the use of *had* to mark the simple preterit (Bailey 1993, 2001; Labov and Harris 1986).

Given this high level of residential segregation, we can expect to find minimal effects of surrounding dialects in studies of AAVE. On the other hand, one can expect greater effects of surrounding groups in studies of the speech of African–American university students and their friends.

16.2   Influence of Surrounding Dialects on AAVE Pronunciation

The studies of adolescent speakers of AAVE in South Harlem showed no participation in the vowel shifts characteristic of the white NYC community (Labov et al.

1968, Labov 1972). This is equally true of the African–American adults interviewed in Harlem and of the African–American subjects in the Lower East Side study (Labov 1966, Ch. 8).[1] Studies of AAVE in West Philadelphia (Labov and Harris 1986) found no trace of Philadelphia sound changes in the speech of members of the core social networks.[2] However, AAVE speakers generally reflect the level of r-pronunciation in the surrounding dialects. In New York City, AAVE speakers show the same consistent vocalization of coda /r/ as the r-less white dialect, but they also extend this pattern to include ambi-syllabic /r/ (Labov et al. 1968, Labov 1972). In basically r-ful Philadelphia, AAVE use of the variable (r) fluctuates around 50 percent (Myhill 1988).

A moderate raising of /æ/ along the nonperipheral track to [æ.] or to [ɛ⁾] is characteristic of the less focused varieties of African–American English as well as of AAVE. Gordon (2000) found this moderate raising of /æ/ among African–American college girls near Chicago. Jones (2003) looked closely at the realization of /æ/ in the African–American community in Lansing and found some raising to the level of short *e* and above, especially among women and older speakers (see also Jones and Preston in press).

Purnell (2008) analyzed the word lists pronounced by nine African–American students from Southeastern Wisconsin, an area in which the Northern Cities Shift is active, but which is differentiated from other Inland North regions by the raising of /æ/ before /g/ – often to the point of merger of /æg/ and /eyg/ (Zeller 1997, ANAE, Ch. 13). For at least two female speakers, Purnell found evidence of the raising of /æ/ before /g/ with the front upglide that marks merger with /ey/.

Eberhardt (2008) examined the low back merger of /o/ and /oh/ among African–Americans in Pittsburgh, where it has been complete among the mainstream white population for over a century. Only three of the thirty-four African–Americans made a distinction in the production of minimal pairs, and these were among the oldest subjects.

These studies all indicate a certain influence of the dialect of the surrounding area on the phonetic output of African–Americans, especially for the relatively small number of adults who have extensive contacts with the white community. As we will see below, such contacts and such dialect influence are not characteristic of children in their formative years. It is unsurprising that adults can absorb and transmit such phonetic features, just as local lexicon is diffused throughout the speech community. African–Americans in Philadelphia ask for a *hoagie* rather than a *sub*, walk on the *pavement* rather than the *sidewalk*, and use the exclamation "Yo!" like everyone else in the city. We are primarily interested here in the diffusion of such complex linguistic structures as the NYC short-*a* pattern and the Northern Cities Shift, as discussed in the geographic diffusion of Chapter 14.

DIFFUSION OF THE PHILADELPHIA SHORT-*A* PATTERN TO THE AFRICAN–AMERICAN COMMUNITY   The Philadelphia short-*a* split into lax /æ/ and tense /æh/ has been

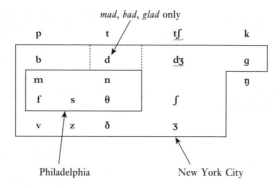

Figure 16.1 Coda consonants determining tense vowels in checked syllables in Philadelphia and New York City

described in considerable detail (Ferguson 1975, Labov 1989b, ANAE, Ch. 13) and has been a focus of attention at many points in the two preceding volumes (see in particular PLC, Vol. 1: 534–7). Figure 16.1 shows the conditioning environments in which closed syllables are tensed in New York City and in Philadelphia. The Philadelphia consonants are a proper subset of the NYC consonants, excluding voiced fricatives and voiced stops except for *mad*, *bad* and *glad*, and excluding all back consonants (specifically /ʃ/). Of the eight additional conditions found in New York City, all but the tensing of *avenue* apply to Philadelphia as well. The Philadelphia system includes two further modifications: (1) the constraint that function words ending in nasals are lax (*can*, *am*, *and*) is extended to include three irregular verbs: *ran*, *swam*, *began*;[3] and (2) there is lexical diffusion in open syllables, with the most tensing in the word *planet*.[4]

Henderson (1996) studied the short-*a* pattern of thirty African–American speakers from Philadelphia; the results are shown in Table 16.2, along with the percentages for the 100 white speakers reported in Labov (1989b). For the normally tense classes, the white Philadelphians are close to 100 percent. African–Americans use equivalent tensing before nasals; come close for the *mad*, *bad*, *glad* sub-class; but fall considerably short for tensing before voiceless fricatives in *path*, *bath*, *pass*, etc., with only 69 percent.

White Philadelphians do not generally tense short-*a* in open syllables; before nasals a small number of particular words like *planet* are tensed, amounting to less than 1%. The open syllable constraint before nasals is much weaker among African–Americans; almost half of the tokens are tense. Finally, the grammatical constraint that laxes irregular verbs ending in nasals (*ran*, *swam*, *began*) is quite weakly diffused to the African–American community: 71 percent of these verbs are tense, in comparison with only 19 percent among white Philadelphians.

Table 16.2 Tensing of short *a* for whites and African–Americans in Philadelphia

Following segment	Euro-Americans (Labov 1989b) % tense	African–Americans (Henderson 1996) % tense
Normally tense in white Philadelphia dialect		
before nasal coda	96	95
before voiceless fricatives	98	69
mad, bad, glad	99	83
Normally lax in white Philadelphia dialect		
before intervocalic nasals	01	43
ran, swam, began	19	71

There is no doubt that the short-*a* pattern of African–Americans in Philadelphia reflects the influence of the surrounding white community. It is not, however, a true copy; that is, it does not appear to be the result of the faithful transmission of the system across generations of child language learners. The diffusion of the short-*a* pattern across communal lines appears to be the work of adults, with loss of detail typical of adult language learning. This will become more evident when we consider the diffusion of grammatical features across communal lines in the second half of this chapter.

DIFFUSION OF THE NORTHERN CITIES SHIFT ACROSS COMMUNAL GROUPS   The studies of African–American English in the North, cited above, were not only looking for phonetic influence of white on black speech in Lansing, Chicago and Milwaukee. In one way or another, they all addressed the question of whether African–Americans were participating in the Northern Cities Shift – the systematic rotation of six English vowels. The Jones and Purnell reports showed some evidence of regional influence on the realization of short *a*. But no further indication of the diffusion of the Northern Cities Shift appears in their data. Jones presents two vowel systems in full: instead of a general raising to mid position, both systems show a continuous short-*a* pattern, with the low front position fully occupied by /æ/ before voiceless stops (Jones 2003: Figures 4.4, 4.6). Short *o* shows no signs of moving forward, and short *e* shows no signs of moving back. Instead, the short-*a* tokens that are raised to lower mid position before voiced fricatives and voiced stops show considerable overlap with tokens of short *e*. All of the Purnell vowel charts show the low front position fully occupied with some tokens of /æ/, and none shows the characteristic vowel shifts that respond to the absence of vowels in this position.

Even though these are small studies, they are focused on just those African–American speakers who are most likely to show the effects of the surrounding white dialect: university students and friends of university students. But in Jones' work, which reached out further into the black community, there was no significant difference in raising that could be attributed to the social networks of the speakers – whether these netwoks were highly focused in the black community or showed wider contacts in the white community (Jones 2003: 119). It therefore seems likely that these limited phonetic effects are typical of the wider influence on the black community as a whole. They are less systematic than the diffusion of the Northern Cities Shift to St Louis, examined in the last chapter.

Preston (2010) brings together a variety of studies of the adaptation of the NCS in the vowel systems of minority groups: African–Americans, Arab–Americans, Mexican–Americans and Polish–Americans. All of these systems show a phonetic approximation of the F1/F2 positions in the following long–short pairs:

/ey/ ~ /i/
/æh/ ~ /e/
/ow/ ~ /u/
/oh/ ~ /ʌ/

The partial influence of the Northern Cities Shift can be seen as follows:

a   The first stage of the NCS is reflected in the tensing and lengthening of /æ/ to /æh/, but /æh/ is not fronted or raised beyond /e/; it remains to be demonstrated whether length consistently differentiates these pairs.
b   The tendency to lower and back /i/ shown in the final stages of the NCS, along with the general upper mid peripheral position of /ey/ in the North, brings /i/ to the same height as /ey/, but makes it distinctively backer.
c   /ʌ/ is not strongly backed, as in the later stages of the NCS, and /oh/ remains in lower mid position, forming the /ʌ/ ~ /oh/ pair.

These convergent phonetic tendencies illustrate again the nature of the phonetic changes common to diffusion, in the perspective outlined by Dinkin in the last chapter. These pairings are not at the abstract level of the morphophonemic alternations of *sane* ~ *sanity*, or *ferocious* ~ *ferocity*, but they show instead the regularization of phonemic targets at the most superficial phonetic level.

16.3   The Diffusion of Constraints on -*t*, *d* Deletion to Children in Minority Communities

Among the more intricate systems of linguistic variation, considerable attention has been given to the constraints on English consonant cluster simplification, or -*t*, *d* deletion. The first examination of internal constraints on a linguistic variable was carried out for the pre-adolescent Thunderbirds and adolescent Jets and Cobras in

South Harlem (Labov et al. 1965; Labov et al. 1968; Labov 1972). The basic constraints were found to be the favoring of retention by the feature of sonority and the grammatical status of the following segment. These were confirmed and elaborated in the studies of AAVE that followed (Wolfram 1969, Fasold 1972; Baugh 1983). The LCV study of Philadelphia in the 1970s expanded this view of constraints on -*t*, *d* deletion to white speakers, who were found to follow the same pattern of deletion as African–Americans at a lower frequency, except for a very strong constraint of following pause (Guy 1980). Since then, this general pattern has been confirmed for many communities throughout the English speaking world.

The same constraints have been found for second and third generation speakers of Latino English, with some exceptions (Wolfram 1974). The cluster /rd/ is never simplified in mainstream dialects, but small percentages of deletion have been recorded in several studies of Latino English (Cofer 1972, Santa Ana 1991). This can be accounted for by the hypothesis that /r/ is phonologically a glide in English with the features [–consonantal, –vocalic], but inherits its Spanish phonological status as a resonant [+consonantal, +vocalic] in Latino English. It has also been found that the favoring of deletion in unstressed syllables is absent in Latino English (Santa Ana 1996), possibly the effect of syllable timing in the substrate language.

The major thesis of this chapter is that language features are diffused across highly segregated communal groups by adults, and that such changes reach children only indirectly. In the case of -*t*, *d* deletion, it appears that a high degree of convergence of black and white speech communities has been reached for some time, but we would not expect such convergence in the more recently developing English of Spanish-dominant children. This is the typical result of first-language interference and the universal effects of articulatory factors, without precise matching to specific norms of the matrix community. For English-dominant Latino children, we might observe the emergence of a community norm more influenced by a general pattern of interaction with adults, including parents and teachers.

One opportunity for examining such a result is found in the work of the Urban Minorities Reading Project (UMRP). This project was designed to test the effect of an Individualized Reading Program on the reading levels of elementary school children in Philadelphia, Atlanta and California (Labov 2003, Labov and Baker in press). Subjects were drawn from four language/ethnic groups: whites (W), African–Americans (A), Latinos who had learned to read in English first (E) and Latinos who had learned to read in Spanish first (S). All schools were in low income areas, where at least 65 percent of the students qualified for the federal free lunch program. Students were selected for the program if they were one or two years behind in reading grade level, or below the 35th percentile in the standardized Woodcock-Johnson Word Attack or Word Identification test. In the first year of the project we recorded the spontaneous speech of 700 students age 8–11, in the second, third and fourth grade. A selection of 397 of the interviews were transcribed and coded for phonological and grammatical variables relevant to AAVE. The selection was randomized by language/ethnic group and section of the country.

Interviewers were researchers/tutors who were practiced in techniques of eliciting spontaneous speech from children of this age. A sample transcription is given in (1):

(1)　IVr: Did you ever get into a fight with a kid bigger than you?

P05-001: Oh yeah. (sucks teeth) but my sister jumped 111 in it.

IVr: What happened, how did it start?

P05-001: (sucks lips) Well, I was at – I was at – I was like, at my grandma's 211 house, and I went 111 back home, cuz my mom, we was, me and Sabrina was here, and then I went 110 back home. And I said, "Sabrina, you got a rope that we can play with?" Sinquetta and 'nem, she said – and I said = – and she had said "Yeah, so then Sinquetta and them had to go back in the house, la, la, la, blah, blah, blah, then some other big girl. I was – we was playin' rope right, (sucks lips), then she gon jump in and she say 230 "You might jump better, and not be 'flicted 811." I said "It's not going to be 'flicted, cuz I know how to turn." She said, and then she only got up to ten. She was mad at me, and she had hit me, so I hit her right back. Sabrina jumped 111 in it. And start 81 hittin' her. I was just 110 lookin. I was just 110 lookin'

Each phonological and grammatical variable was coded with two-to-three-digit codes inserted in the text immediately after the relevant word. These are extracted automatically by the DX program, which reads from the orthography the phonetic structure of clusters, the segmental environment and the grammatical status of clusters, and outputs files for a Varbul analysis. A few of the numerical codes relevant to the present discussion are retained in the sample passage (2):

(2)　111: A coronal complex coda with final /t, d/ retained: *jumped in.*

110: A coronal complex coda with final /t, d/ deleted: *went back, just lookin'*

811: Regular -ed retained after verbal coronal cluster: *be 'flicted*

80: Regular -ed absent after single /t, d/: *start*

211: Possessive {s} present: *grandma's house*

230: Verbal {s} absent *she say.*

To give some idea of the volume of consonant clusters generated in these transcriptions, Table 16.3 displays the numbers of tokens of the (t, d) variable by grammatical status and language/ethnic group.

　Consonant cluster simplification is common to all speakers of English, at varying levels of frequency. In our population of struggling readers, this varies from 28 percent (whites in California) to 64 percent (Latinos (Spanish) in Atlanta). Figure 16.2 shows that, throughout, whites operate at the lowest levels of -*t, d* deletion and Latinos who learned to read in Spanish first at the highest – somewhat higher everywhere than African–Americans. On the other hand, Latinos who

Table 16.3 Numbers of tokens of (t, d) clusters by language/ethnic group and grammatical status in the coded transcriptions of 397 UMRP subjects. A = African–American [N = 112]; W = white [N = 105]; E = Latinos who learned to read in English first [N = 86]; S = Latinos who learned to read in Spanish first [N = 94]

	A	W	E	S	Total
Derivational	683	600	399	363	2,045
Monomorphemic	1,531	1,723	986	899	5,139
Past	718	815	487	332	2,352
Total	2,932	3,138	1,872	1,594	9,536

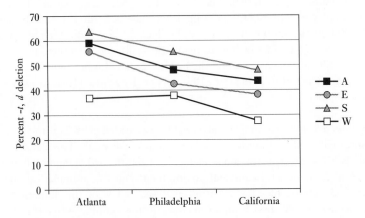

Figure 16.2 Overall frequencies of *-t, d* deletion by language/ethnic group and region for 397 struggling readers (abbreviations as in Table 16.3)

learned to read in English first are intermediate between African–Americans and whites.

When we examine the internal constraints on this process, a radically different picture emerges. The tendency to simplify consonant clusters springs from two distinct sources. There are general constraints on articulatory execution, which is controlled by the sonority of the following segment and by feature combinations with the preceding segment. On the other hand, there are constraints specific to English: the effects of the grammatical status of the cluster and voicing of the final segment. There is no evidence for the universality of these effects,[5] and they are most likely transmitted to the language learner from intimate contact with native speakers.

Table 16.4 presents in the first column the overall analysis of the data set, with social and regional factor groups, followed by runs for each of the four language/ethnic groups considered separately.

Table 16.4   Analysis by logistic regression of (t, d) deletion in the spontaneous speech of 397 UMRP subjects by language/ethnic groups (abbreviations as in Table 16.3)

	All	A	S	E	W
Preceding segment					
sibilant	0.64	0.64	0.74	0.61	0.61
nasal	0.52	0.53	0.39	0.54	0.57
stop	0.41	0.44	0.50	0.36	0.41
other fricative	0.39	0.37	0.47	0.36	0.31
labial	0.33	0.27	0.47	0.40	0.22
Consonants preceding					
2	0.60	0.68			0.66
1	0.49	0.48			0.49
Grammatical status					
derivational	0.61	0.67			0.69
monomorphemic	0.53	0.56			0.54
preterit	0.35	0.24			0.29
Cluster voicing					
voiceless	0.59	0.58		0.63	0.61
voiced	0.42	0.42		0.38	0.40
Voicing agreement					
homovoiced	0.59	0.64		0.60	0.58
heterovoiced	0.18	0.09		0.16	0.19
Following segment					
lateral	0.72	0.76	0.67	0.77	0.69
nasal	0.71	0.72	0.69	0.66	0.77
/w/	0.59	0.62	0.60	0.49	0.66
stop	0.65	0.59	0.62	0.71	0.68
fricative	0.59	0.60	0.49	0.58	0.68
/r/	0.54	0.59	0.56	0.55	0.49
pause	0.44	0.46	0.49	0.41	0.40
/h/	0.43	0.44	0.38	0.49	0.38
vowel	0.38	0.37	0.40	0.37	0.37
/y/	0.33	0.42	0.36	0.59	0.15
Context					
Spontaneous speech	0.51	0.51	0.51		0.51
Story retelling	0.42	0.42	0.42		0.42
Region					
Philadelphia	0.56	0.55	0.59	0.54	0.58
Atlanta	0.53	0.52	0.49	0.60	0.48
California	0.41	0.44	0.41	0.40	0.43
Grade					
2	0.52			0.47	
3	0.51			0.54	
4	0.48			0.44	

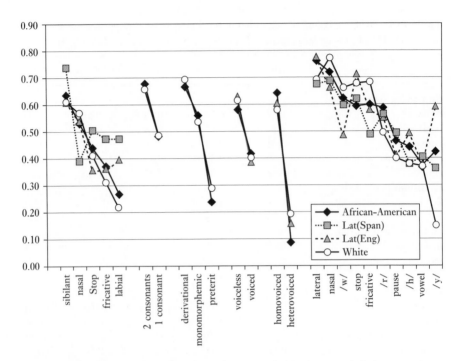

Figure 16.3 Varbrul weights governing /t, d/ deletion by language/ethnic groups in elementary schools (abbreviations as in Table 16.3)

The relations of the significant factor groups in Table 16.4 are displayed in Figure 16.3. The effects of preceding and following segments appear at the extreme left and right of the diagram: significant constraints are found for all four language/ethnic groups. These are the products of general phonological processes; they are based on an articulatory apparatus that is shared by all groups. For the preceding segment, it is found, as usual, that sibilants favor deletion the most, and are followed by nasals, stops, other fricatives and laterals. This ordering has been shown to correlate with the general obligatory contour principle (Guy and Boberg 1997). White and African–American subjects are closely aligned, as shown by the .98 correlation coefficients in Table 16.5. Correlations with the Latino groups are lower. The major effect for the S and E groups is the favoring of deletion by a preceding sibilant, but there is no significant effect among other preceding segments.

The effect of a following segment conforms to the fine-grained divisions developed in Labov (1997). These effects are largely explained by the sonority hierarchy and by the possibility of resyllabification[6] – general phonetic principles (Guy 1991). Here the agreement of the four groups is somewhat greater. All groups show deletion mostly before laterals and nasals, with a parallel fall-off for other obstruents,

Table 16.5 Pearson correlations for effect of preceding segments by communal group (abbreviations as in Table 16.3)

	A	W	E	S
African–American	x	.98	.83	.57
White		x	.52	.41
Latino (Eng)			x	.41
Latino (Span)				x

glides and vowels. For all, pause is not significantly different from a following vowel.[7] The two Latino groups follow the same pattern, with one striking exception: the Latino (English) group shows a high probability of deletion before /y/.

The grammatical constraint, specific to English and so far replicated for all native English speakers, is the most important one for this discussion of group relations. Again, white and African–American struggling readers follow the expected patterns in lock step. The derivational class of *lost, kept, found*, etc. is leading in this group, rather than being intermediate. This is consistent with the finding of Guy and Boyd (1990) that children of this age treat derivational verbs as monomorphemic (see also Labov 1989b).[8] Neither Latino group shows a significant effect of grammatical status.

Figure 16.3 shows significant results for three other factor groups, which again show close agreement between African–American and white groups. Voicing agreement registers the strong favoring of deletion by homovoiced clusters (*just, old*, etc.) as opposed to heterovoiced (*went, help*, etc.). Words with two preceding consonants (*next, helped, rinsed*, etc.) regularly favor deletion over those with only one. Although previous studies of -*t, d* deletion have not focused on the difference between voiced and voiceless finals (/t/ versus /d/), these results show a strong favoring of /t/ deletion as compared to /d/ deletion, all other things being equal. The higher rates of deletion in unstressed syllables, which is frequently found in studies of -*t, d* deletion, do not appear here, probably because of the low number of unstressed syllables in the vocabulary of this age range (516 out of the 9,569 tokens). The Latino (S) group does not show significant effects in any of these factor groups.

The overall result of this study of consonant cluster simplification is that the major outlines of the process are reproduced among young members of the Latino speech community, but in a way that reflects general phonological principles rather than direct transmission. The fine detail is missing, just as in the studies of diffusion from place to place. Most importantly, the more abstract grammatical constraints on -*t, d* deletion are absent. This yields further insight into the difference between transmission within the speech community and diffusion across community lines.

16.4   The Diffusion of Grammatical Variables to Adult Members of the African–American Community

The project on Urban Minorities on Linguistic Change (UMLC) began a study of communication across racial lines in Philadelphia. It was spurred by observations that led us to believe that there was more communication than most people realized. Our conclusions (Labov and Harris 1986, Ash and Myhill 1986, Graff et al. 1986) were in the opposite direction. We found that, as a consequence of increasing residential segregation, the amount of black/white contact was diminishing and that, as a result, linguistic changes within AAVE were leading to increasing divergence between this dialect and the surrounding communities. A major piece of evidence for this conclusion was the study of the social networks shown in Figure 16.4, centering around our chief field worker, Wendell Harris. This figure does not offer a conventional view of social networks – one based on frequency of contact

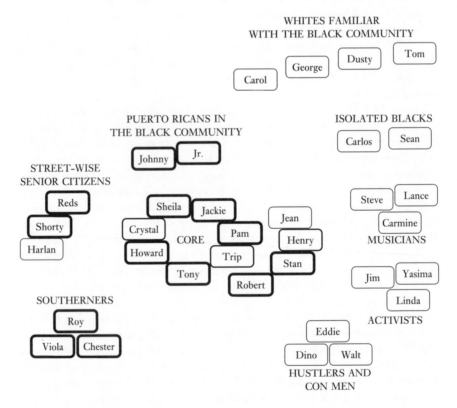

Figure 16.4   Verbal {s} distribution among social networks of West Philadelphia (Labov and Harris 1986)

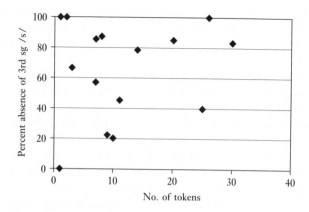

Figure 16.5 Percent absence of third singular /s/ by number of tokens for Philadelphia African–Americans in the UMRP sample of struggling readers

– but rather a display by social histories: people with similar social histories are grouped together. As shown by the key in upper left, the weight of the border surrounding each name is associated with a given percentage of third singular {s} used by that speaker.

In the center is the core group: five men and seven women born and raised in Philadelphia. These are people who answer Baugh's (1983) description of users of the vernacular. In their daily lives, they live with, talk with, and work with African–Americans, and have limited contacts with speakers of other dialects. In a number of long recorded sessions, women spoke with vehemence, anger and amusement about their relations with the men, with each other or with the interviewer, denouncing various others for their violations of the moral code and for various degrees of unfaithfulness. The recordings of this core group come even closer to the target vernacular than did our earlier group sessions in Harlem (Labov et al. 1968).

Several groups are set aside at the left of Figure 16.5 because of their different social histories. These include three members of the core group who were born in the South, three people interviewed at a senior citizens center who had the same knowledge of street life as members of the core group, and two Puerto Ricans, English-dominant, who had married into the black community.

The absence of verbal /s/ in the third singular present form of the verb paradigm in AAVE is the major indicator of the general absence of subject–verb agreement, perhaps the most profound difference between this dialect and others. It shows up in the uniform use of irregular verbs *do*, *have* and *was* in all persons and in considerable variation in subject/verb inversion, all of which indicate the absence of an inflectional node to which tense is attached. The original vernacular target is displayed in Figure 16.5, which shows the frequency of third singular /s/ absence for fifteen African–American children in the Philadelphia subset of the UMRP project discussed in the last section. The horizontal axis shows the total number of tokens for each individual. The group average is 64 percent absence, but the scattergram indicates that this value is actually the product of two distinct distributions. The majority is centered around a mode of 85 percent, and a minority around a mode of 40 percent. It should also be remembered that these were recordings made in a school setting, with an interviewer whom the speaker had known for only a short time, so that some shift away from the vernacular is to be expected for some individuals.

Figure 16.4 is therefore designed to show which adult individuals maintain the vernacular norm of third singular /s/ absence of over 75 percent. A sizeable majority of the names in these groups are labeled with the heavy border that indicates 75–100% absence for the core group, the Southerners and the senior citizens, all of whom have spent most of their lives in the AAVE social context. The Puerto Ricans represent the confluence of Spanish L1 influence and AAVE influence, corresponding to the pattern of Puerto Rican youth with extensive black contacts in Wolfram (1974).

On the right and upper margins of this figure are fifteen individuals in five groups whose symbols show the minimal border weight associated with a high rate – over 50 percent – of subject/verb agreement. At the top are four white speakers with extensive black contacts. Carol is a waitress who lives with an African–American man; her speech is marked by many superficial features of AAVE prosody and vocabulary. George made many close contacts with African–Americans in prison. He was described by a member of the core group, who introduced him by saying, "This boy, if he turned his back when he was talking to you, you wouldn't know if he was black or white." Extracts from his speech were were regularly associated with black ethnicity in the UMLC matched guise experiment (Graff et al. 1986). Yet for these white speakers, intimate contacts with African–Americans did not weaken the pattern of subject/verb agreement that marked their original vernacular.

The individuals Carlos and Sean on Figure 16.5 are African–Americans who had consciously asserted their independence from African–American culture and society, and their speech reflected this isolation in many ways.

The musicians Steve, Lance and Carmine are three of the many African–Americans in Philadelphia who are immersed in the professional music world. Carmine is the most well known and successful, one of the country's best known bass guitarists. Like most musicians, these three often play with, work for and deal with whites on a daily basis.

Jim, Yasima and Linda are political activists, engaged daily in vigorous confrontations with the dominant white politicians of Philadelphia.

Walt, Dino and Eddie are street hustlers and con men, engaged in illegal and semi-legal activities that require frequent interaction with whites.

It is evident from this display that those adults who have interacted extensively with speakers of the surrounding mainstream dialect have absorbed a considerable amount of third singular /s/ marking, without necessarily changing other features of AAVE which mark them as members of the black community.

On the other hand, those who do not engage in such day-to-day interaction with speakers of other dialects retain the original absence of subject/verb agreement in AAVE grammar.

16.5 Directions of Diffusion in the Latino Community

Several studies have indicated that the Latino speech community incorporates a wider variety of diffusion patterns than we find in the African–American community. Most speakers in the African–American community can be ranged along a single dimension, from AAVE to Standard African–American English, which differs from other Standard English dialects by only a few phonological features. On the other hand, Latinos growing up in various American speech communities may be oriented towards three directions of dialect development. A number of published studies of differential linguistic socialization document these shifts: Wolfram's study of Puerto Rican youth with variable relation to the black community (1974); Poplack's 1978 study of a North Philadelphia school with mixed black/white/Puerto Rican population; Fought's report on Latino girls in Northern California (1999, 2003); and Wolford's 2006 investigation of the speech of Latino struggling readers in Philadelphia and California. Labov and Pedraza (1994) studied the linguistic and political identification of Puerto Rican adolescents in New York City.

a   Some Latinos shift in the same direction as speakers of the local white vernacular. This is especially characteristic of females. Thus Poplack (1978) found the Philadelphia centralization of /ay/ before voiceless consonants among some Puerto Rican speakers. Labov and Pedraza (1994) found that girls from the Bronx who adapted New York City vowel shifts were identified uniformly as white by Puerto Rican listeners.

b   Other Latinos who are influenced by black street culture move towards AAVE. This is a tendency heavily concentrated among males. Wolfram (1974) shows a sharp difference between Puerto Ricans with extensive black contacts and Puerto Ricans with none. Poplack (1978) shows a tendency towards monophthongization of /ay/, which is characteristic of some young males. The South Harlem groups studied by Labov et al. (1968) included some Puerto Ricans who were indistinguishable linguistically from the African–American majority; this also applies to the North Philadelphia groups studied by Labov and Harris (1986), as shown in Figure 16.4. Wolford (2006) finds that the zero form of the possessive (*my mother house*) was strongly represented among Puerto Rican youth from Philadelphia, especially males. Labov and Pedraza (1994) reported a consistent attribution of African–American ethnicity to some Puerto Rican males who incorporated features of AAVE in their speech.

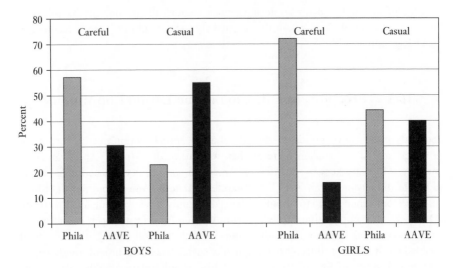

Figure 16.6 Percentage of use of Philadelphia "Canadian raising" vs AAVE monophthongization of /ay/ by style and gender for twenty-four Puerto Rican 6th graders (based on Poplack 1978, Figure 2b)

c A third direction in Latino English is the preservation of some features showing the direct influence of Spanish on the speech of the first or second generation of native speakers of English. Thus Wolford found a strong tendency for the possessive to favor periphrastic forms among Latinos from Southern California, as in *the hand of my mother*. Poplack (1978) identified Spanish influence in the realization of /ay/ by some Puerto Rican speakers in the north Philadelphia school. Mendoza-Denton (2008) describes the use of a high front [i] in the second vowel of *anything, everything* as a symbol of Latino gang identification among girls.

The systematic character of these shifts appears in Figure 16.6, which is based on Poplack's 1978 data on the treatment of /ay/ by Puerto Rican sixth graders in St Veronica's school in Philadelphia: interviews conducted with 24 self-selected groups on the playground. The light grey bars show the percentage of realizations of /ay/ in the white Philadelphia pattern: centralized and backed before voiceless consonants; otherwise a diphthong with low nucleus. The dark bars show the percentage of realizations with the characteristic AAVE monophthongization or weakening of the glide. There are two strong and independent effects: the AAVE variant is favored in casual speech, and it is favored by males.

Wolford's study of the use of the possessive by Latino struggling readers found a similar orientation towards the AAVE pattern on the part of males. Table 16.6 shows the results of a logistic regression analysis of the absence of /s/ in attributive

Table 16.6   Absence of attributive possessive -*s* for Latino groups

Factor group	Factor	Percentage of -*s* absence	Total N	Factor weight
Location	Philadelphia	35	80	0.68
	Atlanta	15	72	0.42
	California	14	76	0.38
Sex	Boys	29	86	0.61
	Girls	18	142	0.43

Source: Tonya E. Wolford, Variation in the expression of possession by Latino children, *Language Variation and Change* 18 (2006): 1–14. Factor groups not significant: group; grade; following segment

possessive forms – the characteristic AAVE form. Philadelphia, where Puerto Ricans are in close contact with African–Americans, shows a much stronger tendency than Atlanta or California, and boys much more than girls. A reverse pattern was found in California, where the periphrastic form characteristic of Spanish influence was favored by girls. Thus in both areas the influence of African–Americans was stronger for males.

These differential movements illustrate the greater complexity of the linguistic economy in Latino communities as opposed to the African–American community, and they reflect in part the differences in racial identification that are possible in Latino groups. Labov and Pedraza (1994) found a close correlation between the adoption of African–American linguistic features and the tendency to identify with blacks in racial politics. This in turn has been found to relate overtly to differences in skin color and hair form among Latino speakers.

So far I have considered diffusion across communal groups to be largely the work of adults. However, this is not necessarily the case when we consider diffusion from the African–American community to the Latino community. Recent studies of Latino youth in Philadelphia find a consistent and native-like use of habitual *be* among speakers, including those who have no particular contact with black speakers of AAVE. This suggests that grammatical influence may have been generalized with a consistency that is characteristic of contact among young speakers with full language learning capacity – that is, of transmission rather than diffusion.

16.6   The Nature of Diffusion across Communal Boundaries

Chapters 5 to 13 of this volume have dealt with linguistic change in progress in the relatively uniform communities of mainstream North American English. The geographic data of ANAE were designed to obtain speakers from the majority ethnic groups of each city sampled (see ANAE, Table 4.2). Of the 762 subjects, 217 were of German origin; 51 Italian; 36 Scandinavian; 52 Polish and other Slavic. ANAE results show that these groups have been assimilated into the linguistic mainstream of the North American community, just as Table 16.1 showed them assimilated in residential patterns. They, became prototypical exponents of the low back merger, the Northern Cities Shift, the Canadian Shift, the Southern Shift and other sound changes of North America. On the other hand, those groups that were isolated through increasing patterns of residential segregation developed other norms, though they were never totally isolated from the mainstream dialect. This chapter has shown how the diffusion of features through adult contact produces various degrees of influence and approximation to the sound systems of the surrounding community. So far, the grammatical system of AAVE has been largely resistant to the norms of the surrounding communities, though this may change over time if residential segregation declines.

17

Conclusion

This volume has presented a broad array of factors responsible for ongoing linguistic change and divergence. It has considered both cognitive and cultural factors in the genesis, development and motivation of linguistic change. The present chapter will consider the relation between these two sets of factors: whether they operate jointly, in alternation or in opposition in the course of change.

17.1 Summary of the Argument

Chapters 2–4 of this volume are concerned with the infrastructure of cognition, as defined in section 1.1. These chapters reported on the effect of linguistic change on the ability to segment and identify phonemes in the stream of speech, and so identify the words intended by the speaker. The basic finding is that the ongoing linguistic changes in Philadelphia, Chicago and Baltimore significantly interfered with these cognitive processes, within the community as well as across communities.

Chapter 6 continued the involvement with the fundamentals of cognition in studying the principles governing the phonemic inventory: mergers, splits and chain shifts. While chain shifts appear to enhance, or at least to preserve, the operation of the phonological system, mergers do not. Sound changes that lead to mergers can hardly be said to enhance the speakers' ability to identify meanings in the stream of speech.[1]

The cognitive basis of sound change is further illuminated by the findings of Chapters 12, which support Bloomfield's formulation of the Neogrammarian view: that the phoneme, and not the word, is the unit of sound change. If the various sound changes presented in this volume actually did proceed word by word, the problem of cross-dialectal comprehension would be many times more difficult. When Chicagoans listened to Philadelphians, it would not be enough to know that /ow/ could be realized as [ɛ:ᵒ]. One would have to know, for each individual word containing /ow/ – *goat*, *go*, *row* – whether this was true or not. And, since lexical diffusion is essentially arbitrary, there would be no other clues as to how each individual word was realized, except brute memorization.

Chapters 9 and 10 consider the driving forces which may be responsible for the continuation, acceleration or completion of change. In one form or another, they involve the association of social attributes with the more advanced forms of a change in progress: local identity, membership in communities of practice, social class, age or gender. We may ask whether the association of a linguistic form with a social group is a cognitive process – a form of knowledge – or a feeling engendered in us by instances of these phonetic forms. The experiments of Hay, Warren and Drager (2006) showed that cognitive processes are involved: subjects' interpretation of a stimulus as *fair* or *fear* was influenced by their perception of the age or social class of the speaker. Thus the grasp of social distributions of linguistic forms might be termed *social cognition*, not different in kind from knowledge of phonological distributions, except that it normally involves gradient rather than discrete judgments. Nevertheless, I will follow the practice of the first two volumes and the argument of Chapter 1 in limiting the term *cognitive factors* to the discrete operation of the linguistic system, as it delivers information on truth-conditional semantics, and opposing it to *social factors* – the association of different ways of saying the same thing with different subgroups of the community.

The attribution of driving forces to social factors is clearest when the learning process is observable in face-to-face interaction. Thus ethnographic studies of small group behavior can correlate the advancement of change with extreme manifestations of local cultural practices (Martha's Vineyard fishermen; burned-out Burnouts). On the other hand, some of the most important social factors invoke broad cultural patterns, which transcend small group behavior. The larger the size of the speech community involved, the more difficult it is to account for uniform patterns of linguistic change. Gender patterns in language change (Chapters 8, 9, 11 of Volume 2) are prototypical of such general cultural factors. Children's initial introduction to gender differences in language may be the contrasting patterns in their parents' behavior. But the generality of male/female differences in language is linked to a cultural pattern that overrides the idiosyncrasies that might stem from local differentiation. How such nation-wide commonalties are transmitted (among children) or diffused (among adults) is a pressing matter for current research.

The most difficult forms of social cognition to account for result from the operation of those social factors that appear to be independent of personal experience and which have here been termed cultural factors. Thus the negative status of the New York City vernacular appears to date from the early nineteenth century, and produces uniform normative responses across the entire population (Labov 1966, Chapter 13). Chapter 10 confronted the enigma of the uniform advancement of the Northern Cities Shift across the Inland North and outlined the possibility that it reflected a long-standing cultural opposition of Yankee morality to Midland individualism.

It cannot be denied that a member of the community who is influenced by the cultural significance of a given linguistic form has received this information through some form of experience. But that experience may be quite remote from face-to-face interaction. The forms of experience involved here are just as subtle and elusive as those which produce long-term trends in the popularity of personal names (Lieberson 2000), profoundly influencing what the individual perceives as a purely personal choice.

No matter how such cultural factors are perceived and transmitted, their relation to the cognitive processing of language forms is at issue. To the extent that they promote and reinforce regional differentiation, they may be seen to interfere with the primary cognitive function of language, in making it harder for those on one side of the boundary to know what those on the other side are talking about. The experiment of Hay et al. (2006) on the New Zealand *fear/fair* distinction can be cited again here. New Zealanders use information on the speakers' age and social class to guess at whether the token [fe:ə] represents *fear* or *fair*. But it also follows that the differential promotion of the merger in the population has led to a situation where this decision will be obscure in many cases. It is worth asking how such a situation has come about in the long-term evolution of language and of the language faculty.

17.2 The Relation of Linguistic Change to Animal Systems of Communication

Human language, as distinct from animal systems of communication, allows us to transfer information on distant times and places, and to use that information to solve the basic problems of living. No matter how cumbersome or inefficient our language may be, it is reasonable to believe that language will serve that purpose better if it remains unchanged, as a common convention accessible to all.

What useful purpose is served by language change? Change is linked with (and opportunistically parasitic on) variation. Most students of linguistic variation have accepted the view of Weinreich et al. (1968), that the speech community displays "orderly heterogeneity." The uniform patterns of social and stylistic stratification suggest that community members can make use of such variation to place speakers on scales of social distance and social power, and many experiments confirm this view (Lambert 1967, Labov 1966, Ch. 12, Labov et al. 2006b, Campbell-Kibler 2005, Conn 2005, Fridland 2003). But Chapters 2–4 show that, when the system changes, community members do not necessarily display the flexibility needed to adapt to what younger speakers are doing. Within the community, it must be the case that youth who are engaged in the incrementation of a sound change (Volume 2, Chapter 14) have some perception of the age vector involved and adults can recognize the new forms used by their children. But it remains to be shown that this age sensitivity leads to an accurate interpretation of speech across generations. The incidence of misunderstanding is of course even greater across dialect boundaries.

Chapters 5–8 outlined the largely mechanical processes that lead to such dialect divergence. Chain shifting is seen as an adjustment or reaction to a disequilibrium created by a triggering event. It is proposed there that the tendency to maximal dispersion in a vowel subsystem, the equilibrating process, is the result of the fundamental mechanics of language acquisition. The child's ability to match the central means of the parents' vowel distribution appears to be based on a capacity for probability matching that is exhibited by many species, from goldfish to ducks to human beings. These chapters may thus be seen as an elaboration of Martinet's view of language change as a long-range readjustment of the system to the effects of an original population disturbance – migration or invasion. If these functional considerations were sufficient to account for language change, the consequent interference with cross-dialectal comprehension might be considered a side effect of a therapeutic process.

Many proposals to explain language change look to a systematic imperfection in transmission (Halle 1962, Ohala 1992, Lightfoot 1999). It seems possible that systematic slippage between perception and production might underlie some of the governing principles in Chapter 6. We are still lacking a conclusive explanation as to why, in chain shifts, tense vowels rise along the peripheral track and lax vowels fall along the nonperipheral track. At the same time these considerations – and others put forward in Chapter 6 – all suffer from their universality. We return always to the opinion of Meillet (1921): no universal cause can account for the sporadic character of language change.

Chapter 8 defines the conditions under which accidental or chance events which are not universal can lead to lasting divergence. This raises a question which may limit our efforts to seek the causes of linguistic change. Gould (1989) argues that, if the evolutionary tape were to be replayed again, the result would be different. To the extent that the evolution of language is determined by contingent events, our explanations will necessarily have an ad hoc or teleological character. The notion of a "driving force" is distinct from an imperfection, a slippage or a mismatch. It implies some positive impulse that satisfies a need or carries out a function. The driving forces reviewed in Chapter 9 are all distinct from the need to transfer information, and all assume an underlying proposition that the new form conveys information about the identity of the speakers, or about their attitude or intentions toward the listener.

The analogies with animal communication systems (ACS), which lack propositional capacities are fairly evident (Marler 1970, Baptista and Petrinovitch 1984, Kroodsma and Pickert 1984, Hauser 1996):

√   Local identity, as established in Labov (1963) or Eckert (2000), is analogous to territorial functions in bird song and other ACS.
√   Reference group behavior, as discussed in Sturtevant (1947) and Le Page and Tabouret-Keller (1985), corresponds to mimicry in ACS.
√   The development of indicators to markers, and the acquisition of style shifting (as in Labov 1966), is analogous to signals of dominance and submission in ACS.
√   Gender differentiation of linguistic change, an almost universal feature of community studies, may have some relation to sexual selection, but here the analogy is not clear.

17.3   More on the Functions of Language

Let us return to the Darwinian Paradox: that the forms of linguistic and biological evolution are strikingly similar, but the functional core of natural selection is missing in linguistic change. The most obvious explanation for this disparity is to ascribe linguistic change to the selection of other functions of language, which have other evolutionary histories, independent of the need to transfer information. The literature on such competing functions is large, though of a general and discursive character (Frei 1929, Bühler 1934, Jakobson 1960, Hymes 1961). Bühler's tripartite approach to the functions of language begins with the recognition of the opposition of representational and social functions and distinguishes two social functions as *expressive* and *directive*. In terms of the data generated by recent sociolinguistic studies, expressive functions provide information on the speaker's emotional state, age, gender, ethnicity, socioeconomic status and local identity – all familiar aspects of sociolinguistic variation. Directive functions would involve accommodation to the audience, adjusting social distance, politeness and deference, style shifting and audience design. The three functional poles can be neatly associated with the three persons of pronominal deixis.

All three functions share the property of providing information, which may in one way or another facilitate or clarify the communicative exchange. These functions are opposed as a whole to facilitative arguments related to the Principle of Least Effort (Chapter 1), which can be interpreted to mean that a linguistic form is more fit if it takes less time or energy to produce. That was indeed the argument of Müller that Darwin (1871) relied upon to complete his analogy between biological and linguistic evolution: words become better as they become shorter (PLC, Vol. 2: 9). The combination of least effort and various communicative functions can render the explanatory enterprise vacuous, since every linguistic change can then be accounted for through one argument or another. Only when we take the representational function as primary can we confront seriously the problem of the direction of linguistic change, admitting that there are historical events that interfere with this function and so make language less fit for communication.

Repair strategies   One approach to the problem is to look for repair strategies that compensate for the loss of representational information. The typical relationship between competing functions is complementary, as in the case of least effort versus representation. Developments in the history of French are among the most commonly cited examples. As information is lost in the attrition of negative particles, it is supplied through the addition of reinforcing adverbs *pas, point, miette, jamais, cap*, etc. (Pope 1934).[2] When information about person and number is lost through the attrition of final /s/, it is supplied through the conversion of optional pronouns to obligatory pronominal clitics.

The loss of information created by phonological merger is sometimes accompanied by a repair mechanism of this type. Thus the merger of /i/ and /e/ before nasals is compensated for by reference to an *ink pen* versus a *safety pin*. In the history of phonetic attrition in Mandarin Chinese, this repair mechanism operates on a grand scale, defying the principle of least effort through the creation of two-character words. When the loss of information is the result of social processes, the same repair mechanism can be seen at work. Considerable information on number was lost through the abandonment of the second person singular *thou* in Early Modern English; it has since been supplied through a variety of mechanisms for distinguishing the plural: *youse*, *youns*, *you all*, *you guys*, etc.

Such compensatory mechanisms imply a give-and-take of forces that are arrayed along the same dimension, the impulse for more information leading to the expenditure of greater effort, the tendency to reduce effort leading to the reduction of information. The relation between least effort and supply of information is *antagonistic*, and the repair mechanism involves a shift in one direction or the other along this single dimension. The question remains as to whether there is a similar repair machinery for the effects of chain shifts. Plichta and Rakerd (2002) showed that subjects from the NCS area had shifted their perceptual category boundary between /æ/ and /o/ in harmony with the shifts in speech production around them. But the evidence of Chapters 2–4 shows that Chicago listeners had not adjusted their hearing to allow themselves to recognize [blæ:k] as a token of *block*, or [sæ:ks] as a token of *socks*. It is possible that this is the result of competing norms, induced by the formality of the experimental situation. The fact that local high school students did better in the Gating experiment than local college students points in this direction. But Figures 4.6 and 4.7 show that, even so, three quarters of these high school subjects did not recognize the words for what they were. There does not appear to be any systematic mechanism by which the informational loss due to chain shifting can be repaired. If this is so, we must conclude that the forces involved in chain shifting are organized along a different dimension, which does not respond to informationally driven considerations. None of the driving forces examined in Chapter 9 are based on the need to transmit propositional information; rather, they relate to some form of social information. One might indeed translate territorial or accommodating behavior into propositional form: "I belong to this corner group," or "I'm irritated by your behavior"; but the important point is that such information is not transmitted in propositional form. Rather, it is transmitted in one of two continuous, quantitative forms: distribution in acoustic space and the frequency of discrete variants.

DENIABILITY   The non-discrete character of this social information is associated with another property. In social interaction one may insult, challenge or defy an addressee by a variety of prosodic or non-verbal devices that share the property of *deniability* (Labov and Fanshel 1977). We are socially responsible for our words, and we may indeed be convicted of perjury for denying them; but we are free to deny the impact of intonation contours and gestures.[3] Sociolinguistic information shares the property of deniability with intonation. To put it simply, one is legally responsible for one's words and for the constructions into which those words are organized, but not for social variation in the realization of those words.

If there are indeed two separate modes of processing information, one may posit a sociolinguistic monitor (Labov et al. 2006b), which processes and stores social information in a form distinct from the storage of propositional information. There is no doubt that social and propositional information are intricately combined in the linguistic signal that is transmitted.

17.4   Social Intelligence and Object-Oriented Intelligence

These considerations point to the possibility that two streams of information processing were inherited in the evolution of human language. The differentiation of social intelligence from object-oriented intelligence is now well established in studies of animal communication systems (Byrne and Whiten 1988, 1997, Hauser 1988). Cheney and Seyfarth (1990) have found that vervet monkeys are expert in the perception of, and response to, intricate sets of social relations, but do not draw inferences from relations of objects that seem transparent to humans: for example, that a dead antelope hanging in a tree indicated the presence of a leopard. Cheney and Seyfarth (2007) reported even more sensitive and intricate manipulations of social information among baboons, in contrast to their limited capacity to reason from information about objects.

Given the possibility of two distinct streams of development in the communicative system, the central question for the study of linguistic change is the relationship between them. We have already seen that information and effort stand in an antagonistic, unidimensional relation. Much of the discussion of social intelligence in the recent literature on the evolution of language implies a unidimensional relation of a different type: reinforcing. Hauser et al. (2002) have argued that the central recursive capacity of the faculty of language, narrowly defined, might have been derived from the recursive character of kinship relations. The implication is that the capacity to manipulate complex kinship terms may be put to productive use in the recursive production and perception of propositions in other domains, and that skill in kinship relations reinforces the capacity to convey information on say, foraging. The "social brain" hypothesis (Dunbar 1998) argues that the mental representation of abstract social concepts led to the general development of intelligence. All of these discussions occur in the context of accounting for the successful development of human language as a communicative system searching for the activities and formative factors which favored that development. However, the findings of this volume indicate that language change limits and reduces the successful communication of propositions. This raises the possibility that, to some extent, the social factors that lead to linguistic change are orthogonal to the representational function of language. By this I mean that there is no fixed relation between a given language change and the loss or gain of information in the propositional system. The centralization of /ay/ and /aw/ in Martha's Vineyard, now generally accepted as a symbolic assertion of local identity (Labov 1963), does not show any signs of reducing the identifiability of *right*, *pride*, *out*, or *proud*, nor does it introduce confusion between *right* and *rate*, *loud* and *layed*. The introduction of consonantal /r/ as a prestige marker in New York City reintroduced and reinforced the distinction between *bad*, *bared* and *beard* (Labov 1966, Ch. 14). However, the development of Philadelphia /aw/ from [æo] to [ɛɔ], whatever its social function may be, has led to the common confusion of *crown* and *crayon* and to the general merger of /æ/, /aw/ and /ey/ before /l/ in *pal*, *Powell* and *pail*. To the extent that such mergers are not easily reversed, we find a significant reduction of communicative efficiency within and across the boundary of the Philadelphia speech community.

Chapter 6 showed that chain shifts are driven by powerful internal factors. Only one of them – the tendency to maximal dispersion within a subsystem – favors communicative efficiency. The unidirectional raising of peripheral vowels and lowering of nonperipheral vowels have no such connection with the representational system. Whatever forces lie behind the Eckert progression – the shift from social class to gender stratification, as a change progresses over time – are not related to the need for representation. Most importantly, we see that there is no adequate repair mechanism for the confusion introduced by chain shifting. The driving forces involved have no systematic relation to the communication of propositional information.[4]

The Northern Cities Shift presents us with a formidable problem in our search for the causes of linguistic change. Local studies show local correlations, but they do not explain the remarkable uniformity of the phenomenon across such a vast area. One may consider the image of a swimmer in an offshore current: sometimes using the Australian crawl, other times the backstroke or the breaststroke. He may have the impression, "I am really making this water move!" and may indeed be responsible for making progress in one direction or another. But the great chain shifts sweeping across North America are more like ocean currents than local eddies, flowing with irresistible force across the Inland North, the South, or Canada. As we found in Chapter 9, they are modified by social factors within their territory. But these currents are arrested abruptly as they reach the 150-year-old social boundary of the North/Midland line.

Chapter 10 suggested that this great uniformity of the Inland North and its abrupt termination at the North/Midland line is the result of large-scale settlement patterns in the nineteenth century, when large numbers of children transmitted the vowel system faithfully across the area. Furthermore, it was proposed that the driving force behind the continued acceleration of linguistic change may be the inherited association of the Northern Cities Shift with the Yankee cultural ideology, which was transformed into a political movement in the ferment of the Second Great Awakening. Chapter 11 added some experimental evidence to support this view.

The implications of this account of the uniformity of the Inland North are that the social factors involved cannot be explained as the effects of local, face-to-face interaction. To cite Fridland again,

> these shared practices do not necessarily require individuals' social cohesion but merely require shared historical experience and a strongly circumscribing environment that places speakers in a similar social position relative to the external social world. (Fridland 2003: 296)

The same argument applies to the uniformity of the direction of linguistic change in metropolitan communities like Philadelphia.

If this is the case, and language change responds to large-scale cultural factors, the connection with the evolution of social intelligence among nonhumans becomes more tenuous. Cultural transmission, the major theme of this volume, is very limited among nonhumans. Indeed there are indications that such normative, uniform movements are not characteristic of small human populations. The linguistic homogeneity of the Inland North is more typical of large urban populations than of linguistic evolution in small family groups. The social evaluation of language differences appears to carry most weight across group boundaries, rather than within them. Thus the individual leaders of linguistic change, who played a major role in Volume 2, begin to recede in importance as we raise the scope of our inquiry to larger domains.

Finally, we return to the uniformitarian question (Christy 1983). Are the processes, events and causes reviewed in these three volumes the same as those that operated to produce the historical record, and are these the same as those that were operating in the earliest periods of the evolution of language? To the first question we have answered throughout with a tentative "yes"; to the second, the answer is more clearly "no." The chances of being right about this earliest prehistory are limited by the Historical Paradox of Volume 1, Chapter 1:

> The task of historical linguistics is to explain the differences between the past and the present; but to the extent that the past was different from the present, there is no way of knowing how different it was –

– or they are even more limited if we apply the maxim of J. B. S. Haldane (cited in R. and P. Grant 1994): "No scientific theory is worth anything unless it enables us to predict something which is actually going on."

These three volumes have attempted to understand the process of language change by paying close attention to what is going on around us. Though we hope always to improve our understanding of how the present situation came to be, these changes in progress tell us much about the human beings who are engaged in them. They are surprising and at times difficult to understand. They mark the limits of our rationality, and illuminate the many sides of human nature.

Notes

Notes to Chapter 1

1 Chapter 16 of Volume 2 argued that the socioeconomic hierarchy, reflected in occupation, education, income, or some combination of these, has just such a generalized
character. In the socially mobile society of North America there is no clear-cut
"membership" in the upper working class, and there are not always well-defined "upper
working-class people" to be identified, admired or stigmatized. There are indeed ethnic
groups, and membership in them, e.g. in the Italian or Jewish American group, is a
social fact. There are also recognized neighborhoods: residence at e.g. Kensington and
Allegheny or 6th & Wolfe in Philadelphia is an established and particular fact about a
given speaker. Factors like these are too particular and too concrete to be identified with
the large-scale linguistic changes that continue to sweep across the city of Philadelphia
or the Inland North. It is therefore no accident that neighborhood and ethnicity play
such a marginal role in the characterization of linguistic change in Chapter 7 (see Vol. 2,
p. 514).

2 This display differs from that of ANAE, Ch. 2 in that the ingliding vowels are here
divided along the front/back dimension through the inclusion of /æh/ in initial position
(see below).

3 The expression "long and ingliding vowels" refers to the fact that members of this set
are normally monophthongal in low or lower mid position, but glide towards a center
target when their nucleus is in upper mid or high position.

4 For more abstract analyses, height can be analyzed as two binary features [±high, ±low],
as in Chomsky and Halle (1968), or as an n-ary dimension to reflect lower-level sound
changes, as in Labov (1966), LYS, Trudgill (1974b).

5 The use of *h* to designate this subset is widespread in the expressive set of long and
ingliding words (*yeah, bah, hah, rah rah*), and generally to indicate the vocalization of
/r/ (*pahk the cah in the Hahvad yahd*) and the results of monophthongization of /ay/
in the South (*mah, ah'm, raht*) and /aw/ in Pittsburgh (*dahntahn*).

6 For example, some speakers in Wisconsin have developed the long monophthongs /u:/
and /o:/ to ingliding vowels, and the results are hard for speakers of other dialects to
identify. Thus their pronunciation of *pole* is identified with *Paul* by speakers of other
dialects (from exploratory interviews conducted by the author).

7   The earlier opposition of *bomb* and *balm* with /o/ and /ah/ is all but gone outside of Eastern New England, where *bother* rhymes with *father*. On the boundary of these two mergers, Johnson (2010) finds almost no trace of speakers who preserve a three-way opposition of /o/, /ah/ and /oh/. Elsewhere the ANAE data are defective on this point, and there are indications of different distributions for /ah/ and /o/ which need to be explored more deeply.

8   The increasing tendency to pronounce /l/ in the second and third words further reduces the contrast.

9   The first evidence for the NCS is found in an unpublished paper of Fasold (1969), which described the first two stages. The NCS was first named, and the first five stages were first identified as a chain shift, in LYS. The backing of /ʌ/ was first identified in Eckert (1986). See also Gordon 2000, 2001, Plichta and Rakerd 2002, Jones 2003, and Evans et al. 2006.

10 The Southern Shift has long been recognized as a chain shift in its realizations in Southern England (Sivertsen 1960, LYS) and in Australia and New Zealand (Mitchell and Delbridge 1965), where it is most often initiated by the backing and raising of the nucleus of /ay/. In Labov (1991) the Southern Shift was shown to include the fronting of /uw/ and /ow/, but in ANAE the latter is recognized as an independent phenomenon, common to the Midland and the South.

11 The Canadian Shift was first reported by Clarke, Elms and Youssef in 1995. See also De Decker and Mackenzie 2000, Boberg 2005, Hollett 2006, Hagiwara 2006, and Roeder and Jarmasz 2009.

12 The status of this merger is difficult to determine, as many /uhr/ words vary lexically with /ohr/: *pour, poor, tour, whore* etc.

Notes to Chapter 2

1   The CDC research project at the University of Pennsylvania was supported by NSF under Grant 509687, "A Study of Cross-Dialectal Comprehension," from 1985 to 1987 and under Grant 8617883, "Comprehension Within and Across Dialects," from 1987 to 1992.

2   Setting aside these two observers, the percentage of dialect-motivated misunderstandings remains at over one quarter, 26.1%.

3   Originally presented in Chapter 11 of Volume 1, and reproduced here in condensed form.

4   In (38) and (39), the dialectal identities of the speakers and of the mechanisms are uncertain, but these examples are added here to complete the *coffee/copy* paradigm. In a similar case, Gillian S.'s *coffee pot* was misunderstood by WL as *copper pot*.

5   This could be observed in an extreme form at a presentation on Natural Misunderstandings at the 2008 meeting of NWAVE in Houston.

6   The cases of uncertainty mostly involve the South. As Feagin (1993) and ANAE (Chapter 9) report, the back upglide that distinguishes /oh/ from /o/ is being lost, with resultant merger in many cities.

7   See Johnson (2010), Chapter 5, for the sudden expansion of the low back merger among young children along the Rhode Island/Massachusetts border.

8   Post-consonantal /l/ is also vocalized in Philadelphia in words like *please, blame,* and *clear*, though this does not play a major role in the discussion of misunderstandings to follow.

Notes to Chapter 3

1   The CDC research project at the University of Pennsylvania was supported by NSF under Grant 509687, "A Study of Cross-Dialectal Comprehension," from 1985 to 1987 and under Grant 8617883, "Comprehension Within and Across Dialects," from 1987 to 1992.
2   We are grateful to Penny Eckert, then at University of Illinois, Chicago Circle, and to Ed Battistella at University of Alabama, Birmingham, for assistance in locating subjects and opportunities for our recordings.
3   The measurements are unnormalized. The speakers are all women in their early twenties, with about the same pitch range.
4   It is important to note that, in Philadelphia, *cad* is always lax; the only words in which /æ/ is tensed before /d/ are *mad, bad* and *glad.*
5   As reflected in the absence of this contrast in most phonics programs.
6   This is not true for the Philadelphian speakers, who were local employees of the University of Pennsylvania, while the subjects were groups of students. It is all the more remarkable that the Philadelphia local error rate was lower than that of the others.

Notes to Chapter 4

1   This conforms to indications from exploratory interviews in Chicago originally reported in LYS, where the raising and fronting of /æ/ was more consistent and further advanced in reading texts than in spontaneous speech.
2   In two cases, both involving the raising and fronting of /æ/, the sentences were drawn from exploratory interviews in Chicago conducted by Labov in 1968.
3   In filling out their residence histories, a number of Fultondale students wrote "Birmingham (Fultondale)."
4   Five of the NCS items and one southern item in word and phrase form are used in the web site "Do you Speak American?" to illustrate the extent of sound change. See http://www.pbs.org/speak/ahead/change/vowelpower/vowel.html.
5   This is an exceptional item, where the full context was less than a complete sentence.
6   This phenomenon is described as "northern breaking" in ANAE, Ch. 13. It is unique to the northern dialect region.
7   Thus Jakobson, Fant and Halle (1967) point out that the phonological system operates in such a way that, when we are introduced to a Mr Miller at a party, we know that it is not Mr Diller or Mr Siller that we are talking to.

Notes to Chapter 5

1 For some of the limitations of animal systems of communication in this respect, see Cheney and Seyfarth (1990, 2007).

2 This notation is neutral as to which element moves first, that is, whether (1) is a push chain or a drag chain.

3 Martinet (1952) attributes the original concept to DeGroot.

4 Though Wells's notation is lexical, the tabular organization he adopts reflects the same subclasses as in Table 1 (ANAE, Ch. 2).

5 This does not apply to the situation before the liquids /l/ and /r/, where mergers of long and short vowels are common (/il/ ~ /iyl/, /ul/ ~ /uwl/, etc.). This leads to the consideration that vowels before /l/ form a separate subset, just as vowels before /r/ do.

6 But see Hollett (2006) for the Canadian Shift in St John's.

7 The phonetic position of the merged class varies considerably throughout the merged areas; in Canada it is quite far back and rounded. It is possible that the backing and raising of /o/ in Figure 5.3 was a small movement, and that /o/ and /oh/ were distinguished primarily by length when Canadian English was first formed.

8 As Chapter 6 will show, peripherality is not defined for low vowels; low /o/ acquires [+peripheral] status when it merges with lower mid back /oh/.

9 Baranowski (2007) points out that in Charleston, where the low back merger is also in progress, one observes a vigorous backing of /æ/. No downward shift of /e/ has been found so far.

10 See Labov and Baranowski (2006) for evidence that the merger of /o/ with /ah/ leads to a phonologically determined increase in length of approximately 50 msec.

11 The mean values of Figure 5.8 are all normalized with the log mean normalization (Nearey 1977; ANAE, Ch. 5.7; Labov 1966).

12 In all such mean calculations, the mean of /æ/ before nasals is calculated separately from the main distribution. The figures shown here are the means for /æ/ placed not before nasals.

13 Most notable are the simultaneous downward shift of /e/ and forward shift of /o/ into the low front position vacated by /æ/ in the Northern Cities Shift (Labov and Baranowski 2006).

14 Many of these communities are of course linked historically, and the low back merger is not an independent development in all sixty of them. However, there is good reason to believe that the merger did occur independently in at least five areas: eastern New England, Canada, western Pennsylvania, northeastern Pennsylvania and the West.

15 In the conditioning of the tensing of short *a*, the front nasals /m/, /n/ are selected; in the tensing of short *o*, the velar nasal.

16 The examples shown are from my own speech, where all common words before voiceless fricatives and front nasals are tense, but uncommon and onomatopoeic words like *Goth, Gothic, wroth, gosh, bosh, tosh, ping-pong, King Kong, ding-dong* are lax. As R. Kim points out (personal communicaton), this also leads to lax "MS-DOS" with a lax vowel before apical /s/.

17 I use here the traditional term "smoothing" in order to avoid confusion with the recent monophthongization of /aw/ to /ah/ in Pittsburgh, discussed in the last section.

18　This was first noted by the spelling reformer Michael Barton (1830), who found that his own New York State speech differed from the New England dictionary writers in just this respect.

19　One could argue that southern US dialects have retained the original /aw/, but the southern back upglide also appears in *lost, often, cloth*, which were never diphthongal in Old and Middle English.

20　The shift to an articulatory framework (ANAE, Ch. 2) converts this third principle to the first. The fronting of [u] to [ü] is there seen as an example of peripheral vowels becoming less open, in parallel with the raising of [a] to [i]. Martinet's argument can be applied in this framework as well.

21　Vowels before /l/ are excluded, since outside of the South they are in extreme back position; and even in the South fronting is quite limited. Only those effects with a probability < .01 are shown.

22　The notation *age * 25* indicates the multiplication of the coefficient for age by 25. Thus it represents the projection of the expected difference between e.g. a speaker 50 years old and a speaker 25 years old. The negative coefficient indicates change in progress in apparent time: increasing age is associated with lower fronting values.

23　This is seen here in the effect of following laterals, which are excluded from this analysis, and in the effect of following nasals. The influence of onset nasals and laterals is always much less than the effect of these consonants in coda position.

24　Melchert (1983) cites similar breaking of *u:* to *iu* after apicals from Oscan, Tsakonian Greek and Boeotian. I am grateful to Ron Kim for drawing my attention to these historical parallels.

25　The status of words with initial palatal consonants is not always clear. The coarticulatory effect on /uw/ in *choose* and *shoes* may be strong enough to eliminate the difference between this /uw/ and /iw/ after palatals in *juice, chew*, etc. Sledd (1955) includes *shoe* with his *dew* class.

26　This use of "peripheral" is of course distinct from its use above, in the description of English vowels. Vachek meant that the glides /h/, /w/, /y/ were peripheral in their lack of integration into the phonological system of English.

27　The unrounding and fronting of /o/ dates from the beginning of the nineteenth century (Barton 1830) and may be almost contemporaneous with the raising of /æ/. The lowering and fronting of /oh/ is quite variable across speakers in many areas, and for some speakers it may be the last stage. Though the backing of /ʌ/ appears as the most recent stage in Eckert (2000), a relatively back position for /ʌ/ can be observed in the North as far east as Providence and as far west as South Dakota.

28　The shift in the direction of /i/ shows a parallel redirection. Early studies of Chicago indicated a strong tendency towards the lowering of /i/, but in more recent studies /i/ shifts back towards a more central position (LYS).

29　The EQ criterion for the NCS (ANAE, Chs 11, 14) selects all speakers for whom /æ/ is higher and fronter than /e/; this is necessarily a superset of dialects in which the raising of /æ/ has reached a mean position above the midline.

30　This function of the Mapinfo program is defined in the documentation for Version 4 as: "The range breaks are determined according to an algorithm such that the difference between the data values and the average of the data values is minimized on a per range basis."

31　And including the exception of Erie, which breaks the inland North into western and eastern regions (ANAE, 14.5, Evanini 2009).

32 Dinkin (2009) finds that Utica is to be included in this series. That city exhibits a complete and consistent use of the NCS.

33 Since the Hudson River is actually an ocean estuary, ice-free year-long, it was a more practical route than the Delaware, which freezes in the winter. From the time when the Erie Canal was completed, New York City rapidly surpassed Philadelphia as the leading metropolis of the United States.

34 This is one of the four criteria which define the NCS: the backing of /ʌ/ and the fronting of /o/ reverses the relative positions of these phonemes found in other dialects, where /ʌ/ is central and /o/ is back. These four criteria are fully described in Chapter 8.

35 In Chapter 8 we will find that three other measures of the progress of the NCS coincide with this North/Midland boundary. ANAE, Ch. 14 shows that several other features of northern phonology fall along this line as well.

36 This lowering was in fact noted by LYS in the speech of the oldest New York City speaker, for whom short *a* was lengthened.

37 A new and vigorous change such as the raising of /aw/ in Philadelphia shows an F1 age coefficient in regression analysis of 3.0 Hz per year. Thus three generations (75 years) will lower the F1 by 225 Hz, which would bring a low front vowel with an F1 mean of 800 Hz to an upper mid front vowel with an F1 mean of 575 Hz. The actual time course will be longer, since 3 Hz per year is at the midpoint of the S-shaped curve, where the speed of change is at its maximum.

Notes to Chapter 6

1 See in particular Vol. 1, p. 332.

2 The best studied vowel split is the Mid-Atlantic separation of short *a* into lax and tense classes (Labov 1989b, ANAE Ch. 13). The best suggestion on its origins traces it to the British broad-*a* opposition (Babbitt 1896, Ferguson 1975), and this in turn to lengthening in open syllables in Early Middle English (Jespersen 1949).

3 Some of the best known cases of merger reversal in the historical record turn out to be cases of "near-merger," where speakers reported two vowels as "the same" but continued to make small but consistent differences in production. Chapters 10 to 14 of Volume 1 are devoted to this question, and include the reported unmerger of the classes of *meat* and *mate* in sixteenth-century English and the classes of *line* and *loin* in eighteenth-century English. The cases of unmerger to be considered in this chapter show no evidence of such a near-merger status.

4 One phonological assumption behind this organization is that only long vowels are found before syllable coda /r/: on this view, *fir*, *her*, *fur* and *world* do not have short vowels, but a syllabic nucleus /r/.

5 In these diagrams, words are unnumbered when elicited, and numbered 2 or 3 when pronounced in the minimal pair test.

6 Such accidental reversals may be the basis of the Utah stereotype of the merger, "Put the harse in the born."

7 The analyst heard /ahr/ and /ɔhr/ as "close," but measurement shows that /ahr/ is actually higher than /ɔhr/.

8   This suggests that a certain amount of attention had to be devoted to the new distribution, since it is characteristic of function words to escape such attention (Prince 1987).

9   It can be noted that *here* and *hair* are frequently singled out as different from other words, but in an inconsistent direction: sometimes merged, sometimes distinct.

10 This merger is in progress in Charleston, where the two sounds are largely merged for speakers under the age of 30 (Baranowski 2007).

11 But see Montgomery and Eble (2004), Bailey (2004).

12 Of these, all but two were in marginal areas, which show few southern features (New Orleans 4, Savannah 2, Atlanta 2, northern Virginia 2).

13 The survey of long-distance telephone operators began with a request for the number of Mr Harry Hawk, with the vowel of the surname pronounced with a low central vowel. When the operator failed to find a number, she was asked if she had looked up "H–A–W–K." In areas of distinction, operators looked for *Hock*; in areas of merger, for *Hawk*. The investigator then proceeded to obtain the operator's own pronunciation of each word and her local status.

14 For Indianapolis, see Fogle (2007); for Pittsburgh African–Americans, Eberhardt (2008); for Erie, Evanini (2009); for Southeastern Massachusetts, Johnson (2010); for Miami, Doernberger and Cerny (2008).

15 Johnson also traced the relation of /o/ to /ah/, the long and ingliding vowel of *father*, *spa*, *taco*, etc. In most communities with the low back merger of /o/ and /oh/, /ah/ was distinct in a fronter position; and when /o/ is distinct from /oh/ it is merged with /ah/. In a few communities all three are distinct, which Johnson believes to be the original configuration.

16 This pattern is characteristic of the Southeastern superregion outside of the South proper. It shows strong fronting of /uw/ and /ow/ along with the South, but it differs from the South in showing the nasal short-*a* system: no monophthongization of /ay/ before obstruents. As a result, the new Charleston system resembles Columbus, Ohio more than Columbia, South Carolina.

17 Becker and Wong (2009) report a replacement of the NYC short-*a* pattern among younger speakers on the Lower East Side, and similar phenomena have been found among isolated neighborhoods in Philadelphia.

18 In both Boston and New York, the general insertion of consonantal /r/ in coda position has influenced formal styles, but not the basic vernacular outside of the upper middle class.

19 An anonymous reviewer introduces some important considerations at this point. "Since the Great Depression, there have been two major waves of population movements in the US. First, urbanization, a huge migration from countryside to cities. This would have brought many regional speakers into the cities, and in smaller cities, might well have overwhelmed the locals. Second, suburbanization, which since the late 1950s saw a huge emigration from cities into the adjacent exurban regions, which brought city dwellers into contact with regional speakers. Together, these may explain the mechanism of regional absorption."

20 A t-test comparing speakers over the age of 40 with those 40 and below shows a .05 probability of this effect being due to chance.

21 A relationship between peripherality and energy appears in the findings of Jacewicz et al. (2004) that the most heavily stressed prosodic positions are realized in the most peripheral positions.

22   Ch. 5 of Vol. 1 showed that phonological space of this type is found in a variety of non-Germanic languages in Europe: Czech, Latvian, Romansh, etc. Kim and Labov (2002) conclude that, in all such cases, this is the result of strong and long-standing influence from West Germanic languages, specifically German.

23   The legend of Figure 6.18 shows 15 vowels which correspond to the initial position of the North American vowel system described in ANAE, Ch. 2. The front vowels /i/, /e/ and /æ/ and the diphthong /aw/ do not include prenasal tokens, and vowels before coda /r/ are not included.

24   There are three subclasses of this diphthong for every dialect, which represent original /iw/ in *dew* and *suit*; /uw/ after coronals in *too, two, do* and *noon*; and the remaining /uw/ after noncoronals, e.g. in *roof* and *move*. These subclasses are not distinguished in the legend, since they are all peripheral.

25   The issue as to whether raised /æ/ in the Northern Cities Shift is a shift of the subsystem to Vh is still open. There is no change of phonemic contrast involved which would justify a new notation, but the phonetic developments, the northern breaking and the consequent chain shift support the view that /æ/ has become phonemically /æh/. The limited distinction of *have ~ halve* and *Sam ~ salm(on)* is thus automatically neutralized.

26   Although it seems that the southern back upglide does represent a spontaneous development /ɔː/ → [ɔo], if it was indeed preceded by a consistent monophthongization of Middle English /aw/.

27   Less complete data are available on a number of other mergers before /l/ involving the opposition of /ʌ/ with /ow/, /oh/ and /u/ in *hull ~ whole, hull ~ hall* and *hull ~ full*.

28   Detailed studies of /e/ show that some tokens fall towards the low front position and others move to the back (LYS, Eckert 2000). The overall trend combines both movements (Labov and Baranowski 2006).

29   But see Jacewicz et al. (2004) on the connection between peripherality and prosodic stress.

Notes to Chapter 7

1   There it will appear that geographical diffusion alters the split short-*a* system to a continuous short-*a* pattern with phonetic conditioning similar to that of New York City, but without any of the finer lexical or grammatical conditioning specific to that dialect.

2   This reversal of the relative positions of short-*a* and short-*e* is the "EQ criterion" – one of the four measures that define the NCS (ANAE, Ch. 14).

3   Examples of /a/ ~ /ɔ/ fluctuation can be found in a wide range of languages.

4   Note, however, the findings of Dinkin (2009), cited above. Dinkin also shows that the resistance of the NCS to the low back merger is not absolute. Speakers in the fringe area of the Inland North, who share most features of the NCS, also show many signs of influence from the low back merger. On the other hand, the raising of /oh/ appears to provide a much more solid basis for resisting the low back merger.

Notes to Chapter 8

1 See the maps in Chapter 18 of Volume 1.
2 As defined in ANAE, *homogeneity* denotes the proportion of speakers within the isogloss who show the defining feature, and *consistency* denotes the proportion of all speakers with the defining feature who are located within the isogloss. See ANAE, Appendix 11.1, p. 151.
3 In the Midland we also find that fronting is favored by population size and disfavored by education.
4 Most notable are the simultaneous downward shift of /e/ and forward shift of /o/ into the low front position vacated by /æ/ in the NCS (Labov and Baranowski 2006).
5 The same quantitative criterion, 700 Hz, was used in ANAE to distinguish upper mid /æ/ from moderately raised variants (AE1, see above).
6 The West is the only area where the low back merger is regularly accompanied by unrounding; in Canada, Eastern New England and Western Pennsylvania the merged vowel is lower mid back, rounded.
7 And most likely differentiated by length.

Notes to Chapter 9

1 This certainly seems to be the case with the progress of *do*-support in early Modern English, as traced in Kroch (1989).
2 Two later studies of Martha's Vineyard also examined the effect of local identity on this sound change. Blake and Josey (2003) found that the sound change was no longer operating; but Pope et al. (2007) found a continuation of centralization of /ay/ and /aw/, with a maximum for those born in the years 1917–31, and a parallel correlation with positive orientation towards the island.
3 As Eckert makes clear, there is a large intermediate class between these polar groups, who sometimes define themselves as "in-betweens" but orient themselves to this binary opposition in one way or another. Figure 9.2 includes data only for the polar groups.
4 At the same time it should be noted that Hindle was not able to find a significant correlation of vowel variation with any smaller unit of the social context, or to describe the social meaning of any individual act of employment of the variable (aw).
5 Thus the 1971 Montreal sample gave equal representation to the highest and lowest social groups, though they represented a small percentage of the total population (Sankoff and Sankoff 1973).
6 Earlier formulations of the curvilinear hypothesis associated monotonic functions of age with curvilinear social patterns. Chapter 14 of Volume 2 pointed out that purely monotonic functions are not actually possible, since children begin with the level of the variable they acquire from their caretakers. Change in progress is associated with a monotonic function among adults, with a peak somewhere in late adolescence. See also Tagliamonte and D'Arcy 2009.

7 The figures shown here and all the figures from the Philadelphia study to follow are based on the normalized mean values of acoustic measurements of F1 and F2, derived by the log-mean normalization to eliminate the main effects of differences in vocal tract length (see Vol. 2, Ch. 5).

8 Some people are aware that *crown* and *crayon* are homonyms in Philadelphia, but this is not connected with the rise of [æo] to [eɔ]. The only element of the Philadelphia vowel system that is frequently mentioned by our subjects is the realization of tense /æ/ as [e:ə], often called the "harsh, nasal *a*."

9 Regression analyses show that the upper working-class advantage is significant (Volume 2, Table 5.4).

10 It is useful here to distinguish between *custom*, the transmission of stable forms across generations, and *fashion*, the rapid change of forms within and across generations. While most language forms are stable and customary, a few rapidly changing variables may be closely compared to fashions. In the study of personal influence by Katz and Lazarsfeld (1955), the closest parallels to patterns of linguistic change are found in the domains of fashion and cosmetics, where younger women are the opinion leaders.

11 Four years after Lieberson named his daughter *Rebecca*, he found a half-dozen Rebeccas responding when he called his daughter's name at preschool. I had the same experience with my own daughter Rebecca.

12 The social class groups represent divisions of a 16-point index equally weighted for education, occupation and house value. For details, see Chapter 5 of PLC, Vol. 2.

13 Setting aside the St Louis corridor, where the NCS is in the process of diffusion, advancing from Chicago to St Louis.

14 Although the Atlas procedures required that any telephone respondent who was born and raised in an area be accepted as representative of that area, there was an additional policy that each community be represented by at least one woman under 40, if possible.

15 The correlation with social status that is most consistent in the Atlas data employs the measure of number of years of school completed, which ranges from 6 to 20.

16 This is a Boolean function that ranges from 0 to 1. Values are here multiplied by 100, to show roughly the same range as other features.

17 As an illustration of the need for regional specificity, consider the fact that Canadian Raising, the centralization of /ay/ before voiceless consonants, is a strongly male-dominated change in Philadelphia (see Vol. 2, Ch. 9) but a strongly female-dominated change in the inland North (Eckert 2000).

18 That is, not necessarily along the lines of the gravity model of Trudgill (1974a). Efforts to apply the gravity model to the data of Callary (1975) on the correlation of the raising of short *a* in northern Illinois with city size have not been successful.

19 The name "Northern Cities Shift" may therefore turn out to be a misnomer, but it is too firmly established in the literature to be changed at this point.

20 Furthermore, a number of individual vowel shifts show such a significant relation to city size: fronting of /æ/, $p < .05$; lowering of /e/, $p < .05$; fronting of /o/, $p < .05$; backing of /ʌ/, $p < .01$.

21 Wagner (2008) is a step in this direction, as she follows high school students through their first year after graduation.

Notes to Chapter 10

1 This chapter enters into a domain of cultural history in which my own experience is limited. I am particularly indebted to Christopher Grey, William McDougall and Richard Cawardine for directing me to the important sources on the Second Great Awakening and on the intersection of religious and political thought in the nineteenth century.

2 Early accounts of linguistic differences often opposed "Yankee" to "Western" features, and some of the latter turn out to be Northern in the DARE data. Holbrook (1950: 113) reports that "in extreme Northern Indiana, a harrow was called a *drag* and a drag was a *stone boat*. They *geared* their horses instead of harnessing them, said *hit* for it, *Aprile* for April, *cheer* for chair; *shet* for rid."

3 Fischer's insights into American cultural geography play an important role in the exploration of ideological parallels to dialect development in this chapter. I am aware of the extensive critiques that have been made of this work (see Fischer 2008, Zelinsky 2009). In so far as these criticisms deal with the geographic patterns of emigration from England to America, they are not relevant to the use of Fischer's constructs here; this use deals with the patterns of westward settlement that followed and with the cultural contrast across the North/Midland line. Indeed, Fischer's account of the continuity of speechways from England to America can be seriously flawed (as one might expect from a historian's treatment of linguistic data), without bearing in any way on the linguistic opposition of North and Midland dialects and on their origins in the Eastern US.

4 For an early analysis of this opposition between coastal and upland South, see McDavid (1964).

5 Persistence figures are the result of large-scale comparisons of successive population lists. Refined persistence calculations used here distinguish mortality from individual migration (Fischer 1989: 184).

6 In summarizing the data underlying Figure 10.9, Elazar (1986) notes: "The simple mapping of such patterns has yet to be done for more than a handful of states and communities, and while the gross data that can be used to outline the grand patterns as a whole are available in various forms, they have been only partially correlated. However, utilizing the available data, it is possible to sketch with reasonable clarity the nationwide geography of political culture" (p. 96).

7 This was of course before the NCS had fully developed.

8 Carwardine remarks on this parallel in the introduction to his study of evangelicals in US politics before the Civil War: "Evangelical Protestants, to a degree unrivaled since the Civil War, have thrust themselves into the political mainstream, moving away from the political fringes that they inhabited for much of the first two thirds of this century. The ideological divisiveness and bitter political conflicts of the 1970s and 1980s, like those of the antebellum years, were rooted in divergent religious and ethical undertakings" (1993: ix).

9 Some cities with a population of less than 50,000 are included in the Atlas, in cases where a subject interviewed in a larger city turned out to have been raised in a smaller city up to the age of 17. Most of these smaller cities were also county seats.

10 Alaska and Hawaii have no death penalty either; but they are not listed, since Figure 10.11 covers only the continental US.

11 The Liberty Party was an early advocate of the abolitionist cause; it first gathered in Warsaw, New York and it held a national convention in Albany in 1840. In 1848 the party met with other groups in Buffalo, New York, to form the Free Soil Party.

12 The term *evangelical* has a long and complex history, which makes it resist a single definition. Generally it refers to a church that stresses the importance of the individual act of faith for salvation – as opposed to the rituals, ceremonies and institutions of the established churches.

13 More specifically, if 48% or more of the 1880 population that had been born outside of Indiana was born in New York, Pennsylvania or Ohio.

14 Played by Michael Beschloss during an interview with Terry Gross on May 8, 2007, and summarized in Beschloss (2007).

Notes to Chapter 11

1 http://www.cnn.com/SPECIALS/1998/schools/gun.control/, retrieved 12/5/09. See also http://en.wikipedia.org/wiki/Gun_laws_in_the_United_States_(by_state).

2 http://en.wikipedia.org/wiki/Category:Abortion_maps.

3 I am grateful to Gregory Guy for suggesting this direction of analysis.

4 The total is 85, since only 85 of the 90 subjects gave ratings for both subjects on the affirmative action scale.

Notes to Chapter 12

1 See PLC, Vol. 2: 487 for the mathematical definition of skewness, in terms of the ratios of the third moment around the mean to the second moment.

2 Raising and fronting of /aw/ to mid position is primarily characteristic of the prenasal or postnasal allophones, but it is sometimes found in oral environments as well.

3 The original separation of Philadelphia (uw) allophones distinguished free /uw/ as uwF from checked /uw/ as uwC. The ANAE distinction of /uw/ after coronals (Tuw) from /uw/ after non-coronals (Kuw) is adapted by Conn. In practice the two analyses produce almost the same results, since in spontaneous speech most Tuw are free (*too*, *do*) and most Kuw are checked (*move*, *roof*).

4 The temporal progression projected here goes beyond the interpretation given in Eckert (2000), which is consistent with the possibility that the raising of /æ/ was a gender oriented change from the outset. The idea that gender association rises and falls as a change goes to completion is derived primarily from the gender developments presented in Chapters 8 and 9 of Volume 2.

Notes to Chapter 13

1   From the psycholinguistic point of view, it might seem that the lemma will be selected. Yet lemmas are often realized as forms with segmental sequences inconsistent with the sound change in question. For example, the word *ran* is a realization of the lemma *run*, which has no relation to short-*a* tensing.

2   It can be noted that this fronting of *tool*, *school*, *fool*, etc. is the most sharply receding of all southern features.

3   Pursuing F1 and F2 into that voiceless portion of the vowel assigned to the acoustic realization of /h/ does not find marked higher values of F2.

4   None of these social effects applies to the South, where the fronting of /uw/ is most advanced, but there is no significant effect of the speaker's age, city size or style.

5   Although the Brown corpus is based on written English, the lexicon covers the ANAE data fairly well, with only 377 out of 6,755 items missing – a better match than is found with the larger British National Corpus. When the missing values are assigned an arbitrary low value of 1 or 10, no difference in the value of the coefficient is found.

6   The number of items in each split half differs slightly, as some speakers talked considerably more than others.

7   This contrast between /uw/ and /ow/ played a major role in the identification of the triggering event in the fronting of /uw/ in Chapter 5.

8   The word *know* is appropriate to use here rather than the stem *know#*.

9   This phenomenon was first noted in LYS, where Tony from Chicago showed more advanced raising of /æ/ in his reading style than in speech. In general, the Northern Cities Shift is not subject to social correction and shows no recession in word lists. In this respect it contrasts sharply with the behavior of /ow/ fronting in the southeastern region, where a much higher level of social consciousness is accompanied by style shifting away from the vernacular form when attention is paid to speech.

10   Two of these appear with $p < .01$, but, as those with only $p < .05$ are removed one by one from the model, all but *unhappy* fail to meet the .01 criterion.

Notes to Chapter 14

1   The evidence is not yet clear on whether /o/ is totally merged with /ah/ in the various dialects where it remains distinct from /oh/.

2   An older exception with a short final vowel was the *r*-less form of *her*, *fur*, etc., pronounced /hʌ/, /fʌ/ in New York City (Labov 1966, Ch. 10). A current exception is the much discussed word *meh* /me/, meaning "I don't care."

3   This class is expanded greatly in *r*-less dialects, where *beard*, *fear*, *weird*, etc. are included.

4   This effect is so strong that words with such obstruent/liquid onset combinations are excluded from the mean calculations of the Plotnik program.

5   With the exception of the Jewish community in Montreal (Boberg 2004).

6   Beyond the outer limits of this region we find monophthongization before resonants (*fire*, *time*, *I'll*, etc.), but not before obstruents.

7   In most areas of the South this is a social class distinction: (ay0) is stigmatized as a feature
     of lower-class speech (Feagin 1994).
8   Of the 49 Telsur subjects in this region, 17 use monophthongs 100% of the time for
     the (ayV) allophone, but only 7 of these show 100% monophthongization for (ay0).

Notes to Chapter 15

1   The parenthetical insertion "(or dialect)" should not be taken as an extension of the
     family tree model; it simply conforms to the general linguistic position that there is no
     substantive difference between language and dialect; see the Linguistic Society of
     America resolution on the Oakland "Ebonics" controversy. RWT insert this phrase, in
     line with their general emphasis on the evidence drawn from sociolinguistic studies of
     change in progress at the dialect level.
2   This terminology does not imply higher or lower positioning in the socioeconomic
     scale. Changes from above may involve the diffusion of nonstandard elements from
     other systems, as in the recent spread of London features to other British cities (Trudgill
     1974b, Kerswill 2004).
3   It has been argued that branches of a family tree can become differentiated by random
     drift after separation (Hockett 1958). The general rates of lexical replacement (Dyen
     and Guy 1973, Guy 1982) ensure that separated languages or dialects will eventually
     drift apart. However, language changes often move with such speed (e.g. from one
     end of the vowel space to the other, in three or four generations) and with such clear
     directionality that random drift alone seems an implausible mechanism. Furthermore,
     studies of change in progress show differentiation of dialects in close contact with
     each other (e.g. across the North/Midland line; ANAE, Ch. 11). RWT argue that the
     principles of descent adopted in their analysis will apply even when there is no "clean
     separation."
4   Halle (1962) argued that linguistic change is the result of children's imperfect learning
     in another sense: that late additions to adults' grammar are reorganized by children into
     a simpler model, which does not exactly match the parents' original grammar. Although
     Lightfoot (1997, 1999) argues for this model as a means of explaining completed changes,
     such a process has not yet been directly observed in the study of changes in progress.
5   More precisely, adults borrow observable elements of language, the same elements that
     can be socially evaluated. As argued in Chapter 13, the objects of social evaluation are
     one step more abstract than words or sounds. The adult speakers in a community assign
     prestige or stigma to the word stem, irrespective of its appearance in a word with
     various inflections. Thus *piss* is not considered more or less vulgar than *pisses*. Adults
     also assign prestige or stigma to the use of specific allophones for a given phoneme.
     Thus the sound [i:ə] is stigmatized in *bad*, but not in *idea*.
6   Brian Joseph (personal communication, June 8, 2006) points out that the issue of
     grammatical vs lexical borrowing may be a moot one in current linguistic theories, in
     which structures are located in the lexicon.
7   Trudgill's gravity model described the Brunlanes development and the spread of non-
     standard features from London, and provided the direction for a further modeling of
     hierarchical diffusion. The "cascade" model, in which change proceeds from the largest

to next largest city in an area, has proved more general, but other studies indicate that it is only one of many possible models of territorial diffusion (Bailey et al. 1993).

8   For other variables, it may be the frequency or the scope that is incremented.

9   Montreal English may be an exception (Boberg 2004), along with some sections of the Mexican–American community in the US.

10 *Tense* is used here as a cover term for a complex association of phonetic features: raising, fronting, lengthening and the development of an inglide, as opposed to *lax*: a short low front monophthong.

11 Babbitt (1896) observed older New Yorkers with a higher vowel in broad-*a* words than in others; but, for the majority, all words before front nasals, voiced stops and voiceless fricatives were tensed equally, except for function words (p. 461).

12 Newark, along with Jersey City, Hoboken and Weehawken, is fully representative of the New York City system.

13 The steady outflow of New Yorkers to the suburbs of Bergen County, NJ and Westchester, NY has not effectively modified the basic vernacular of those communities. The eastward line of demarcation in Long Island has not been well defined in any recent studies.

14 There were a number of differences in areas of lexical diffusion, like /oh/ vs /a/ in *walrus, wash, moral*.

15 Vowel-initial polysyllabic words are normally lax in NYC; Alex O.'s lax class includes *Amtrak* and *ancestor*.

16 The derivational forms *classic* and *classify* are located in the most conservative area of the tense class distribution. If they had been members of the lax class, they would have been located at the lower right of the lax group, near *Allentown*.

17 John E. was an engineer in a local Albany firm. He was 46 years old when interviewed in 1995.

18 The larger sample interviewed by Boberg and Strassel indicates that Cincinnati is retreating from its traditional short-*a* system. While the interviewed speakers who were over 50 years of age were completely consistent, those aged between 31 and 50 years were consistent only before nasal consonants; otherwise short *a* was tense before the other tensing environments only 60 percent of the time. Speakers under 30 years of age showed tensing in the non–nasal environments only 25 percent of the time. Cincinnati then follows the general shift of Midland short *a* towards the nasal system, in which tensing takes place before (and only before) front nasals.

19 Stites named the city Losantiville; in 1790, two years later, it was renamed Cincinnati.

20 The most general formulation is that *weak words* are excluded from the tense class; weak words are those whose only vowel can be shwa. We note that the word *can't* is a function word which cannot have shwa, and it is never lax (Labov 1989b). For the general characteristics of the Mid-Atlantic dialects, see ANAE, Ch. 13.

21 A common explanation given for this constraint is that function words are lax in their unstressed form, and so they are lax by analogy in their restressed form. Though this may be a correct explanation, it is recognizably post hoc.

22 Since Cajun English speakers show substrate influence from French (Dubois and Horvath 1998), one must also consider this language as a potential influence on New Orleans in general.

23 Like many such abbreviations, *Dan* can be assigned the tense/lax status of the full form *Daniel*; the glide /y/ only variably closes the syllable in NYC, as in *spaniel, annual*.

With an initial *gr-* and two following syllables, *grandparents* is frequently lower than all other tense vowels. *After* is exceptionally tense in NYC; in New Orleans, it follows the general rule of lax realization of word-initial /æ/ in polysyllables.

24   Elizabeth G. was a teacher of French/Irish/German background.

25   This broadcast is currently available at: http://www.amroutes.com/programs/shows/20050316.html.

26   Both directions are of course possible, and it is plausible that palatalization of *work*, *third*, etc. is indeed derived from the South. Kurath and McDavid (1961) show that it is widely used in several southern areas.

27   Korn's book refers to Charleston on 43 pages, Savannah on 5, and Boston on 6.

28   Mr Kohlmeyer referred to an oral tradition in his family according to which the New York City influence in New Orleans was from a single teacher from Brooklyn, who arrived in the 1890s. Marc Caplan of New Orleans told me of an oral tradition in his family that attributed New York City influence to the period, late in the nineteenth century, when New Orleans docks were rebuilt with the help of large numbers of laborers from New York City. I have found no written evidence for this.

29   The influence of the Jewish community, detailed above in the historical data, appears phonetically in the raised /oh/ of New Orleans. There is a marked tendency for second and following generations of Jews to raise this vowel to upper mid and lower high position, more so than other ethnic groups does; see Labov (1966) for New York City and Laferriere (1979) for Boston.

30   ANAE, Ch. 8 shows that the distinctions between /hw/ and /w/, /ohr/ and /ohr/, /iw/ and /uw/ have all but disappeared in the United States, although they were strongly maintained both in the North and in the South in the records of the mid-twentieth century (Kurath and McDavid 1961). The low back merger of /o/ and /oh/ has expanded in some areas with comparable speed. The Philadelphia LVC project interviewed adolescents at a Pottsville recreational park in 1977. When Herold (1990) returned to the same site eleven years later, she found that the percentage of those judging *cot* and *caught* as "the same" had jumped from 17 percent to 100 percent for girls, and from 29 percent to 67 percent for boys.

31   Martin H., of German background, worked as a manufacturer's wholesale representative.

32   Fairbury is a small town with a population of 3,600; it is included in ANAE because the subject who responded to the telephone inquiry had recently moved to a larger city and had a linguistic system fully representative of Fairbury, thus adding to our ability to trace the St Louis corridor. The city of Peoria is not far from I-55, but it is not on the direct route.

33   The Midland distribution is 75 to 1, but, since the null hypothesis for the nine tokens within the corridor would have fewer than five tokens in a cell, Fisher's Exact Test is appropriate, yielding p = .00026.

34   The difference in homogeneity between the St Louis corridor and the Inland North has a chance probability of .0017 by Fisher's Exact Test.

35   Rose M. was 38 when she was interviewed in 1994. She had worked as a dancer and as a seamstress.

36   There is of course a limit to how many newcomers a speech community can absorb. "Dialect swamping" occurs when the incoming population is ten times the original population, as in the AAVE communities of the North and in the coalmining communities of northeastern Pennsylvania (Herold 1990, 1997).

37 Mean family size for New England settlements was 7, as compared to 3 for the Virginia Tidewater South and 5 for the Quaker-oriented settlements of the Delaware Valley (Fischer 1989: 815).

38 Fischer's "refined persistence rate" is defined as the percentage of living adults persisting in a given community through ten years.

39 *Cruller, school leaves out, sick to one's stomach, pavement, smearcase, smearcheese, haycock, quarter to.*

40 Figures 15.20–15.21 show the boundaries of the Inland North, the region defined by the NCS. However, the Inland North is only a portion of the larger Northern region, in which the preconditions for the NCS are present, but the shift as a whole is not.

41 In nominating Lincoln in 1860, the Republican Party confirmed its opposition to the extension of slavery to the newly admitted states.

42 The interstate highway I-55, built just after World War II, is now the main route for Chicago–St Louis travel, but it follows the path of earlier traffic, in particular the Illinois Central Railroad, which was built in 1856 to connect Cairo at the southern tip of Illinois with Galena and Chicago.

Notes to Chapter 16

1 One near exception was Doris H., an African–American woman raised in a white neighborhood of Staten Island (Labov 1966, Table 4.5). She showed the full range of *r*-pronunciation, from 0 to 100%, and moderately raised (oh), but her use of (æh) was the typical [æ.] of the black community.

2 But see below for grammatical influence. Characteristic Philadelphia vowel shifts are heard from a small scattering of individuals of two types: older speakers who grew up in the period preceding the Great Migration of southern blacks into Philadelphia, and isolated individuals who explicitly reject black cultural patterns.

3 And *wan*, the vernacular past of *win* in Philadelphia.

4 More recently the Philadelphia tense class has expanded to include short *a* before nasals.

5 When a comparable study of Spanish was conducted, first results showed the opposite effect, inflectional segments being deleted more often than monomorphemic sequences (Ma and Herasimchuk 1968); and all following studies showed similar results.

6 As shown most clearly in the higher rate of deletion before /l/ than before /r/ for all groups.

7 In this respect, this population differs from the report of Guy (1980), who found high pause effects on deletion for African–American adults.

8 On collapsing the derivational and monomorphemic factors, the decrease in log likelihood (* −2) yields a chi-square of 2.92 for African–Americans, with p = .08, but 15.1 for whites, with p < .0001. This significant difference indicates that, for some children and for some verbs, the final /t/ or /d/ is not present in the underlying form.

Notes to Chapter 17

1 Yang (2009) shows that the diffusion of mergers may be understood in terms of increases in the fitness of a grammar in its capacity to account for variation in the input.

2 A competing view holds that the act of negation is reinforced first with negative adverbs, and the attrition of the negative particle is then accelerated by its increasing redundancy.

3 As a classic example, "I didn't yell or scream. I only went like *this* [passing finger across the table], 'You call that clean?'" (Labov and Fanshel 1977).

4 Recent experiments on adaptation of phoneme boundaries do indicate some adjustment on exposure to dialect differences, though they are not sufficient to prevent the confusions documented in Chapters 2–4. See Plichta and Rakerd 2002, Dahan et al. 2008.

References

Abdel-Jawad, Hassan R. 1987. Cross-dialectal variation in Arabic: Competing prestigious forms. *Language in Society* 16: 359–67.

Allen, Harold B. 1964. The primary dialect areas of the Upper Midwest. In H. B. Allen (ed.), *Readings in Applied English Linguistics*. New York: Appleton-Century-Crofts. Pp. 31–41.

Allen, Harold. 1973. The use of Atlas informants of foreign parentage. In Harald Scholler and John Reidy (eds), *Lexicography and Dialect Geography: Festgabe for Hans Kurath*. Wiesbaden: Franz Steiner Verlag (*Zeitschrift für Dialektologie und Linguistik*, Beihefte, Neue Folge, Nr 9 of *Zeitschrift fürMundartforschung*). Pp. 17–24.

Ash, Sharon. 1982a. The vocalization of /l/ in Philadelphia. University of Pennsylania dissertation.

Ash, Sharon. 1982b. The vocalization of intervocalic /l/ in Philadelphia. *The SECOL Review* 6: 162–75. [Reprinted in H. B. Allen and M. D. Linn (eds), *Dialect and Language Variation*, Orlando: Academic Press, pp. 330–43.]

Ash, Sharon. 1988. Contextless vowel identification. Paper given at NWAV XVII, Montreal.

Ash, Sharon. 1999. Word list data and the measurement of sound change. Paper given at 28th annual meeting of New Ways of Analyzing Variation (NWAV), Toronto.

Ash, Sharon. 2002. The distribution of a phonemic split in the Mid-Atlantic region: Yet more on short a. In D. E. Johnson and T. Sanchez (eds), *University of Pennsylvania Working Papers in Linguistics 8.3: Papers from NWAVE 30*. Philadelphia: Penn Linguistics Club.

Ash, Sharon, and John Myhill. 1986. Linguistic correlates of inter-ethnic contact. In D. Sankoff (ed.), *Diversity and Diachrony*. Amsterdam and Philadelphia: John Benjamins Publishing Co. Pp. 33–44.

Atlas of American History. 1984. 2nd rev. edn. New York: Scribner's.

Auer, Peter and Frans Hinskens. 1996. The convergence and divergence of dialects in Europe. New and not so new developments in an old area. *Sociolinguistica* 10: 1–30.

Babbitt, E. H. 1896. The English of the lower classes in New York City and vicinity. *Dialect Notes* 1: 457–64.

Bailey, Charles-James. 1972. The integration of linguistic theory. In R. Stockwell and R. Macaulay (eds), *Linguistic Change and Generative Grammar*. Bloomington: Indiana University Press. Pp. 22–31.

Bailey, Guy. 1993. A perspective on African–American English. In Dennis Preston (ed.), *American Dialect Research*. Philadelphia: John Benjamins. Pp. 287–318.

Bailey, Guy. 1997. When did southern American English begin? In E. Schneider (ed.), *Englishes Around the World: Studies in Honour of Manfred Görlach*. Amsterdam/ Philadelphia: John Benjamins. Pp. 255–75.

Bailey, Guy. 2001. The relationship between African–American vernacular English and white vernaculars in the American South. In Sonja Lanehart (ed.), *African American English: State of the Art*. Philadelphia: John Benjamins. Pp. 53–92.

Bailey, Guy. 2004. Digging up the roots of southern American English. In Anne Curzan and Kimberly Emmons (eds), *Studies in the History of the English Languge: II. Unfolding Conversations*. Berlin: Mouton de Gruyter. Pp. 433–44.

Bailey, Guy and Garry Ross. 1992. The evolution of a vernacular. In M. Rissanen et al. (eds), *History of Englishes: New Methods and Interpretations in Historical Linguistics*. Berlin: Mouton de Gruyter. Pp. 519–31.

Bailey, Guy, Tom Wikle and Lori Sand. 1991. The focus of linguistic innovation in Texas. *English World-Wide* 12(2): 195–214.

Bailey, Guy, Tom Wikle, Jan Tillery and Lori Sand. 1993. Some patterns of linguistic diffusion. *Language Variation and Change* 5: 359–90.

Banuazizi, A. and M. Lipson. 1998. The tensing of /ae/ before /l/: An anomalous case for short-*a* rules of white Philadelphia speech. In C. Paradis et al. (eds), *Papers in Socio-linguistics: NWAVE-26 à l'Université Laval*. Quebec: Editions Nota bene. Pp. 41–51.

Baptista, Luis A. and Lewis Petrinovitch. 1984. Social interaction, sensitive phases, and the song template in the white crowned sparrow. *Animal Behavior* 32: 172–81.

Baranowski, Maciej. 2006. Phonological variation and change in the dialect of Charleston, SC. University of Pennsylvania dissertation.

Baranowski, Maciej. 2007. *Phonological Variation and Change in the Dialect of Charleston, South Carolina*. Publications of the American Dialect Society 92.

Barton, Michael. 1830. *Something New, comprising a New and Perfect Alphabet*. Boston and Harvard: Marsh, Capen and Lynn.

Baugh, John. 1983. *Black Street Speech: Its History, Structure and Survival*. Austin: University of Texas Press.

Becker, Kara and Amy Wong. 2009. The short-*a* system of white and minority speakers of New York City English. Paper given at the 2009 Annual Meeting of the Linguistic Society of America, San Francisco.

Beecher, Henry Ward. 1863. *Sermon. The Home Missionary 35*. New York: The American Missionary Society.

Benediktsson, Hreinn. 1970. *The Nordic Language and Modern Lingusitics*. Reykjavík: Societas Scienarium Islandica.

Berger, Marshall D. 1980. New York City and the ante-bellum South: The maritime connection. *International Linguistic Association* 31(1): 47–53.

Beschloss, Michael. 2007. *Presidential Courage*. New York: Simon and Schuster.

Blake, Renee, and Meredith Josey. 2003. The /ay/ diphthong in a Martha's Vineyard community: What can we say 40 years after Labov? *Language in Society* 32: 451–85.

Blanc, Haim. 1964. *Communal Dialects in Baghdad*. (Harvard Middle Eastern Monographs, X). Cambridge, MA: Harvard University Press.

Blankenhorn, M. A. 1950. Visit to the grave of Daniel Drake. *Bulletin of the Historical and Philosophical Society of Ohio* 8: 297–300.

Bloomfield, Leonard. 1933. *Language*. New York: Henry Holt.

Boberg, Charles. 1997. Variation and change in the nativization of foreign (a) in English. University of Pennsylvania PhD dissertation.

Boberg, Charles. 2001. The phonological status of western New England. *American Speech* 76: 3–29.

Boberg, Charles. 2004. Ethnic patterns in the phonetics of Montreal English. *Journal of Sociolinguistics* 8: 538–68.

Boberg, Charles. 2005. The Canadian Shift in Montreal. *Language Variation and Change* 17: 133–54.

Boberg, Charles and Stephanie M. Strassel. 2000. Short-a in Cincinnati: A change in progress. *Journal of English Linguistics* 28: 108–26.

Bowie, David. 2003. Early development of the Card–Cord merger in Utah. *American Speech* 78: 31–51.

Bradley, David. 1969. Problems in Akha phonology: Synchronic and diachronic. Unpublished paper.

Britain, David. 1997. Dialect contact, focusing and phonological rule complexity: the koineisation of Fenland English. *Penn Working Papers in Linguistics: A Selection of Papers form NWAVE* 25(4): 141–69.

Brody, Stephanie. 2009. The status of planets: Development and transmission of Philadelphia short-*a*. Paper given at *Penn Linguistics Colloquium* 33, Philadelphia.

Brown, Vivian. 1990. The social and linguistic history of a merger: /i/ and /e/ before nasals in southern American English. Texas A & M University dissertation.

Bühler, Karl. 1934. *Sprachtheorie*. Jena: Gustav Fischer.

Bybee, Joan. 2002. Word frequency and context of use in the lexical diffusion of phonetically conditioned sound change. *Language Variation and Change* 14: 261–90.

Byrne, Richard W. and Andrew Whiten (eds). 1988. *Machiavellian Intelligence: Social Expertise and the Evolution of Intellect in Monkeys, Apes, and Humans*. Oxford: Clarendon Press.

Byrne, Richard W. and Andrew Whiten (eds). 1997. *Machiavellian Intelligence II: Extensions and Evaluations*. New York: Cambridge University Press.

Callary, R. E. 1975. Phonological change and the development of an urban dialect in Illinois. *Language in Society* 4: 155–70.

Campbell, Lyle. 1993. On proposed universals of grammatical borrowing. In Henk Aertsen and Robert J. Jeffers (eds), *Historical Linguistics 1989: Papers from the 9th International Conference on Historical Linguistics 1989*. (Rutgers University, 14–18 August 1989.) Amsterdam: John Benjamins. Pp. 91–109.

Campbell-Kibler, Kathryn. 2005. Listener perceptions of sociolinguistic variables: The case of (ING). Stanford University dissertation.

Carnes, Mark C. and John A. Garrity. 1996. *Mapping America's past: A Historical Atlas*. New York: H. Holt.

Carver, Craig M. 1987. *American Regional Dialects: A Word Geography*. Ann Arbor: University of Michigan Press.

Carwardine, Richard J. 1993. *Evangelicals and Politics in Antebellum America*. New Haven: Yale University Press.

Cedergren, Henrietta. 1973. On the nature of variable constraints. In C.-J. Bailey and R. Shuy (eds), *New Ways of Analyzing Variation in English*. Washington: Georgetown University Press. Pp. 13–22.

Chambers, J. K. 1993. "Lawless and vulgar innovators": Victorian views of Canadian English. In S. Clarke (ed.), *Focus on Canada*. Amsterdam: John Benjamins. Pp. 1–26.

Chambers, J. K. and Peter Trudgill. 1980. *Dialectology*. Cambridge: Cambridge University Press.

Chen, Matthew and William S.-Y. Wang. 1975. Sound Change: Actuation and implementation. *Language* 51: 255–81.

Cheney, Dorothy L. and Robert M. Seyfarth. 1988. Social and non-social knowledge in vervet monkeys. In R. Byrne and A. Whiten (eds), *Machiavellian Intelligence*. Oxford: Clarendon Press. Pp. 255–70.

Cheney, Dorothy L. and Robert M. Seyfarth. 1990. *How Monkeys See the World: Inside the Mind of Another Species*. Chicago: University of Chicago Press.

Cheney, Dorothy L. and Robert M. Seyfarth. 2007. *Baboon Metaphysics: The Evolution of a Social Mind*. Chicago: University of Chicago Press.

Cheng, Chin-Chuan and William S.-Y. Wang. 1977. Tone change in Chaozhou Chinese: A study of lexical diffusion. In W. S.-Y. Wang (ed.), *The Lexicon in Phonological Change*. The Hague: Mouton. Pp. 86–100.

Chomsky, Noam and Morris Halle. 1968. *The Sound Pattern of English*. New York: Harper and Row.

Christy, Craig. 1983. *Uniformitarianism in Linguistics*. Amsterdam/Philadelphia: John Benjamins.

Clarke, Sandra, Ford Elms and Amani Youssef. 1995. The third dialect of English: Some Canadian evidence. *Language Variation and Change* 7: 209–28.

Cofer, Thomas. 1972. Linguistic variability in a Philadelphia speech community. Univerity of Pennsylvania dissertation.

Cohen, Paul. 1970. The tensing and raising of short (a) in the metropolitan area of New York City. Columbia University Master's Essay.

Conn, Jeffrey. 2005. Of "moice" and men: The evolution of a male-led sound change. University of Pennsylvania dissertation.

Cook, Stanley. 1969. Language change and the emergence of an urban dialect in Utah. Unpublished University of Utah dissertation.

Cooper, Franklin S., Pierre Delattre, A. M. Liberman, J. M. Borst and Louis J. Gerstman. 1952. Some experiments on the perception of synthetic speech sounds. *JASA* 24: 597–606.

Cravens, Thomas D. 2000. Sociolinguistic subversion of a phonological hierarchy. *Word* 51: 1–19.

Cravens, Thomas D. 2002. *Comparative Historical Dialectology: Italo-Romance Clues to Ibero-Romance Sound Changes*. Philadelphia: John Benjamins.

Cross, Whitney R. 1950. *The Burned-Over District: The Social and Intellecual History of Enthusiastic Religion in Western New York, 1800–1850*. Ithaca, NY: Cornell University Press.

Cukor-Avila, Patricia. 1995. The evolution of AAVE in a rural Texas community: An ethnolinguistic study University of Michigan dissertation.

Dahan, D., S. J. Drucker and R. A. Scarborough. (2008). Talker adaptation in speech perception: Adjusting the signal or the representations? *Cognition* 108: 710–18.

Darwin, Charles. 1871. *The Descent of Man, and Selection in Relation to Sex.* 1st edn, 2 vols. London: John Murray.

Davis, Lawrence M. 2000. The reliability of dialect boundaries. *American Speech* 75: 257–9.

De Decker, Paul and Sara Mackenzie. 2000. Slept through the ice: A further look at lax vowel lowering in Canadian English. *Toronto Working Papers in Linguistics* 25.

Di Paolo, Marianna. 1988. Pronunciation and categorization in sound change. In K. Ferrara et al. (eds), *Linguistic Change and Contact: NWAV XVI*. Austin, TX: Dept of Linguistics, University of Texas. Pp. 84–92.

Di Paolo, Marianna and Alice Faber. 1990. Phonation differences and the phonetic content of the tense–lax contrast in Utah English. *Language Variation and Change* 2: 155–204.

Dinkin, Aaron. 2008. The real effect of word frequency on phonetic variation. *Penn Working Papers in Linguistics* 14(1): 97–106.

Dinkin, Aaron. 2009. Dialect boundaries and phonological change in upstate New York. University of Pennsylvania dissertation.

Disner, Sandra. 1978. Vowels in Germanic languages. UCLA Working Papers in Phonetics 40. University of California Los Angeles dissertation.

Doernberger, Jeremy and Jakob Cerny. 2008. The low back merger in Miami. Paper given at NWAV 37, Houston, TX.

Donegan, Patricia J. 1978. On the natural phonology of vowels. Ohio State University dissertation.

Dubois, Sylvie and Barbara Horvath. 1998. From accent to marker in Cajun English: A study of dialect formation in progress. *English World-Wide* 19: 161–88.

Dunbar, R. I. M. 1988. *Primate Social Systems.* London: Chapman & Hall.

Dyen, Isidor and Jucquois Guy. 1973. *Lexicostatistics in Genetic Linguistics II: Proceedings of the Montreal Conference.* Montreal: Centre de recherches mathématiques, Université de Montréal.

Eberhardt, Maeve. 2008. The low-back merger in the Steel City: African American English in Pittsburgh. *American Speech* 83: 284–311.

Eckert, Penelope. 1986. The roles of high school social structure in phonological change. Paper presented at the Chicago Linguistic Society.

Eckert, Penelope. 1989. *Jocks and Burnouts: Social Categories and Identities in the High School.* New York: Teachers College Press.

Eckert, Penelope. 2000. *Linguistic Variation as Social Practice.* Oxford: Blackwell.

Eckert, Penelope and Sally McConnell-Ginet. 2003. *Language and Gender.* Cambridge: Cambridge University Press.

Elazar, Daniel J. 1972. *American Federalism: A View from the States.* 2nd edn. New York: Thomas Y. Crowell.

Elazar, Daniel J. 1986. *Cities of the Prairie Revisited: The Closing of the Metropolitan Frontier.* Lincoln: University of Nebraska Press.

Eliasson, Stig. 1997. The cognitive calculus and its function in language. In J. Gvozdanovic (ed.), *Language Change and Functional Explanations.* Berlin: Mouton de Gruyter.

Evanini, Keelan 2009. The permeability of dialect boundaries: A case study of the region surrounding Erie, Pennsylvania. University of Pennsylvania dissertation.

Evans, Betsy E., Rika Ito, Jamila Jones, and Dennis R. Preston. 2006. How to get to be one kind of Midwesterner: Accommodation to the Northern Cities Chain Shift. In T. Murray and B. L. Simon (eds), *Language Variation and Change in the American Midland.* Amsterdam: John Benjamins. Pp. 179–97.

Fasold, Ralph W. 1969. A sociolinguistic study of the pronunciation of three vowels in Detroit speech. Unpublished manuscript.

Fasold, Ralph W. 1972. Tense marking in Black English. Paper presented at the Center for Applied Linguistics, Washington, DC.

Fastovsky, David E. and Peter M. Sheehan. 2004. The extinction of the dinosaurs in North America. *GSA Today* 15: 4–10.

Feagin, Louise Crawford. 1979. *Variation and Change in Alabama English*. Washington, DC: Georgetown University Press.

Feagin, Louise Crawford. 1993. Low back vowels in Alabama: yet another merger? Poster paper given at NWAVE 22, Ottawa, Canada.

Feagin, Louise Crawford. 1994. "Long i" as a microcosm of southern states speech. Paper given at NWAVE 23, Stanford, CA.

Ferguson, Charles A. 1975. "Short a" in Philadelphia English. In M. Estellie Smith (ed.), *Studies in Linguistics in Honor of George L. Trager*. The Hague: Mouton. Pp. 259–74.

Fidelholtz, J. L. 1975. Word frequency and vowel reduction in English. *Chicago Linguistic Society* 200–13.

Fischer, David Hackett. 1989. *Albion's Seed: Four British Folkways in America*. Oxford: Oxford University Press.

Fischer, David Hackett. 2008. Albion and the critics: Further evidence. *The William and Mary Quarterly*, 3rd series, 48(2) 260–308. Also available at: http://www.jstor.org/pss/2938075.

Fischer, Olga, Muriel Norde and Harry Perridon. 2004. *Up and Down the Cline: The Nature of Grammaticalization*. Amsterdam: Benjamins.

Flanagan, J. 1955. A difference limen for vowel formant frequency. *JASA* 27: 613–17.

Fogle, Deena. 2008. Expansion or approximation: The low-back merger in Indianapolis. Paper given at NWAV 37, Houston, TX.

Foner, Philip S. 1941. *Business and Slavery: The New York Merchants and the Irrepressible Conflict*. Chapel Hill: The University of North Carolina Press.

Fought, Carmen. 1999. A majority sound change in a minority community: /u/-fronting in Chicano English. *Journal of Sociolinguistics* 3: 5–23.

Fought, Carmen. 2003. Chicano English in context. New York: Palgrave Macmillan.

Frazer, Timothy C. 1978. South Midland pronunciation in the North Central States. *American Speech* 53: 40–8.

Frazer, Timothy C. (ed.). 1993. *"Heartland" English*. Tuscaloosa: University of Alabama Press.

Frei, Henri. 1929. *La Grammaire des fautes*. Paris: Librairie Paul Geuthner.

Fridland, Valerie. 2003. Tie, tied and tight: The expansion of /ay/ monophthongization in African–American and European–American speech in Memphis, Tennessee. *Journal of Sociolinguistics* 7: 279–98.

Friesner, Michael and Aaron J. Dinkin. 2006. The acquisition of native and local phonology by Russian immigrants in Philadelphia. *Penn Working Papers in Linguistics* 12(2): 91–104.

Fruehwald, Josef. 2007. The spread of raising: A case of lexical diffusion. University of Pennsylvania Honors Senior Thesis.

Garde, Paul. 1961. Réflexions sur les différences phonétiques entre les langues slaves. *Word* 17: 34–62.

Gauchat, Louis. 1905. L'Unité phonétique dans le patois d'une commune. In *Aus Romanischen Sprachen und Literaturen: Festschrift Heinrich Mort*. Halle: Max Niemeyer. Pp. 175–232.

Gilliéron, Jules. 1918. *Pathologie et thérapeutique verbale*. Paris.

Gordon, Elizabeth and Margaret A. Maclagan. 1989. Beer and bear, cheer and chair: A longitudinal study of the ear/air contrast in New Zealand English. *Australian Journal of Linguistics* 9: 203–20.

Gordon, Elizabeth et al. 2004. *New Zealand English: Its Origins and Evolution*. Cambridge: Cambridge University Press.

Gordon, Matthew J. 2000. Phonological correlates of ethnic identity: Evidence of divergence? *American Speech* 755: 115–36.

Gordon, Matthew J. 2001. *Small-Town Values and Big-City Vowels: A Study of the Northern Cities Shift in Michigan*. Publications of the American Dialect Society 84.

Gould, Stephen Jay. 1989. *Wonderful Life*. New York: W. W. Norton.

Graff, David, William Labov and Wendell Harris. 1986. Testing listeners' reactions to phonological markers. In D. Sankoff (ed.), *Diversity and Diachrony*. Philadelphia: John Benjamins. Pp. 45–58.

Grant, Peter R. and B. Rosemary Grant. 1994. Predicting microevolutionary responses to directional selection on heritable variation. *Evolution* 49: 241–51.

Gregg, R. J. 1957. Notes on the pronunciation of Canadian English as spoken in Vancouver, BC. *Journal of the Canadian Linguistic Association* 3: 20–6.

Guy, Gregory R. 1980. Variation in the group and the individual: The case of final stop deletion. In W. Labov (ed.), *Locating Language in Time and Space*. New York: Academic Press. Pp. 1–36.

Guy, Gregory R. 1991. Contextual conditioning in variable lexical phonology. *Language Variation and Change* 3: 223–39.

Guy, Gregory R. and Charles Boberg. 1997. Inherent variablilty and the obligatory contour principle. *Language Variation and Change* 9: 149–64.

Guy, Gregory R. and Sally Boyd. 1990. The development of a morphological class. *Language Variation and Change* 2: 1–18.

Guy, Jacques B. M. 1982. Bases for new methods in glottochronology. In Amran Halim, Lois Carrington and S. A. Wurm (eds), *Papers from the Third International Conference on Austronesian Linguistics*, Vol 1: *Currents in Oceanic Pacific Linguistics*, C–74. Pp. 283–314.

Haeri, Niloofar. 1996. *The Sociolinguistic Market of Cairo: Gender, Class and Education*. London: Kegan Paul International.

Hagiwara, Robert. 2006. Vowel production in Winnipeg. *Canadian Journal of Linguistics* 51: 127–41.

Halle, Morris. 1962. Phonology in generative grammar. *Word* 18: 54–72.

Harrington, Jonathan, Sallyanne Palethorpe and Catherine Watson. 2000. Monophthongal vowel changes in received pronunciation. *Journal of the International Phonetic Association* 30: 63–78.

Haspelmath, Martin. 2004. On directionality in language change, with particular reference to grammaticalization. In Olga Fischer, Muriel Norde and Harry Perridon (eds), *Up and Down the Cline: The Nature of Grammaticalization*. Amsterdam: John Benjamins. Pp. 17–44.

Haudricourt, A. G. and A. G. Juilland. 1949. *Essai pour une histoire structurelle du phonétisme français*. Paris: C. Klincksieck.

Hauser, Marc D. 1988. Invention and social transmission: New data from wild vervet monkeys. In R. Byrne and A. Whiten (eds), *Machiavellian Intelligence: Social Expertise* and the Evolution of Intellect in Monkeys, Apes, And Humans. Oxford: Clarendon Press. Pp. 327–44.

Hauser, Marc D. 1996. *The Evolution of Communication.* Cambridge, MA: MIT Press.

Hauser, Marc D., Noam Chomsky and W. Tecumseh Fitch. 2002. The faculty of language: What is it, who has it, and how did it evolve? *Science* 22: 1569–79.

Hay, Jennifer, Paul Warren and Katie Drager. 2006. Factors influencing speech perception in the context of a merger-in-progres. *Journal of Phonetics* 34: 458–84.

Hazen, Kirk. 2002. Identity and language variation in a rural community. *Language* 78: 240–57.

Heeringa, Wilbert and John Nerbonne. 2001. Dialect areas and dialect continua. *Language Variation and Change* 13: 375–400.

Heine, Bernd and Tania Kuteva. 2005. *Language Contact and Grammatical Change.* Cambridge: University of Cambridge Press.

Henderson, Anita. 1996. The short-a pattern of Philadelphia among African American speakers. *Penn Working Papers in Linguistics* 3: 127–40.

Hermann, E. 1929. Lautveränderungen in der individualsprache einer Mundart. *Nachrichten der Gesellschaft der Wissenschaften zu Göttingen. Phil.-hist. Klasse* 11: 195–214.

Herold, Ruth. 1990. Mechanisms of merger: The implementation and distribution of the low back merger in eastern Pennsylvania. University of Pennsylvania dissertation.

Herold, Ruth. 1997. Solving the actuation problem: Merger and immigration in eastern Pennsylvania. *Language Variation and Change* 9: 165–89.

Hershberg, Theodore (ed.). 1981. *Philadelphia: Work, Space, Family and Group Experience in the Nineteenth Century.* New York: Oxford University Press.

Hershberg, Theodore et al. 1981. A tale of three cities: Black, immigrants and opportunity in Philadelphia. 1850–1880, 1930, 1970. In T. Hershberg (ed.), *Philadelphia: Work, Space, Family and Group Experience in the Nineteenth Century.* New York: Oxford University Press. Pp. 461–95.

Herzog, Marvin I. 1965. *The Yiddish Language in Northern Poland.* Bloomington and The Hague (= special issue of *IJAL* 31(2), Part 2).

History of McLean County, Illinois. 1879. Chicago: W. LeBaron Jr. & Co.

Hindle, Donald. 1978. Approaches to vowel normalization in the study of natural speech. In D. Sankoff (ed.), *Linguistic Variation: Models and Methods.* New York: Academic Press. Pp. 161–72.

Hindle, Donald. 1980. The social and structural conditioning of phonetic variation. University of Pennsylvania PhD dissertation.

Hock, Hans Heinrich. 1986. *Principles of Historical Linguistics.* Berlin: Mouton de Gruyter.

Hock, Hans Heinrich and Brian Joseph. 1996. *Language History, Language Change and Language Relationship.* Berlin: Mouton.

Hockett, Charles. 1958. *A Course in Modern Linguistics.* New York: Macmillan.

Hoenigswald, Henry. 1960. *Language Change and Linguistic Reconstruction.* Chicago: University of Chicago Press.

Holbrook, Stewart H. 1950. *The Yankee Exodus: An Account of Migration from New England.* New York: Macmillan.

Hollett, Pauline. 2006. Investigating St. John's English: Real- and apparent-time perspectives. *Canadian Journal of Linguistics* 51: 143–60.

Holmes, Janet and Allan Bell. 1992. On shear markets and sharing sheep: The merger of EAR and AIR diphthongs in New Zealand English. *Language Variation and Change* 4: 251–73.

Hooper, J. B. 1976. Word frequency in lexical diffusion and the source of morphophonological change. In W. M. Christie (ed.), *Current Progress in Historical Linguistics*. Amsterdam: North Holland. Pp. 95–105.

Hopper, Paul and Elizabeth Traugott. 2003. *Grammaticalization*. Cambridge: Cambridge University Press.

Hymes, Dell. 1961. Functions of speech: An evolutionary approach. In F. C. Gruber (ed.), *Anthropology and Education*. Philadelphia: University of Pennsylvania Press.

Irons, Terry. 2007. On the status of low back vowels in Kentucky English: More evidence of merger. *Language Variation and Change* 19: 101–36.

Jacewicz, Ewa, Joseph C. Salmons and Robert A. Fox. 2004. Prosodic domain effects and vocalic chain shifts. Paper given at the 9th Conference on Laboratory Phonology.

Jakobson, Roman. 1960. *Style in Language*. Cambridge, MA: Technology Press of Massachussetts.

Jakobson, Roman. 1972. Principles of historical phonology. In A. R. Keiler (ed.), *A Reader in Historical and Comparative Linguistics*. New York: Holt, Rinehart and Winston. Pp. 121–38.

Jakobson, Roman and Morris Halle. 1956. *Fundamentals of Language*. The Hague: Mouton and Co.

Jakobson, Roman, Gunnar Fant and Morris Halle. 1967. *Preliminaries to Speech Analysis, the Distinctive Features and Their Correlates*. Cambridge, MA: MIT Press.

Janda, Richard D. and Brian D. Joseph. 2001. Reconsidering the canons of sound-change: Towards a "Big Bang" theory. In B. Blake and K. Burridge (eds), *Selected Papers from the 15th International Conference on Historical Linguistics*. Amsterdam: John Benjamins. Pp. 205–19.

Jensen, Richard. 1971. *The Winning of the Midwest: Social and Political Conflict, 1888–1896*. Chicago: University of Chicago Press.

Jespersen, Otto. 1946. *Language: Its Nature, Development and Origin* [1921]. New York: W. W. Norton and Co.

Jespersen, Otto. 1949. *A Modern English Grammar on Historical Principles. Part I: Sounds and Spellings*. London: George Allen and Unwin.

Johnson, Curtis D. 1989. *Islands of Holiness: Rural Religion in Upstate New York*. Ithaca: Cornell University Press.

Johnson, Daniel Ezra. 2010. *Stability and Change across a Dialect Boundary: The Low Vowels of Southeastern New England*. Publications of the American Dialect Society.

Johnson, Jacqueline S. and Elissa L. Newport. 1989. Critical period efforts in second-language learning: The influence of maturational state on the acquisition of English as a second language. *Cognitive Psychology* 21: 60–99.

Johnstone, Barbara, Netta Bhasin and Denise Wittkofski. 2002. "Dahntahn" Pittsburgh: Monophthongal /aw/ and representations of localness in southwestern Pennsylvania. *American Speech* 77: 148–60.

Jones, Jamila. 2003. African Americans in Lansing and the Northern Cities Vowel Shift. Michigan State University unpublished PhD dissertation.

Jones, Jamila and Dennis R. Preston. In press. The language varieties of African–Americans in Lansing. *Journal of African Language Learning and Teaching* (*Festschrift* volume for David Dwyer).

Joseph, Brian D. 2000. Processes of spread for syntactic constructions in the Balkans. In C. Tzitzilis and C. Symeonidis (eds), *Balkan Linguistik: Synchronie und Diachronie*. Thessaloniki: University of Thessaloniki. Pp. 139–50.

Katz, Elihu and Paul Lazarsfeld. 1955. *Personal Influence*. Glencoe, IL: Free Press.

Kenyon, John and Thomas Knott. 1953. *A Pronouncing Dictionary of American English*. Springfield, MA: G. C. Merriam.

Kerswill, Paul. 1996. Children, adolescents, and language change. *Language Variation and Change* 8: 177–202.

Kerswill, Paul. 2004. Dialect leveling and geographical diffusion in British English. In D. Britain and J. Cheshire (eds), *Social Dialectology: In Honour of Peter Trudgill*. Amsterdam: John Benjamins. Pp. 223–43.

Kilpinen, Jon. 2010. Political map for geography 200. Available at: http://www.valpo.edu/geomet/pics/geo200/politics/elazar.gif (accessed 2/5/10).

Kim, Ronald and William Labov. 2002. The diffusion of West Germanic diphthongization in Central and Eastern Europe. Paper given at the Penn Linguistics Colloquium, Philadelphia, February.

King, Robert. 1969. *Historical Linguistics and Generative Grammar*. New York: Holt, Rinehart and Winston.

King, Ruth. 2000. *The Lexical Basis of Grammatical Borrowing: A Prince Edward Island French Case Study*. Amsterdam and Philadelphia: John Benjamins.

Kiparsky, Paul. 1988. Phonological change. In F. Newmeyer, (ed.), *Linguistics: The Cambridge Survey*. Cambridge: Cambridge University Press. Pp. 363–415.

Kniffen, Fred B. and Henry Glassie. 1966. Building in wood in the eastern United States. *Geographic Review* 56: 40–66.

Kohlberg, Lawrence. 1966. A cognitive–developmental analysis of children' sex role concepts and attitudes. In E. E. Maccoby (ed.), *The Development of Sex Differences*. Stanford, CA: Stanford University Press. Pp. 82–173.

Korn, Bertram W. 1969. *The Early Jews of New Orleans*. Waltham, MA: American Jewish Historical Society.

Kretzschmar, William A., Jr. 1992. Isoglosses and predictive modeling. *American Speech* 67(3): 227–49.

Krishnamurti, B. 1998. Regularity of sound change through lexical diffusion: A study of s > h > 0 in Gondi dialects. *Language Variation and Change* 10: 193–220.

Kroch, Anthony. 1978. Toward a theory of social dialect variation. *Language in Society* 7: 17–36.

Kroch, Anthony. 1989. Reflexes of grammar in patterns of language change. *Language Variation and Change* 1: 199–244.

Kroodsma, Donald E. and Roberta Pickert. 1984. Sensitive phases for song learning: Effects of social interaction and individual variation. *Animal Behavior* 32: 389–94.

Kucera, Henry and W. Nelson Francis. 1967. *Computational Analysis of Present-Day American English*. Providence: Brown University Press.

Kurath, Hans. 1949. *A Word Geography of the Eastern United States*. Ann Arbor: University of Michigan Press.

Kurath, Hans and Raven I. McDavid, Jr. 1961. *The Pronunciation of English in the Atlantic States*. Ann Arbor: University of Michigan Press.

Kurath, Hans, Miles L. Hanley, Bernard Block, Guy S. Lowman, Jr and Marcus L. Hansen. 1931. *Linguistic Atlas of New England*. Providence, RI: American Council of Learned Societies.

Labov, William. 1963. The social motivation of a sound change. *Word* 19: 273–309. [Revised as Ch. 1 of W. Labov, *Sociolinguistic Patterns*, Philadelphia: University of Pennsylvania Press].

Labov, William. 1966. *The Social Stratification of English in New York City*. Washington, DC: Center for Applied Linguistics. Cambridge: Cambridge University Press.

Labov, William. 1972. *Language in the Inner City*. Philadelphia: University of Pennsylvania Press.

Labov, William. 1974. Language change as a form of communication. In Albert Silverstein (ed.), *Human Communication*. Hillsdale, NJ: Erlbaum. Pp. 221–56.

Labov, William. 1976. The relative influence of family and peers on the learning of language. In R. Simone et al. (eds), *Aspetti sociolinguistici dell' Italia contemponea*. Rome: Bulzoni.

Labov, William. 1980. The social origins of sound change. In W. Labov (ed.), *Locating Language in Time and Space*. New York: Academic Press. Pp. 251–66.

Labov, William. 1981. Resolving the Neogrammarian controversy. *Language* 57: 267–309.

Labov, William. 1984. Field methods of the Project on Linguistic Change and Variation. In J. Baugh and J. Sherzer (eds), *Language in Use*. Englewood Cliffs: Prentice Hall. Pp. 28–53.

Labov, William. 1989a. The child as linguistic historian. *Language Variation and Change* 1: 85–97.

Labov, William. 1989b. The exact description of the speech community: Short a in Philadelphia. In R. Fasold and D. Schiffrin (eds), *Language Change and Variation*. Washington: Georgetown University Press. Pp. 1–57.

Labov, William. 1990. The intersection of sex and social class in the course of linguistic change. *Language Variation and Change* 2: 205–54.

Labov, William. 1991. The three dialects of English. In P. Eckert (ed.), *New Ways of Analyzing Sound Change*. New York: Academic Press. Pp. 1–44.

Labov, William. 1994. *Principles of Linguistic Change*, Vol. 1: *Internal Factors*. Oxford: Basil Blackwell.

Labov, William. 1997. Resyllabification. In F. Hinskens, R. van Hout and W. L. Wetzels (eds), *Variation, Change and Phonological Theory*. Amsterdam and Philadelphia: John Benjamins. Pp. 145–79.

Labov, William. 1998. Co-existent systems in African American vernacular English. In S. Mufwene, J. Rickford, G. Bailey and J. Baugh (eds), *The Structure of African-American English: Structure, History and Use*. London and New York: Routledge. Pp. 110–53.

Labov, William. 2001. *Principles of Linguistic Change*, Vol. 2: *Social Factors*. Oxford: Blackwell.

Labov, William. 2003. When ordinary children fail to read. *Reading Research Quarterly* 38: 131–3.

Labov, William. 2007. Transmission and diffusion. *Language* 83: 344–87.

Labov, William and Bettina Baker. In press. What is a reading error? *Applied Psycholinguistics*.

Labov, William and Maciej Baranowski. 2006. 50 msec. *Language Variation and Change* 18: 223–40.

Labov, William and David Fanshel. 1977. *Therapeutic Discourse: Psychotherapy as Conversation*. New York: Academic Press.

Labov, William and Wendell A. Harris. 1986. De facto segregation of black and white vernaculars. In D. Sankoff (ed.), *Diversity and Diachrony*. Philadelphia: John Benjamins. Pp. 1–24.

Labov, William and Pedro Pedraza. 1994. The reinterpretation of English: On Hispanic responss to linguistic change. Paper presented to the Third Annual UNM Conference on Hispanic Language and Social Identity.

Labov, William, Sharon Ash and Charles Boberg. 2006a. *Atlas of North American English: Phonology and Sound Change*. Berlin: Mouton de Gruyter.

Labov, William, Paul Cohen and Clarence Robins. 1965. A preliminary study of the structure of English used by negro and Puerto Rican speakers in New York City. Final Report, Cooperative Research Project 3091. [ERIC ED 03 019].

Labov, William, Mark Karan and Corey Miller. 1991. Near-mergers and the suspension of phonemic contrast. *Language Variation and Change* 3: 33–74.

Labov, William, Malcah Yaeger and Richard Steiner. 1972. *A Quantitative Study of Sound Change in Progress*. Philadelphia: US Regional Survey.

Labov, William, Paul Cohen, C. Robins and J. Lewis. 1968. A study of the non-standard English of negro and Puerto Rican Speakers in New York City. Cooperative Research Report 3288. Vols I and II. Available through the ERIC system, at www.eric.ed.gov (accessed 4/1/10).

Labov, William, S. Ash, M. Baranowski, N. Nagy, M. Rabindranath and T. Weldon. 2006b. Listeners' sensitivity to frequency. *Penn Working Papers* 12: 105–29.

Laferriere, Martha. 1979. Ethnicity in phonological variation and change. *Language* 55: 603–17.

Lambert, Wallace. 1967. A social psychology of bilingualism. In J. Macnamara (ed.), *Problems of Bilingualism*. Special issue of *Journal of Social Issues* 23: 91–109.

Langstrof, Christian. 2006. Acoustic evidence for a push-chain shift in the intermediate period of New Zealand English. *Language Variation and Change* 18: 141–64.

Lau, Chun-fat. 2003. Labovian principles of vowel shifting revisited: The short vowel shift in New Zealand English and southern Chinese. In Barry Blake and Kate Burridge (eds), *Historical Linguistics 2001. Selected Papers from the 15th International Conference on Historical Linguistics*. Pp. 293–301.

Lave, J. and E. Wenger. 1991. *Situated Learning: Legitimate Peripheral Participation*. Cambridge: Cambridge University Press.

Le Page, Robert B. and Andree Tabouret-Keller. 1985. *Acts of Identity: Creole-Based Approaches to Language and Ethnicity*. Cambridge: Cambridge University Press.

Lennig, Matthew. 1978. Acoustic measurement of linguistic change: The modern Paris vowel system. University of Pennsylvania dissertation.

Lieberson, Stanley. 2000. *A Matter of Taste: How Names, Fashions and Culture Change*. New Haven: Yale University Press.

Liebling, A. J. 1961. *The Earl of Louisiana*. New York: Simon and Schuster.

Lightfoot, David. 1997. Catastrophic change and learning theory. *Lingua* 100: 171–92.

Lightfoot, David W. 1999. *The Development of Language: Acquisition, Change, and Evolution*. Oxford and Malden, MA: Blackwell Publishers.

Liljencrants, J. and Lindblom, B. 1972. Numerical simulation of vowel quality systems: The role of perceptual contrast. *Language* 48: 839–62.

Lillie, Diane. 1998. The Utah dialect survey. Brigham Young University Master's Essay.

Lindblom, Bjorn. 1988. Phonetic content in phonology. *Phonologica* 1988: In W. Dressler, et al. (eds). Proceedings of the 6th International Phonology Meeting. Cambridge: Cambridge University Press. Pp. 181–96.

Luick, K. 1903. *Studien zur Englischen Lautgeschichte*. Vienna and Leipzig: W. Braunmullier.

Lutz, Angelika. 2004. The first push: A prelude to the Great Vowel Shift. *Anglia* 233: 209–24.

Ma, Roxana and Eleanor Herasimchuk. 1968. The linguistic dimensions of a bilingual neighborhood. In J. Fishman, R. Ma and R. Cooper (eds), *Bilingualism in the Barrio*. Washington, DC: Office of Education.

Maclaglan, Margaret A. and Elizabeth Gordon. 1996. Out of the AIR and into the EAR: Another view of the New Zealand diphthong merger. *Language Variation and Change* 8: 125–47.

Majors, Tivoli. 2004. Low back vowel merger in Missouri speech: Acoustic description and explanation. *American Speech* 80: 165–79.

Malkiel, Yakov. 1967. Every word has a history of its own. *Glossa* 1: 137–49.

Marler, Peter. 1970. A comparative approach to vocal learning: Song development in white-crowned sparrows. *Journal of Comparative and Physiological Psychology* 71: 1–25.

Martinet, André. 1952. Function, structure and sound change. *Word* 8: 1–32.

Martinet, André. 1955. *Economie des changements phonétiques*. Berne: Francke.

Massey, Douglas S. and Nancy A. Denton. 1993. *American Apartheid: Segregation and the Making of the Underclass*. Cambridge, MA: Harvard University Press.

McCone, Kim. 1996. *Towards a Relative Chronology of Ancient and Medieval Celtic Sound Change*. Maynooth Studies in Celtic Linguistics 1. Maynooth: Department of Old Irish, St Patrick's College.

McDavid, Raven I., Jr. 1955. The position of the Charleston dialect. *Publications of the American Dialect Society* 23: 35–49.

McDavid, Raven I., Jr. 1964. Postvocalic /r/ in South Carolina: A Social Analysis. In D. Hymes (ed.), *Language in Culture and Society*. New York: Harper & Row. Pp. 469–82.

McKelvey, Blake. 1949a. A panoramic view of Rochester's history. *Rochester History* 11: 1.

McKelvey, Blake. 1949b. Rochester and the Erie Canal. *Rochester History* 11: 3, 4.

McNabb, Donald, and Louis E. Madère, Jr. 1983. A history of New Orleans. Available at: http://www.madere.com/history.html (4/1/10).

Meillet, Antoine. 1921. *Linguistique historique et linguistique générale*. Paris: La société linguistique de Paris.

Melchert, H. Craig. 1983. The second singular personal pronoun in Anatolian. *Münchener Studien zur Sprachwissenschaft* 42: 151–64.

Mendoza-Denton, Norma. 2008. *Home Girls: Language and Cultural Identity among Latina Youth Gangs*. Oxford: Blackwell.

Milroy, James and Lesley Milroy. 1978. Belfast: Change and variation in an urban vernacular. In P. Trudgill (ed.), *Sociolinguistic Patterns in British English*. London: Edwin Arnold. Pp. 19–36.

Milroy, Lesley. 1980. *Language and Social Networks*. Oxford: Basil Blackwell.

Mitchell, A. G. and A. Delbridge 1965. *The Pronunciation of English in Australia*. Sydney: Angus and Robertson.

Mitchell-Kernan, Claudia. 1969. Language behavior in a black urban community. Monographs of the Language-Behavior Research Laboratory 2. Berkeley: University of California.

Modaressi, Yahya. 1978. A sociolinguistic investigation of modern Persian. University of Kansas dissertation.

Sivertsen, Eva. 1960. *Cockney Phonology*. Oslo: Oslo University Press.

Sjodahl, Lars H. 1964. The Kibbys and Kibbeys of Early Cincinnati. *Cincinnati Historical Society Bulletin* 22: 38–40.

Sledd, James. 1955. Review of G. Trager and Henry Lee Smith, *An Outline of English Structure*. *Language* 31: 312–45.

Stampe, David. 1972. On the natural history of diphthongs. *Chicago Linguistic Society* 8: 578–90.

Stevens, Harry R. 1952. Cincinnati's founding fathers: Isaac Burnet. *Bulletin of the Historical and Philosophical Society of Ohio* 10: 231–9.

Stockwell, Robert and Donka Minkova. 1997. On drifts and shifts. *Studia Anglica Posnaniensia* 31: 283–303.

Sturtevant, Edgar. 1947. *An Introduction to Linguistic Science*. New Haven: Yale University Press. [Ch. 8, esp. pp. 81–4.]

Tagliamonte, Sali A. and Alexandra D'Arcy. 2009. Peaks beyond phonology: Adolescence, incrementation, and language change. *Language* 85: 58–108.

Terrell, Tracy. 1975. The merger of the low vowel phonemes in the English of Southern California: A preliminary report. Paper given before the American Dialect Society.

Thelander, Mats. 1980. *De-Dialectalisation in Sweden*. Uppsala: Instiuionen för Nordisksa Sprak vid Uppsala Unirsitet.

Thiemann, C., F. Theis, D. Grady, R. Brune and D. Brockmann. 2010. The structure of borders in a small world. Manuscript. Department of Engineering Sciences and Applied Mathematics, Northwestern University.

Thomason, Sarah and Terrence Kaufman. 1988. *Language Contact, Creolization, and Genetic Linguistics*. Berkeley: University of California Press.

Toon, Thomas E. 1976. The variationist analysis of Early Old English manuscript data. In W. M. Christie Jr. (ed.), *Proceedings of the Second International Conference on Historical Linguistics*. Amsterdam: North Holland. Pp. 71–81.

Trager, George L. 1930. The pronunciation of "short A" in American Standard English. *American Speech* 5: 396–400.

Trager, George L. 1934. What conditions limit variants of a phoneme? *American Speech* 9: 313–15.

Trager, George L. 1942. One phonemic entity becomes two: The case of "short a." *American Speech* 17: 30–41.

Trudgill, Peter. 1972. Sex, covert prestige and linguistic change in urban British English. *Language in Society* 1: 179–95.

Trudgill, Peter. 1974a. Linguistic change and diffusion: Description and explanation in sociolinguistic dialect geography. *Language in Society* 3: 215–46.

Trudgill, Peter. 1974b. *The Social Differentiation of English in Norwich*. Cambridge: Cambridge University Press.

Trudgill, Peter. 1986. *Dialects in Contact*. Oxford and New York: Basil Blackwell.

Trudgill, Peter. 1996. Dialect typology: Isolation, social network and phonological structure. In G. Guy, C. Feagin, D. Schiffrin and J. Baugh. *Towards a Social Science of Language: Papers in Honor of William Labov*, Vol. 1. Amsterdam: John Benjamins. Pp. 3–22.

Trudgill, Peter. 2004. *New-Dialect Formation: The Inevitability of Colonial Englishes*. Oxford: Oxford University Press.

Montgomery, Michael and Connie Eble. 2004. Historical perspectives on the pen/pin merger in Southern American English. In Anne Curzan and Kimberly Emmons (eds), *Studies in the History of the English Langue: II. Unfolding Conversations*. Berlin: Mouton de Gruyter. Pp. 415–34.

Morain, Thomas J. 1988. *Prairie Grass Roots: An Iowa Small Town in the Early Twentieth Century*. The Henry A. Wallace Series on Agricltural History and Rural Studies. Ames, IA: Iowa State University Press.

Moravcsik, Edith. 1978. Language contact. In J. Greenberg (ed.), *Universals of Human Language*, Vol. 1. Stanford, CA: Stanford University Press. Pp. 93–122.

Moreno, J. L. 1953. *Who Shall Survive*. Rev. edn. New York: Beacon House.

Moulton, William G. 1960. The short vowel systems of northern Switzerland: A study in structural dialectology. *Word* 16: 155–82.

Murray, Thomas E. 1993. The language of St. Louis, Missouri: Dialect mixture in the urban Midwest. In Timothy C. Frazer (ed.), *"Heartland" English: Variation and Transition in the American Midwest*. Tuscaloosa: University of Alabama Press. Pp. 125–236.

Murray, Thomas E. 2002. At the intersection of regional and social dialects: The case of like + past participle in American English. *American Speech* 77: 32–69.

Myhill, John. 1988. Postvocalic /r/ as an index of integration into the BEV speech community. *American Speech* 63: 203–13.

Nearey, Terence. 1977. Phonetic feature system for vowels. University of Connecticut dissertation.

Newport, Elissa L. 1990. Maturational constraints on language learning. *Cognitive Science* 14: 11–28.

O'Cain, Raymond K. 1972. A social dialect survey of Charleston, South Carolina. University of Chicago dissertation.

Ohala, John J. 1992. What's cognitive, what's not, in sound change. In Günter Kellermann and Michael D. Morrissey (eds), *Diachrony within Synchrony: Language History and Cognition*. Duisburger Arbeiten zur Sparch-und Kulturwissenschaft 14. Frankfurt am Main: Peter Lang.

Orton, Harold and Eugen Dieth. 1962–7. *Survey of English Dialects*. Leeds: E. J. Arnold and Son.

Osthoff, Hermann and Karl Brugmann. 1878. *Morphologische Untersuchungen auf dem Gebiete der indogermanischen Sprachen*, Vol. 1. Leipzig: Hildesheim.

Oyama, Susan. 1973. A sensitive period for the acquisition of a second language. Harvard University dissertation.

Paul, Hermann. 1970. *Principles of the History of Language* [1888]. Translated from the 2nd edn of the original by H. A. Strong. New and rev. edn. London: New York, Longmans, Green.

Payne, Arvilla. 1976. The acquisition of the phonological system of a second dialect. University of Pennsylvania dissertation.

Payne, Arvilla. 1980. Factors controlling the acquisition of the Philadelphia dialect by out-of-state children. In W. Labov (ed.), *Locating Language in Time and Space*. New York: Academic Press. Pp. 143–78.

Pederson, Lee, Susan L. McDaniel and Carol M. Adams (eds). 1986. *Linguistic Atlas of the Gulf States*, 7 vols. Athens, GA: University of Georgia Press.

Peterson, Gordon E. and Harold L. Barney. 1952. Control methods used in a study of the vowels. *JASA* 24: 175–84.

Phillips, B. S. 1980. Lexical diffusion and southern Tune, Duke, News. *American Speech* 56: 72–8.

Phillips, B. S. 1984. Word frequency and the actuation of sound change. *Language* 60: 320–42.

Phillips, Betty S. 2006. *Word Frequency and Lexical Diffusion*. New York: Palgrave Macmillan.

Pierrehumbert, Janet 2002. Word-specific phonetics. In C. Gussenhoven and N. Warner (eds), *Laboratory Phonology VII*. Berlin: Mouton de Gruyter. Pp. 101–40.

Plichta, Bartek and Brad Rakerd. 2002. Perceptions of /a/-fronting across two Michigan dialects. Paper given at NWAVE 31, Stanford.

Pope, Jennifer, Miriam Meyerhoff and D. Robert Ladd. 2007. Forty years of language change on Martha's Vineyard. *Language* 83: 615–27.

Pope, M. K. 1934. From Latin to modern French with especial consideration of Anglo-Norman. Manchester: Manchester University Press.

Poplack, Shana. 1978. Dialect acquisition among Puerto Rican bilinguals. *Language in Society* 7: 89–104.

Power, Richard Lyle. 1953. *Planting Corn Belt Culture: The Impress of the Upland Southerner and Yankee in the Old Northwest*. Indianapolis: Indiana Historical Society.

Preston, Dennis R. 2010. Transmission and diffusion, contact, and space and symmetry in the acquisition of norms. Annual Linguistic Society of America Conference, Baltimore, January.

Primer, Sylvester. 1888. Charleston provincialisms. *American Journal of Philology* IX: 198–213.

Prince, Ellen. 1987. Sarah Gorby, Yiddish folksinger: A case study of dialect shift. *International Journal of the Sociology of Language* 67: 93–116.

Pulleyblank, Edwin G. 1978. Abruptness and gradualness in phonological change. In M. A. Jazayery et al. (eds), *Linguistics and Literary Studies in Honor of Archibald A. Hill*. The Hague: Mouton. Pp. 181–91.

Purnell, Thomas. 2008. AAE in Milwaukee: Contact at a vowel shift frontier. Paper given at annual meeting of LSA, Chicago. To appear in a volume edited by Malcah Yaeger-Dror and Erik Thomas.

Rickford, John. 1999. *African American Vernacular English: Features and Use, Evolution, and Educational Implications*. Oxford: Blackwell.

Rickford, John and Christine Théberge Rafal. 1996. Preterite had + V-ed in the narratives of African-American pre-adolescents. *American Speech* 71: 227–54.

Rickford, John R, Arnetha Ball, Renee Blake, Raina Jackson, and Nomi Martin. 1991. Rappin on the copula coffin: Theoretical and methological issues in the analysis of copula variation in African–American vernacular English. *Language Variation and Change* 3: 103–32.

Ringe, Donald, Tandy Warnow and Anne Taylor. 2002. Indo-European and computational cladistics. *Transactions of the Philological Society* 100: 59–129.

Roberts, Julia. 1993. The acquisition of variable rules: t, d deletion and –ing production in preschool children. University of Pennsylvania dissertation.

Roberts, Julia and Labov, William. 1995. Learning to talk Philadelphian: Acquisition of short *a* by preschool children. *Language Variation and Change* 7: 101–12.

Roeder, Rebecca and Lidia-Gabriela Jarmasz. 2009. The lax vowel subsystem in Canadian English revisited. Paper given at the Toronto Working Papers in Linguistics.

Sankoff, David and William Labov. 1979. On the uses of variable rules. *Language in S[ociety]* 8: 189–222.

Sankoff, David and Gillian Sankoff. 1973. Sample survey methods and comp[uter]-assisted analysis in the study of grammatical variation. In R. Darnell [(ed.),] *Canadian Languages in their Social Context*. Edmonton, Alberta: Linguistic Res[earch]. Pp. 7–64.

Sankoff, Gillian. 2002. Linguistic outcomes of language contact. In Peter Trudg[ill,] Chambers and N. Schilling-Estes (eds), *Handbook of Sociolinguistics*. Oxford: Blackwell. Pp. 638–68.

Sankoff, Gillian. 2004. Adolescents, young adults and the critical period: Two case s[tudies] from "Seven Up." In Carmen Fought (ed.), *Sociolinguistic Variation: Critical Refl[ections]*. Oxford and New York: Oxford University Press. Pp. 121–39.

Sankoff, Gillian and Hélène Blondeau. 2007. Language change across the lifespan: Montreal French. *Language* 83: 560–88.

Sankoff, Gillian, and Diane Vincent. 1977. L'emploi productif du *ne* dans le frança[is] à Montréal. *Le français moderne* 45: 243–56.

Sankoff, Gillian, Hélène Blondeau and Anne Charity. 2001. Individual roles in a r[eal-time] change: Montreal (r > R) 1947–1995. In Hans van de Velde and Roeland va[n Hout] (eds), *'r-atics: Sociolinguistic, Phonetic and Phonological Characteristics of /r/*. [Brussels:] Travaux. Pp. 141–58.

Santa Ana, Otto. 1991. Phonetic simplification processes in the English of the B[arrio: A] cross-generational sociolinguistic study of the Chicanos of Los Angeles. Univ[ersity of] Pennsylvania dissertation.

Santa Ana, Otto. 1996. Sonority and syllable structure in Chicano English. *Langu[age Variation] and Change* 8: 63–89.

Saussure, Ferdinand de. 1949. *Cours de linguistique générale* [1916]. 4th ed[. Paris:] Payot.

Scargill, M. H. and H. J. Warkentyne. 1972. The Survey of Canadian English: [A Report.] *English Quarterly* 5: 47–104.

Scherre, Maria Marta Pereira and Anthony J. Naro. 1992. The serial effect on in[ternal and] external variables. *Language Variation and Change:* 4: 1–13.

Schmidt, Johannes. 1871. *Zur Geschichte des indogermanischen Vocalismus (Part I)*[. Weimar:] H. Böhlau.

Scovel, Thomas. 2000. A critical review of the critical period research. *Annua[l Review of] Applied Linguistics* 20: 213–23.

Scoville, John. 1870. *The Old Merchants of New York City, by Walter Barrett, Cl[erk]*. New York: Carleton.

Shen, Zhongwei. 1990. Lexical diffusion: A population perspective and a numer[ical model.] *Journal of Chinese Linguistics* 18: 159–200.

Shepard, Lee. 1949. When, and by whom, was Cincinnati founded. *Bulletin of t[he Historical] and Philosophical Society of Ohio* 7: 28–34.

Shepard, Lee. 1957. News from North Bend: Some Early Letters. *Bulletin of t[he Historical] and Philosophical Society of Ohio* 15: 316–29.

Shibata, Chickako. 2006. Chain shifts and merger in New Zealand English. *Engl[ish]* 23: 27–57.

Shuy, Roger W. 1962. The Northern–Midland dialect boundary in Illinois. *[Publication of] the American Dialect Society* 38: 1–79.

Trudgill, Peter and Tina Foxcroft. 1978. On the sociolinguistics of vocalic mergers: Transfer and approximation in East Anglia. In P. Trudgill (ed.), *Sociolinguistic patterns in British English*. London: Edwin Arnold. Pp. 69–79.

Vachek, Josef. 1964. On peripheral phonemes of modern English. *Brno Studies in English*. Praha: St'atn'i Pedagogick'e Nakladatelstv'i.

Wagner, Suzanne Evans. 2008. Language change and stabilization in the transition from adolescence to adulthood. University of Pennsylvania dissertation.

Wang, William S.-Y. and C.-C. Cheng. 1977. Implementation of phonological change: The Shaungfeng Chinese case. In W. S.-Y. Wang (ed.), *The Lexicon in Phonological Change*. The Hague: Mouton.

Wang, William S.-Y. and C.-C. Cheng. 1977. Implementation of phonological change: The Shaungfeng Chinese case. In W. S-Y. Wang (ed.), *The Lexicon in Phonological Change*. The Hague: Mouton.

Weinberg, Maria Fontanella de. 1974. *Un aspecto sociolinguistico del Espanol Bonaerense: La -S en Bahia Blanca*. Bahia Blanca: Cuadernos de Linguisticca.

Weiner, E. Judith and William Labov. 1983. Constraints on the agentless passive. *Journal of Linguistics* 19: 29–58.

Weinraub, Marsha et al. 1984. The development of sex role stereotypes in the third year. *Child Development* 55: 1493–503. (Society for Research in Child Development.)

Weinreich, Uriel. 1968. *Languages in Contact: Findings and Problems*. The Hague: Mouton. [Originally published as Publications of the Linguistic Circle of New York, no. 1, 1953.]

Weinreich, Uriel, William Labov and Marvin Herzog. 1968. Empirical foundations for a theory of language change. In W. Lehmann and Y. Malkiel (eds), *Directions for Historical Linguistics*. Austin: University of Texas Press. Pp. 97–195.

Wells, J. C. 1982. *The Accents of English*, Vol. 1: *An Introduction*. Cambridge: Cambridge University Press.

Wenger, Etienne. 1998. *Communities of Practice: Learning, Meaning and Identity*. Cambridge: Cambridge University Press.

Williams, Ann and Paul Kerswill. 1999. Dialect levelling: Continuity vs. change in Milton Keynes, Reading and Hull. In P. Foulkes and G. Docherty (eds), *Urban Voices*. London; Arnold.

Winford, Donald. 2003. *An Introduction to Contact Linguistics*. Oxford: Blackwell.

Wolf, Clara and Elena Jiménez. 1979. El ensordecimienteo del yeismo porteño, un cambio fonológico en marcha. In A. M. Barenchea et al. (eds), *Estudios Linguisticos y Dialectologicos*. Buenos Aires: Hachette, 1979.

Wolford, Tonya E. 2006. Variation in the expression of possession by Latino children. *Language Variation and Change* 18: 1–14.

Wolfram, Walt. 1969. *A Sociolinguistic Description of Detroit Negro Speech*. Arlington, VA: Center for Applied Linguistics.

Wolfram, Walt. 1974. *Sociolinguistic Aspects of Assimilation: Puerto Rican English in New York City*. Arlington, VA: Center for Applied Linguistics.

Wolfram, Walt. 1994. Dialects and the Ocracoke Brogue: The modeling of a dialect. Ocracoke School Experimental Education, March 1994.

Wolfram, Walt. 1999. *Dialect Change and Maintenance on the Outer Banks*. Tuscaloosa: University of Alabama Press.

Wolfram, Walt and Natalie Schilling-Estes. 2003. Dialectology and linguistic diffusion. In Brian Joseph and Richard Janda (eds), *The Handbook of Historical Linguistics*. Malden, MA: Blackwell. Pp. 713–35.

Woods, Nicola 2000. New Zealand English across the generations: An analysis of selected vowel and consonant variables. In Alan Bell and Koenraad Kuiper (eds), *New Zealand English*. Amsterdam: John Benjamins. Pp. 84–110.

Wyld, Henry Cecil. 1936. *A History of Modern Colloquial English*. London: Basil Blackwell.

Yang, Charles. 2009. Population structure and language change. Unpublished manuscript.

Zelinsky, Wilbur. 1992. *The Cultural Geography of the United States. A Revised Edition.* Englewood Cliffs, NJ: Prentice Hall.

Zelinsky, Wilbur. 2009. Review of *Albion's Seed: Four British Folkways in Americ*a by David Hackett Fischer. *Annals of the Association of American Geographers* 81: 526–31.

Zeller, Christine. 1997. The investigation of a sound change in progress: /æ/ to /e/ in Midwestern American English. *Journal of English Linguistics* 25: 142–55.

Ziegeler, Debraq. 2004. Redefining unidirectionality: Is there life after modality? In Olga Fischer, Muriel Norde and Harry Perridon, *Up and Down the Cline: The Nature of Grammaticalization*. Amsterdam: Benjamins. Pp. 115–36.

Index